Pride in Our Past, Promise for the Future

— A —

MONUMENTAL

STORY

Pride in Our Past, Promise for the Future

— A —

MONUMENTAL

STORY

Rosemary Riesett Limmen

MONUMENTAL LIFE
INSURANCE COMPANY

1858 — 2008

FIRST EDITION

February 2008

ISBN 978-0-615-17853-0

Produced and published by

Monumental Life Insurance Company

2 East Chase Street

Baltimore, Maryland 21202

www.monlife.com/ml

PRINTED IN THE USA

Produced for the Monumental Life Insurance Company by

The Chesapeake Book Company, Baltimore, Maryland

Designed by James F. Brisson, Williamsville, Vermont

Photo scanning and photography of Monumental Life Insurance Company

artifacts by Peter M. Riesett, Brooklyn, New York

This book is dedicated to the thousands of employees and retirees—past and present—who have contributed to Monumental Life's fifteen decades of growth and success, and to the many generations of policyholders with whom we have built relationships over the last 150 years. Thank you for your loyalty, your commitment, and your trust. Thank you for allowing us to come into your homes to meet needs and protect your families.

Pride in Our Past, Promise for the Future—A MONUMENTAL Story presents the history of one of America's oldest and largest insurance organizations. It is also *your* story. Without *you*, there would have been no Monumental Life. Without *you*, there would have been no story to tell.

THE MUTUAL LIFE INSURANCE COMPANY

OF BALTIMORE.

Amount $5000

N° 1.

Age 41

Ten ANNUAL PREMIUMS $288 15/ each.

This Policy of Insurance

Witnesseth that

The Mutual Life Insurance Company

Of Baltimore,

In consideration of the representations made to them in the application for this Policy, and of the sum of _____ *Two hundred and eighty eight* _____ Dollars and _____ *fifteen* _____ Cts to them duly paid by _____ *John Willcox Jenkins* _____ and of the _____ annual payment of a like amount on or before the _____ *tenth* _____ day of *March in each year for Ten years* _____ during the continuance of Policy, *after which it is a paid up policy.*

Do Assure the Life of the said *John Willcox Jenkins* of *Hampden village* in the County of *Baltimore* State of *Maryland* for the sole use of _____ *John Willcox Jenkins* _____ in the amount *Five Thousand* _____ dollars, for the term of *his* natural life.

And, the said Company do hereby PROMISE AND AGREE to pay the amount of the said Insurance at their Office in the City of BALTIMORE, to the said insured _____ *John Willcox Jenkins* _____ *His Heirs* or assigns, within ninety days after due notice and proof of the death of the said party whose life is hereby insured

FOREWORD

By Henry G. Hagan

Not many companies can celebrate being in business for one hundred and fifty years. Few can claim they have remained in the same city throughout their entire history. Fewer still can say they have remained committed to their core business yet have evolved to meet the changing needs of the families they've served.

But Monumental Life Insurance Company can!

Since 1858, Monumental Life has provided protection and peace of mind for millions of policyholders. We survived the Great Baltimore Fire, the Great Depression, world wars, Wall Street crashes, and hostile takeover attempts. Through mergers and acquisitions, growth and growing pains, we retained our traditional home service values. We've earned our customers' loyalty and the respect of our peers. We're proud of our past and our dedicated, talented people.

Pride in Our Past, Promise for the Future: A MONUMENTAL Story salutes the company's history of strength and success. But like the life insurance business itself, our story is really about people. The gentlemen who built our organization in the turbulent pre–Civil War years. The Baltimore businessmen, merchants, landowners, watermen, factory workers and farmers who were the company's first policyholders.

FACING PAGE: *Policy issued by the Mutual Life Insurance Company of Baltimore in 1870 on the life of Baltimorean John Willcox Jenkins*

The clerks who hand-wrote hundreds of policies by oil lamp light in the early 1900s. The thousands of men (and women), each fondly known by their customers as the "insurance man," who wore out shoe leather walking door-to-door for decades, meeting needs and collecting premiums in inner-city neighborhoods. The generations of families who trusted us and welcomed us into their homes. The widows and children we helped when their husbands and fathers died unexpectedly.

Monumental's story is also about promises. Promises made and promises kept to millions of families for over 150 years. Promises to be there—long after contracts were signed, when families needed us the most—to protect lives, incomes, dreams and futures. Hand-delivered checks that helped bury deceased loved ones and take care of the living.

We are proud of our past, our deep roots, our home service traditions, and the relationships we've built over more than a dozen decades. We are also proud of our ability to innovate and remain responsive to changes within our industry, our country, and society as a whole. We look forward to the opportunities and challenges that will help us build a strong and successful future.

We thank the millions of people who have contributed to Monumental Life's growth and success. Without our field and home office employees, our sales representatives and distributors, our policyholders and stockholders, our officers, directors and retirees, we wouldn't be here today. Without you, we couldn't continue to meet needs. Without you, there would be no celebration of 150 years of commitment to our customers and the communities we serve. Without you, there would be no "Monumental Life."

So to all, let me offer a hearty "Hats Off!" for the role you have played in our Monumental story. I am proud of what we have accomplished together over all of these years, and I am very proud of what we continue to do!

Henry G. Hagan
Chairman, President and CEO
Monumental Life Insurance Company

ACKNOWLEDGMENTS

Write a book? You've got to be kidding! I never even considered myself a "writer" until I joined Monumental in 1984.

Writing has never been easy for me. In fact, putting just the right words down on paper has sometimes felt like pulling teeth . . . pure torture! How could I possibly write for a living? And yet, for more than twenty years, I've been writing press releases, advertising and marketing copy, articles for company publications, letters and speeches for officers, even songs, invocations, and silly skits for company events.

When I suggested that we write a book to celebrate Monumental Life's 150th Anniversary in 2008, senior management looked right back at me. I'd been responsible for telling the company's story ever since 1984. "Who knows more about Monumental than you?" they asked. "Who could do the job better?" Maybe the question should have been, "Who, besides you, would be crazy enough to try?"

Writing this history has been the most challenging, frustrating, rewarding and enjoyable assignment of my Monumental career. Challenging because of the mountains of data I found hiding behind solid steel doors in the company's underground vault. Challenging too because handwritten board meeting minutes provided the only source of information documenting the company's first sixty years. Frustrating because—despite an exhaustive search of city and state records—we never did find photographs of the company's founders and first directors, its first policyholders, and four of its first five presidents. Rewarding and enjoyable because of the information we *were* able to find, thanks to the many wonderful people who shared their stories, photos and mementos.

When I began this project more than two years ago, I had no idea how much digging, sifting, sorting and decision-making it would take to tell Monumental Life's story, accurately and with as many interesting anecdotes and "people stories" as possible.

Thanks to free-lance writer Gary Hornbacher, I was able to interview more people and include many more stories than I could ever have completed on my own. Former assistant Michele Terveer, retiree Maggie Gregory, and interns Blair

Hagan, Ashleigh Smith, and Kellie Bland also helped with research—including transposing taped interviews and plotting policyholder addresses from the 1870s on an old Baltimore map. But the ultimate responsibility for selecting details and events, as well as putting them in their proper historic perspective, was mine and mine alone. As readers of this history—each with your own knowledge, experience and perspective—you will have to determine how well I accomplished that task.

Pride in Our Past, Promise for the Future—A MONUMENTAL Story would not have been possible without the support and encouragement I received from Monumental Life's officers— especially Henry Hagan, Ralph Arnold, Stacey Boyer and Duane Davies. Thank you for trusting me to tell the story of one of the country's largest life insurance organizations—not as an accountant or actuary would tell it—but in my own, very personal and somewhat unconventional way.

Thank you, too, to the dozens of current and retired officers, field and home office employees who agreed to be interviewed. Though I have not quoted all of you, or included notes from every interview, speaking with you provided the background and details I needed to shape each chapter. I couldn't have told this story without your valuable insight and experiences.

Monumental's story would also have been incomplete were it not for the hundreds of photographs and negatives provided by Jim Lighter, unofficial "company photographer" for almost forty years. Between the 1950s and the mid-1990s he documented promotions and employee social events, company meetings, milestones and training sessions and took almost every photo included in Chapters 8 through 11. Thank you, Gail Matzen and Dick Lippert, for your help in identifying, sorting and cataloguing this "treasure chest" of historic images.

Thank you also to the research staffs at the Maryland Historical Society and the University of Baltimore who assisted in locating information and photographs to document the company's earliest years, and to photographer Bob Stockfield who provided the most recent images of company officers and events.

I especially want to thank the group of retired officers and directors—Jim Gentry, Bos Ensor, Bob McGraw, Larry Jenkins,

Les Disharoon, and Harvey M. ("Bud") Meyerhoff—who read drafts, corrected errors and offered positive feedback. Comments like "it's really interesting!" . . . "I stayed up all night reading!" . . . and "I'd pay money to buy this book!" kept me going and helped confirm that I'd selected a format that would engage readers.

And what would I have done without the professionals who helped me bring the words and images together?

Thank you, Robert I. ("Ric") Cottom, former director of the Press at the Maryland Historical Society, for your advice and answers to my many questions —"Is it working? Is it interesting? Will anyone read this?"—since I sent you first drafts in July 2006. You appreciate Monumental's place in Baltimore and Maryland history, encouraged me to explore it within these pages, and have edited this text to make sure it is historically accurate.

Hats off to book designer Jim Brisson, working from a small village in rural Vermont, for filling these pages with just the right mix of "classic" and "classy" design. We agreed immediately on the look we wanted, collaborated on the selection of type faces and formats, and communicated almost daily for many months to agree on page layouts, colors, and placement of six hundred photographs. You've earned a halo for your efforts!

So has my son, Peter Riesett, who did all the on-site photography of artifacts and documents and scanned more than five hundred images. Thank you, Pete, for being such a painstaking perfectionist. Your experience and expertise as head photographer in the New York Public Library's Photographic Services and Permissions Department helped us preserve parts of Monumental's past saved, until now, only in employee publications printed more than eighty years ago.

Thank you also to interns Kristin Burkett and Ashley Vinkemeier who spent the summer of 2005 in the company vault (dressed in sweats!) helping me create a system to organize and catalog the thousands of documents, publications, reports, photographs and artifacts in our archives. Without your commitment to this first critical step, I would not have known what we had, or where it was. More recently, intern Tiffany Gibson provided valuable support locating and securing permission to use historic photographs, and Alisha Social, a senior at Baltimore's Mergenthaler Vocational-Technical High School, provided the minority student perspective needed to create Chapter 9's opening story about the 1968 riots in Baltimore. Thank you both!

A big "thank you" also to my children and family who understand how obsessed and single-focused a creative person can be, and to my friends and co-workers who challenged me, and kept me writing for almost eighteen months.

Finally, words cannot express all that I owe my new husband, partner and best friend . . . Jan Limmen, that's *you* . . . who has literally "lived" the creation of this book with me from start to finish. As someone who enjoys writing, you didn't know what you were getting into when you asked me to marry you on Valentine's Day 2005. This book has been part of our daily life since our wedding day. Your insight, input, people-loving perspective, and early reading of my first drafts helped me get started on the right track. Night after night, you waited for me to get home and listened as I laid out chapter-opening ideas over late-night dinners. Thank you for being there. Thank you for being you. Soon, you will have a partner (a published author!) who gets home before 9:00 p.m. without her head full of dates, details and looming deadlines.

Because of the many people who have helped make this book become a reality—including those whom I may have inadvertently forgotten to mention here by name—I too am "proud of my past" and look forward to a retirement filled with "promise for the future." Writing this book has been a stress-filled but unbelievably satisfying experience . . . a real, once-in-a-lifetime, "monumental" ride!

Rosemary Riesett Limmen
November 2007

CONTENTS

Pride in Our Past, Promise for the Future

A

MONUMENTAL

STORY

CHAPTER 1

Caught in the Middle
(1858–1869)

IN THE MISTY predawn morning, dockworkers hoist bundles of tobacco and flour onto ships anchored in the harbor. Barrels of sugar, wheat and imported coffee, piles of hides, and bales of raw cotton sit waiting on worn wooden wharves. Railroad locomotives whistle impatiently in the city's Bolton, Camden and President Street stations. Watermen call to one another as they transfer the morning's catch of Chesapeake Bay crabs, oysters and fresh fish into waiting wagons. Immigrants, newly arrived from Germany and Ireland, step off gangplanks to begin new lives in America.

The date is March 5, 1858, and Baltimore—the country's third largest city, burgeoning commercial center and port of entry—is alive with activity!

Along the waterfront, foreign accents compete with the familiar sounds of arriving ships. Sails luff in the wind. Steam engines shudder and shut down. Merchants haggle. Horses clip-clop, pulling wagons along cobblestone streets. The aromas of tea, spices and leather mingle with the unmistakable stench of fish, fertilizer, wet wool, sweat, sewage and Pigtown's slaughterhouses. Well-dressed businessmen, bankers and financiers walk to imposing downtown offices. Free blacks rush to jobs as laborers, porters, ships' caulkers, and housekeepers. And in ethnic neighborhoods throughout the city, immigrant workers wake to begin long days in nearby canneries, mills, and shipyards.

On this day, like others in recent weeks, Baltimore residents rich and poor will meet on street corners to debate politics and the dominant issues of the day—slavery, secession, and the growing conflict between North and South.

Thirty miles away in the state capital of Annapolis, lawmakers in Maryland's General Assembly grant a charter, by legislative act, incorporating the Maryland Mutual Life and Fire Insurance Company as the state's first life insurance company.

FOUNDING FATHERS

In 1858 the idea of creating a mutual life insurance company, through which policyholders would share in the profits, was gaining popularity among knowledgeable

FACING PAGE: *Baltimore Harbor was bustling with activity in the years before the Civil War. Steamships and Federal Hill can be seen in the distance.* (Courtesy of the Maryland History Society)

Birds-eye view of Baltimore City, 1859.
(Courtesy of Enoch Pratt Free Library, Central Library/State Library Resource Center, Baltimore, Maryland)

businessmen. Life insurers headquartered in Massachusetts, New York, New Jersey, and Pennsylvania offered permanent protection to qualified applicants, based on written applications and medical examinations. New York Life, founded in 1845, had already appointed dozens of sales agents in all settled areas of the country.

What prompted a group of businessmen to form Maryland's first life insurance company? Baltimore, the largest city south of the Mason-Dixon Line, had several established banks, investment houses and financial institutions, but no insurance company that accepted risks on individual lives. In the late 1850s, the city was not a safe place to live or work. Overcrowding, disease, poor hygiene, frequent fires, and outbreaks of violence posed life-threatening conditions on downtown streets. More than ever before, people needed life insurance to bury the dead and take care of the living.

The gentlemen listed on the Maryland Mutual Life and Fire Insurance Company's original charter recognized the opportunity to respond to a growing need. Established and successful citizens, they represented a sampling of Baltimore businesses and professions.

Gilbert H. Bryson, a civil engineer and surveyor, had assisted Benjamin Henry Latrobe, architect of the U.S. Capitol and Baltimore's Basilica of the Assumption, constructed between 1806 and 1821, in laying out the route of the Baltimore & Ohio Railroad. James H. Bond was an established merchant. David Mauldin Perine, register of wills in Baltimore City and County, owned the Homeland estate north of the city. He was the fourth generation of the Perine family of West Baltimore potters. Edmund Smith served as president of the Republican Association of Baltimore. Samuel G. Spicer was a lawyer specializing in buying and selling real estate. Dr. James S. Stevenson had received his medical degree from the University of Maryland School of Medicine in 1841 and joined the school's Medical-Chirurgical faculty in 1843. James L. Young, carpenter and builder, owned a business begun by his father.

The charter approved by the Maryland General Assembly on March 5, 1858, served as the new corporation's organizational document. It provided guidelines for selecting directors and officers, setting premiums, assessing risks, building capital and surplus, and paying benefits, as well as preparing annual reports and scheduling annual meetings.

Most important, the charter created a mutual life insurance company, owned by its policyholder-members, who had a vote in making corporate decisions. Membership included "every person whose life shall be insured in this Company for the benefit of his or her family, or who shall procure a policy of insurance on his or her own life, or on the life of another . . . during the period of such insurance, and until said policy shall be paid, cancelled or surrendered."

Two years later, in 1860, James H. Bond, Samuel G. Spicer and James L. Young, acting for the corporation, placed an advertisement in three Baltimore daily newspapers. The ad notified "all applicants for insurance in the Maryland Mutual Life and Fire Insurance Company . . . to meet at the office of Elisha Harrington, No. 91 Second Street, Room No. 9, up stairs, on Tuesday, May 22nd, at 3½ o'clock, P.M. for the organization of said company."

Meeting attendees presented life insurance applications totaling $121,000—$21,000 more than required by the charter—and voted for a board of ten directors. On May 29 the directors elected officers and appointed a finance committee. George P. Kane, Baltimore's newly appointed marshal of police and former colonel in the First Maryland Artillery Regiment, was elected president unanimously. George W. Weems was elected vice president; Abram Requa, secretary; and Dr. John S. Chapman, medical examiner. By July 5, the board had found office space

at No. 3 Franklin Building renting for $300 annually. Meeting again on July 24, they appointed a committee "to arrange a Tariff of rates" that "would be universally popular with the American people." The premiums they approved were adapted from rates used by the Mutual Benefit Life Insurance Company of Newark, New Jersey.

On August 30, 1860, the board appointed W. A. Gold, Esq., from Texas, Maryland, a small quarrying community twelve miles north of Baltimore City, as the company's first agent. He was paid a 10 percent commission and received $25 to spend on advertising.

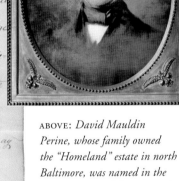

ABOVE: *David Mauldin Perine, whose family owned the "Homeland" estate in north Baltimore, was named in the charter as one of the company's members and founders.*
(Courtesy of the Maryland Historical Society)

LEFT: *This hand-written charter documents the creation and incorporation of the Maryland Mutual Life and Fire Insurance Company on March 5, 1858, by the General Assembly of Maryland.*

The Maryland Mutual Life and Fire Insurance Company, Maryland's first life insurer, announced its May 22, 1860, organizational meeting of applicants through this advertisement placed in three Baltimore newspapers.

LIFE INSURANCE . . .

European Import Grew Well on American Soil

THE FIRST LIFE INSURANCE POLICY was written in London in 1583 on an English citizen, for a term of one year. Like many immigrants and imports bound for the New World, life insurance barely survived its trans-Atlantic voyage, only to flourish once rooted in American soil.

Our country's earliest explorers, traders, settlers and pioneer families saw little need for life insurance protection. Self-sufficient, hearty risk-takers by nature, they relied on and took care of themselves and one another. "It is a strange anomaly," wrote Benjamin Franklin, "that men should be careful to insure their houses, their ships, their merchandise and yet neglect to insure their lives, surely the most important of all to their families and more subject to loss."

Over time, American religious groups, professional societies, and fraternal organizations began to provide "pooled" benefits for their members. Still, demand was so low in 1800 that just over a hundred individual life insurance policies were in force. The first life insurance agency business in the U.S., in fact, was not established until 1807 when Israel Whelan, an agent for London-based Pelican Life Insurance Company, set up shop in Philadelphia.

Between 1813 and 1845, groups of businessmen formed life insurance companies accepting risks in Pennsylvania, Massachusetts, New York, and New Jersey—all states with large and growing cities. Some companies began offering life insurance through agents who met face-to-face with customers. "Life insurance needed the help of many money-motivated advocates," wrote industry historian J. Owen Stalson. "It needed to be taken to market by able and adequately compensated salesmen."

In 1854, with per capita wealth in the U.S. estimated at $300 annually, life insurance sales totaled $15 million. By 1860, two years after the Maryland Mutual Life and Fire Insurance Company received its charter, that figure had more than doubled to $36 million.

Several factors converged to produce this mid-nineteenth century "boom" in life insurance sales. The nation began its move toward industrialization. Though the country was still predominantly rural, factories appeared where farms once prospered and manufacturing began to replace small-scale craftsmanship. Cities and transportation systems grew, creating jobs and new opportunities. Ships filled with immigrants arrived from Europe as farmers and freed slaves migrated north looking for work.

In cities like Boston, New York, Philadelphia and Baltimore, more and more Americans began to buy homes, wear store-bought clothing, and work for wages. Families had more to lose, and more to protect, should breadwinners die unexpectedly. With the help of a growing number of sales agents, citizens at all income levels began to understand why they needed life insurance.

By 1870 industry sales of individual life insurance (measured by the face value of policies) reached $588 million. The first billion dollar sales year was 1891.

> *"It is a strange anomaly, that men should be careful to insure their houses, their ships, their merchandise and yet neglect to insure their lives, surely the most important of all to their families and more subject to loss."*
>
> —Benjamin Franklin

Stage coaches, Conestoga wagons and push carts were familiar sights on Baltimore's Calvert Street in 1859. (Courtesy of the Maryland Historical Society)

POSITIONED FOR SUCCESS

On the surface, economic conditions in and around Baltimore City seemed ripe to support not only the sale of life insurance but also Maryland Mutual's ultimate success. With easy access to the sea, fertile farmland, and abundant waterpower, the city was prospering as a processing, manufacturing, warehousing, financial and commercial center.

Steamboats crisscrossed the Chesapeake Bay ferrying people, produce and fresh seafood. Clipper ships, built in Baltimore, left daily for Europe and the Orient, South America and the Caribbean. Merchants traveled in and out of the city along a network of roads and "turnpikes" extending into neighboring counties and states. Five railroad lines, including the Baltimore & Ohio, linked Baltimore businesses to points north, south and as far west as the Ohio River.

Thanks to rapid industrialization and an influx of European immigrants, the city's population had grown almost 600 percent, from 35,583 in 1814—the year Francis Scott Key wrote the *Star-Spangled Banner* as the British bombarded Baltimore's Fort McHenry during the War of 1812—to 212,418 in 1860. Location, transportation systems, population growth, housing, prosperous agricultural and manufacturing industries, and the availability of capital for expansion all combined to create a positive climate for growth of new goods and services.

But discontent was growing in Baltimore, and a political storm was gathering force. Over the next few years, both would have an impact on the company's progress and change forever the country's history.

DISCONTENT DIVIDES CITY

In the years leading up to the Civil War, congestion and overcrowding plagued the city. Downtown streets, the first in the country to be illuminated by gaslights, overflowed with people. The police department was staffed with political appointees. The fire companies, all volunteer, were undisguised centers of political activity. Neither was of the caliber a city of Baltimore's size required. Educational, cultural and social institutions benefited few of the city's poor, who were forced to compete with arriving immigrants for the lowest-paying jobs. Just as critical, a powerful, anti-immigrant American Party called the "Know Nothings" had seized control of city and state governments. Bigotry, corruption, and scare tactics were common.

Campaigning for mayor of Baltimore in 1860, reform candidate George W. Brown promised better law enforcement, safer streets and an end to political corruption. Though he received more than 65 percent of the popular vote, he soon faced challenges no mayor could have anticipated.

Half northern, half southern by location and heritage, Baltimore was a city divided in 1860. Its population included abolitionists and slave owners, industrialists and skilled craftsmen, laborers and elements of a landed, privileged aristocracy with close ties to the South. Twenty-five percent of the city's residents were European-born. Another 12 percent were black. Of that number, 90 percent were free.

As agitation grew over the issue of slavery, the state's many Southern sympathizers believed strongly in a U.S. Constitution that gave each state the power to defend itself from outside aggression and to decide for itself if slavery should exist within its borders. Even so, many Maryland citizens continued to support the Union, preferring compromise and peace to war—*if* peace could be achieved with the Union intact. When presidential candidate Abraham Lincoln declared "a house divided against itself cannot stand" and determined that "this government cannot endure permanently half slave and half free," many residents took his comments as a challenge to the concept of states' rights.

Elected president of the United States on November 6, 1860, Lincoln received only 2,294 votes in Maryland. In the weeks that followed, the people of Baltimore and Maryland watched in astonishment and dismay as seven Southern states seceded from the Union. Caught between North and South by personal and business ties, many Maryland families, friendships and business partnerships were torn apart by the conflict. Despite attempts by Baltimore's police department to maintain order, opposing political factions fought openly in the streets.

Fear of rioting in "Mob Town," the city's well-earned nickname in those unruly years, caused President-elect Lincoln to reschedule a midday ride through Baltimore on his way to Washington in February 1861. Amidst rumors of an assassination attempt, Lincoln avoided exposure to Southern sympathizers by sneaking through the city in the middle of the night. Baltimore citizens ridiculed the president for what they perceived as an act of cowardice.

BLOODSHED IN BALTIMORE

Less than two months later, just one week after the Confederate attack on Fort Sumter in Charleston, South Carolina, mob violence in Baltimore caused the Civil War's first real bloodshed and deaths.

Responding to Lincoln's call for troops to protect the nation's capital, the 6th Massachusetts Volunteer Militia Regiment and a larger unit from Pennsylvania arrived by train at Baltimore's President Street Station on the morning of April 19, 1861. Before continuing on to Washington on the B&O line, the cars containing two regiments of 1,700 men had to be pulled by teams of horses along Pratt Street and the waterfront to the B&O depot at Camden Station. The 6th Massachusetts set out first, but before they could cover a mile, an angry pro-Southern mob blocked the tracks with ships' anchors and piles of sand, forcing the last four cars to return to President Street. Four companies, 220 men, then set out for Camden Station on foot.

They had barely begun the march when the mob surrounded them, heaving rocks and paving stones. Rioters rushed into the ranks of the militia and attempted to snatch their rifles. Both sides fired shots.

Baltimore's Mayor Brown hurried to the front of the column, which stretched out nearly a third of a mile, to meet the officer in charge. At the rear of the line, between Light and Charles Streets, Marshal George P. Kane, who had resigned as Maryland Mutual's president, and dozens of policemen held back the mob with drawn revolvers. Under police protection, the troops continued their march to Camden Station without further violence, but by then, four soldiers and a dozen Maryland citizens had been killed.

"The authorities of the city did their best to protect both strangers and citizens, and to prevent any collision, but in vain," Mayor Brown wired President Lincoln. "Under these circumstances it is my solemn duty to inform you that it is not possible for more soldiers to pass through Baltimore, unless they fight their way at every step. I therefore hope and trust, and most earnestly request, that no more troops be permitted or ordered by the Government to pass through the city. If they should attempt it, the responsibility for the blood shed will not rest upon me."

The following day, a mob attacked two Baltimore newspaper offices and destroyed a press owned by a German-Jewish abolitionist. The city council appropriated $500,000 for defense against further incursions. Hearing that more troops were on their way, Marshal Kane and Mayor Brown met with Governor Thomas Hicks. The three men agreed that key railroad bridges should be destroyed to prevent additional troop trains from entering the city. Meanwhile, groups of secessionists tore down telegraph wires connecting Baltimore and Maryland to points north. Northerners were outraged. New York newspaper editor Horace Greeley called for Baltimore to be burned to the ground in retaliation.

George W. Brown was mayor of Baltimore in 1861.
(Courtesy of the Maryland Historical Society)

Four soldiers and twelve citizens died when Baltimore's Southern sympathizers attacked Federal troops passing through the city on April 19, 1861. It was the first bloodshed of the Civil War. (Courtesy of the Maryland Historical Society)

Colonel George P. Kane...

Baltimore Marshal of Police, Mayor, Monumental Life's First President

Elected president of the Board of the Maryland Mutual Life and Fire Insurance Company in 1860, Colonel George P. Kane turned out to be both a good risk and a worthy representative of the life insurance business, despite the fact that he spent time in federal prison for his Southern sympathies. His life and civic contributions serve as examples of the difficult role played by many Baltimore citizens during the war. Like Baltimore itself, Kane's beliefs, background, position and commitment to the city often found him caught between North and South.

Born in Baltimore in 1820, George P. Kane received a liberal arts education and, while still a young man, opened a grain and grocery business on Light Street Wharf. As president of Baltimore's Hibernian Society for many years, he served as an advocate for the welfare of Irish-American citizens and the education of their children. In 1849, President Zachary Taylor appointed Kane Collector of the Port of Baltimore, a federal position he held until 1853. In 1855 he was one of four businessmen to purchase Baltimore's old Merchants Exchange, on Second Street, for $90,000. Subsequently, they sold it back to the U.S. government for use as a customs house and post office.

Active in military and fire company matters throughout his life, Kane rose to the rank of colonel in the First Maryland Artillery Regiment. In 1858 he commanded the Montgomery Guards, a company composed exclusively of Irishmen. A former president of the Independent Fire Company, he belonged to an association whose members had served in the city's old volunteer fire companies. He suggested creating the city's first paid fire department.

On May 29, 1860, Kane was unanimously elected president of the Maryland Mutual Life and Fire Insurance Company—a position he held for only two

months. As talk of slavery, secession, and civil war increased on city streets, Baltimore's reform-minded citizens appointed Colonel Kane Marshal of Police in 1860. Serving as executive head of the police force, he reorganized the department and inspired in its members a new spirit and commitment to restore order and protection to the city.

That resolve was soon tested. On the morning of April 19, 1861, the 6th Massachusetts Volunteer Militia arrived at Baltimore's President Street Station. Responding to orders from President Lincoln to protect the nation's capital, the regiment had to change rail lines in Baltimore on its way to Washington, D.C. Marching through the city, four companies of Union soldiers were met by a crowd of taunting, stone-throwing Southern sympathizers. At Charles and Pratt Streets, Kane reportedly waved a revolver and shouted, "Keep back, men, or I'll shoot." Despite his attempts to prevent violence, twelve rioters and bystanders and four soldiers were killed in the first bloodshed of the Civil War.

On June 27, 1861, a detachment of federal officers arrested Kane in his home on St. Paul Street and took him to Fort McHenry. Military authorities eventually transferred him to Fort Warren in Boston Harbor along with Mayor George Brown, the city's police

ABOVE: The directors of Maryland Mutual Life and Fire Insurance Company elected George P. Kane the company's first president on May 29, 1860, a position he held for only two months. History remembers Kane as Baltimore's marshal of police during the riot of April 19, 1861. He was elected mayor of Baltimore in 1877 and died in office a year later.

his death on June 23, 1878.

A defender of the city and an avowed Southern sympathizer, Kane was admired during his lifetime and mourned in death by many Baltimoreans.

"It is not so much as a politician that [he] will be sincerely mourned," noted an editorial in the Baltimore *Sun*, "—for his principles were too rigid for partisans—but as a citizen of Baltimore who by native force of character raised himself to the highest positions in the city of his birth, both federal and municipal, and who as a merchant and official commanded their trust and confidence, because he proved he deserved it."

commissioners and several members of the Maryland legislature. Suspected secessionists, they were held as political prisoners for fourteen months without ever being tried or charged with a crime. In November 1862, Secretary of War Edwin M. Stanton released them all unconditionally.

Kane moved south to Richmond following his release. According to one account, he received a commission on General Robert E. Lee's staff and was with Lee at the Battle of Gettysburg. According to another, he left with Jefferson Davis when the Confederacy evacuated Richmond after the surrender at Appomattox Courthouse.

Records document that Kane was manufacturing tobacco in Danville, Virginia, in 1865. He returned to Baltimore in 1867, served on the Jones Falls Commission and was elected sheriff of Baltimore by the Democratic Party in 1873. Elected mayor four years later, he served briefly in that position until

John N. McJilton
(1860–1869)

John N. McJilton, D.D., born in 1805, had a long and distinguished career in Baltimore before the outbreak of the Civil War. City records confirm that he was interested in literature, science and the arts from a young age. Recognized as editor of both the *Baltimore Athenaeum* and the *Baltimore Literary Monument*, he was a teacher at Public School #1 on Fayette Street in 1837. The same year, he helped found the Maryland Academy of Fine Arts. In 1847, Matchett's Baltimore Directory listed his address as 103 Hanover Street and his occupation as "treasurer of public schools."

McJilton was so well known in Baltimore literary circles in the 1840s that even Edgar Allan Poe knew of him. In a letter to McJilton dated August 11, 1841, Poe wrote the following about a piece of encoded writing he thought McJilton had published under a fictitious name: "As my solution in this case will fully convince you of my ability to decipher the longer but infinitely more simple cryptograph, you will perhaps excuse me from attempting it—as I am exceedingly occupied with business. Very truly yours. Edgar A. Poe." McJilton responded: "This is certainly intended for someone else. I know nothing of the matter whatever. . . . I suppose some wag has addressed you anonymously whom you have mistaken for me. JNM."

Ordained an Episcopal minister in 1843, Reverend McJilton remained interested in the arts. On January 6, 1848, he delivered the opening address of the Maryland Association for the Encouragement of Literature and the Arts. While pastor of the Trinity Chapel on North Avenue in the mid-1850s, he was also a member of the Maryland Institution for the Instruction of the Blind and served as trustee of Hampden Hall, a literary institution in Baltimore County.

McJilton joined the board of directors of the Maryland Mutual Life and Fire Insurance Company on July 23, 1860. A few days later, he was unanimously elected the company's president. Board minutes from December 1869 indicate that, like his predecessor, George P. Kane, McJilton "was removed from the city" during the Civil War, but we do not know when he left Baltimore or when he enlisted as a Union soldier. We do know that he wrote a letter to Maryland governor Augustus W. Bradford on October 18, 1862, in which he discussed hospital conditions near the battlefields. Along with other Civil War veterans, he helped found the Maryland Soldiers Relief Association for disabled soldiers and their families in 1864.

As chaplain for the Maryland Hospital in the late 1860s, McJilton officiated at Sunday services in the hospital chapel. A published report to the state's medical superintendent states, "his visits [were] looked for with much pleasure by those patients who have a religious sentiment and who wish to be present for worship."

Reverend McJilton died in 1875 at the age of seventy. The Maryland Historical Society has preserved and archived many of his writings and papers.

Edgar Allan Poe wrote the following about a piece of encoded writing he thought McJilton had published under a fictitious name: "As my solution in this case will fully convince you of my ability to decipher the longer but infinitely more simple cryptograph, you will perhaps excuse me from attempting it—as I am exceedingly occupied with business.

Very truly yours. Edgar A. Poe."

Samuel Kramer
(1869–1870)

When the directors of the Maryland Mutual Life and Fire Insurance Company resolved to cease taking risks on January 3, 1862 "owing to the . . . unsettled conditions of the country," Samuel Kramer was secretary of the Executive Committee. He continued to be listed as a member of the Executive Committee throughout the war, though the company had ceased writing business.

Like George P. Kane, Kramer was involved in the April 1861 skirmish with the 6th Massachusetts, but he was neither arrested nor sent to prison. A staunch Unionist, he enlisted on November 1, 1861, as a chaplain and was promoted to the rank of major a year later. He fought for the Union as a major in the 3rd Maryland Volunteer Infantry Regiment.

Formed in August 1861, the 3rd Regiment was sent to Harpers Ferry, Virginia, on May 24, 1862, to protect the town from General Stonewall Jackson and his advancing Confederate troops. The regiment also fought at Antietam, Chancellorsville and Gettysburg. Though thousands of Union troops were killed in those battles, Kramer survived, was discharged on August 21, 1863, and returned to Baltimore to resume his board position at Maryland Mutual.

Meeting on December 6, 1869, Samuel Kramer and other members of the company's Executive Committee resolved to resume operations. Because Reverend McJilton was no longer able to "occupy the position of president . . . Samuel Kramer was elected in his stead" as Maryland Mutual's third president. He resigned as both a director and the company's president just two months later on January 27, 1870. Surviving company records give no reason why.

On the morning of May 14, 1861, Baltimore awoke to find 1,500 Massachusetts soldiers camped on Federal Hill on the south side of the harbor, with cannons covering the city. Their commander, General Benjamin F. Butler, had acted without orders and was severely reprimanded, but the troops remained. These men, photographed months later, are from New York. (Courtesy of the Maryland Historical Society)

Fearing the loss of Maryland to the Confederacy, President Lincoln moved cautiously but firmly. On the morning of May 14, 1861, Baltimoreans awoke to find 1,500 Union soldiers camped on Federal Hill, overlooking the harbor. Martial law was declared and the writ of habeas corpus suspended. Between June and September of 1861, Marshal Kane, Mayor Brown, several city commissioners and state legislators, and a number of citizens were arrested and held at Fort McHenry without charges for their role in the riots or out of suspicion that they intended to aid the rebellion.

Seven months later, on January 3, 1862, the directors of the Maryland Mutual Life and Fire Insurance Company met and "resolved that owing to the present unsettled condition of the country and present great prostration of business, the Company do cease for the present to take risk of life or fire insurance." With Marshal Kane in federal prison, and businessmen reportedly loading their money and valuables onto ships in the harbor, the company stopped accepting applications for the duration of hostilities.

Between 1861 and 1865, almost 30,000 Baltimore citizens left the city—women and children, to safety; men, to fight for either the Union or the Confederacy. Among them were several of the company's officers and directors.

Two prominent Baltimore citizens—John N. McJilton, an Episcopal minister, and Samuel Kramer—both elected directors in 1860, succeeded George P. Kane as president of the company's board. Board minutes dated December 6, 1869, note that McJilton, "having removed from the city and being unable . . . to occupy the position of president. . . . Samuel Kramer was elected in his stead."

CHAPTER 2

Mutual Life Marches On
(1870–1898)

"ICOULD PAINT THIS PICTURE from memory," notes the Mutual Life agent. "Row upon row of red brick houses. Horse-drawn carts parked on crowded streets. Outhouses sitting in narrow alleys. Laundry stretched on lines across tiny backyards. Everywhere I go the scene is the same, regardless of the street." On this early summer evening, bits of conversation escape from open doors and windows to remind him where he is. Neighbors meet and exchange news. Guttural German, lilting Irish brogues, Italian, Polish, Yiddish, Russian and Greek—the words are different, depending on the neighborhood. Almost all are foreign, or English overlaid with a distinct accent.

The working-class communities near Baltimore's downtown harbor are the agent's assigned territory, his "debit." He is responsible not only for sales but also for providing service. Working in densely populated ethnic neighborhoods, he will walk from call to call. Week after week, he climbs the same wooden or white marble steps and knocks on similar doors —to greet familiar faces, update information and collect his clients' premiums. Should one of them die, he will be there, representing the company, to deliver promised benefits to the family.

Five years as a Mutual Life agent, he knows these neighborhoods well, and people know him. They wave to him on the street. They welcome him into their homes. He listens to their hopes and dreams, drinking coffee at the kitchen table. Clients seem to enjoy his visits and the personal, face-to-face attention as much as he does. Best of all, they introduce him to their family members and friends. This job gives him the opportunity to help people. That's why he likes it. His customers, mostly European immigrants like himself, came to America hoping to improve their lives. And, in many ways, they have. If only their children could go to school instead of having to work for scant wages in the city's sweatshops.

Life is better in Baltimore since the war, but money is still tight. Most of his clients work twelve-hour days. Many earn less than $450 annually and pay about $75 a year to rent their modest homes. Even so, on average they give him sixty

FACING PAGE: *These rowhouses in Baltimore's Fells Point were typical of the working-class neighborhoods in which Mutual Life agents wrote business in the late 1800s.*

(Courtesy of Enoch Pratt Free Library, Central Library/State Library Resource Center, Baltimore)

In the 1870s, horse-drawn wagons still delivered merchandise to merchants on Baltimore streets paved with cobblestones.
(Courtesy of the Maryland Historical Society)

cents a week for their life insurance premium. In a few homes, like the Engels' on Light Street, he collects as much as $1.82 weekly, because both the husband and wife are insured. Mr. Engel, a barrel maker by trade, and his wife, a housekeeper, are typical of Baltimore's working class in the late 1870s. Thanks to him, they seem to understand the importance of having life insurance and pay their premiums weekly to keep it in force.

If his clients are not home when he stops to collect, the agent knows where to find them. Most work nearby—in the city's shops and garment factories, on the docks, in the downtown packinghouses, shoveling coal in the rail yards or laying bricks on neighborhood streets. Sometimes he'll catch up with out-of-work craftsmen looking for jobs in one of Baltimore's guildhalls. He may even find "the oysterman," a real character, sitting on a barstool, beer in hand, at his favorite Fells Point saloon.

Walking these neighborhoods, block by block, the agent will not go home until he makes a sale and collects all premiums due. No wonder the soles of his shoes wear out so quickly. Luckily, a few of his customers are shoemakers.

On March 1, 1873, the Mutual Life Insurance Company of Baltimore issued a life insurance policy to a German-born immigrant tailor named Valentin Bauscher. Mr. Bauscher paid ninety cents a week for $1,000 of coverage. His was the first individual, paid-weekly "Industrial" life insurance policy issued in the United States.* Policies sold by agents and paid weekly by tradesmen, small business owners, farmers, watermen and inner-city, blue-collar workers provided the foundation for the company's growth and success in Baltimore for more than one hundred years.

NEW NAME, NEW FOCUS

Occupied for four years by Federal troops, Baltimore sustained no physical damage during the Civil War. Though caught between North and South, the city's economy was not so much hurt by the war as reordered by it. Before the war, Baltimore had been a major provider of goods and services to the South. This changed as fighting in neighboring states, the military's use of the railroads, and the Union blockade of Southern ports disrupted commerce and the normal flow of raw materials, manufactured products and people in and out of the city. On the other hand, Baltimore became an even more important railroad, supply and medical center during the war, and many firms became prosperous equipping Union troops.

Following Robert E. Lee's surrender to General Ulysses S. Grant at Appomattox Courthouse in 1865, soldiers who had fought on both sides made their way home. Trade and business increased as Baltimore investors poured resources into rebuilding the South. Lives gradually returned to normal, with one noteworthy change. In 1864, the Maryland legislature had outlawed slavery. In 1867 the Fifteenth Amendment to the U.S. Constitution, which Maryland did not ratify, proposed giving black men the right to vote. In 1870, the first black voter cast his ballot, without incident, in a Baltimore City election.

As peace and prosperity returned, the directors of the Maryland Mutual Life and Fire Insurance Company met in December 1869. They resolved to resume operations and authorized officers to issue insurance policies as prescribed by the company's charter.

In January 1870 board member Benjamin Griggs Harris went to Annapolis to ask the Maryland General Assembly to change the company's name to the "Mutual

---

* Industrial insurance is characterized by death benefits of $2,000 or less, minimum underwriting requirements and weekly, bi-weekly or monthly payments collected in the policyowner's home by a sales agent. Also called debit insurance. (Life Office Management Association Glossary of Terms, 1992).

Life Insurance Company of Baltimore." On February 16, directors approved the name change, deleting all reference to fire insurance. (By then, the city of Baltimore was better protected against fire with a paid, professional fire department.) The amended by-laws stated: "the business of the company shall be confined exclusively to insurance on lives, and to insurance appertaining to, or effecting lives, and on a purely mutual plan." The same day, board members elected directors and officers to fill vacancies caused by the war. The men they selected would be responsible for leading the company back into the business of selling life insurance.

The directors then elected Benjamin G. Harris president, at an annual salary of $3,000. Augustus C. Pracht was elected vice president and James H. Cox, secretary. Directors agreed to pay Cox $1,200 per year, plus any commissions earned as a solicitor/agent. The board also elected Dr. Riggin Buckler chief medical examiner. He received $3 for examinations performed in his own

office or the company's office, and $5 for each examination performed elsewhere.

Board members John Willcox Jenkins, a wholesale shoe dealer, and John Bowes, a dry goods merchant, were appointed to the Finance Committee. John Baptist Piet, a printer and bookseller, and Ernest Knabe, whose father had founded the world-famous Wm. Knabe & Co. piano manufacturing company, were appointed to the Auditing Committee. John E. Weatherby, a stove dealer, and James E. Stansbury, owner of an oyster and fruit packing business on South Broadway, headed the Agencies Committee. William H. Read, a mineral water manufacturer, and William G. Scarlett, a mercantile owner, became responsible for claims. All but three were Baltimore natives; two had been born in Europe.

On February 22, 1870, the Finance Committee reported that President Harris and each of the directors had personally pledged bonds and securities, as required by the company's charter, to create a Guarantee Capital

Baltimore, looking south toward the Inner Harbor from Mt. Vernon Square and the Washington Monument, 1862. The monument was completed in 1829.
(Courtesy of the Maryland Historical Society)

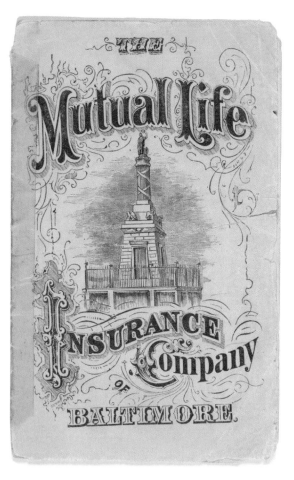

Mutual Life of Baltimore rate book, 1870.

Fund of $100,000 "payable in case of losses beyond the ability of the company to meet in such sum and at such times as may be required."

After leasing office space at 196 West Baltimore Street for $2,500 for one year, the board approved the design for a company seal, authorized the printing of signs and advertising with the company's new name, and republished its book of rates. Equally important, they authorized the Agencies Committee to "grant commissions to solicitors, from 20 to 30%, but not to exceed an average of 25%." They set Ordinary policy limits at $5,000, with the excess over $5,000 covered by reinsurance, and agreed that "all premiums be paid in cash in annual, semi-annual or quarterly installments, according to the rates established for deferred payments."

Maryland's first life insurer was finally back in business.

FIRST POLICYHOLDERS

Officers and directors immediately submitted applications for $5,000 of life insurance on their own lives. Director John Willcox Jenkins was issued the first policy under the company's new name, for which he paid a $288.15 annual premium.

Eager to issue more insurance, board members passed a resolution on March 3, 1870, authorizing Mutual Life's Superintendent of Agencies to "proceed to Frederick to solicit life insurance policies from the members of the Methodist Conference there assembled" and to "make arrangements with some of the ministers to act as our agents . . . at a commission of 25% on the first year's premium." The prospecting trip was very profitable. In the spring of 1870, Mutual Life issued dozens of policies to farmers and their relatives living in this agricultural

community forty-five miles west of Baltimore City. By year-end, applications from Frederick County farm families accounted for almost 25 percent of the company's sales.

On March 25, 1870, the mayor and City Council of Baltimore authorized the company to begin providing $1,000 in insurance on the life of every member of the Baltimore City Fire Department on what was essentially a group contract. The city of Baltimore paid the premium of $24.78 per person per year.

The company's first policies were Ordinary insurance, primarily endowments and limited pay contracts. Considered quite progressive at the time, most nonetheless included geographical and occupational restrictions, such as the following clause, that limited the company's liability:

> If a person whose life hereby insured shall travel or reside beyond the settled limits or the protection of the Government of the United States . . . or shall enter upon a voyage upon the high seas (except as hereinafter specified); or shall be personally engaged in blasting, mining, submarine operations or the production of highly inflammable or explosive substances; or in working or managing a steam engine or circular saw in any capacity; or as mariner, engineer, fireman, conductor, express manager, or laborer in any capacity upon service on any sea, sound, inlet, river, lake or railroad; or shall enter any military or naval service whatsoever (the militia, when not in actual service excepted) without the consent of the Company in each or either of the foregoing cases, previously given in writing; or if he shall die in, or in consequence of, a duel, or of the violation of the law of any nation, state or province, or if his death shall be caused by the use of intoxicating drink or opium; this policy shall be null and void.

Despite such restrictions—which speak volumes about the hazards of nineteenth century life and the reluctance to insure against them—Mutual Life's policies provided individual life insurance protection at competitive rates that, until then, had not been offered to Maryland residents by a Maryland-based insurer.

The company's first policyholders were business owners, merchants, manufacturers, millers, printers, doctors, lawyers, farmers, hotelkeepers, housekeepers, clerks, blacksmiths and citizens who simply listed their occupations as "lady," "gentleman" or "farmer's wife."

The information provided on their applications paints an interesting picture of the culture, life, work, causes of death and challenges faced by some Maryland families during the company's earliest years.

One applicant's mother died of malaria. Another's sister "had cancer on her hand and in amputation died from the effects." Other applicants had lost family members to scarlet fever, cholera, consumption, pneumonia, typhoid fever, childbirth and "change of life." A man named Myerly said his father was murdered. W. T. Russell's father "drowned at sea." A Mr. Gaither noted that his mother died after she "was thrown from a carriage, broke her shoulder and died from hemorrhages six months later." Answering the question "Have you ever had a serious illness?" another man wrote that he "was shipwrecked in 1862" but suffered "no injury, merely prostration." One forty-year-old woman simply responded "Yes" to the question "Are your habits of life correct and temperate?"

Several applicants —including Charles Willey, shot in

the leg while fighting in 1862; Thomas Kramer, who lost a brother; George Boulder, whose brother died from exposure in prison; and Mary Owings, whose brother served in the Confederate army—had been injured themselves or lost siblings during the Civil War.

One application dated 1870 shows that not all wounds and animosities were healed by war's end. Responding to the question "Have you ever lived outside the United States?" applicant Ernest LaGarde wrote: "Yes, in the Confederate States of America as a soldier in the Confederate Army." Born in New Orleans, Mr. LaGarde was a professor at Mount St. Mary's College in Emmitsburg, Maryland, when he applied for his Mutual Life policy.

LEFT: *Mutual Life of Baltimore was insuring the city's industrial workers, as well as the child seated among them, by 1879.*
(Courtesy of the Lacy Foundry, Baltimore)

BUILDING A BUSINESS

For these and other Maryland families, the war years brought home the reality that life is precious and unpredictable, that tragedy can strike without warning, and that loss of life and livelihood can change forever one's plans and dreams. Looking toward the future, surviving family members began to recognize the value and purpose of having life insurance. And Mutual Life was ready with products to protect their lives and incomes.

In 1870, its first active year in business after the war, the company issued more than three hundred policies to Maryland natives and immigrants living in Baltimore and its rural surrounding counties. Mutual Life's offices moved to 17 South Street in March 1871. On June 27, 1871, board members approved payment of the company's first claim, for $1,000, on the life of policyholder Joshua Gilbert Jordan. Two years later, death claims paid to ten Maryland families totaled $3,650.

Over the next ten years, Mutual Life continued to prosper, grow, and pay promised benefits, reaching a major milestone in 1883 of 3,961 policies and $1,000,000 of life insurance in force "upon lives of the citizens of the State of Maryland."

Why did Mutual Life succeed when other, more established competitors struggled to survive a decade of severe economic depression and unemployment? Several reasons stand out. One was that, unlike some life insurers in those years, Mutual Life accepted applications on women's lives. In 1873 alone, coverage on women accounted for about 11 percent of the company's new business. In 1879 the board also approved coverage for infants and children. The expanded product line and larger base of potential insureds no doubt influenced the company's growth and success.

But the real surge in policy count and premium resulted from two key decisions made by Mutual Life's forward-thinking board early in the decade. First, in 1871 the directors voted to open a German Department. Then, in 1873 they authorized a new policy form that provided individual life insurance coverage for policyholders paying premiums on a weekly basis. The popularity of these small, paid-weekly "Industrial" policies changed forever Mutual Life's future and its way of doing business.

INDUSTRIALIZATION ATTRACTS IMMIGRANTS

In the years following the Civil War, the city's leaders actively supported reconstruction, industrial development, and the growth of foreign trade. Wealthy Baltimore citizens like financier Alex. Brown, merchant Johns Hopkins and B&O Railroad president John Work Garrett helped fuel economic recovery by investing in new rail lines, streetcars, lumber companies, and mines. Entrepreneurs financed the building of new mills, factories, foundries, machine shops, slaughterhouses, meatpacking plants and canneries. Between 1870 and 1900, the number of Baltimore industries tripled as capital investment increased six-fold. The city became a major importer of raw materials—grain, coal, cotton, leaf tobacco, coffee, sugar and fruits—and a leading exporter of men's clothing, straw hats, boots, shoes, seafood, liquor, canned fruits and vegetables, processed oysters, fertilizer, coal, iron and steel.

As industry expanded to meet the growing demand for manufactured goods, so did the city's need for workers. European families, Pennsylvania and Virginia farmers, former Confederates and freed slaves—all flocked to Baltimore looking for opportunities to improve their lives.

Most immigrants arrived in Baltimore with little or no money, no promise of a job and no place to live. Before long, though, shoemakers, tailors, and seamstresses found work in the Garment District. Less skilled workers—including thousands of women and children—earned between forty cents and $1.25 a day cutting fabric, sewing buttons, operating machines and performing repetitive tasks in the city's sweatshops. Entire families worked side-by-side in Fells Point and Canton canneries—shucking oysters, shelling peas and skinning tomatoes. Muscled men stoked foundry furnaces, built ships and rail cars, and laid miles of track for the coming Railroad Age. Along with blacksmiths, barrel makers, carpenters, ship caulkers and bricklayers, they contributed to Baltimore's reputation as a tough, gritty city.

In 1877, B&O Railroad workers earned just $400 a year. When railroad owners cut wages by 10 percent, angry and desperate B&O workers called strikes that prevented trains from leaving Martinsburg, West Virginia, and Cumberland, Maryland. On July 20, 1877, B&O President Garrett met with Maryland governor John Carroll at Baltimore's Camden Street Station. Anticipating similar strikes or worse in Baltimore, Governor Carroll called up the Fifth and Sixth Regiments of the Maryland National Guard. As he had feared, the crowds that gathered that Friday evening at Baltimore's Camden Street and Mt. Clare Stations included not only striking railroad workers and their families—many of whom were Irish immigrants—but also sympathetic neighbors, city shopkeepers, factory workers and laborers.

The strike, subsequent riots, and deaths of more than one hundred citizens in Baltimore and elsewhere along the nation's railways called attention to the rigors of railroad

life, raised public awareness of railroad working conditions and generated support for worker grievances. In response to the riot and public outcry, the B&O established an Employees' Relief Association in 1880 that provided workers with benefits—including sick pay, time off for accidents, and eligibility for death benefits—in return for each worker paying a monthly premium equal to one day's wage. In 1884, the B&O also established the nation's first pension plan. (Eighty years later, in 1964, more than 25,000 active and retired B&O workers would be covered by life and disability insurance benefits provided by Mutual Life, then named Monumental Life. Many of those benefits were still in force in 2007.)

Looking for better wages and benefits, immigrants applied for jobs at the new Hampden-Woodberry cotton mills, located on land annexed from Baltimore County in 1888. Hampden-Woodberry, one of the largest mill sites in the country, was connected to downtown Baltimore by streetcar, employed nearly 4,000 workers, and produced almost 80 percent of the world's cotton duck cloth. Because it provided workers with affordable, company-owned housing, Meadow Mill, owned by William E. Hooper, whose son James became a Mutual Life director, was considered a haven for women and working-class families.

Immigrant women found work as seamstresses in Baltimore's Garment District.
(Courtesy of the Maryland Historical Society)

An 1877 strike by B&O Railroad workers prompted railroad management to establish an Employee Relief Association to provide sick pay, death benefits and the nation's first pension plan.
(Courtesy of the B&O Railroad Museum)

LEFT: *Following the Civil War, thousands more European immigrants arrived in Baltimore looking for jobs and opportunities to begin new lives. Mutual Life hired German-speaking agents, opened a German Department, and insured many German families.*
(Courtesy of the Maryland Historical Society)

By the late 1880s, the city's immigrants could also find moderately priced, affordable housing in "row house" neighborhoods in East Baltimore, around the harbor, and near the city's rail and stockyards. In fact, thanks to the creation of neighborhood building and loan associations in those years, Baltimore's rate of home ownership among blue-collar, working-class families was the highest of any American city.

But many of the most skilled European immigrants could not read, write or understand English. They gravitated to Baltimore because they found communities and ethnic neighborhoods where they could speak their own language. They built churches and synagogues and established their own schools, mutual aid societies,

fraternal organizations, newspapers and building & loan associations. Butchers and bakers opened shops to meet their neighbors' needs. Though newcomers mingled with Americans and other European-born immigrants on the job, at night they retreated to the familiar sights, sounds, and smells of their own close-knit ethnic neighborhoods.

These lower and middle-income, ethnic communities became home for many of the European-born immigrants who later purchased Mutual Life policies. When addresses of the company's policyholders are overlaid on an 1870s map of the city, it is interesting to note how many are clustered in the industrial, working-class neighborhoods near the Garment District, cotton mills, canneries and rail yards.

THE PROVIDENTIA

It was no coincidence that 70 percent of the company's policies issued in 1873 covered the lives of German-born immigrants. In 1860, Germans made up 25 percent of the city's population. When in 1868 the owners of the B&O started direct steamship service between Bremen and Baltimore, thousands more Germans booked passage to the United States. By 1870 thirty thousand Baltimore residents, 35 percent of the city's population, claimed German descent. Though they were joined by large groups of Irish Catholics, Italians, Poles, Russians and Greeks between 1870 and 1910—and to a smaller degree by natives of Bohemia, Lithuania and Scandinavia—Germans continued to be the largest foreign-born group living in Baltimore until 1920.

By creating a German Department, Mutual Life's directors recognized the size and importance of the city's German population. Working through the Providentia Society of the City of Baltimore, they signed a contract with Dr. William S. Landsberg, future board secretary, giving him the authority to "appoint German agents, procure German risks and establish Bunds or Societies in the territory now worked by the company."

The Providentia was a beneficial association for immigrants of German descent, chartered by the Maryland legislature on October 4, 1871. Though the society did not directly insure the lives of its members, it did procure policies for them with a life insurance company. The Mutual Life Insurance Company of Baltimore was the Providentia's underwriter. Policies were "conducted on the Mutual Plan . . . to better the situation of those whose families are dependent on them for support." As policyholders, members of the Providentia were also members of Mutual Life. Coverage insured their lives and provided money to family members in case of death, "or the same sum to themselves, should they attain a given age." Member benefits also included a "weekly sick annuity" paying a fixed weekly sum, usually $7 per week, to members "incapacitated by sickness from attending to work."

By the end of 1872 agents for the Providentia had procured 663 applications from 481 participating members. In return for coverage, members paid "weekly dues" installments and received receipt books with Certificates of Membership at the end of each quarter. They met regularly throughout the 1870s, 1880s and early 1890s at Raine's Hall—the local bricklayers' union hall at the corner of Baltimore Street and Customs House Avenue—to discuss issues, review benefits and elect officers. As one might expect, minutes for all Providentia meetings were recorded in both German and English.

ABOVE: *A meeting notice, in German, invited German immigrants to a January 1899 meeting of the Providentia Society of Baltimore.*

Providentia members met regularly at Raine's Hall, the local bricklayer's union hall at the corner of Baltimore Street and Customs House Avenue.

LEFT: *Many members of the Providentia were insured by Mutual Life. This certificate provided a $500 death benefit plus a weekly sick annuity of seven dollars to society members who became incapacitated by illness or injury.*

Valentin Bauscher . . .
Immigrant, Tailor, Providentia Agent and Officer

On March 1, 1873, Mutual Life issued a life insurance policy to a forty-seven-year-old German immigrant tailor named Valentin Bauscher, who lived with his wife Sara at 60 Milliman Street, not far from the Johns Hopkins Hospital. His was the first of thousands of individual weekly premium life insurance policies issued by Mutual Life beginning in the 1870s. For $1,000 of coverage, Bauscher made weekly payments of 90 cents "on or before the second day of each week in each and every year" until his eightieth year.

Bauscher had been living in Baltimore for at least ten years in 1873, and had probably arrived in the 1840s or 1850s as part of the first large wave of German and Irish immigrants. Where he practiced his trade, and for how long remains unknown. Mutual Life's applications asked only for occupation, not for an employer's name or address. He might have found work in the city's Garment District, where over 6,000 workers produced more than a third of the South's clothing, especially men's tailored suits and coats. L. Grief & Sons, owned by a German-Jewish immigrant, was just around the corner from Bauscher's rowhouse.

The first paid-weekly life insurance policy in the country was written on the life of a German immigrant tailor named Valentin Bauscher who lived with his wife Sara in this rowhouse at 60 Milliman Street in Baltimore, not far from the Johns Hopkins Hospital. Bauscher later became an agent and Providentia board member.

Bauscher evidently saw the need to protect his family against mishap and joined the Providentia Society, which led to his purchase of life insurance. Out-of-state insurers were writing life insurance in Baltimore, but only Mutual Life sold small, paid-weekly, policies to the city's working-class immigrants. We believe that his policy was the first individual paid-weekly "Industrial" life insurance policy issued by a U.S. insurer.

In 1874, Bauscher was listed in Providentia meeting minutes as one of the society's eighty member agents. Assigned by Dr. William S. Landsberg, Superintendent of Agencies, to the city's Northeast District, he was responsible for soliciting new members and collecting premiums near his home. He became a Providentia director in 1876 and served as vice president of the Providentia's board from 1883 to 1888.

Bauscher's name disappeared from Providentia meeting minutes after 1888, when he was sixty-three, but it is unlikely that he passed away before 1902, the year the Providentia canceled formal meetings. It was customary for associations to remember deceased board members and officers with formal resolutions, but none was drafted or approved for Valentin Bauscher. No deed, census, tax or death records could be found for Valentin Bauscher or his family. His whereabouts during his last years remain a mystery.

Industry mortality tables for 1873 estimated that Bauscher, then age forty-seven, might live another 23.17 years. In 1888 he had worked as a tailor, served the Providentia and Mutual Life for almost fifteen years, and was still seven years shy of turning seventy. If he had inherited his German parents' genes, he lived to experience "old age" and, like them, celebrated his eightieth birthday.

to form a new agreement, separate entirely from the Providentia, or find another solution that would benefit the company, "it being understood that we hereby assent our intention of complying in every particular with all contracts heretofore made by its policies issued."

The Providentia's agents received a 15 percent commission on first-year premiums and were expected to recruit at least one new member within eight weeks of their own application. They could use their commissions, paid by Mutual Life, to accumulate funds for future loans. Agents who collected weekly dues at the homes of members also received an allowance of one dollar per day, "provided the money collected [was] delivered to the office promptly and without any necessary delay." Applicants living outside of Baltimore paid an extra dollar to have their policies delivered.

In 1874, Dr. Landsberg, the Providentia's Superintendent of Agencies, divided his eighty agents into five district agencies or "committees"—South Baltimore, Central, Northwest, Northeast and Eastern—based on where business was concentrated in the city. By then, a separate branch of the Providentia also existed in Woodberry for members working in the cotton mills.

In 1875 directors of Mutual Life and the Providentia agreed to merge the two organizations' businesses and use a single policy form. For almost two more decades, Providentia agents continued to solicit members whose lives were protected by Mutual Life against death, accident, disability and illness.

In the early 1890s, with claims for sick benefits from Providentia members increasing rapidly because of disease and disability, Mutual Life's directors agreed that the relationship had ceased to be profitable or advantageous to the company. They gave the Executive Committee power

From these early seeds, grew Mutual Life's weekly premium business, its district agency system, and the company-defining tradition of providing home service and collections that survived into the twenty-first century.

INSURING MARYLAND'S WORKING CLASS

At a meeting of the company's directors in July 1892, President Harris proposed increasing business by "adding an Industrial Branch as conducted by the Metropolitan and Prudential Companies." The board voted unanimously to approve the plan and directed a committee consisting of Harris, Medical Director Dr. Henry M. Wilson and John F. Harris to "complete the organization and put it in operation."

Why were board members so enthusiastic about the new Industrial Branch? Since issuing the country's first weekly premium "Industrial" policy to Valentin Bauscher in March 1873, the company's weekly business had continued to grow. Despite the nationwide economic depression that began the same year, or maybe because of it, the small, paid-weekly policies appealed not just to Providentia members and immigrants but to Maryland's working-class citizens—including coal miners, farmers, and Chesapeake Bay watermen.

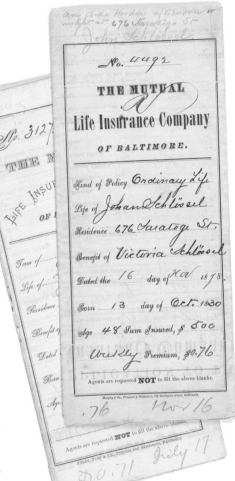

Forty-eight-year-old Johann Schlossel of 676 Saratoga Street in Baltimore paid seventy-six cents a week for his $500 Mutual Life policy issued in 1878.

Sold door-to-door by agents who collected premiums in their customers' homes, the Industrial Branch's policies and payment plan were so popular that, by year-end 1895, Mutual Life reported 6,039 weekly premium "Industrial" policies in force compared with 6,110 Ordinary policies paid annually, semi-annually or quarterly. Meeting in 1896, the board voted to discontinue the Ordinary plan, create a uniform table of rates, change policy forms, and begin issuing all policies on a weekly basis.

With that decision, President Harris and his board planted roots deep in fertile ground that would eventually make Mutual Life one of the country's oldest and largest providers of life insurance for lower- and middle-income families.

"It is a duty that every man owes to himself and family to afford such protection as his means will afford against his death," urged an insurance industry rating agency publication in 1898. "In these days, one can secure insurance [with a] reputable company. In the city of Baltimore, the Mutual Life Insurance Company, of Baltimore, has the highest standing and influence, and has paid many thousands of dollars to deserving families. This company operates in this city, and does an immense business in industrial insurance."

In the first six months of 1897 alone, Mutual Life's agents wrote more than $225,000 of new paid-weekly Industrial premiums. At year-end 1897, with 19,430 total policies and $209,369 in assets, Mutual Life hit its second major milestone—$2 million of insurance in force.

INVESTING IN THE REGION'S GROWTH

An insurance company collects premiums from its policyholders and invests those premiums to increase its assets, build surplus and create reserves to cover losses and claims. In its earliest years, Mutual Life's assets included home and farm mortgages as well as bonds and securities received from directors. These were held in its

vault as collateral. Annual statements submitted to the Maryland insurance commissioner in 1876 show shares in the Maryland Hotel in Annapolis from directors Robert Fowler, mill owner and Maryland State Treasurer from 1862 to 1870, and his son David, who became a Maryland circuit court judge in 1881. Other assets included shares in Baltimore's new Fountain Hotel, Baltimore City bonds valued at $7,000, and Kent County, Maryland, bonds worth $5,000.

As sales and premium income increased, the company's directors began investing in local housing, businesses, industry, public utilities and the region's transportation systems. In fact, at the board's request, the General Assembly amended Mutual Life's charter "so that the funds of the company might be loaned upon mortgages and leasehold property."

A list of Mutual Life's assets from the late 1890s shows over $90,000 in Baltimore City real estate and ground rents and $43,500 in mortgages—including one mortgage for $11,000 (earning 5 percent interest) on a Catonsville property owned by James Cardinal Gibbons, Catholic Archbishop of Baltimore. By the end of Maryland's "Railroad Age" in 1900, Mutual Life also held stock in several banks as well as bonds financing the Mt. Vernon Woodberry Cotton Duck Company, the Baltimore & Ohio Railroad, the Annapolis & Baltimore Short Line Railroad, the Chesapeake & Ohio Railroad, the Norfolk & Western Railroad, and other smaller rail lines serving the East Coast and Midwest.

The company's commitment to its policyholders' financial security, and to the growth and development of Baltimore and the State of Maryland, would continue into the new century, despite changes in company leadership in 1897.

CHANGING OF THE GUARD

As the century drew to a close, so did almost three decades of Benjamin G. Harris's leadership as president of Mutual Life. When he passed away in June 1897, he left a legacy of industry innovation and a company solidly positioned for continued success.

Mutual Life's directors issued a resolution expressing "their sorrow at the loss they have sustained in the death of their late President, Mr. B. G. Harris. From a long and intimate acquaintance extending over many years and affording every opportunity to observe his bearing in the responsible and exacting duties of his office, [we] declare it fitting thus formally to testify [our] appreciation of his courtesy and integrity as a man, his untiring faithfulness as an officer."

On July 8, 1897, Benjamin Harris's son, John F. Harris, was elected president of Mutual Life. A director since 1891, he had served as vice president under his father since 1892. When Mr. Harris announced that he was not a candidate for president in 1898, "his declination was received with regretful surprise by all the directors, and though urged to reconsider his determination, [he] refused to accept the nomination offered him." Harris nominated Matthew S. Brenan, board vice president and a director since 1892, to succeed him as president of the company. Elected unanimously, Matthew Brenan served as Mutual Life's president from 1898 to 1923.

Legacy of Leadership . . .

Benjamin G. Harris, President

Born in New Jersey on July 21, 1821, Benjamin Griggs Harris was the son of English immigrants. In 1854 city newspapers reported that he married Eleanor Neale, daughter of Baltimore businessman Francis Neale, at St. Peter's Catholic Church on Poppleton Street. By 1860, Harris lived with his wife's family in a large house at 23 Franklin Street, and he and his father-in-law were partners and general commission merchants in Neale Harris & Co. If their business was like others at the time, they made their money charging 5 percent commission on orders placed through their company.

Sometime between 1860 and 1870, Harris became president of the Patapsco Guano Company, a company on Philpot Street near Baltimore's Little Italy that produced and exported fertilizer. He sold the business shortly after being elected president of the Mutual Life Insurance Company of Baltimore in 1870. Census records document that by 1870 he had also moved his family—including his wife, their five children (aged five to fifteen), his father-in-law, and several servants—to a home in the Hampden-Woodberry area of Baltimore County.

Harris moved back to St. Paul Street in Baltimore City sometime in the 1880s, and it was there that he died in June 1897 after having served as Mutual Life's president for twenty-seven years. His son, John F. Harris, elected a director in 1891, succeeded his father as president and served for approximately one year.

Dr. Henry M. Wilson, Medical Director

A leading practitioner of medicine in Baltimore throughout the second half of the nineteenth century, Dr. Henry M. Wilson's name first appears as one of Mutual Life of Baltimore's medical examiners in February 1870. As the company's Medical Director for several decades, he never missed a board meeting until 1914. There was "a case of contagion in his household," note the board minutes from that year, "and the doctor, with his usual consideration, did not wish to endanger the health of the Directors by attending this meeting."

Born in Baltimore on February 2, 1829, Henry Merryman Wilson attended Dickinson College in Pennsylvania and received his medical degree from the University of Maryland in 1850. He joined the university's Medical-Chirurgical Faculty in 1853 and served as faculty secretary from 1859 to 1873, as vice president from 1873 to 1874, as president from 1874 to 1875, and as president of the University of Maryland Alumni Association in 1886 and 1887.

During the years he was Mutual Life's Medical Director, Dr. Wilson also served as physician to Baltimore's Aged Men's and Aged Women's Homes. His home and office were located at 306 W. Fayette Street in the 1860s and at 251 Madison Avenue in the 1870s and 1880s.

When Dr. Wilson's death was reported to the board on May 9, 1918, Mutual Life's directors endorsed the following resolution: "Dr. Wilson, connected with the company since its foundation and by his uniform courtesy, unselfish interest and valuable advice has largely contributed to the success which the company has achieved."

CHAPTER 3

Helping Baltimore Rebuild
(1900–1916)

USINESSMEN STARE in disbelief at blocks of burned out buildings. Men, women and children, huddled against the icy wind, gather on street corners to see the destruction. Exhausted firemen, covered in soot, aim hoses at heaps of smoldering debris. Where the rubble has cooled, the water freezes immediately, forming icicles on shattered windows, downed power lines, and charred telephone poles.

FACING PAGE: *After the fire of 1904, a businessman opens his "fireproof" safe to find the contents, in the basket at right, charred beyond recognition.*
(Courtesy of the Maryland Historical Society)

BELOW: *Baltimore policemen prevent crowds of curious spectators from entering downtown Baltimore's "Burnt District" on Sunday afternoon, February 7, 1904.*
(Courtesy of the Maryland Historical Society)

On this frigid February day in 1904, teams of firefighters pull down dangerous, crumbling facades. Baltimore's mounted police patrol debris-filled streets and wharves. Two thousand Maryland National Guardsmen control growing crowds of curious spectators. Along cordons surrounding what is being referred to as the "Burnt District," uniformed soldiers and sailors restrain citizens not holding passes issued by the city's Board of Police Commissioners. Ignoring the danger, anxious merchants and factory owners find ways past the barricades to reach their buildings.

Two days ago, on a quiet Sunday morning, a discarded cigar or cigarette started a small fire in the basement of the Hurst Dry Goods Company, a six-story brick warehouse on German Street between Liberty Street and Hopkins Place. Had a watchman been on duty inside the building, he might have quickly smothered the flames. Unfortunately, by the time passersby saw smoke escaping from windows and sidewalk grates, the fire had reached the fourth floor.

Firefighters from twenty-four fire companies worked night and day for thirty hours to control the raging blaze that began at the Hurst Dry Goods Company on German Street.
(Courtesy of the Maryland Historical Society)

At 10:48 A.M. a heat-activated alarm rang in the Fifth District Fire Station. Within two or three minutes, fire companies arrived at the scene. At 10:53 A.M. the Hurst building exploded in a loud roar, shooting flames and flying debris through the neighborhood. Falling bricks and glass buried an aerial ladder truck, a steam engine and a hose wagon. Narrow downtown streets, just thirty to forty feet wide curb to curb, created a funnel that fueled the flames. Hampered by a driving wind, intense heat, hydrants that lacked standardized fittings, and aging steam engines that could send water no higher than third story windows, overwhelmed firefighters quickly lost control of the blaze.

Baltimore's Great Fire of 1904 raged for thirty hours, consuming seventy square blocks (140 acres) of the downtown business district. Though twenty-four fire companies from as far away as New York and Atlantic City responded to Mayor Robert M. McLane's desperate calls for help, the blaze destroyed 1,500 buildings valued at $13 million and shut down 2,500 businesses. By Tuesday morning, February 9, more than 35,000 of Baltimore's 539,000 citizens were out of work. Remarkably, only one life was reported lost.

Some business owners were able to remove critical files, customer records, cash, securities and merchandise before flames reached their buildings. Unfortunately, time locks on bank doors prevented many depositors from rescuing cash and the contents of safety deposit boxes until Monday morning, when it was too late. Days later, bankers, financiers and merchants dug through ashes and hired teamsters to haul away safes and vaults containing valuables that could not be replaced. Millions of dollars in assets were recovered intact. When opened, some "fireproof" safes contained only charred paper.

CLOSE CALL!

Whether it was through good fortune, premonition, sound business decisions, or a combination of all three, the Mutual Life Insurance Company of Baltimore survived the Great Fire of 1904 without loss of life, business, property or investments.

Having deleted the word "fire" from its name in 1870, the company no longer offered fire coverage or accepted

RIGHT: *Mutual Life employees numbered just fifty-two in 1900 when this photograph was taken outside the company's 2 South Holliday Street offices. President Matthew S. Brenan is sitting center front, fourth from the right.*

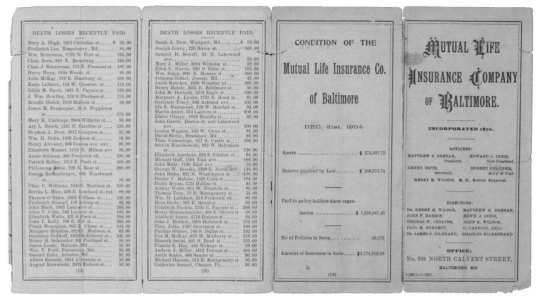

fire risks. Mutual Life continued to thrive, as it had following the Civil War, by selling life insurance to working-class families. As business grew, so did the need for more office space. In 1890 board members signed a new lease and moved the company's offices from 17 South Street, where they had been since 1871, to 2 South Holliday Street in the city's financial district.

When the century turned, Matthew S. Brenan had already been president of Mutual Life's board of directors for two years. On January 10, 1901, he reported that the lease on the South Holliday Street location would expire in September 1902. Considering the company's size and growing importance in the city, he suggested that Mutual Life purchase its own building. Expecting to have close to $3 million of life insurance in force on more than 27,000 lives by year-end 1901, the directors approved a bid limit of $25,000 and appointed Brenan and directors Thomas W. Jenkins, a cabinetmaker, and attorney Paul M. Burnett to a Building Committee charged with finding appropriate space. Jenkins had served as a Mutual Life director since 1886, Brenan since 1892, and Burnett since 1898.

Properties for sale in the downtown business district included the American National Bank Building at the corner of Gay and High Streets and a three-story brick building with thirty feet of frontage on the west side of Calvert Street, between Lexington and Saratoga Streets. At its April 1902 board meeting, Mutual Life's directors approved the purchase of 208 North Calvert Street for $12,300 and $200 in annual ground rent, with possession scheduled for September 15, 1902. They awarded the bid for needed improvements, estimated at $11,040, to a contractor and father of four named Luther Wright who had been born in England in 1858.

On January 22, 1903, President Brenan proudly opened Mutual Life's Calvert Street doors and invited directors to examine both the interior and exterior of their new offices. All agreed it was "an up to date building of the modern type, and well-constructed."

On the night of the great fire less than thirteen months later, the Calvert Street building sat directly in the inferno's path. Had the thirty mile-per-hour winds not shifted, halting the fire's northeastward march at Lexington and St. Paul Streets, Mutual Life's new building as well as the federal court house, the post office and Baltimore's city hall might have been destroyed. Turning south and east toward the piers and the Jones Falls, the blaze did engulf the Chamber of Commerce, the Stock Exchange, the Merchant's Club, the Maryland [Art] Institute, and the South Holliday Street block where Mutual Life's offices had been the year before.

ABOVE: *This Condition of the Mutual Life Insurance Company of Baltimore report, dated December 31, 1904, lists death claims paid in 1904. None were attributed to the Great Baltimore Fire.*

BELOW: *The 1904 fire destroyed seventy square blocks (140 acres) of downtown Baltimore, including the building at ● 2 South Holliday Street where Mutual Life offices had been located until January 1903. The company's new building at ● 208 North Calvert Street was spared when shifting winds turned the fire to the southeast.*

(Courtesy of the Maryland Historical Society)

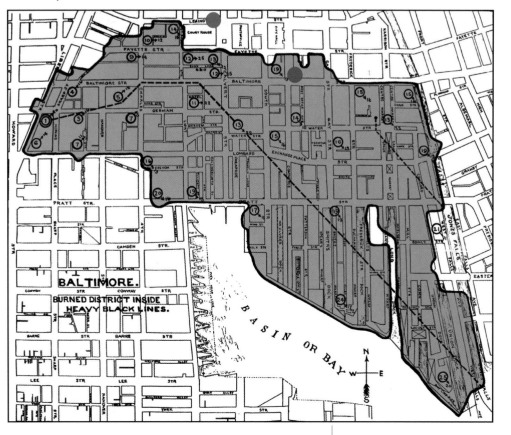

Also burned out was the office of Maryland insurance commissioner Lloyd Wilkinson on the seventh floor of the Merchants Bank Building—including charters, reports, and powers of attorney for over 250 insurance companies authorized to operate in the state. Only a few daybooks and ledgers that would fit in safes were saved. All other public records had to be replaced.

As fire enveloped the city's financial district later that evening, Mutual Life's officers had other concerns. Company securities valued at $111,000 were stored in a vault at the Continental Trust Building on Calvert and Baltimore Streets. At 10:15 P.M. flames shot up the sixteen-story skyscraper. Across the street, the Baltimore & Ohio Railroad Building was already burning. The corner soon became the hottest spot in the city—a "hellish maelstrom" wrote *Baltimore Sun* reporters—with temperatures reaching 2,500 degrees. By morning, the blaze had burned out many of the city's banks, investment houses, insurance companies and the offices of four daily newspapers—including the *Baltimore Herald*, where twenty-three-year-old H. L. Mencken was city editor. On Monday morning, all that remained of the Continental Trust Building was a gutted shell.

Reporting to Mutual Life's board on April 7, 1904, President Brenan told directors: "owing to the unsafe conditions of the Continental Trust Building, which was damaged by fire," the Executive Committee "had transferred the securities of the company to the vaults of the Safe Deposit & Trust Company." Like Alex. Brown & Sons on Baltimore and Calvert Streets, and the Mercantile Trust & Deposit Company one block away, the Safe Deposit & Trust Company had survived the Great Baltimore Fire with only broken windows and a few singed desks.

BALTIMORE BATTLES THE BLAZE

At the turn of the century, Baltimore's major banks, insurers, merchants, import/export firms and steamship lines were concentrated on or near Charles, Light, Calvert and South Streets, within a few blocks of the harbor basin. This commercial area and the central retail corridor along Howard Street provided employment for thirty thousand bankers, merchants, wholesalers, bookkeepers, secretaries and sales clerks. Though lower-paid workers and clerks still lived near the harbor and their jobs, many business

owners and merchants had already bought houses in the city's more affluent neighborhoods to the north and west, away from congestion and crowded narrow streets.

As flames consumed the downtown business district on Sunday, February 7, 1904, wealthy citizens gathered at the Belvedere Hotel, on the corner of Charles and Chase Streets north of the Washington Monument. Newly opened in 1903, the hotel's thirteenth floor provided an unparalleled view of the fire raging only eleven blocks to the south. Across the harbor basin, working families atop Federal Hill also watched the spectacle as the fire spread across the waterfront.

Irish-born Thomas O'Neill drove to the Carmelite Convent on Biddle Street and asked the nuns to pray that the fire would spare the magnificent department store he had begun to build upon arriving in Baltimore in 1866. Though well-constructed and protected by sprinkler systems and a fifteen-thousand-gallon rooftop water tank, his store at Charles and Lexington Streets stood directly in the fire's path. When firefighters asked permission to dynamite it as they had numerous other buildings, O'Neill refused. Quick-thinking employees stuffed rags in the downspouts as the flames approached, and smashed the water tank to soak the store's roof. As a result, only one corner of the building suffered any damage. To give thanks for his good fortune, O'Neill left the Catholic Archdiocese of Baltimore $7 million when he died in 1919.

By 1959 his legacy had doubled to $14 million, enough to fully fund the construction of Baltimore's new Cathedral of Mary Our Queen on Charles Street at the city's northern limits.

As the fire raged Sunday evening, Mayor McLane himself reportedly climbed into City Hall's belfry and tolled a warning bell. Within minutes, city workers arrived to move critical records to more secure vaults. Others grabbed brooms and formed bucket brigades to keep embers at bay. From the harbor, tugboats and fireboats poured water on wharves, lumberyards, and packinghouses. At the Consolidated Gas, Electric, Light & Power Company, employees rescued blueprints showing the location of the city's gas mains. These would later prove to be invaluable in rebuilding the downtown business district.

On St. Paul Street, citizens helped move three hundred patients from City Hospital to safer facilities. At the Central Telephone Exchange operators wrapped in wet blankets stayed on duty until 9:20 P.M., when their building caught fire and they had to be relocated, but their efforts had kept communication lines open and prevented downtown Baltimore from losing contact with surrounding cities and towns.

Flames continued to spread south and east well past midnight, threatening businesses and jobs in Little Italy, Fells Point and Canton, where many of Mutual Life's

O'Neill's Department Store, visible in the distance, was spared through the efforts of quick-thinking employees.
(Courtesy of the Maryland Historical Society)

ABOVE: *National Guardsmen prevent looting on blocks of gutted downtown buildings.*
(Courtesy of the Maryland Historical Society)

RIGHT: *Despite continuing clean-up and construction along the tracks, the St. Paul Street trolley was taking men and women to work within days of the blaze.*
(Courtesy of the Maryland Historical Society)

all bars closed and kept them closed for ten days, citizens simply stopped drinking. On Thursday morning, February 11, three thousand workers pitched in to clean up the streets.

At the White House in Washington, President Theodore Roosevelt considered dashing to Baltimore to help fight the blaze, but cooler heads prevailed. On Saturday, February 13, he sent his oldest daughter, Alice, to tour the Burnt District, see the full extent of the devastation, and deliver his message of good will and encouragement. Proving once again that they were as tough and gritty as their reputation, the hard-working people of Baltimore—including many Mutual Life policyholders—had helped save their city.

immigrant, blue-collar policyholders lived. As they put their children to bed that Sunday night, many no doubt worried that their neighborhoods, homes and livelihoods would go up in smoke. "Stop it at the Jones Falls!" became a rallying cry heard round the city. When the flames were indeed halted at the Jones Falls, thankful Italian families danced in the streets. Citizens delivered coffee, food and blankets to exhausted firefighters and horses. Restaurants remained open all night.

During the fire and the days that followed, there was no crime, no looting, and no rioting. No one was killed by violence. When the city's police commissioners ordered

BUSINESSES REBUILD

With trade and commerce so critical to economic survival, civic leaders, bankers, financiers, merchants and factory owners had long recognized the importance of adequately protecting their assets against loss. Even before smoldering embers cooled, Baltimore businessmen were optimistic about their ability to rebuild.

Two days before the fire broke out, the City Board of Estimates had approved a loan for new sewers, street paving, schools, firehouses and parks. The day after firefighters brought the blaze under control, business and financial leaders called emergency meetings to discuss reconstruction, including long-needed improvements to the downtown infrastructure. Baltimore's fire insurance companies also joined forces, creating the General Loss Committee to quickly resolve claims. During the next five months, the committee handled 3,778 claims and paid out over $29 million. Another 1,000 to 1,200 claims were settled directly by individual insurance companies.

When the *New York Times* reported that "Baltimore plans a greater city, millions in safe deposit vaults found intact . . . banks are sound," wholesalers, jobbers and creditors breathed a collective sigh of relief, and New York banks and financial institutions rushed to offer financing. One month later, Baltimore voters approved a $6 million loan to modernize their harbor.

Within two years, most burned out businesses had relocated to larger, more modern three- and four-story office buildings. Wider, smooth-paved roads replaced many cobblestone streets. Tangled overhead wires and utility poles disappeared. By 1906 city leaders could boast of new sewer connections, 150 miles of new gas mains and steam pipes, twenty-eight acres of harbor docks and markets, and new fire hydrants, alarm boxes and equipment.

The transformation was remarkable. Even more so was the city's refusal to accept "hand outs" or charity of any kind. Baltimore's business leaders—including Mutual Life—invested in rebuilding their city without the benefit of federal or state subsidies.

Though devastating, the Great Fire of 1904 spared most working-class neighborhoods, destroyed many aging, rat-infested wharves and warehouses, started a construction boom, created jobs, and provided the city's progressive, reform-minded leaders and politicians with the opportunity to create a safer, healthier, more vibrant downtown business center.

REFORMERS PUSH FOR SOCIAL CHANGE

Like many East Coast industrial cities, Baltimore still had its share of slums. Many less-skilled immigrants and factory workers spent long days living and working in stifling heat or freezing cold, in conditions that were both unsafe and unsanitary. Disease ran rampant in working-class neighborhoods and factories. Health care for the poor was minimal. Children did not have to attend school, and crooked politicians and political machines controlled Baltimore's mayors, the city council, and many service contracts.

As early as 1895, Baltimore's Reform League had pushed for safer streets, more efficient garbage removal, food inspections, sewers, and significant health and safety regulations. In local and national elections in 1900, concerned citizens supported progressive reform candidates, including vice presidential

Baltimore's city council passed the first law requiring city inspection and licensing of "sweatshops" in 1902. By 1908, Baltimore taxpayers supported twenty-eight park and schoolyard playgrounds as well as public baths where lower-income families could bathe and wash clothes. A year later, the city opened a hospital for the treatment of infectious diseases. In 1910 the General Assembly passed laws regulating slaughtering and food processing. With financial support from companies like Mutual Life, the city completed its long-awaited, much needed $20 million sewer system in 1911.

The country's life and health insurers approved of such social reforms because they would help control the spread of disease, improve policyholder health and quality of life, extend life expectancy, and ultimately reduce the cost of life insurance and the number of death claims. The most startling effect of the era's reforms was the drop in mortality during the first year of life, from 154.70 deaths per thousand between 1848 and 1860 to 112.46 deaths per thousand between 1900 and 1918. Nationwide, the reforms also increased life expectancy at birth for working-class men during the same periods from forty-one years to fifty-five.

ABOVE: *Early nineteenth-century social reforms included parks, playgrounds and compulsory education for children, including these saluting the flag in Baltimore's Reid Memorial Settlement House.*
(Courtesy of the Maryland Historical Society)

candidate Theodore Roosevelt, who emphasized education, order, cleanliness, and health. Meeting in Baltimore in 1906, the National American Women's Suffrage Association—whose members included Susan B. Anthony, Jane Addams and Clara Barton—lobbied not only for women's right to vote but also for such wide-ranging reforms as clean water and streets, pure food and milk, compulsory schooling and more playgrounds for children.

INSURING THE AMERICAN DREAM

In 1900, Baltimore's labor force included 156,449 men and 60,901 women employed in a hundred different trades and professions. Over 200,000 workers, aged twelve to ninety, labored ten or twelve hours a day, six days a week in clothing factories, foundries and machine shops, railroad shops, shipyards and steel mills. They processed copper, tin and sheet-iron, and packed fruits, vegetables and oysters for export.

Skilled or unskilled, Baltimore's working class took pride in their work. Most viewed education, training and self-improvement as a way to climb the socio-economic ladder, possibly start small businesses of their own, and enter the middle class. Influenced by the decade's

RIGHT: *By 1910, trolleys competed with a growing number of automobiles on Baltimore's congested downtown streets.*
(Courtesy of the Maryland Historical Society)

																																		No. of Weeks	
RIL.			MAY.				JUNE.					JULY.				AUG.					SEP.				OCT.				NOV.				DEC.		In Arrear	In Advance
13	20	27	4	11	18	25	1	8	15	22	29	6	13	20	27	3	10	17	24	31	7	14	21	28	5	12	19	26	2	9	16	23	30	7	14	21	28		

Quarter ending June 30th, 1912. Quarter ending September 30th, 1912. Quarter ending December 31st, 1912.

2

progressive reformers, many skilled craftsmen belonged to the city's remaining trade unions, where they took an active role in politics and exercised their right to vote.

Remembering lives of poverty in the rural South or starvation and persecution in Europe, Baltimore's working men and women seemed determined never again to be cold or hungry or to sleep on a dirt floor. They willingly labored for long hours for low wages to support their families and earn their piece of the "American Dream." For many of Mutual Life's immigrant, working-class policyholders, the dream included decent clothes, a variety of healthy foods, and ownership of a modest two-story house in neighborhoods like Old Town, Fells Point, Canton and Highlandtown that were safe, stable and community-centered.

As vacant land around the harbor basin became scarce, industry expanded east and south of the central business district. Looking for higher pay and new opportunities, workers followed. By 1916 thousands of Baltimore workers and their families had found jobs, benefits, homes, shopping, entertainment and social lives in "company towns" and communities built around Bethlehem Steel's Sparrows Point steel mill, near the Baltimore Railroad Car Works in Curtis Bay, and in the shipbuilding centers of Locust Point and Dundalk. Many Dundalk families, in fact, took advantage of the company's offer to finance their new homes through payroll deductions.

West of downtown, along Edmondson Avenue near Gwynns Falls Park in a "suburban" area annexed by the city in 1888, builder James Keelty was also helping Baltimore workers become homeowners. In 1912 his blocks of twelve-foot-wide "rows," advertised for between $1,200 and $1,400 each, were attractive to many middle-income buyers.

Wherever working-class Baltimoreans lived, Mutual Life agents found them, offering paid-weekly policies to insure their lives and protect family income and dreams from the unexpected. Finding new customers and collecting premiums in policyholder homes became easier with the arrival of Henry Ford's mass-produced "Model T." By 1914, ten thousand Fords filled city and suburban Baltimore streets. Driving at least a few of them, no doubt, were Mutual Life's most successful, higher-paid sales leaders. They no longer had to depend on streetcars to service customers living outside the central business district.

Before long, Mutual Life's volume of business grew large enough to support branch offices in local Baltimore neighborhoods from which agents could make sales, provide customer service, and build their books of business. Three of the company's earliest field offices within the city limits were located on Cross Street in south Baltimore; at North Avenue and Gay Streets, where "Mutual Life Insurance Company of Baltimore" is still carved in granite over the front door; and at North Avenue and Bloomingdale, near Walbrook Junction.

ABOVE: *This Mutual Life agent's debit book shows small weekly premiums collected and credited during 1912.*

BELOW: *A Baltimore family in their new automobile, 1909.*
(Courtesy of Enoch Pratt Free Library, Central Library/State Library Resource Center, Baltimore)

Baltimore's Bonaparte . . .

Reformer, U.S. Attorney General, Founder of the FBI

CHARLES JOSEPH BONAPARTE (1851–1921) was the Baltimore-born grandson of Jerome Bonaparte, youngest brother of French Emperor Napoleon I, and Baltimore socialite Elizabeth "Betsy" Patterson. After graduation from Harvard College and Harvard Law School he became a practicing attorney in Baltimore in 1874.

Bonaparte, nominally a Republican, believed efficiency and expertise, not political connections, should determine government service, and for decades he fought the notoriously corrupt Democratic "machine" that dominated Baltimore politics. In 1885 he and B&O president John Cowan established the city's Reform League to replace crooked political appointees with honest and competent men.

Because he served as Mutual Life's general counsel and advisor from the late 1880s until 1894, Bonaparte's name is frequently mentioned in executive board minutes. Though there is no direct evidence, he may well have influenced the directors' decision to focus on providing life insurance for Baltimore's working class.

Bonaparte was an avid and outspoken "Progressive," supporting candidates who wanted to address urban problems—slums, poor gas and electric service, mismanaged city departments, the telephone monopoly, and the lack of safe food and building codes. Between 1900 and 1918 he and other well-educated, like-minded men and women sought federal intervention to correct abuses in the country's burgeoning industrial society.

Bonaparte first met Theodore Roosevelt, Commissioner of the U.S. Civil Service and another outspoken "Progressive," in 1892 when both spoke at a meeting of the Baltimore Civil Service Reform Association. Roosevelt boasted of his efforts to reform federal law enforcement by filling positions with skilled men. Border patrol applicants, he said, were now required to demonstrate marksmanship. Bonaparte, who doubted that one found the best men via target-shooting, countered that "Roosevelt should have had the men shoot each other and given the jobs to the survivors."

ABOVE RIGHT: *Mutual Life General Counsel Charles J. Bonaparte and his wife, early in his career.*
(Courtesy of the Maryland Historical Society)

When then–Vice President Roosevelt ascended to the nation's highest office in 1901 in the wake of William McKinley's assassination, he called on Bonaparte. From 1902 to 1904 Bonaparte served on the Board of Indian Commissioners, and in 1904 he was appointed chairman of the National Civil Service Reform League. The following year he was appointed secretary of the navy, and in 1906 he became U.S. attorney general. Two years later he created a tiny corps of well-disciplined former detectives and Secret Service men to investigate crime and fight corruption across state borders. In 1909, as he was leaving office, Roosevelt and Bonaparte recommended that these thirty-four Special Agents become a permanent part of the Justice Department. The new administration of William Howard Taft complied, naming the force the Bureau of Investigation on March 16, 1909.

Charles J. Bonaparte died in Baltimore County, Maryland in 1921. He is buried at Baltimore's Loudon Park Cemetery. Married to Ellen Channing Day, he had no heirs.

CUMBERLAND, HERE WE COME!

By 1914, Mutual Life had enough business west of the city to justify opening the company's first branch office outside Baltimore. With a population of 21,288 in 1910, Cumberland, the economic capital of Western Maryland and the state's second largest city, was a logical choice. Located at the entrance to the Cumberland Gap, through which the National Road (today's Route 40) to the Ohio Valley had threaded since the early 1800s, the city was a strategic trading center and the gateway to Maryland's Allegany and Garrett Counties. By 1900, the Chesapeake & Ohio Canal ended there, and five railroads stopped in its train yards to load coal, iron, glass, leather and textiles.

Just west of Cumberland, in a four-mile wide, twenty-five-mile long valley known as George's Creek Basin, was one of the East Coast's largest veins of semi-bituminous coal. Working the mine in 1902 were six thousand "pick and shovel men," a work force that included native-born Americans as well as Scottish, English, Irish, Welsh and German immigrants. Considered the most highly valued, best-paid miners in all of Maryland, Pennsylvania and West Virginia, they encountered less danger and reported fewer accidental deaths than coal miners working in neighboring states.

The George's Creek miners dressed well, owned nice houses and lived comfortable and cultured lives in a community that included shops, mills, breweries and distilleries, two business colleges, nine banks and twenty-nine factories. Because of the area's diversity, its working-class families were better able to endure depressions and economic downturns than residents of other, less industrial Maryland counties. These factors all made Cumberland an excellent source of life insurance prospects.

Mutual Life opened its branch office in Cumberland in 1914. Since no deeds in the Allegany County Courthouse document property ownership in those years, it is likely that the company rented space along Baltimore Street, a few blocks from the Potomac River, in the center of the downtown business district. The office served many square miles of mountainous countryside in Western Maryland and West Virginia near the southern border of Pennsylvania. Then as now, many of the office's agents, were licensed to write business in all three states. Though Peoples Life Insurance Company of Washington, D.C., opened an office nearby a decade or so later, there seemed to be enough business to keep all agents busy.

In 1950 the company purchased property at 107 South Centre Street in downtown Cumberland. When the district office moved from that site almost fifty years later, the city designated the building an historic landmark.

BELOW: *Because the western Maryland city of Cumberland was a strategic trading center and gateway to the state's Allegany and Garrett Counties, Mutual Life opened its first branch office outside Baltimore there in 1914.* (Courtesy of the Maryland Historical Society)

The Mutual Life Insurance Company of Baltimore.

ANNUAL STATEMENT

DECEMBER 31st, 1913.

ASSETS.

Book value of Bonds,	$430,219.00
Book value of Baltimore City Stock,	120,083.75
Mortgages on Real Estate,	361,025.80
Ground Rents,	125,890.63
Real Estate,	26,300.00
Loans on Company's Policies,	4,627.82
Deferred Premiums,	2,940.70
Interest due and accrued,	19,914.47
Cash in Office and Bank,	47,314.50
	$1,138,316.67

LIABILITIES.

Legal Reserve on Policies,	$746,128.26
Book value of Bonds over market value,	49,560.25
Agents' cash bond deposit,	3,060.00
Loans in excess of reserve,	400.29
Interest paid in advance,	30.00
All other liabilities,	1,545.82
Surplus,	337,592.05
	$1,138,316.67

Income during the year 1913,	$464,390.24
Disbursements,	311,958.29
Income over disbursements,	152,431.95
Insurance in force December 31st, 1913,	$12,992,369.00
Amount paid Policy Holders since organization,	2,622,329.52

MILLION-DOLLAR MILESTONE!

Mutual Life prospered and grew in the decade following the Great Fire. In the first nine months of 1905 alone, agents wrote 4,036 new policies for $511,156 of basic life insurance protection on the city's working class. Because of this increase in business, directors assigned medical examinations in the territory east of the Jones Falls to Medical Director Dr. Henry M. Wilson and agreed to pay Dr. James D. Iglehart, also a member of the Executive Committee, $300 per year plus fifty cents per examination to assist him.

At the quarterly meeting of directors in April 1908—the company's Fiftieth Anniversary year—President Matthew Brenan proudly reported that Mutual Life had invested assets valued at $335,000 as well as 56,468

policies and $6.6 million of insurance in force. By 1910, Ordinary life insurance in force—paid annually, quarterly or monthly—had declined to the point that directors no longer reported figures for the Ordinary Branch. The number of paid-weekly policies, on the other hand, continued to climb. Annual financial statements submitted to the Maryland Insurance Commission confirm that Mutual Life had 71,023 weekly premium "Industrial"* policies and $11.5 million of insurance in force at year-end 1912.

In the spring of 1913, the company celebrated a significant milestone—one million dollars in assets—with a dinner at Baltimore's famed Hotel Rennart. Addressing attendees, Dr. Wilson complimented officers and directors for "their faithful attention and untiring efforts" in making Mutual Life a "One Million Dollar Company." Wilson also presented President Brenan with an impressive "emblem of victory"—an Italian onyx marble pedestal topped by a handsome bronze figure. Thanks to Brenan's leadership and efforts, the doctor noted, Mutual Life had become "recognized by the public and the business community as one of the [city's] leading companies."

Mutual Life's $1.1 million in assets at year-end 1913 included $120,083 invested in Baltimore City stock and $361,025 in local mortgages. In 1915, following a favorable examination of its records by the Maryland State Insurance Department, Mutual Life's directors agreed to deposit $100,000 of its city securities with the treasurer of the State of Maryland, "to be held by him as trustee for the benefit and protection of the [company's] policyholders." Though not required by charter, the transaction demonstrated the company's strength and concern for its customers. As expected, policyholders and the public reacted positively to the decision.

---

* Industrial insurance is characterized by death benefits of $2,000 or less, minimum underwriting requirements and weekly, bi-weekly or monthly payments collected in the policyowner's home by the sales agent. Also called debit insurance. (Life Office Management Association Glossary of Terms, 1992).

PUBLIC CALLS FOR INSURANCE REGULATION

Mutual Life's directors had good reason for considering public opinion when it deposited company assets with the Maryland treasury. Since the turn of the century, "muckraking" journalists had taken great pleasure in exposing scandalous business practices and improprieties in many industries, including life insurance. Newspapermen frequently wrote stories about high agent commissions and bonuses, executive salaries and lobbying expenses, shady investment practices, nepotism, and cutthroat sales tactics in a highly competitive marketplace.

Worried that the country's life insurers were acting irresponsibly and playing "fast and loose" with its money, the public demanded closer scrutiny of the nation's insurers by legislators and state insurance departments.

Customers throughout the U.S. lost faith in the industry and canceled policies. Finding it difficult to make sales, many agents resigned.

The National Association of Life Underwriters (NALU), a professional association of life insurance agents, was not surprised by the uproar. It had been warning the industry about its tarnished image for twenty years. Meeting annually from 1890, NALU members were committed to agent education, professionalism and ethical business practices. As negative press about the industry increased, NALU agents mobilized for action. In just one year, from 1905 to 1906, membership grew from forty-five local associations with two thousand members to fifty-two associations and 2,260 members.

By February 1906 public outcry against life insurers had reached the point that President Roosevelt called a

ABOVE: *The Democratic Party held its national convention at Baltimore's Fifth Regiment Armory in 1912, six years after President Theodore Roosevelt called governors and attorneys general to Chicago to design uniform legislation to regulate the insurance industry.*

(Courtesy of Enoch Pratt Free Library, Central Library/State Library Resource Center, Baltimore)

conference of governors and attorneys general in Chicago to design uniform legislation to regulate the industry. The resulting proposal, known as the Ames Bill, died in the House when congressmen concluded that the U.S. Constitution did not give them the power to interfere in the insurance business.

Though insurance companies were excluded from participating in the Chicago Conference, Ernest J. Clark, a John Hancock Insurance Company general agent working in Baltimore, was part of a delegation of agents that later testified before Congress in support of the Ames Bill. One man who did attend the Chicago Conference was U.S. Attorney General Charles J. Bonaparte, who had received an appointment to Roosevelt's Cabinet in 1905. The grandson of Betsy and Jerome Bonaparte, Charles Bonaparte had co-founded Baltimore's Reform League in 1885 and served as counsel and advisor to Mutual Life from the late 1880s until 1894.

Possibly because of Bonaparte's influence, Mutual Life did not suffer the setbacks that plagued many of its competitors in those years. President Matthew Brenan could hold his head high when he attended NALU's 1902 convention in Cincinnati and again a year later when he welcomed NALU members to Baltimore. Sales soared as the company's positive image and presence in the city continued to grow.

In 1909 and 1910, NALU's *Life Association News* (*LAN*) cautioned agents about deceptive insurance sales practices such as rebating premiums and using underhanded means (called "twisting") to replace a rival company's policies. At about the same time, *LAN* also published articles about the psychological aspects of selling and using the power of suggestion to persuade prospects to buy. When the federal government introduced the income tax a few years later, NALU officers sent a letter to President Woodrow Wilson protesting the taxing of insurance policy dividends.

Despite these efforts to educate agents about issues affecting their business, there was still no industry-wide training program or life insurance textbook. Speaking to association members early in 1913, NALU president Ernest Clark, still a John Hancock general agent, emphasized that "the life insurance agent of the future must be educated and trained along the most careful and scientific lines, in order to give his clients the intelligent and conscientious service that their individual needs, according to varying conditions and circumstances, require."

In December 1913, NALU hired a professor from the University of Pennsylvania's Wharton School of Finance and Commerce to write the industry's first life insurance textbook. Two years later, an advertisement in *LAN* announced to agents the publication of *Life Insurance: Its Principles and Practice*. At its annual convention in 1918, NALU adopted an agent *Code of Ethics* that became a model for similar professional organizations.

As Baltimore prepared to host the Democratic Party's national convention in 1912 at the Fifth Regiment Armory, Americans cast apprehensive glances at rising militarism across the Atlantic and a shaky economy at home. By the end of 1914, war had flared in France and Belgium, and forty-three of ninety-one life insurance companies reported lower sales and profits than the year before.

Mutual Life was not among them. Though many of the city's immigrants worried about families they had left behind in Europe, business in Baltimore was booming. In January 1916, President Brenan thanked the Mutual Life board for the "splendid increase of $1.4 million and 11,367 new policies in 1915." In January 1917, Mutual Life purchased a five-story marble front building at 15 South Street in Baltimore for $100,000. On April 5, 1917, one day before the United States entered a war that had been raging in Europe for two and a half years, company directors held their first meeting at the new and much larger home office location.

As the focus shifted from domestic social reform to the war effort, the Progressive Era ended and, for the company and the country, a new one began.

Competitors Share Common Goals

I N 1897, as Mutual Life's presence in Baltimore grew, the Immediate Benefit Life Insurance Company, later the Sun Life Insurance Company of America, received its charter to do business in Maryland. Two years later, the Home Life Insurance Company of America was incorporated in Delaware. By 1906 still other life insurers destined to become part of the "Monumental Melting Pot" had opened their doors in Washington, D.C., and states farther south.

Before World War I, each company concentrated its activities in the state where it had been founded. Decades later, though competing with Mutual Life in many of the same communities and neighborhoods, these companies were united by three common goals— to provide affordable Industrial life insurance protection for working-class Americans, to retard the flow of capital to the insurance "giants" in the Northeast, and to keep premium money at home to benefit the local economies.

Consolidation naturally occurred throughout the late 1900s as size and market share became critical factors to successful competition. The largest single consolidation of companies with "Industrial" roots occurred in 1997 as part of one of the most publicized life insurance company acquisitions in U.S. history. As a result of this merger, the company became responsible for 6,124,361 active policies and its annualized premium in force on the combined home service life, health and annuity business grew from $145 million to $548 million.

PEOPLES COMES TO LIFE

Early in the twentieth century, a young man from Buckeystown, Maryland, met an insurance prospect in the Foggy Bottom neighborhood of Washington, D.C. After making the sale, he jumped on his bicycle and peddled up Virginia Avenue, application tucked under his arm. As he paused briefly to look back, he could not have imagined that near that very spot in 1959 a company he had founded would build a magnificent new home office. The young man was W. Wallace Chiswell, first president of Peoples Life Insurance Company.

A veteran of the Spanish-American War, Chiswell left his family's farm to make good as a "debit agent," selling industrial life insurance for the Peoples Mutual Benefit Association of the District of Columbia. He worked long hours, wrote lots of business, and at age thirty bought the company for $3,000. On September 3, 1903, it was incorporated under the laws of the District of Columbia as the "Peoples Mutual Benefit Life Insurance Company." Chiswell's first act of business was to reinsure all existing coverage.

With the help of his brother, Benjamin W. Chiswell, the company's first Agency officer, and his sister, who served first as chief clerk and as secretary-treasurer, the family-owned company opened for business in rented space on F Street, N.W., a few blocks from the nation's capitol. Its five agents sold weekly premium health and accident insurance for twenty-five cents a week. Policyholders received $50 at the time of death, or $8 a week if an accident or illness stopped their paychecks.

The rapidly expanding company relocated to larger quarters at 518 6th Street, N.W. in 1911. In 1913 it opened its first office outside Washington in Richmond, Virginia. In 1916, Peoples' agents began selling Industrial life insurance policies with $250 to $1,000 face amounts as their counterparts working for Mutual Life in Baltimore had done forty years earlier. By 1920, with almost $17.7 million of insurance in force, the company was licensed to conduct business in the District of Columbia, Virginia and Maryland. In 1924, with eighteen district offices and over five hundred home office and field employees, the home office moved to 14th and H Streets, N.W.

ABOVE: *Peoples Life Insurance Company employees shortly after the new organization opened for business in 1903.*

BELOW: *Peoples Life Insurance Company home office in Washington, DC, 1959.*

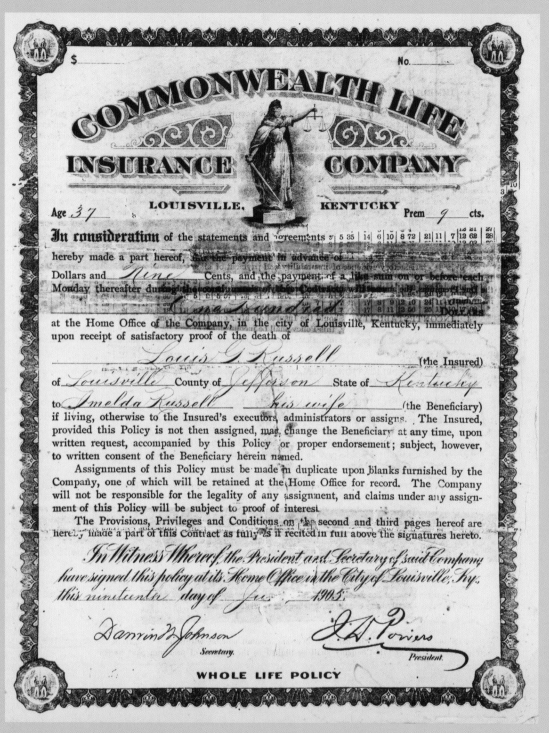

ABOVE: *Louisville's Commonwealth Life Insurance Company issued its first weekly premium life insurance policy in 1905.*

W. Wallace Chiswell died on August 3, 1950, after serving as chairman of the board until 1943. Though active in Peoples Life until the end, he never saw the company's magnificent new building at 601 New Hampshire Avenue, N.W., in Foggy Bottom. Its cornerstone was laid on April 2, 1959, on almost the exact spot where he had written that application more than five decades earlier.

COMMONWEALTH KEEPS CAPITAL IN KENTUCKY

On Sunday, June 4, 1905, an ad in the *Louisville Courier-Journal* introduced the city's new life insurer to the public with the slogan: "A Square Deal for Every Policyholder." The next day, eleven months after being incorporated in the Commonwealth of Kentucky for 2,000 shares of $100 par value stock, the Commonwealth Life Insurance Company opened for business.

Colonel Joshua D. Powers, Commonwealth Life's first president, and Darwin W. Johnson, secretary-treasurer, ran the company as a team. Powers's name opened doors and Johnson managed the business. Operating only in Kentucky, Commonwealth Life sold both Industrial and Ordinary life insurance. The company's first weekly premium application was written in 1905.

During its formative years, the company paid claims in cash. Agents with a $44 book of collected business, called a "debit," received 15 percent of their collections. Sales commissions could not exceed $15 per week. Company historian Victor B. Gerard credits Commonwealth Life's early growth—it had $9.6 million of insurance in force by year-end 1909—to innovative products, successful recruiting, and its agents' willingness to ride horseback into the Kentucky hills. They often accepted chickens, eggs, and vegetables from customers as payment for premiums!

Like Mutual Life in 1914, Commonwealth sought to expand its Industrial business by opening

That same year the company changed its name to Peoples Life Insurance Company and expanded its portfolio to include Ordinary policies. Operating under the motto "Peoples Life Insurance Protects the Entire Family," the company stressed service and fair and prompt payment of claims. Its Agent's Creed referred to it as a "company of the people, by the people, for the people."

branch offices in cities with high concentrations of blue-collar workers earning weekly paychecks. The first of these outside Kentucky was in Birmingham, Alabama. Over the next twenty years, under the leadership of Darwin Johnson, who became president in 1922, the company opened additional offices in Indiana, West Virginia and several southeastern states.

NEW LIFE INSURERS IN NORTH CAROLINA

Another insurer of working-class families destined to join the "Monumental Melting Pot" was planting roots in Durham, North Carolina. Originally chartered as an assessment institution in 1906, the Durham Mutual Protective Association later became the Durham Mutual Life Insurance Company. Out of Durham Mutual Life grew the Durham Life Insurance Company and Home Security Life, both reorganized after the original founders went their separate ways.

Durham Life Insurance Company was incorpo‐rated in North Carolina in 1913. Its founder and first president was A. M. Moize. The company's home office was located on Market Street until 1920 when, despite urging from many civic and business organizations to stay in Durham, directors voted to move the company to Raleigh. By 1940, Durham Life had sixteen branch offices in the Carolinas and Virginia.

Home Security Life Insurance Company was organized on May 30, 1916, by three of Durham's leading citizens—John Sprunt Hill and brothers E. N. Moize and A. M. Moize, who had founded Durham Life three years earlier. The company's name came from its founders' desire to help policyholders "Make Your Home Secure with Home Security." The business grew rapidly, writing over $660,000 of insurance in the first six and a half months. In 1920 officers moved the home office to larger quarters at Main and Market Streets. On December 31, 1930, the company had ten home office employees and $13 million of insurance in force.

Commonwealth Life Insurance Company and Peoples Life Insurance Company became subsidiaries of the Louisville, Kentucky–based Capital Holding Corporation in 1969. In 1975, Capital Holding acquired Home Security. Peoples Security Life Insurance was formed in 1985 when Capital Holding merged Peoples Life and Home Security. Durham Life acquired Baltimore's Sun Life of America in 1988. Capital Holding acquired Durham Life and merged it into Peoples Security in 1992. By 1997, Capital Holding had been renamed "Providian" and its three life insurance companies—Commonwealth Life (CLI), Peoples Security (PSI), and Capital Security Life Insurance (CSI)—were acquired by AEGON USA and merged into Monumental Life.

BELOW: *Alvis M. Moize founded Durham Life in 1913. Three years later, he was named first president of Durham's Home Security Life Insurance Company, which he also founded with John Sprunt Hill and his brother E. N. Moize.*

CHAPTER 4

Attacked on Two Fronts
(1917–1922)

FOUR CHILDREN watch as a Model T Ford stops at their front door. Though the number of automobiles on Baltimore streets has multiplied since the war began, the black Fords are not a common sight in their neighborhood. The few they have seen, with uniformed drivers at the wheel, do not bring good news.

The children's older brother Frankie is a "doughboy," serving with the American Expeditionary Force in France. Drafted in June 1918, fourteen months after the U.S. declared war on Germany, he trained at Camp Meade in Maryland. Two weeks ago, he stopped home to see his family before shipping overseas. His mother had boasted to friends: "My Frankie looks so handsome in his Army uniform!" She also noticed that Frankie spoke much better English since completing language lessons at the camp.

The Ford's arrival has frightened the children. So has the non-stop tolling of bells from St. Leo's Catholic Church in Little Italy. They hope nothing has happened to their brother. They run to find their parents as the doorbell rings.

The Ford's driver is not an army officer but their family physician. He has come to examine their father, who has missed several days of work since Frankie left in September. "It's just the grip," says the doctor. "Nothing to worry about. Stay off your feet and get some rest." But the children are worried. Their father is still young, just forty years old. They've never seen him sick. He's always been so strong and

healthy. He has to be strong, he tells them, to keep his job at the steel mill. Since the war in Europe began in 1914, he's been working overtime and bringing home more money.

Within the next week, the children see the doctor enter many of their neighbors' homes. Wherever he goes, people with masks covering their mouths beg for medicine, but none of his usual remedies—camphor, aspirin and quinine—seem to stop this influenza. Everyone is sick. After reading the daily newspapers, the doctor begins to wonder if Frankie brought the deadly virus to his Baltimore neighborhood from Camp Meade when he visited. Reports say the epidemic began in army training camps. Like Frankie's brother and sisters, he too worries about the young recruit. He's heard that life in the trenches is filthy and lice-ridden, with more soldiers succumbing to influenza, pneumonia and disease-carrying parasites than to injuries inflicted by German bayonets and bullets.

On October 7, the city closes all schools and the children cannot go out to play. The same week, the health commissioner cancels the Liberty Loan parade they had hoped

FACING PAGE: *Private T. P. Laughlin was one of the first New York National Guardsmen called into active duty in World War I. Sent to France in June 1917, he was in combat by October. The U.S. Army had fewer than 130,000 men when America entered the war.*
(Courtesy of the National Archives)

to attend with their mother. Over 25,000 women were expected to march to raise money for the war. On October 10 the Baltimore City Health Department confirms 1,962 new cases of influenza.

"What's happening?" the children ask their mother. Down the street, someone has left several coffins on the sidewalk. Frankie's brother and sisters know what they are. Now they experience death firsthand. Their father dies that day, along with two hundred other Baltimore residents. Their mother washes his body herself and prepares it for the undertaker.

By October 12, families are forbidden to attend church services. Friends are cautioned not to shake hands, dance or talk face to face. Trolley tokens are washed daily and policemen have begun to arrest citizens who spit on the street. City services become strained when 186 policemen, 105 firemen and sixty garbage collectors call in sick. Down 250 telephone operators, C&P Telephone begs customers to limit telephone use.

On October 15, a young Baltimore mother-to-be is ready to give birth. Doctors are so stressed and hospitals so unsafe that the family calls a midwife to deliver the baby at the couple's home near 31st Street. Because of the chaotic conditions, she lists the newborn's birth date as October 18.

Sixty years later, Joseph Willis, discovers in city records that he is actually three days older than he thought.

On November 10, 1918, one day before the Armistice is signed ending the war in Europe, another black Ford pulls up in front of Frankie's family home. This time, the driver is not a doctor but a man in uniform bringing more tragic news. Young Frankie has died fighting in France. The officer tells Frank's mother that she will receive a check for $5,000 from the federal government. A U.S. citizen for less than two years and a soldier just five months, Frankie purchased War Risk Insurance before he shipped out. The army had deducted the premiums from his pay.

A widow left with four young children and no men to bring home income, Frankie's mother is also thankful that she and her husband agreed to speak to the Mutual Life agent who knocked on their door a few years ago. Though she couldn't convince her husband to purchase a policy on her life, he did agree to apply for a small policy covering his own. The benefits from that policy will help pay the bills and keep the family comfortable until she can find work.

"OVER THERE"

When war first broke out in Europe, most Americans believed it would not affect their lives. At first neutral about the conflict, many Baltimore families of European descent—including Mutual Life policyholders—eventually took sides. Those with English roots believed that Great Britain must be preserved. Irish Americans opposed helping the British, whose government resisted Ireland's drive for independence. Residents of Little Italy supported Italy, which eventually allied itself with Britain and France. Baltimore's Polish community hoped an Allied victory would free their homeland from German-Austrian domination. Proud to be living in America but still supporting their own schools and newspapers, many German families in Baltimore refused to denounce their heritage and wanted to avoid waging war on land of their fathers.

Baltimore's proud citizens welcomed home returning World War I veterans with a victory parade on Howard Street in 1918.
(Courtesy of the Maryland Historical Society)

INSURERS SUPPORT SALE OF LIBERTY BONDS

In addition to soldiers, the war effort also required money for clothing, training, tents, arms and ammunition, vehicles, fuel and medical supplies. To raise needed funds, the U.S. government sold Liberty Loan Bonds. Baltimore's quota was $25 million.

In June 1917, the industry's *Life Association News (LAN)* reported that life underwriter associations—enthusiastic about the slogans "Enlist or Invest" and "Liberty Bonds for Liberty"—were actively supporting bond sales. In Richmond, Virginia, local agents led the Chamber of Commerce in a citywide fundraising effort. By June 1918 life insurance agents around the country had proudly participated in three Liberty Bond campaigns, selling 1.2 million bonds valued at $830 million.

Shortly after former president Theodore Roosevelt appeared at a Liberty Bond rally in Baltimore on September 25, 1917, Mutual Life's directors authorized President Matthew Brenan to invest $20,000 in the war effort. By mid-1918 the company had purchased Liberty Bonds worth $65,000 and invested another $36,000 in U.S. War Certificates and Stamps. In July 1919, Liberty Bonds accounted for $150,000 (20 percent) of the company's portfolio of invested assets. Six months later, Liberty Bond counts had grown to $235,000 and 26 percent, respectively.

LEFT: *"Baltimore's Own" 313th and 115th Infantry Regiments, part of Maryland's 29th Division, march proudly after fighting in France with the American Expeditionary Force.*
(Courtesy of the Maryland Historical Society)

BELOW: *Posters like this one encouraged Americans to buy Liberty Bonds during World War I. Mutual Life supported the war effort by investing $235,000—over 20 percent of its assets—in Liberty Bonds between 1917 and 1919.*
(Courtesy of the University of Baltimore)

By the time the United States entered World War I on April 6, 1917, most Americans supported President Woodrow Wilson's decision to get involved. Hundreds of thousands of eligible men, including 61,000 Baltimore citizens, registered for the draft. Nationwide, 18 percent of those drafted—nearly half a million men—were immigrants to the United States. Among them were many German-Americans who felt the need to prove their loyalty before it could be questioned. Between 1917 and 1920, sixteen thousand Baltimoreans served in the U.S. armed forces.

Dozens of Mutual Life field and home office employees, as well as life insurance agents throughout the U.S., joined the trainloads of men who enlisted, shouldered rifles and shipped out to Europe. "Baltimore's Own" 313th and 115th Infantry Regiments, part of Maryland's 29th Division, fought in France with General John J. "Black Jack" Pershing.

A Soldier's Story . . .
Baltimore's Robert Moreland

*D*ECORATED WORLD WAR I HERO Alvin C. York, later immortalized by Gary Cooper in the movie *Sergeant York*, was unsure how he would behave in the heat of battle. Drafted out of the Tennessee hills, York was an excellent marksman. During the Meuse-Argonne Offensive on October 8, 1918, he single-handedly killed fifteen Germans and captured 132 others.

Monumental Life retiree Ann Moreland remembers her father talking about having similar fears. Robert M. Moreland told his daughter that he, too, was "scared to death in France, until he saw one of his buddies shot by German gunfire." The frightened young man quickly became a fighting man.

Robert Moreland enlisted in the U.S. Army at the age of sixteen. His mother had passed away; his father was at sea in the Merchant Marine. An older sister signed his enlistment papers, unaware that he had lied about his age. Sent to France in July 1918, young Moreland served alongside other Maryland men in the 29th Infantry Division. Fighting not far from Sergeant York's unit along the French-German border, he too saw action in the Meuse-Argonne. His division—nicknamed the "Blue and Gray" because it comprised Maryland and Virginia regiments that had fought on both sides of the American Civil War—sustained 5,570 casualties, including 787 deaths.

Ann remembers seeing her father's gas mask when she was a child. "Gas caused many of our casualties," he told her. Ann also remembers hearing her father say he still missed the horse he'd ridden overseas. When U.S. troops pulled out at the end of the war, their horses were given to local farmers.

Having served in Europe for two years, Robert Moreland was one of the lucky soldiers who came home in 1919 with only minor shrapnel wounds. Already a "veteran" at age eighteen, he did not leave the armed services. After returning to Baltimore aboard a U.S.

troop ship, he realized that he liked being at sea and immediately enlisted in the navy. Upon his discharge six years later, he took a job with the U.S. government.

Robert Moreland married Ann's mother Margaret in 1926. Two years later, Ann was born. After graduating from high school, she joined Monumental Life in 1949 in the Addressograph Department and later served as manager of the Payroll Department and Assistant Treasurer. Ann retired in 1996 with forty-six years of service. Two years later, her father, the World War I veteran, died at age eighty-six, having experienced no ill effects from his years in the service.

RIGHT: Baltimorean Robert Moreland enlisted in the U.S. Army at sixteen. Sent to France in July 1918, he fought beside other Maryland men in the 29th Division along the French-German border. A World War I "veteran" at age eighteen, he reenlisted in the navy after returning home.

Baltimore citizens also bought Liberty Bonds to support the war. Even children saved their pennies. As anti-German sentiment increased throughout the country, Baltimore's German-American community demonstrated its patriotism by purchasing almost $500,000 of the bonds. At the same time, many German Americans applied for naturalization and went to court to adopt more American names. Early in the war, Baltimore's city council had changed the name of German Street, where many German immigrants owned shops (and where the Great Fire of 1904 had begun), to Redwood Street in honor of George Buchanan Redwood, the first Maryland army officer to die in France.

With food in short supply and prices escalating (near panic developed when the city ran out of potatoes!), Baltimore citizens planted "liberty gardens" and promoted "sugarless Tuesdays." Young women at Baltimore's Goucher College harvested 256 bushels of potatoes on Dr. John Goucher's estate. Women made bandages for the Red Cross. Heeding their parents' advice to prevent waste, small children even collected coal that had fallen from passing trains.

WOMEN JOIN THE WORK FORCE

World War I brought changes not only to Baltimore, but also to Maryland. The federal government opened new installations—including Camp Meade, the Edgewood

Arsenal, and the Aberdeen Proving Ground. Industries, especially the Bethlehem Steel Plant at Sparrows Point, expanded and production boomed to meet the demand for U.S. warships and freighters. Wages increased; unemployment decreased. Employment in shipbuilding alone grew from 2,000 to 20,000 jobs.

As men went off to war, women were welcomed where previously they had not been able to find work. In Baltimore and around the country, women joined assembly lines, drove streetcars, and replaced men in respected business positions.

At Mutual Life, President Brenan hired Emily Crowley, then just nineteen years old, as his secretary. She became the company's first female employee. Thirteen years later, with responsibility for the company's investment records, she married Charles J. Linke, an employee with more than forty years' service who had joined the company as an office boy at age nine.

On June 1, 1918, a young woman named Margaret Conner also began her career with Mutual Life in the Cumberland, Maryland, branch office. Hired into a sales position, she was the company's only female agent for more than eighteen years. Making "very creditable increase," she built several of the office's debits, overcame many obstacles, and was well liked by all of her policyholders. The men she regularly out-paced in office sales contests saluted her sportsmanship with the cheer "Long live Miss Conner!"

As a result of World War I, women earned the right to vote in 1920 and also their place in the insurance industry. Between 1918 and 1923, Mutual Life hired seventy-five women to fill positions previously held only by men.

One female employee wrote the following in the "Women's Page" of the company's employee publication, The *Old Black Hen*:

A few years ago, no one believed that women possessed much business ability, but during the war they proved to themselves and to others that they were capable of achieving great things. The war is past. Conditions are gradually becoming normal.

Mutual Life hired Margaret Conner, its first female agent, in 1918.

LEFT: *Bethlehem Steel's plant at Sparrows Point just outside Baltimore expanded production during World War I to meet the demand for warships and freighters.*
(Courtesy of the Maryland Historical Society)

ABOVE: *Between 1918 and 1923, Mutual Life hired seventy-five women, like these in the Industrial Policy Writing Department, to fill positions previously held only by men.*

ABOVE RIGHT: *"Suffragettes" marched through Baltimore to draw attention to a woman's right to vote.*
(Courtesy of the Maryland Historical Society)

There is no time for us to look backward to see what we have done. We must look forward and see what we can do.

Six months later, another woman in the home office wrote:

It's common gossip that there was a time when the Mutual conducted its business without the assistance of women. Maybe that's so . . . but we are here to say that it could not be done now.

There is no business in the world which offers richer or more diversified careers for the ambitious woman or for the girl who is just starting to make her way in the business world than insurance. . . . It is true all of us cannot be executives; but faithful and efficient services will in all cases reap their own reward.

For Miss Helen Cummings, an assistant in the Policy Writing Department, "faithful, intelligent and conscientious work" did produce its own reward. The *Old Black Hen* reported in February 1923 that she was the first woman "to win an executive position with the Company."

NO SLUMP IN SALES

As early as 1915 industry research analyst Edward A. Woods was optimistic that life insurers would fare well during the war. Even with military casualties and claims, his predictions came true. "Stock exchanges closed, many corporations almost ceased doing business, even the Standard Oil Company for a while stopped buying oil; but there was not a single default, hardly a delay in the conduct of life insurance."

War brought economic prosperity, but casualties had a sobering effect on society. When the federal government made War Risk Insurance available to all members of the armed forces, men heading into combat could buy up to $10,000 of life insurance protection at bargain rates through payroll deduction. Most forward-thinking life insurance agents and company executives welcomed the program, recognizing that War Risk Insurance would introduce the benefits of life insurance to an increasing number of families. As a result, they reasoned, their own postwar sales would increase.

At Mutual Life, sales never did slump. During the nineteen months that America was at war, Maryland's working class continued to purchase paid-weekly policies, increasing the company's life insurance in force by more than $4.4 million—from $17.8 million on March 31, 1917, to almost $22.2 million by the end of 1918. Other companies selling Industrial life insurance—including Commonwealth Life of Louisville, Kentucky; Peoples Mutual Benefit Life, headquartered in Washington, D.C.; and Home Security Life in Durham, North Carolina— reported similar growth.

ABOVE: *This 1917 war bond rally at Baltimore's Mount Vernon Place attracted thousands, including James Cardinal Gibbons, Roman Catholic Archbishop of Baltimore from 1877 to 1921, and former president Theodore Roosevelt.* (Courtesy of the Maryland Historical Society)

LEFT: *Illustrations like this one, from Mutual Life's employee publication, encouraged agents to go "over the top" in sales in the early 1920s as "doughboys" had done at the front during World War I.*

To protect themselves from the "invisible enemy" during the 1918 influenza epidemic, policemen on duty in large U.S. cities began wearing masks. The epidemic claimed 650,000 American lives.

ATTACK ON THE HOMEFRONT

What industry analyst Woods had not predicted was the influenza epidemic that attacked the U.S. in 1918 and claimed 650,000 American lives—a number many times greater than all U.S. soldiers killed in the war. The flu cut across social classes. In Baltimore, dockworkers, hotel bellmen and society ladies were infected. Some of the city's wealthiest, strongest citizens were the first to succumb. Attacking the immune system of healthy, robust young adults while largely sparing infants and the elderly, the deadly virus killed quickly.

The first Marylander to die was twenty-eight-year-old Henry Scott from Elkton, a baseball player and lineman for the Pennsylvania Railroad. He passed away on September 4, 1918, six months after the first (and milder) wave of the influenza had infected soldiers at an army training camp in Kansas. The Baltimore Health Department reported its first ten cases on September 26. During the next six weeks, 150,000 of the city's 600,000 residents became sick, and 5,000 died.

Other U.S. cities reported statistics that were no less astounding. In Louisville, disaster struck the 84th Division stationed at Camp Zachary Taylor. The epidemic put 13,000 men in the hospital and killed 824. People living nearby remembered seeing stacks of caskets tied on trucks leaving the camp. With 195,000 deaths attributed to the flu and its complications, October 1918 was the deadliest month in U.S. history.

What caused the epidemic of 1918 to spread so quickly?

First, citizens received little accurate information about the virus. There were even rumors that it was a form of "German warfare unleashed by Kaiser Wilhelm." Second,

BELOW: *Mutual Life's death claims spiked 177 percent during the influenza epidemic—from $205,686 in 1917 to $365,221 in 1918. The virus spread so quickly that several beneficiaries died before they could even cash their checks.*

few precautions were taken to prevent its spread. Third, families did not know what to expect, or how to treat victims who suddenly became ill. More concerned about battlefield casualties in Europe, news reporters almost ignored the epidemic attacking the home front. By the time doctors and health departments around the world realized this was something more than the "same old flu," it was too late. Desperate to give parents at least some hope, one Baltimore doctor simply filled tiny bags with camphor and tied them around sick children's necks.

The sudden loss of workers and parents crippled the smooth running of businesses, institutions and families. The extraordinary number of death claims also severely strained the reserves of many U.S. life insurance companies. An article in the November 1918 issue of *LAN* magazine estimated that epidemic-related losses would reach $40 million.

Mutual Life's results helped that prediction become a reality. For calendar year 1918, the company's death claims spiked 177 percent—from $205,686 on 1,882 lives in 1917 to $365,221 on 3,432 lives in 1918. During the height of the epidemic in 1918, two clerks were so busy paying claims that at least fifty people were waiting in line at all times. The epidemic spread so quickly that several beneficiaries died of the flu before they could even cash their checks.

In October 1918, the Executive Committee authorized borrowing $100,000 from the National Marine Bank of Baltimore at 5 percent interest, with Liberty Loan Bonds as collateral, to "cover extraordinary claims arising against the company as a result of the recent influenza epidemic." With both World War I and the pandemic over in 1919, Mutual Life repaid the loan, and claims returned to more normal pre-war levels.

Personal tragedies notwithstanding, the war and the influenza increased public awareness of how quickly life and health can change without warning. Many of the families who lost loved ones were not prepared, either for death or for going on with their lives. Widows often had no other source of income. Children who lost parents were often placed in orphanages or raised by relatives who never again spoke of what had happened.

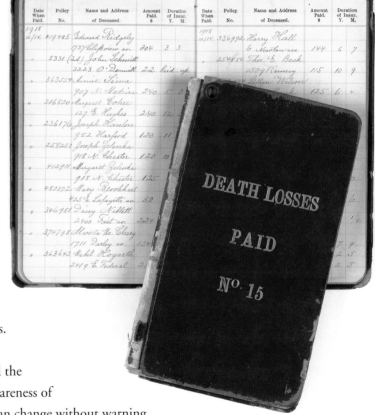

LEFT: *One of Mutual Life's leading sales staffs in the early 1920s. Both World War I and the influenza epidemic helped increase sales by raising public awareness of the need for life insurance.*

BELOW: *Mutual Life's employee publication,* The Old Black Hen, *got its name from a poem printed on the cover of the very first issue. For almost fifty years, agents were encouraged to approach sales like the hen that scratches the earth until she finds worms.*

MUTUAL LIFE INSURANCE · THE OLD BLACK HEN · COMPANY OF BALTIMORE

Mr. Agent: *"Meanwhile the Old Black Hens are out and gobbling up the worms."*

| Volume 1 | OCTOBER 1922 | No. 1 |

"The Old Black Hen"

Said the little red rooster, "Gosh all hemlock. Things are tough,
Seems that worms are getting scarcer, and I cannot find enough.
What's become of all those fat ones is a mystery to me;
There were thousands through that rainy spell—but now where can they be?"

The old black hen who heard him didn't grumble nor complain,
She had gone through lots of dry spells, she had lived through floods of rain,
So she flew upon the grindstone, and she gave her claws a whet,
As she said, "I've never seen the time that there weren't worms to get."

She picked a new and undug spot; the earth was hard and firm.
The little rooster jeered, "New ground! That's no place for a worm."
The old black hen just spread her feet, and she dug both fast and free,
"I must go to the worms," she said, "the worms won't come to me."

The rooster vainly spent his day, through habit, by the ways
Where fat round worms had passed in squads back in the rainy days.
When nightfall found him supperless, he growled in accents rough,
"I'm hungry as a fowl can be. Conditions sure are tough."

He turned then to the old black hen and said, "It's worse with you,
For you're not only hungry, but you must be tired too.
I rested while I watched for worms, so I feel fairly pert;
But how are you? Without worms too? And after all that work?"

The old black hen hopped to her perch and drooped her eyes to sleep,
And murmured in a drowsy tone, "Young man, hear this and weep:
I'm full of worms and happy, for I've dined both long and well,
The worms are there as always—but I had to dig like hell."

Oh, here and there red roosters still, are holding sales positions,
They cannot do much business now because of poor conditions,
But soon as things get right again, they'll sell a hundred firms—
Meanwhile the old black hens are out and gobbling up the worms!

(Author Unknown.)

From "Insurance Salesman"

BRANCHING OUT

Speaking to Mutual Life's directors in July 1919, company president Matthew Brenan announced: "In view of the business for insurance in the state of Maryland being thoroughly canvassed, and in order to maintain the increase in new business the company has enjoyed in the past, it [will] be necessary . . . to open a branch office in some other state, and I would suggest the state of Ohio."

Over the next few years, Mutual Life opened offices and appointed agents in the industrial cities of Cleveland and Columbus, Ohio, and St. Louis, Missouri, and applied for licenses to operate in Kansas, Kentucky, Indiana, Minnesota, Louisiana and Illinois. Insurance in force grew rapidly, reaching $41.8 million by year-end 1921.

At about the same time, management began promoting the "Mutual Spirit" to field and home office employees through the *Old Black Hen*. "What is this spirit anyway?" one field manager was asked by an acquaintance who worked for another insurance company. "Well, the best way I can describe it," answered the manager, "is to tell you that everything about our organization is intensely human. . . . Each one gives the other a lift, and everybody lifts together! The best proof that such a thing is alive and active is to talk to the men who occasionally leave, for any reason at all, whether of his own accord or not, there is always that feeling of regret."

First edited by Howard M. Emmons, director and vice president of the board, with articles contributed by associate editors in each field office, the *Old Black Hen* was published for more than fifty years. Full of sales tips, reports from the field, and pep talks from company officers, the first issue of the publication included the following message from President Matthew Brenan:

> The [home] office and field forces have been steadily advancing the interests of the Company and have been loyal to its principals and faithful to their duty. . . . It has not been without considerable effort that progress has been made. . . . Good, steady, conscientious work is bound to bring results. . . . In no other way can permanent achievement be made.

Eager for additional increase and growth, board vice president Paul M. Burnett also challenged the field force in the same publication:

> The Mutual Life Insurance Company can go backwards, stand still or forge forward according to the loyalty, honesty and ambition of its young men. Which shall it be? Shall we be content with progress we have made and stand on our record or shall we strive for greater things? No company and no business can offer better opportunities to deserving young men willing to progress by hard knocks and efficient service. . . . Westward we wish to weld [our] chain of offices—a chain with no weak links—until it reaches from the Chesapeake Bay to the Golden Gate.

BURNETT ELECTED PRESIDENT

Early in 1922, Matthew Brenan's physician recommended that he take a six-month leave of absence to rest and recuperate from a lingering illness. While he was on leave, Mutual Life's directors voted to create the position of chairman of the board and elected Paul M. Burnett to fill the new post. Burnett had "full and complete power to control the policies of the company and superintend and manage its affairs . . . as though he were president."

One of the chairman's first decisions as acting president was to consult industry actuary S. H. Wolfe about getting the company back into the Ordinary business. Following Wolfe's suggestion, Mutual Life designed and introduced new Ordinary products—including straight life, 15, 20 and 30-year endowments and 15, 20 and 30-pay life policies—to "compete with others in the field." Wolfe prepared the necessary forms and rates. Permitted to write up to $5,000 of coverage on one life, Mutual Life's agents sold 193 Ordinary policies for $238,000 of coverage by March 31, 1923.

Though Matthew Brenan returned to his position as Mutual Life's president by the end of 1922, he never fully recovered his health. He passed away in May 1923. Following Brenan's death, the board he had served on faithfully for twenty-five years elected Paul M. Burnett the company's next president.

Matthew S. Brenan . . .
Mutual Life President 1898–1923

BORN ON September 26, 1859, one year after Mutual Life received its charter, Matthew S. Brenan grew up in Baltimore during the turbulent years of the Civil War. His grandfather, an immigrant from Bordeaux, founded a lumberyard in Baltimore in the mid-1800s. After graduating from Baltimore's Loyola College in 1877 with a Master of Arts degree, Brenan joined his uncle in the family's hardwood business. He was associated with P. E. Brenan & Company at the corner of Howard and West Streets for twenty-five years.

Elected a director of the Mutual Life Insurance Company of Baltimore in 1892, Brenan served on the company's Auditing Committee from 1895 until 1897, when he became vice president of the board. Elected unanimously by his peers to head the board in 1898 at thirty-nine years of age, Brenan was Mutual Life's president for twenty-five years, from 1898 until 1923. Under his leadership, Mutual Life prospered, accumulated more than one million dollars of assets, invested in Baltimore's reconstruction, and earned a position of prominence and respect among the city's business leaders.

Active in community affairs throughout his life and career, Brenan was a member of the University Club, the Merchants & Manufacturers Association, and the Real Estate Board. He was a director of the National Marine Bank, treasurer of the Baltimore Life Underwriter's Association, and vice president of both the Loyola Building Association and the French Benevolent Society.

Matthew Brenan passed away in May 1923 following a leave of absence from his duties as Mutual Life's president, recommended by his physician. Company directors agreed that Brenan should take the time needed for "complete relaxation from business and an effort to recover his health." In announcing Brenan's death, Paul M. Burnett, vice president and chairman of the board, commented: "An irreparable loss has been sustained, for by his many virtues, the purity of his life, the strength of his character, exercised with a tenderness and love for those with whom he associated, he has contributed not only to the success of the company but to the moral welfare of its many employees."

Brenan's widow donated to the company a life-size, "handsomely framed" portrait of her deceased husband, which had been presented to Brenan shortly before his death by Mutual Life's field force. Directors displayed the portrait in their board room.

CHAPTER 5

Twenties Roar!

(1923–1929)

TWO YOUNG COUPLES enter the dimly lit Owl Bar on the first floor of Baltimore's Belvedere Hotel, the women in high heels and short dresses with dropped waists. Their hair is bobbed in the fashion of the day. Wisps of curls escape from beneath their small, close-fitting hats. One wears a feather boa and fringe, the other drapes a fur coat casually over one shoulder. Dressed for a night "on the town" in one of Baltimore's most fashionable neighborhoods, their evening will include a vaudeville show at the Lyceum Theater a block north on Charles Street.

Spotting friends at the bar, they take seats, light cigarettes and order drinks. Watching them from his perch high above the bar amid an array of liquor bottles is a wooden owl with glowing eyes that blink mysteriously. Regular customers know this means the bar's liquor shipment has arrived, the feds aren't around, and it's safe to enjoy themselves. When the owl's eyes stare straight ahead, unblinking, patrons know it's best to behave like the wise old bird who "sat on an oak, the more he saw the less he spoke, the less he spoke, the more he heard." To speak out now might prompt a raid by the feds.

Despite Prohibition, Baltimore is known as a "wet" town. Local breweries never stopped producing beer, and distilled liquor flows regularly through the port. The United States Industrial Alcohol Corporation, largest producer of alcohol in the nation, is located here, and those in the know can obtain a gallon for three dollars. So much alcohol is available that Baltimore has no need for "speakeasies." Restaurants display a red crab in their windows to announce the availability

ABOVE: *Hand-painted New Year's Eve 1918 menu from the Belvedere Hotel's Owl Bar.* (Courtesy of the Owl Bar)

LEFT: *Despite approaching Prohibition, men didn't storm the doors of Baltimore liquor stores. Alcohol flowed freely through the city during the 1920s.*
(Courtesy of the Maryland Historical Society)

of liquor "in the back," or advertise their "wetness" with a tongue-in-cheek sign proclaiming "fresh sea food." The city's mayor and Governor Albert Ritchie have never appropriated money to enforce the Eighteenth Amendment. Baltimore police don't even have the right to arrest those caught drinking.

Since returning from France five or six years ago, the young men spend money freely and live more frivolously than their parents. Having endured harrowing months in the trenches, they have learned, as soldiers do, to "eat, drink and be merry for tomorrow we may die." Their dates, having won the right to vote in 1920, eagerly embrace cars, canned foods, appliances, ready-made clothes, and anything else that will remove the drudgery of daily housework from their lives.

Like most young people of their generation, they smoke cigarettes, dance the Charleston, and question traditional values. In a time of rising prosperity, they are optimistic about the future. Their heroes are the decade's achievers and outspoken rebels—editor H. L. Mencken and novelist F. Scott Fitzgerald, who frequent the Owl Bar; pilot Charles A. Lindbergh; and Babe Ruth, the Baltimore-born slugger who struck it rich playing baseball.

But tonight's talk is not about baseball, booze or "jazz," the current music craze.

"What's happening across the street?" they ask the bartender. The beautiful home and carriage house with a high garden wall that once stood at 1101 Charles Street has been torn down. Construction crews are clearing the site. "The Mutual Life Insurance Company bought the place," answers the bartender. "They're putting up a new building here. Six stories."

"Great location," says one young man, referring to the corner of Charles and Chase. "Impressive address, even for this neighborhood. The house belonged to Louis McLane, Jr., didn't it?"

Other well-dressed couples join the conversation. Someone remembers hearing that Louis McLane, Jr., grew up in Delaware. "His father was a U.S. senator, secretary of state, secretary of the treasury, minister to England and president of the B&O Railroad in the mid-1800s." Another notes that the younger McLane served in the navy, married a Baltimore woman and sailed to San Francisco in 1850, where he operated several steamship lines.

"Did you know that he founded the Pioneer Stage Coach Line, the Pony Express and was president of Wells Fargo?" asks one young woman. "He came back East in 1866, lived in New York for a few years, then moved down here."

"When did he buy the house?" someone asks. "Around 1870," the young woman replies, "but he didn't move his whole family household here until about 1884. That's when they added rooms and gardens for servants and guests. He had six children."

"My grandfather knew him when he was Executive Committee Chairman of the Mercantile Trust Company," she adds. "We drove up Charles Street the other day, to Penn Station. He said the construction site reminded him of a party he attended there in June 1899 to celebrate the McLanes' fiftieth wedding anniversary. They served punch from a large Chinese porcelain bowl decorated inside and out with landscapes, flowers, birds and butterflies. It must have been beautiful. Apparently, he bought the punch bowl in San Francisco in the 1860s. Grandfather remembered it so vividly."

"Looks like this new building is going to be something too," says the bartender. "The architect stopped in for a drink the other day. He says it'll have eight huge granite columns and a lobby with marble floors and real gold leaf painted on the ceiling. Mutual Life must be doing very well."

BIGGER IS BETTER

With life insurance sales booming in the early 1920s, *LAN* Magazine reported that "more," "bigger," and "better" had become the industry's bywords. Like many of its competitors in those years, Mutual Life soon outgrew existing office space at 15 South Street. In late 1923, Paul Burnett, the company's newly elected president, announced to directors that larger quarters were needed to accommodate the company's expected future growth.

Through business contacts in Baltimore, Burnett had learned that the McLane property, on the northeast corner of Charles and Chase Streets, "134 feet on Charles Street and 186 feet on Chase," could be bought for about $225,000. Improved with a new office building, the location would meet all the company's requirements. In November 1923, Mutual Life's directors approved purchase of the property for a price not to exceed $225,000. Shortly thereafter the company bought the McLane home and outbuildings for $221,000. In January 1924, Burnett reported that Howard M. Emmons, a company director, had completed the title search and transferred the title. Board members agreed to pay Emmons $730.35 for his legal work.

In July 1925 directors reviewed and approved plans—submitted by Baltimore architects Parker, Thomas & Rice, who designed the Belvedere Hotel—for the design and construction of Mutual Life's new home office building. "Such a building typifies the kind of institution this company has been endeavoring to erect," said Emmons, "the kind that years will not weaken nor age dim the luster. The architects have blended strength with beauty, as our contracts [combine] safety with attractiveness, and our dealings with the public combine justice to all with fairness to the individual."

This large Chinese porcelain bowl once belonged to Louis McLane, Jr.—founder of the Pony Express and president of Wells Fargo—who built and owned the townhouse on the northeast corner of Charles and Chase Streets until 1923, when Mutual Life purchased the property. McLane brought the bowl to the U.S. from China in the 1860s. His grandson D. K. Este Fisher, Jr., donated it to the company in 1974.

BELOW: *By the time construction of the Belvedere Hotel began in 1902 or 1903, the four-story McLane townhouse had been standing on the corner of Charles and Chase streets for twenty or thirty years.*
(Courtesy of the Maryland Historical Society)

Belvedere means "Beautiful View"

THE LAND at Charles and Chase Streets that Mutual Life purchased in 1923 for its new home office is on a hill in Baltimore that was once at the edge of an estate owned by Revolutionary War hero John Eager Howard. In 1812, Howard's property extended from present day Biddle Street south to Monument Street, and from near Eutaw Street eastward to Guilford Avenue. "Belvedere," the family mansion, faced northwest on land that today is just south of where Chase Street crosses Calvert. Looking south from their home, the Howard family enjoyed one of the most beautiful views in the city.

John Eager Howard inherited Belvedere from his grandfather George Eager, who purchased the land from Lord Baltimore in 1688. In 1815, Howard donated "Howard's Woods," at the estate's southern boundary, for construction of Baltimore's Washington Monument. After his death in 1827, John Eager Howard's heirs donated additional land in the shape of a cross for a park around the base of the monument at Mount Vernon Square. The rest of the estate was divided into lots and sold to prosperous Baltimore citizens. By the 1850s and 1860s, the neighborhood surrounding the Washington Monument had become the center of the city's social life.

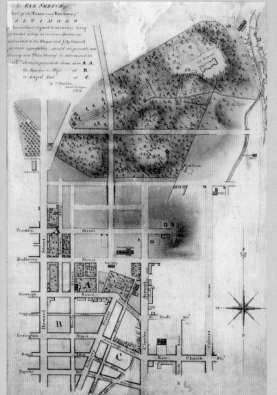

ABOVE: *The Poppleton Survey Map, dating from 1812, shows the extent of John Eager Howard's Baltimore estate. At the time, Charles Street ended at the estate's southern boundary. Howard's "Belvedere" mansion sat where, today, Chase Street crosses Calvert Street.*

(Courtesy of the Maryland Historical Society)

RIGHT: *Architect's original drawings of the McLanes' Charles Street townhouse show skylights, bay windows, an elegant spiral stairway, a servants' back stairs, several bedrooms and an attic billiard room.*

(Monumental Life archives)

Sometime between 1870 and 1884, Louis McLane, Jr., purchased property on the northeast corner of Charles and Chase Streets for a family home. Designed by Baltimore architects Niernsee and Nielson, the four-story townhouse had skylights, bay windows, a billiard room in the attic, a spiral front staircase and servants' back stairs. A carriage house and stables in the rear contained stalls for eight horses plus rooms for equipage and a coachman.

Like many of its neighbors, the McLane townhouse included a parlor, library, dining room and butler's pantry on the first floor; three bedrooms with dressing rooms and wardrobes, two bathrooms and a "water closet" (toilet) on the second; five bedrooms, a bathroom and water closet on the third; and bedrooms for servants in the attic. Those servants—probably either Irish immigrants or African Americans—prepared meals and washed the family's clothes "below stairs" in a basement that included a large kitchen, laundry, servants' hall and delivery entrance. Coal was delivered directly into the cellar below through two chutes facing on Chase Street.

When investors decided to build a hotel across the street from the McLane house in 1900, they called the beautiful mansard-roofed structure the Belvedere Hotel after the Howard estate. Opened in 1903, the Belvedere was the largest, most luxurious hotel in the city. For decades it hosted visiting heads of state, actors of stage and screen, musicians, composers, sports heroes, politicians and other famous folk. The Belvedere's "Owl Bar" was the hottest and "sassiest" spot in town—*the* place to be seen in the Twenties and Thirties. Divorcée Wallis Warfield Simpson, who married Britain's Duke of Windsor, and columnist Emily Post both lived in the neighborhood.

Mutual Life's directors no doubt appreciated the history and prestige associated with the Charles and Chase Street address.

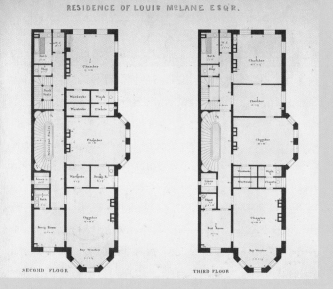

RESIDENCE OF LOUIS McLANE ESQR.

SECOND FLOOR   THIRD FLOOR

As construction of the new building neared completion in the fall of 1926, Mutual Life's directors sent 1,200 letters to businessmen and insurance and financial industry associates in Baltimore and its branch office locations, inviting them to the official opening on October 7. Board minutes from that day reflect that the company received a "hearty response" to its invitation.

The same day, the board approved the purchase of a messenger's uniform and small thank you gifts for five female and twenty-eight male employees who "very willingly rendered more or less unusual service by working at night and taking a great deal of interest in preparing the new building for inspection by the public."

Obviously proud of the Mutual Life's new 70,000-square-foot building—"one of the handsomest in the city of Baltimore"—Burnett reported that many in the financial and business community had attended the open house. Several businesses that could not send officers or representatives to the opening recognized the event with gifts of floral bouquets. The list of companies wiring flowers included the Merchants National Bank of Baltimore; the National Bank of Baltimore; the New Amsterdam Casualty Company, Baltimore; Lincoln National Life Insurance Company, Fort Wayne, Indiana; Mercantile Trust & Deposit Company, Baltimore; Parker, Thomas & Rice, Architects; and the Fidelity Storage & Trust Company.

Of special interest to visitors who toured the building that day was a bronze wheel inlaid in the lobby's marble floor. Each spoke of the wheel represented a U.S. city in which Mutual Life had opened a district office since 1870. On October 7, 1926, there were twenty-six spokes.

Anxious to begin construction, the board instructed the architects to complete their work and go to bid with plans and specifications as quickly as possible. J. Henry Miller Construction Company of Baltimore won the project with a bid of $623,000. Additional building costs included $4,000 for demolition of the McLane house; $65,000 for electrical work, elevators and vaults; and $3,386 to Hutchinson Brothers for kitchen and cafeteria equipment.

At the board's quarterly meeting in January 1926, Burnett announced that contractors had completed the new building's foundation and had begun to install ironwork specified in the plans. Six months later, a copper box containing company artifacts and historic documents was set in the building's cornerstone.

Over the next four years, directors approved spending over $6,000 to furnish executive offices, an executive dining room and kitchen, and a three-room Medical Suite with desks, chairs, rugs, a large clock, china, silver, a refrigerator and range, three beds, linens, and medicine. One of the most impressive purchases was a dining room table and twelve chairs, bought from an antiques dealer in New Orleans who certified it had once belonged to the Empress Eugenie, widow of Napoleon III. An informed and committed antiques collector, Paul Burnett personally selected many of the pieces.

D.C. (1924), Newark and Akron (1924 and 1925), Wilmington, Delaware (1925), Pittsburgh and Beaver Falls (1925), Evansville, Indiana (1925), New Orleans (1925), and the first of four offices in Chicago (1926).

Postwar growth and prosperity also created new sales opportunities within Mutual Life's home state. During the Roaring Twenties, forty-four companies—including Lever Brothers, Proctor & Gamble, Crosse & Blackwell, Revere Copper, Armco Steel, Western Electric and the Glenn L. Martin Aircraft Company—located plants in the Baltimore area. Adding four thousand middle-income jobs to the region, they provided families with additional reasons to purchase life insurance protection. To meet this growing need, Mutual Life appointed managers and opened additional Maryland offices in South Baltimore, Annapolis, Salisbury, and Hagerstown in 1925.

The nation's economy and consumers were on the move, and so were Mutual Life's agents! Gas cost twenty-three cents a gallon. Newly paved highways made driving easier. By the middle of the decade, most areas of the state were accessible by automobile. Even on Maryland's once isolated Eastern Shore, farmers could afford to buy cars

and trucks. Americans had more time and money for leisure and the country's travel and tourism industries grew quickly. Between 1921 and 1927, for example, the assessed value of land in Maryland's Ocean City beach resort climbed from $200,000 to $6 million.

Upon reaching a major milestone—$5.5 million of assets on October 1, 1924—

WHEEL OF PROGRESS KEEPS ROLLING

ABOVE: President Paul Burnett (seated at left, with dogs) celebrated a Mutual Life milestone—$5.5 million in assets—by hosting a luncheon for directors at his summer home, St. Helena Island, in Round Bay on Maryland's Severn River.

BELOW: "Busy bees" from the home office were also invited to join Burnett and directors for the celebration on St. Helena Island. Arriving by boat, they enjoyed a relaxing afternoon.

LOWER RIGHT: Four generations of Mutual Life policyholders from Zanesville, Ohio.

When Paul Burnett was elected president in May 1923, Mutual Life had nine district offices outside Baltimore in four states—Maryland, Ohio, Missouri and Kentucky. Eager to see the company push westward, "all the way to San Francisco," Burnett urged Mutual Life's directors to open district offices in other states. He was so confident that the expansion would succeed that he asked for and received authority to appoint additional vice presidents to help him manage the growing business. In January 1924, Agency Manager Charles C. Ewell was elected second vice president and moved from Baltimore to St. Louis.

As Mutual Life's "Wheel of Progress" rolled along in the mid-1920s, the company opened additional field offices in Indianapolis (1923), Philadelphia (1924), Washington,

Mutual Life's directors celebrated the company's success with a leisurely luncheon hosted by President Paul Burnett at his summer home, St. Helena Island, in Round Bay on Maryland's Severn River.

The general prosperity in the first half of the decade demonstrated that there was a market for weekly premium life insurance not only in industrial cities, where factory workers took home weekly paychecks, but also in small towns and rural communities where farmers and watermen earned their living. To make sales and service calls on the Maryland's Eastern Shore, Mutual Life agents drove miles of roads bordered by corn and soybean fields, wrote insurance on chicken farmers, prospected among oystermen on Tilghman Island, and began collecting premiums from crab pickers in Crisfield.

As contractors erected the new home office in Baltimore in 1926, agents in each office were also laying foundations—for both Industrial and Ordinary business—following "sales-building plans" constructed by their management teams. A new rate book and eight new juvenile policies, for children aged six months to ten years, helped agents open doors. The policies paid death benefits ranging from $25 to $1,000 and enabled parents to save for their children's education and future business interests.

On April 7, 1927, President Burnett reported that Mutual Life's Industrial business had passed another milestone, growing almost $10 million in a single year— from $92.9 million of insurance in force at year-end 1925, to $102.8 million at year-end 1926. In just three years, agents had also written almost $17 million of Ordinary life insurance. During the month of November 1926 alone, Burnett noted, processing Ordinary applications totalling $5.7 million in coverage "necessitated night work by the company's Ordinary clerks."

Mutual Life's plans for expansion and growth did not end at the Mississippi River. On a trip to the Pacific Coast in 1925, Burnett visited Spokane, Seattle, Portland, San Francisco and Los Angeles. With "less competition than on the East Coast and having large 'industrial'

populations," Burnett reported, these five cities presented an unusual opportunity for the company to open offices and develop business. With business growing in Chicago, the company opened another office there in July 1928. But the stock market crash the following year and the resulting Depression abruptly curtailed Burnett's grander plans.

Burnett and Mutual Life's officers had every reason to roar loudly about the company's progress and success during the Roaring Twenties. Clearly, they had earned the bonuses, approved by charter amendment in January 1924, that provided both an incentive and a reward for expanding the company's Industrial and Ordinary lines of business.

"DELEGATES" ATTEND FIRST SALES CONVENTION

World War I had created an abundant supply of eager, disciplined, combat-toughened young veterans looking for civilian jobs and a chance to prove themselves on the home front. As Mutual Life opened new offices in the mid-1920s, it needed agents, and there were plenty of qualified candidates. Fueling the company's remarkable growth, the field agents, office "superintendents" and assistants hired in those years provided all-important sales, service and support.

Weekly "board call" results list agent and staff sales for the week of May 19, 1923. The special campaign honored Paul M. Burnett, elected Mutual Life's new president that month.

Sales tips and production reports appeared regularly in the company's monthly publication, the *Old Black Hen*, beginning in October 1922. From St. Louis came the following recipe for a successful agent's "Mutual Cake":

> Mix 2 cups FAITH and 8 tablespoons ENERGY together with 6 tablespoons ABILITY and 3 cups AMBITION. Then add 1 cup SINCERITY and 3 cups CONFIDENCE. Last, but not least, mix in LOYALTY and flavor with plenty of MUTUAL SPIRIT. (No eggs needed.)

And from the Newark District in Ohio came this timely advice which editor Howard M. Emmons encouraged agents to digest:

> Think big and you will accomplish big things. Always be an optimist; do not let conditions control you, control them instead. When you make a sale in a home, sell yourself as well as your policy so that in the future you will have a good foundation to build upon. Watch your new business; make it a point to collect several weeks' premium on date of delivery. Policies are like infants; you sometimes have to nurse them. When things go wrong, go into some quiet place and take an inventory of yourself. Then you will have a different outlook and can go forth with renewed zeal.

Like the company's officers, agents who produced results were rewarded for their efforts. Prior to 1924, each Mutual Life field office had held its own annual recognition banquet. Early in 1924, Paul Burnett proposed holding an annual "convention of certain superintendents, assistants and agents each January at a place and time to be arranged." The board agreed, setting aside $3,000—a sum equal to the total then being spent for individual office banquets—for such a convention in 1925.

The conventions would increase business, Burnett explained, because they would include "special inducements" and proficiency standards that agents and managers had to meet in order to be selected as convention "delegates." Burnett also believed that conventions of seventy-five to eighty successful agents and managers would result in new ideas, needed reforms and the sharing of plans for the "future betterment of the company."

Mutual Life's first formal sales convention was held in New Orleans, January 25–31, 1925, at an actual total cost of $9,859. Reporting at the directors' quarterly meeting in April of that year, Burnett noted that the convention "was the best move yet on the part of the company in the interests of new business and the company's future." There was "full attendance at all meetings, great enthusiasm on the part of the delegates, instructive speeches by those appointed to address [attendees], a wonderful spirit . . . and a determination to make this the company's banner year."

Borchers & Sons Market...

Butchers to the Board, Agent Networking Base

LEFT: *H. H. Borchers & Sons Meat Market at Poplar Grove Street and Edmondson Avenue in West Baltimore delivered meat to Mutual Life's home office on Charles Street for many years.*

BORCHERS MEAT MARKET at Poplar Grove Street and Edmondson Avenue in West Baltimore attracted customers like a magnet. Huge sides of beef and pork hung from hooks on the wall. Bratwurst curled on the counter next to mountains of sausage links and frankfurters. Neatly trimmed hams, steaks and chops were proudly displayed next to scales sitting just a few feet from the market's dirt (not "dirty"!) floor.

Wearing traditional white butcher's aprons, Herman Henry Borchers and his sons William and Herman, Jr., greeted customers, took orders, cut, and sold some of the freshest, most tender and tasty meat in all of Baltimore.

The elder Borchers emigrated from Germany's Black Forest at the turn of the century. Before opening his shop in 1915 he sold meat from a stall in Baltimore's Hollins Market. Borchers' was typical of the immigrant-owned, customer-focused neighborhood markets that flourished in Baltimore in those years. By the 1920s and 1930s, H. H. Borchers & Sons was so highly respected that its list of customers included hotels, schools, businesses, and some of the city's most popular restaurants.

Retired Monumental Life Agent John Borchers remembers Borchers Meat Market as a young boy. When his uncle made deliveries, John often accompanied him. For many years, one of the delivery truck's regular stops was Mutual Life Insurance Company on Charles Street. "They buy the best for their executive dining room," John remembers his uncle saying.

Two Mutual Life employees, Clarence Bowen and Fred Wehr, were regular customers. Bowen managed the West Baltimore branch office, four blocks from the butcher shop. Wehr, like John's father William, belonged to the Masonic Lodge. William Borchers also knew Leo Rock, who was elected company president in 1936.

When John Borchers was looking for a career in the 1950s, his father suggested that he talk to Leo Rock and Clarence Bowen. "How can you miss working for an insurance company that's almost one hundred years old?" his father asked. After the interview, Bowen, a thirty-year insurance veteran, agreed that the outgoing young man who wanted to help people would fit well on his team of thirty agents. John would be a "phenomenon," however—the office's first new agent in ten years!

Young Borchers wrote policies on his father and uncle, who referred him to others in the meat business, including a few of the city's most respected chefs. He insured its employees, left his business cards on the counter, and stopped by at least two or three times a week to talk to customers about life insurance.

"When I received my first week's pay of $35," John remembers, "I thought I was making a fortune." Fifty dollars for his second week's work was even better. Borchers sold ten to twelve new weekly premium policies per week in those years. He also collected weekly premiums of five cents to three dollars on many policies written in the 1920s and 1930s by agents who had since retired.

Borchers' first "debit" was in the heart of Baltimore near Mount Saint Joseph High School. It included Edmondson Avenue, Irvington and Hilton Streets. Later, his area included the neighborhoods around Edmondson Village. He will never forget delivering his first $10,000 claim check to a widow. "That was a lot of money back then . . . like a million dollars today!"

During his forty-year career, Borchers sold life insurance to generations of the same families, including five generations of the Clarence Bollinger family, owners of a fruit stand business in Baltimore that today is in Westminster, Maryland. He insured the descendants of immigrant Carl Doederlien, his mother's uncle, whose family founded a jewelry, clock and watch shop in Munich in 1856 that later became Baltimore's Nelson Coleman Jewelers.

Always looking for prospects, John Borchers talked insurance to everyone he met. Watching his grandfather, father and uncle serving customers at H. H. Borchers & Sons as a boy, he learned that "the customer always comes first." Little did he know that, years later, he would be working for a few of those customers and serving others as their life insurance agent.

German immigrant Carl Doederlien opened a jewelry, clock and watch shop at Charles and Saratoga Streets in 1925. Several generations of Doederlien's descendants, including the current owners of Nelson Coleman Jewelers in Baltimore County, have been Mutual Life policyholders for decades.

The Real Estate Trust Company and Mutual Life shared directors as well as first floor office space in Mutual Life's 1926 building. The real estate company remained as tenants for more than sixty years, long after it became part of Baltimore's highly respected Mercantile Bank & Trust Company.

(Monumental Life archives)

Looking for additional opportunities to promote business and reward production, the executive board approved payment of $100 for a company advertisement on the back page of a minstrel show program in July 1924. Mutual Life agents produced the show to benefit a local charity. Later that year, Burnett also paid $107 to rent Baltimore's City Club and provide refreshments for members of the President's Club "to instill enthusiasm in the men for securing policies in new homes."

Building on this success, Burnett brought managers from the Philadelphia, Wilmington and Cleveland offices to Baltimore in September 1925 for a pep talk and training. The following month he reported to directors that District Manager Leo Rock and his Cleveland agents had contributed $120 for "advertising purposes in order that they might gain access to new homes." Directors agreed to match the office's contribution.

In the fall of 1926, several managers, assistants and "men who looked promising for promotion" traveled from Ohio, Pennsylvania, Delaware and Washington, D.C., to Baltimore in their own automobiles to inspect the new building, become better acquainted with the home office organization, and discuss important matters regarding the future of the business. The company reimbursed each attendee for the cost of gasoline. The following year, the company held a similar two-day convention just for managers.

With the lines of communication open between home office and field, agent production and professionalism continued to grow. At the same time, Mutual Life's agents and officers were benefiting from participation in industry meetings.

At the Annual Meeting of the National Association of Life Underwriters (NALU) in 1927, the industry announced the creation of the American College of Life

Underwriters and its new Chartered Life Underwriter ("CLU") designation for agents. In December 1927, Burnett himself attended the annual convention of life insurance presidents in New York City. Returning from that meeting, he decided to hire an "efficiency expert" to recommend ways for the company to "consolidate debits, reduce canvassing expenses, and make other reforms needed to reduce operating expenses."

DIRECTORS VOTE TO DEMUTUALIZE

As the decade drew to a close, the words "more," "bigger" and "better" continued to be the industry's bywords. In Baltimore, Mutual Life celebrated its success in a very big way.

With just under $8.8 million in assets and over $140 million of life insurance in force on December 31, 1927, the company had existed as a mutual life insurer, owned by its policyholders, for almost seventy years. It was one of the twenty oldest life insurance companies in the country. Baker, Watts & Company, a Baltimore investment firm, noted in the June 1927 issue of its monthly publication that Mutual Life occupied a "distinctive place" among the three hundred life insurance companies actively operating in the United States.

On October 6 of that year, Director Milton Roberts proposed a startling change in the company's corporate structure. Addressing directors at their quarterly meeting, he read a resolution recommending that the company "demutualize" and reorganize as a stock life insurance company, subject to the laws applicable to such corporations.

At the time, Roberts was president of the Real Estate Trust Company, an organization incorporated in 1924 under laws of the State of the Maryland to conduct general mortgage and real estate business. Mutual Life had invested $50,000 in Real Estate Trust Company's initial stock offering. Over the next decade, the two companies built a close and profitable business relationship. In fact, the Real Estate Trust offices were located in Mutual Life's new building.

In order to convert Mutual Life to a stock company, reported Roberts, "the president is directed to give notice of the proposal . . . at a meeting of the policyholders of the corporation to be held . . . on January 5, 1928 . . . at the company's offices." As required by law, the company also had to publish notice of the meeting in two Baltimore newspapers. Roberts's resolution also noted: "the president is authorized and directed to take such steps as in his judgment may be best to obtain consent in writing from the policyholders. If not in writing, to have as many policyholders as possible present in person to vote at the meeting."

The following notice appeared in both the *Baltimore Sun* and the *Daily Record* from October 13 through November 17, 1927:

> Notice is hereby given under Section 99, Article 48A, Bagby's Code of Maryland, that a meeting of all members and policyholders of the Mutual Life Insurance Company of Baltimore is hereby called to be held on Thursday, January 5, 1928, at 11 o'clock A.M., at the Company's office, northeast corner of Charles & Chase Streets, Baltimore, Maryland, to vote in person upon or give their consent in writing to, a resolution to the change the form of the corporate organization to a stock company.
>
> —Paul M. Burnett, President
> Mutual Life Insurance Co.
> of Baltimore

By year-end 1927, the entire board concurred with the proposed change, provided that two-thirds of the company's policyholders also approved. With business spread over several states, directors agreed to pay the company's agents ten cents per signature to assure that as many policyholders as possible were contacted and proxies were returned.

WHY DEMUTUALIZE? . . .

HY would the directors of a successful and growing seventy-year-old mutual life insurance company propose to change the company's corporate structure? Board meeting minutes from 1927 and 1928 noted what was required for Mutual Life to convert from a mutual to a stock company but provided little to explain why directors gave their unanimous approval to this significant change.

Traditionally, insurance companies demutualize to raise capital for expansion and growth. In the process, ownership of the organization passes from thousands or millions of policyholders to investing "shareholders" who purchase shares of the company's stock. Some companies distribute stock and/or stock options to policyholders. Others, like Mutual Life in 1928, raise capital by inviting policyholders to purchase stock.

Policyholders who become stockholders retain their contractual insurance benefits, their voting rights, and their ownership in the company, based on the number of shares purchased. With equity in their own hands, shareholders can also benefit financially from selling the company's publicly traded stock on the open market.

By concentrating the power to make decisions in fewer hands, demutualization increases an insurance organization's flexibility. As a stock company, an insurer can operate more efficiently, compete more aggressively in the marketplace, and raise operating funds more easily by selling additional shares of its stock to the public.

When companies demutualize, their focus sometimes shifts from providing policyholder benefits to maximizing profits and their shareholders' return on investment. This change in goals, coupled with a more competitive "bigger is better" atmosphere, can bring change to an organization's workplace and affect both employee morale and productivity. Based on reported growth in the years following its change in corporate structure, becoming a stock company was the right decision for the future of Maryland's first life insurance company.

During the late 1990s, several of the ninety-one mutual companies operating in the U.S. and Canada reorganized as stock companies to compete more effectively in the marketplace. Going through the same process in 1928, Mutual Life's directors had recognized the benefits —to policyholders, employees, directors and the company—of converting to a stock company several decades before many of the country's oldest and largest mutual life insurers even considered such a bold move.

Concentrating the power to make decisions in fewer hands increases an insurance organization's flexibility.

Board members also agreed to amend the corporate charter to fix capital for the new stock company at $500,000 through the issue of 5,000 shares of common stock at $100 per share. The following Executive Committee members and directors signed the resolution dated December 29, 1927: Paul M. Burnett, president; Howard M. Emmons, first vice president; Henry Roth, secretary; Dr. James D. Iglehart, medical director; John B. H. Dunn; C. Fred Hutchinson; Adelbert W. Mears; Milton Roberts; Thomas F. Shriver; and Alfred J. Tormey.

Policyholders met at Mutual Life's home office on January 5, 1928, but it was a very short meeting. When Arthur L. Jackson, the company's general counsel, announced that actuaries had been unable to complete the necessary calculations, the meeting was recessed early and rescheduled.

On January 30, 1928, with fifty-seven policyholders physically present at the rescheduled meeting, Directors Burnett, Emmons and Roberts presented signed proxies giving them authority to vote on behalf of 376,982 of the company's 489,073 policyholders. The 377,049 total votes in favor of changing to a stock company structure included policyholders present at the meeting and

represented 77 percent of all policyholders—more than the two-thirds needed to approve the change. Charles C. Ewell, Agency Manager and Actuary Department supervisor, and Miss Rebecca Sharry, the company's first female actuary, certified the election results. Mutual Life employee Emily T. Crowley, a notary public, signed and affixed her seal to the document.

Four days later, Burnett reported that sixty-three Mutual Life policyholders had submitted stock subscription forms by the required deadline. The board determined that each subscribing policyholder would receive "five shares at par" valued at $500. Remaining shares were allotted to policyholders of the company holding an executive, officer or department manager position "in order that the present management, control and operation of the company may continue in the same hands and under the same management which has successfully conducted the company for years past."

On February 6, 1928, Carville D. Benson, State Insurance Commissioner of Maryland, certified that "the Mutual Life Insurance Company of Baltimore [had] complied with all the laws of Maryland . . . and [was] fully authorized to transact the business of life insurance as a stock life insurance company."

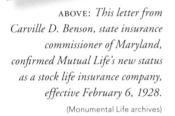

ABOVE: *This letter from Carville D. Benson, state insurance commissioner of Maryland, confirmed Mutual Life's new status as a stock life insurance company, effective February 6, 1928.*
(Monumental Life archives)

RIGHT: *Mutual Life issued its first stock certificate for seventy-five shares of capital stock at $100 per share to James C. Harris on February 10, 1928.*

FIFTY-THREE YEARS OF SERVICE

Absent from the first stockholders meeting in July 1928 was Henry Roth, secretary of Mutual Life's Executive Committee for forty years, who had passed away on April 26. With fifty-three years of continuous service, Roth had been the company's oldest employee. Working under three Mutual Life presidents, he had personally participated in dozens of milestone decisions that had contributed to the company's significant growth and success as a mutual life insurance company.

Writing to Roth's family, the board noted:

> Those of us who have been intimately associated with him for so many years feel that we have lost a friend as well as a faithful, conscientious and industrious official. He was an example to all for punctuality and loyalty. Never more contented than when sitting at his desk, he was ever-ready with helpful suggestions to those around him and greeted the public in an affable and friendly manner, thereby cementing a close relationship between the policyholder and the company.

Roth's son, Harry Roth, Jr., took over his father's responsibilities in the Cashier's Office. At the same time, the officers acted on three recommendations made by consulting actuaries S. H. and Lee J. Wolfe. They appointed R. O. Wehrheim as Agency Manager; employed an "expert accountant," Harold Loweree, with authority to manage and control accounting systems in all departments throughout the company; and appointed an executive with responsibility for investments.

$11 MILLION MILESTONE!

On June 28, 1928, Burnett moved close to $4 million of company securities from the Safe Deposit & Trust Company, where they had been stored since 1904, to a Real Estate Trust Company vault with four burglarproof safes in Mutual Life's new home office building.

Mutual Life ended 1928 with $11 million dollars in assets and $147 million of insurance in force. On April 4, 1929, the board voted to pay a 6 percent dividend totaling $30,000 to all stockholders of record out of surplus earnings. Later in the year, the company sold the property it still owned at 15 South Street for $175,000 and borrowed $50,000 from both the Real Estate Trust Company and the National Marine Bank "in order that the company not be temporarily hampered for want of cash in the event the same was needed."

These decisions at such a critical time no doubt contributed to the company's long-term financial security and safety. As in 1903, when the directors' decision to move the home office saved it from being destroyed in the 1904 Baltimore Fire, Mutual Life's executives seemed to have had either ESP or a "guardian angel" whose wisdom, advice and foresight saved the company—as well as its policyholders and investors—from financial disaster when the stock market crashed on October 24, 1929.

Mutual Life ended 1928 with $11 million in assets and $147 million of insurance in force.

LEFT: *Henry Roth, Mutual Life secretary for forty years, passed away in 1928 after fifty-three years of continuous service.*

CHAPTER 6

New Deal, New Name

(1930–1939)

S HE ARRIVED at the same time every evening, regardless of the weather, and went right to work. Night after night, her routine was as drab and colorless as the day's news. After most employees had gone home, she cleaned the bathrooms; polished the furniture in the executive dining room, boardroom and offices; emptied the wastebaskets; and put out the trash. She was always careful when dusting the valuable china and antiques, knowing she couldn't replace anything she might break. More importantly, she couldn't lose her job.

FACING PAGE: *The Depression years were difficult for many widows and orphans, especially if breadwinners had had to cancel life insurance policies to heat homes and feed their families.*

One evening the cleaning woman was so hungry she fainted and had to be sent home. She admitted that she hadn't eaten all day. An investigation revealed that she lived in Baltimore with her family. Her normally hard-working husband, recently let go from his job, was ashamed that he could not provide food and clothing for his wife and three children. The family's only income was the seven dollars a week she earned cleaning Mutual Life's home office building.

How would the family survive if she was too weak to work?

Recognizing a desperate situation, Mutual Life employees quickly collected money to provide the family with coal and enough food for immediate relief. When he heard about it, President Paul Burnett immediately referred the case to the Family Welfare Association of Baltimore. In addition to finding temporary employment for the husband, the company

also helped cover the family's basic needs until he received his first pay.

The cleaning woman and her family never knew who helped them through this difficult time. With so many people out of work and struggling to survive in 1931, Burnett preferred to provide relief anonymously, out of the company's Special Fund.

Through life insurance, Mutual Life had been helping families take care of their loved ones for decades. During the Great Depression, the company—including its field agents and home office employees—were there, once again, providing hope, protection, advice and support when people needed it most.

ABOVE: *During the Great Depression, unemployed men in Baltimore and other U.S. cities waited in "breadlines" to receive free soup.* (Courtesy of the FDR Library)

ROOSEVELT CREATES JOBS, HOPE

Desperation became commonplace during the early 1930s. Across the country factories were idle. Commerce and trade barely moved through once-booming ports. Locked gates, empty storefronts, rusting boxcars and fields of rotting crops greeted men and women looking for work.

When the stock market crashed in 1929, wealthy families lost fortunes made during the "Roaring Twenties." The poor, who had been struggling in the years just before the crash as the economy began to slow, now faced bleaker times ahead. By 1933 breadlines in every major city reminded Americans that more than fourteen million workers were unemployed. Unable to pay mortgages or rent, families lost their homes. Some ended up living in makeshift shantytowns, derisively called "Hoovervilles" after President Herbert Hoover.

Many Americans accused Hoover of having ignored economic indicators that signaled the coming crash. Believing that federal intervention would create unnecessary bureaucracy, Hoover in fact did little at first. When pressured to act by legislators and the public, he eventually approved state funding of local relief programs, passed the Smoot-Hawley Tariff to protect U.S. industry from foreign competition—a measure so excessive it provoked retaliation and had the effect of reducing American exports—and established the Reconstruction Finance Corporation. These measures proved to be wrong-headed, too little, or too late.

During his campaign for the presidency in 1932, Franklin D. Roosevelt—whose Baltimore connections included having served as a director for the Fidelity & Deposit Insurance Company, headquartered a dozen blocks south of Charles and Chase Streets—stressed his own conservatism but promised to do more to bring about economic recovery. His "New Deal" platform was based in part on ideas conceived during World War I to mobilize federal resources in a national emergency. The country, Roosevelt insisted, could wait no longer for the economy to recover on its own.

America's working class—including many Mutual Life policyholders—elected "F.D.R." by a large margin. In him, voters saw someone with compassion for the country's ordinary citizens. During his famous first "Hundred Days" in office in 1933, Roosevelt feverishly pushed program after program through Congress to provide relief, create jobs, and stimulate economic recovery.

The Federal Deposit Insurance Corporation (FDIC) insured bank deposits. The National Industrial Recovery Act (NIRA) helped boost declining prices. The Civil Works Administration (CWA) created jobs building or repairing roads, parks and airports. The Civilian Conservation Corps (CCC) put 2.5 million men and

ABOVE: *During his first hundred days in office in 1933, President Franklin D. Roosevelt pushed "New Deal" programs through Congress to provide relief, create jobs, and stimulate the economy.*

(Courtesy of the FDR Library)

RIGHT: *Creation of the Civilian Conservation Corps provided jobs and income for unemployed workers in the 1930s.*

(Courtesy of the FDR Library)

8,500 women to work maintaining and restoring forests and beaches. Between 1935 and 1943, the Works Progress Administration (WPA) created work for eight million Americans constructing schools and hospitals and improving the country's infrastructure. Roosevelt's New Deal and weekly "fireside chats" on radio did much to improve the country's morale, provide hope, and increase confidence that recovery was coming.

Maryland's diverse economy and its proximity to Washington, D.C., made the state less vulnerable than many other areas of the country. Though numerous Baltimore businesses failed during the Great Depression, companies such as General Motors opened plants and created new jobs. Just as important, none of the city's major financial institutions closed permanently.

Touched by the Depression in many ways, Mutual Life nevertheless kept on growing.

MUTUAL LIFE MEETS NEEDS

Before the 1930s, no state agencies existed to provide unemployment or welfare relief. If families needed help, they went to locally funded organizations like the Family Welfare Association of Baltimore, the Salvation Army, the Bureau of Catholic Charities, and Jewish Social Services. In February 1931, the city's Chamber of Commerce created the Citizens Emergency Relief Committee. By year's end, the committee had raised $650,000 from Baltimore businessmen and collected another $2 million during the city's annual Community Chest drive.

Unfortunately, it would not be enough. When FDR took office in January 1933, just over twenty thousand Baltimore families were on relief, and the Emergency Relief Committee was distributing more than $50,000 per week in aid. Despite these efforts, the lives of families hardest hit by the Depression had been reduced to little more than a struggle for survival.

On January 5, 1933, Mutual Life's president, Paul Burnett, reported that he had received a letter from the Family Welfare Association asking the company to increase its annual contribution to the Community Chest. The letter also urged company executives to "make a special request of employees to set aside a small sum regularly to donate to the Community Fund to benefit the poor." Home office employees responded generously with donations totaling $2,740. The Executive Committee approved a corporate donation of $1,500.

Benefit checks provided much-needed relief to beneficiaries struggling to make ends meet during the Depression. This check for $160.05 included a five-cent refund of one week's premium.

Mutual Life agents were also encouraged to help in their local communities. Editor Howard Emmons wrote in the *Old Black Hen* in 1932:

It is going to be very difficult for some families to have a Merry Christmas this year. Where want, poverty, hunger and cold are in the home, happiness is absent. The majority of us can help to bring relief to at least one home, even at a sacrifice of something we would like to do or have. . . . A gift of clothing which you no longer really need, a basket of groceries and simple food will mean much. . . . With present prices, a good Christmas dinner is not hard to purchase for the average pocketbook.

Executive committee minutes from the 1930s document that Mutual Life's directors approved regular contributions to the Community Chest, Catholic Charities, Jewish Social Services, the Maryland General Hospital, and the Western Maryland Dairy to provide milk for sick children.

Paul M. Burnett . . .

Leader, Benefactor, Builder of Men

President Paul M. Burnett's oil portrait, commissioned in 1923, hung in Mutual Life's board room and lobby for more than sixty years.

(Courtesy of the Burnett/Clifford family)

AUL M. BURNETT, Monumental Life's president and chairman of the board from 1923 to 1944, passed away in office at age seventy-seven. He left behind a legacy that had begun in 1894, when he succeeded Charles J. Bonaparte as the company's general counsel. Elected to the board of directors in 1898, Burnett contributed ideas and seconded motions at his very first meeting.

"Nothing was more pleasing to him than to watch men grow and to help build them," noted his secretary, Irene Reaney, in 1932. "No one appreciates more than he a man who is truthful, honest and loyal to the company." Burnett exemplified that loyalty throughout his career. Once elected to the company's board of directors, he came into work nearly every day for fifty years.

Burnett lived to see Mutual Life of Baltimore grow from a small local company into one of the largest Industrial-Ordinary life insurance companies in the country. He inspired officers, executives, managers and field agents with his vision. He was determined to expand the company's presence outside Maryland, and he saw that happen in 1918. Elected president in 1923, he guided the construction of Mutual Life's impressive new home office at Charles and Chase Streets.

He was responsible for changing the organization's structure from a mutual to a stock company in 1928 and for changing the company's name to "Monumental Life" in 1935. He was chairman of the board when directors voted to expand the home office with a new addition in 1939.

"Mr. Burnett is generous to a fault with anything belonging to him personally," noted his secretary, "but he is a conscientious guardian of the company's funds and 'tight' as the proverbial Scotsman unless he can be absolutely convinced that the company will receive dollar for dollar in every transaction."

Burnett's desire for privacy was legendary. So were his lack of confidence in banks and his distrust of an overly invasive federal government. On hearing that President Franklin Roosevelt had created the Securities and Exchange Commission in 1934, he asked Mutual Life's attorneys if it was legal for a federal organization to have such far-reaching authority and oversight. When told that it was, he recommended that the company invest in bearer bonds, which did not have to be registered. He also built one of the city's most secure vaults to keep the company's assets safely locked up behind its own doors.

Burnett was so adamantly opposed to having his personal income taxed by the federal government that he did everything he could to hide it. His grandson, Paul Clifford, a retired Monumental Life officer, tells the story of a set of fourteen-karat gold-trimmed plates that belonged to his mother Ellinor, Burnett's only daughter. The plates are now in his possession along with a note that reads: "Hide these from Teddy [Roosevelt]; he'll want his share."

Grandson Paul also has a silver trophy, engraved with the words "Major Paul M. Burnett, 3rd Battalion, 4th Maryland Infantry, February 12, 1917" documenting that Burnett—as patriotic as he was private—served with the Maryland National Guard.

Burnett has been described as bright, creative, and shrewd—a "self-made man," a "savvy businessman" and a "risk taker." Had he not been a successful attorney and insurance executive, he could easily have been an architect, a landscape gardener, a gentleman farmer, or an antiques dealer. Burnett not only built an insurance company and designed its tastefully furnished home office, he also imported Arabian horses from England, invested in antiques, bought and developed a twelve-acre island estate on Round Bay in Maryland's Severn River, where he entertained family and friends, and built a hospital ward to benefit Baltimore's crippled children.

The Burnett Memorial Ward of the Maryland General Hospital opened in September 1935 in the midst of the Depression. Dedicated to his mother, Mrs. M. Amelia Burnett, the construction of a hospital or ward for crippled children had long been one of Burnett's dreams. Built at a cost of $20,000 and furnished with up-to-date equipment and appliances— including beds, cribs, bassinettes and sun porch furniture donated by his wife—the Burnett Ward accommodated up to thirty infants and children whose parents could not afford to pay for needed surgery and treatment.

Still not satisfied, Burnett wanted to provide diversion, fresh air and sunlight as well as medical care for the convalescing children. In the spring of 1936, just six months after the ward at Maryland General opened, Burnett began to transform his summer home on St. Helena Island in the Severn River into an island hospital and retreat. The Burmont Hospital for Crippled Children—consisting of two wards, an examination room, nurses' quarters, a kitchen, dining room, playroom, porches and fenced-in riverfront playground— opened later that year with six children. The staff included two resident nurses, two playground instructors, and a visiting doctor from Baltimore.

Hearing about the facility, the city's social workers began to refer children who were undernourished or in need of orthopedic care. At about the same time, President Leo Rock announced that ten beds would be reserved for the children of Monumental Life's Baltimore policyholders. By the fall of 1937, every Burmont Hospital bed was full.

Though employees and other individuals contributed funds to operate the facility, Burnett remained the hospital's and the children's primary benefactor until he died in 1944. Shortly thereafter, the private island was sold and the proceeds donated to the Children's Hospital.

Burnett's daughter, Ellinor, married Dr. Stewart Clifford, but not before her father hired a detective to thoroughly investigate who he was and how he lived. Elected to Mutual Life's board following the death of director Dr. James Iglehart in 1934, Dr. Clifford was a well-respected pediatrician who developed the PKU test for infants. President John F. Kennedy asked for Dr. Clifford's help in saving the life of his infant son, Patrick, in the 1960s.

Following in the footsteps of his grandfather and father, Dr. Clifford's son, Stewart, a senior vice president with Citibank of New York, also served as a Monumental Life director until the 1980s. He left the board knowing that his family had given over ninety years of continuous service to Maryland's first and oldest life insurance company.

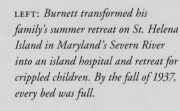

ABOVE: *Paul Burnett's 14k gold cuff links represent both his interest in horses and an era when "gentlemen" always dressed formally in suit, tie, vest and shirts with French cuffs.*
(Courtesy of the Burnett/Clifford family)

LEFT: *Burnett transformed his family's summer retreat on St. Helena Island in Maryland's Severn River into an island hospital and retreat for crippled children. By the fall of 1937, every bed was full.*

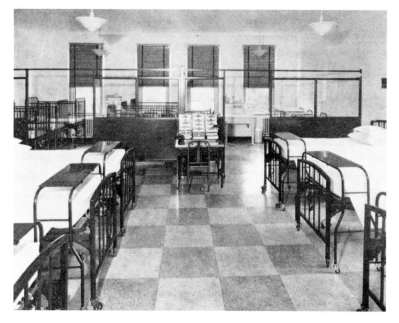

ABOVE: *The Burnett Memorial Ward of the Maryland General Hospital opened in 1935 in the midst of the Depression. Dedicated to his mother and costing $20,000, the ward for crippled children had long been one of Paul Burnett's dreams.*

BELOW: *Irene Reaney, executive secretary and personnel officer, and Bertha Hatten, elevator operator.*

RIGHT: *Mutual Life's Actuarial Department in 1932.*

The company also made large donations to the Burnett Memorial Ward at Maryland General Hospital. Built in memory of Paul Burnett's mother, M. Amelia Burnett, the ward benefited the children of Mutual Life policyholders living in Maryland who needed, but whose families could not afford, orthopedic treatment and care.

Throughout the Depression—long before companies commonly offered employee medical, disability, vacation and retirement benefits—Mutual Life's directors also continued their generous practice of helping employees with special financial needs such as medical bills, the cost of hospital stays, travel expenses, and leaves of absences deemed necessary for "rest and relaxation." The company's directors considered each situation and expense on an individual basis without formal guidelines, often to reward an employee's years of loyal, faithful service.

In 1932 and again in 1937, for example, the Executive Committee approved payment of hospital bills and surgery costs for Irene Reaney, executive secretary and personnel officer. When Charles J. Limke, the company's oldest employee with forty-four years' service, became very ill in 1936, the company paid for round-the-clock nursing care.

In 1936 company executives also approved a two-week leave of absence and fifty dollars spending money for elevator operator Bertha Hatten to take a trip to the country or seashore. An employee since 1926, Mrs. Hatten was known and loved by all for her sunny and charitable disposition. During the Depression's severe winters, when there was so much poverty and need, the *Old Black Hen* reported that she "scouted around the home office for clothing and necessities for those unfortunates whose appeals she could not ignore." When she lost her own husband, several officers reported that she appeared "tired and distressed" and could benefit from a vacation.

In these difficult years when numerous banks and financial institutions failed, Mutual Life continued to prosper by focusing on the real needs of its employees, its agents, its working-class policyholders and its stockholders. Between 1930 and 1939, the company never missed a claim payment, paid promised death claims totaling more than $8.6 million, and distributed dividend checks annually to all stockholders. In home after home, Mutual Life checks protected lives, provided financial support, and prevented many families from falling prey to poverty following the death of a loved one.

Speaking on NBC Radio during Life Insurance Week in May 1935, Alfred E. Smith, Roosevelt's rival for the Democratic presidential nomination in 1932, noted: "Although many people have lost their life savings during the depression, nobody lost a cent in the well-managed life insurance companies."

Instead, despite the sacrifice it may have required, most of Mutual Life's Industrial policyholders continued to dig deep into their pockets to pay the nickel or dime-a-week premium to keep their valuable insurance coverage in force. The manager of the company's McKeesport, Pennsylvania, district explained clearly "What One Nickel Did" for a family insured through his office:

> Starting with the baby's five-cent policy in 1932 . . . there has since been placed 58 cents Industrial and $1,500 Ordinary in this particular home. It is a 100% Mutual family now. As a result of our first five cent contract, and the diligent cultivation of the family connections, there is an additional $1.45 in [weekly] premium on uncles, aunts and other relatives. . . . From leads supplied by parents of the insured child, $2,000 Ordinary and almost $3.00 additional Industrial premium has been placed. . . . The nickel keeps rolling on and on.

In 1932, U.S. insurers reported $110 billion of life insurance in force. As the Depression dragged on, agents throughout the industry were counseled to point out that cash values in life insurance had steadily increased while stock values plummeted. "Life insurance," agents reassured policyholders, "is still a safe place to put your money."

But rising unemployment inevitably meant more lapsed policies and a tougher climate for life insurance sales. As early as October 1931, Burnett expressed his concern to directors about the agents in Mutual Life's branch offices: "It is necessary to be in constant touch with them,"

he said, "to keep up enthusiasm and not lose our business." Leo Rock, appointed vice president of Field Services in 1930, was charged with this task.

"Let us not compare our income or resources with what they were in 1927 or 1928, because few men have either," wrote the *Old Black Hen*'s editor in early 1933. "But rather let us take the situation with which we are confronted now, this year, and determine we will make some increase. Thousands upon thousands of people were obliged to cash in on their life insurance policies, but they will buy new ones, and you will get your share if you keep going."

Despite the uncertainty of the Depression, or maybe because of it, Mutual Life's insurance in force increased from $170.6 million at year-end 1930 to $233.2 million in 1936 as the company opened additional offices in Cleveland (1930), Baltimore East (1930), Chicago (1934), Atlanta, (1935), Detroit (1935), and Flint, Michigan (1936).

BELOW: *Mutual Life's Baltimore branch office at North and Gay Streets opened in 1932.*

HARDSHIP RELIEVED

Beginning in 1935, workers across America lined up to complete applications for Social Security insurance. Each applicant received a small record book to keep track of his or her payments.

One sale, made by Agent Edward Page in the new Detroit office, illustrates why families continued to purchase life insurance throughout the 1930s. Canvassing door to door in the 3700 block of Detroit's Meldrum Avenue, Agent Page met a twenty-nine-year-old young man named Louis Vansaghi. Employed with a moderate income but still living with his elderly parents, Mr. Vansaghi had a small Industrial policy with another company. When the agent pointed out that the policy would not provide enough income to take care of his parents should anything happen to him, the young man completed an application for $1,000 of additional coverage.

Agent Page delivered the Twenty Pay Life policy to Mr. Vansashi on Saturday, April 18, 1936. The medical examination had confirmed that the young man was in good health. He was pleased that he had taken a step forward toward securing his own future. He also saw the look of pride in his parents' eyes when they learned what he had done to protect them as well.

The next day, Sunday, April 19, Louis Vansaghi lost control of his car in Monroe, Michigan, and died instantly in the crash. When Agent Page delivered the claim check, he was greeted with a smile by the young man's parents. Though suffering from their loss, they were grateful to the agent for talking to their son. They thanked him and the company for the benefits and service they provided.

"This incident should be an inspiration to every agent in the company," wrote Detroit manager C. Waldvogel. "Think of the sorrow and heartaches . . . caused by lack of contact and calls necessary to unfold the story of life insurance. The service we are rendering is a godsend to the ones left behind."

INDUSTRY RESPONDS TO SOCIAL SECURITY

The widespread suffering caused by the Depression prompted President Roosevelt to ask Congress for legislation establishing a broad-based federal system of "social security" to assist children, the elderly, the disabled and the unemployed. The Social Security Act of 1935 established old-age pensions and welfare programs supported by "contributions" in the form of taxes paid by both individual workers (on their wages) and employers (on their payrolls).

Many U.S. employers and corporations considered the mandatory payment of payroll taxes an invasion of their corporate boardrooms and budgets. Mutual Life had always taken care of its own. The company's officers would have preferred fewer federal handouts and more New Deal incentives for private business to create jobs.

Insurance executives also wondered how life insurance would fit into the New Deal economy. Social Security taxes, they feared, would be a drain on corporate profits as well as the first step toward government-sponsored insurance. At the quarterly directors' meeting in July 1937, Paul Burnett noted that payment of Social Security taxes had already placed an "unusually heavy burden" on the company. On the other hand, some industry officers believed that Social Security—like World War I and the influenza epidemic—would raise public awareness about the value of life insurance, old age security, and planning for retirement.

Addressing the National Association of Life Underwriters' Annual Convention in 1934, NALU president Holgar Johnson advised agents to use Social Security as the basis for a life insurance sale: "Inasmuch as no system of subsidized aid has provided more than bare necessities, we can be certain that [Americans'] high standard of living as well as the ingrained individualism of the American people will express itself, no matter what changes may take place."

Merle Thorpe, editor of *National Business*, suggested that the insurance industry take a new approach during the Depression's security-minded times. Enough doom and gloom, wrecked homes, improvident husbands and fathers, helpless widows and orphans, he said. "I plead for more emphasis on the joy of living. In a very real sense, life insurance is for life. Death is not its goal. The idea of protection plus investment for future dividends of happiness and ease of mind is a golden text for the times."

At the same time, Roosevelt looked to the country's life insurers to do even more to protect the working class. In 1937 he sent the following message to delegates attending the annual NALU convention: "The records of life insurance companies, more than any other business, express the relative growth of the spirit of social and economic responsibility for others. The contributions which life insurance companies make toward safeguarding the security of American home life go a long way in protecting our standard of living."

FLOOD!

The following stories from the *Old Black Hen* illustrate the company's commitment to protecting its assets and its customers' quality of life during some very difficult times.

When the swollen waters of the Allegheny, Monongahela and Ohio Rivers overflowed their banks in March 1936, Pittsburgh was hit by a catastrophe greater than the Depression. As water flooded downtown, closed businesses and destroyed homes, District Manager James C. Harris, "using considerable strategy and nerve," crossed National Guard lines and made his way to the district's office. Though the entire area was under martial law, he removed files and supplies and "left notice for his men and the public to come to his home to transact their business." Using the dining room and kitchen tables and any other furniture they could find, the three "office girls" set up an improvised office.

With hundreds of families left homeless and housed in schools, churches or with out-of-town relatives, the Pittsburgh agents began the difficult task of locating their customers. Despite the challenges, Harris proudly reported that his men collected 119 percent of premiums due that week. No policies lapsed and no families lost coverage because of the flood.

Ten months later, as the rising waters of the Ohio River threatened Louisville, Evansville and Cincinnati in January 1937, the offices' district managers sent letters and telegrams to the home office. "Worst flood in the history to the city. Four debits under water!" wrote Mr. Montgomery from Cincinnati. "City under water. Entire sections evacuated," wired Mr. Clancy from Evansville. "Office cut off by water," wrote Mr. Gillespie from Louisville. "Train service stopped. Many agents removed from their homes."

ABOVE: *When the Ohio River overflowed its banks in 1936 and 1937, businesses in downtown Pittsburgh, Louisville and Evansville—including Mutual Life field offices—had to evacuate, relocate and serve customers out of temporary space.*

MONUMENTAL LIFE INS. CO.

80 YEARS OF PROGRESS

1858   1938

TOP: *Flood waters got so high in some cities and neighborhoods that a few Mutual Life agents used boats to reach customers and collect premiums..*

INSET: *Though the Cumberland, Maryland office was damaged during the 1937 flood, it did not prevent local agents and managers from celebrating the company's eightieth anniversary in 1938. Margaret Connor, the company's first female agent, seated at right, celebrated her twentieth service anniversary the same year.*

In Louisville, hit hardest by the flood, Gillespie set up his entire organization in a temporary office in one of the city's hotels. "Working under severe handicaps," they continued to conduct business as usual until the water receded. Several agents and the office's two cashiers were separated for days from their families. Hanging over all was the fear of disease. "Fortunately, there was no shortage of preventative serums and . . . every company man was inoculated before going into the flooded areas."

Leo Rock arrived from Chicago and, using local newspapers, succeeded in notifying policyholders in the flooded cities that the grace period for paying their premiums would be extended. "To our knowledge," noted the *Old Black Hen*, "we were the first company to offer an extension to Industrial policyholders."

"Living at night by candle and oil lamps in a heatless hotel," company officers, agents and cashiers "adeptly handled situations as they arose." One Louisville agent, unable to contact his manager as flood waters continued to rise, wrote the home office to find out what to do with the money he had collected, without fail, on his debit. From Assistant Manager Paul Rock in Evansville came word that he had "arranged to cover a portion of his territory the following day by boat."

The "never say die" spirit exhibited during these and other disasters explains why the company succeeded during a decade plagued by economic hardship. A few weeks after the flood, Louisville's district manager wrote to Leo Rock that the way the situation had been handled was "an inspiration" to everyone involved—company employees, policyholders, and citizens of Louisville. "It is regrettable that you cannot receive all the expressions of kindness that have [come] from our policyholders in the stricken area." Hereafter the company's name would stand for "more than just an insurance company, but rather a real human institution that recognizes a crisis and is willing to alleviate the suffering."

SHARING THE WEALTH

In April 1930, just five months after the stock market's crash, Mutual Life directors voted to increase the company's capitalization from $500,000 to $1 million by issuing five thousand additional shares of stock at $100 per share. One year later, shareholders exchanged their $100 shares for ten $10 shares. Despite warnings from insurance commissioners in several states "not to pay too large a dividend to policyholders unless the condition of the company was sufficiently satisfactory," Mutual Life director Milton Roberts considered it a duty to pay a dividend when the company had done so well. In a letter to Paul Burnett dated January 6, 1932, Roberts pointed out that, although times were difficult, the firm had been "so successfully managed and so efficiently operated" that

"it will undoubtedly occupy a unique position among the companies engaged in the same . . . business and with the same high rating." Furthermore, he added, "the soundness of the company . . . is certainly a justification and compliment to the wisdom which has so controlled the investment policy that the company has passed through the severest upheaval, economically and financially, the world has ever witnessed without disturbing its financial stability or impairing its operating efficiency." The company paid a dividend of one dollar per share on 100,000 outstanding shares in February 1932, and again in February 1933.

When Congress enacted the Revenue Act of 1934, it required corporations throughout the country to determine if they were accumulating gains and profits beyond the reasonable needs of their business. Successful companies like Mutual Life were urged to distribute as much of their profits as possible to stockholders in order to place more money in circulation, to increase taxes on individual incomes, and to hasten economic recovery. Companies that did not meet federal guidelines and adequately distribute profits to shareholders were subject to a surtax.

With a surplus close to $3 million in July 1933, Mutual Life's directors moved to increase capitalization once again, from 100,000 to 200,000 shares valued at $10 per share. When company assets—including stocks, bonds, U.S. Treasury bills, mortgages and Baltimore ground rents—exceeded the $20 million mark in 1934, board members also resolved to set aside a fund of $100,000 out of surplus to help employees purchase company stock through payroll deduction. With the approval of Mutual Life's president and secretary, employees could borrow up to 75 percent of the stock's purchase price at 5 percent interest. The company held the stock until the loan was fully paid.

To further comply with the Revenue Act of 1935, Mutual Life paid its regular 10 percent dividend per share, a total of $300,000, to all stockholders, plus $109,529 in dividends to its Ordinary participating policyholders.

NEW NAME, NEW PRESIDENT

Having changed its corporate structure from a mutual to a stock insurance company in 1928, Mutual Life's directors continued to discuss the need for a more appropriate name for Maryland's oldest insurer. On April 4, 1935, Director A. W. Mears offered a resolution to "change the name of this company wherever it may occur in its charter . . . from the Mutual Life Insurance Company of Baltimore to a name selected by stockholders." After forming a committee composed of Directors Howard M. Emmons, Leo Rock and F. Harold Loweree to consider suggested names, the board published the required notice in local newspapers. It announced a meeting of Mutual Life stockholders on July 5, 1935, for the purpose of changing the corporation's name.

From the many suggested, committee members agreed that "Monumental Life Insurance Company" was the most suitable and appropriate name to recommend to stockholders. It reflected both the company's size and its history of strength and success in Baltimore, the "Monumental City." When stockholders expressed their wholehearted agreement, the company began to include the new Monumental Life name on all documents, contracts, company letterhead, letters and publications.

Early in 1936, President Paul Burnett reported that Monumental Life was the ninth largest life insurer in the U.S. and Canada writing both Ordinary and Industrial insurance. He also noted proudly that since 1898, when he was first elected a director, the company had improved its methods of agency operation; reduced agent turnover and losses; reduced the cost of collections, agent supervision and operating expenses; improved the quality of business written; and undertaken a careful inspection of risks.

On resigning as president, effective June 1, 1936, Burnett recommended that the board elect Leo P. Rock as his successor. Directors "regretfully accepted [Burnett's] resignation on behalf of policyholders and stockholders and offered [the company's] gratitude and appreciation for his years of service and untiring efforts for the company's welfare."

But Burnett did not relinquish control of the company in 1936; he merely changed titles. Elected chairman of the board, he remained Monumental Life's ranking officer for several more years, with the ability to exercise all power and authority conferred on the president by the company's by-laws. As chairman, Burnett had no vote in business decisions brought before the board. He did, however, retain control of the Investment Committee. In addition to appointing Milton Roberts and F. Harold Loweree as Investment Committee members, he received the board's approval to make changes in the company's investment policy, "as may be deemed advisable."

Addressing the company's executive officers—Leo P. Rock, president; Howard M. Emmons and Milton Roberts, vice presidents; F. Harold Loweree, secretary; Dr. Fred Vinup, medical director; and Harry C. Roth, controller—in 1937, Burnett expressed concerns about the company's "inability to invest money profitably and securely" in the current economic conditions. The bond market had declined since January 1937, and the company had more than $15 million invested in U.S. government and City of Baltimore bonds. Also disappointing was the common stock portfolio's net yield of 4.82 percent.

MONUMENTAL LIFE

INSURANCE COMPANY

Vol. 11   BALTIMORE, MARYLAND, JULY, 1935   No. 7

MONUMENTAL LIFE INSURANCE COMPANY

NOTHING CHANGED BUT THE NAME

CONTINUE TO MAKE IT AS NOTED, IMPRESSIVE AND ENDURING AS ITS NAME!

Looking for advice on how to best invest over $25 million in cash held in twenty-four banks, Burnett sent Milton Roberts to New York to meet with trust officers and economists from two New York banks. The bank officers agreed that it was dangerous to maintain large cash balances and advised Monumental Life's directors to "invest funds even at current low interest rates with the realization that such securities would have to be held to maturity." The situation was further complicated, reported Roberts, "by the uncertainties of the political situation and the antagonistic and punitive attitude exhibited by the national administration."

In 1938 the board of directors resolved to invest only in U.S. Treasury bonds, notes and bills, railroad bonds (Class "A"), mortgages, public utilities, industrial companies, and dividend-paying preferred and common stocks of domestic companies. Its goal was to promptly but safely maximize the company's return on policy reserves.

In the depths of the Depression, U.S. life insurance companies continued to pay promised benefits—totaling more than $3.8 billion in 1933—to protect families against loss of life and property.

Leo P. Rock . . .
Agent to President

Leo P. Rock

AS A NEW AGENT in Mutual Life's St. Louis District Office in 1921, Leo Rock was skeptical about remaining in the insurance business. Listening to officers speak at agency meetings, he wondered if the company was all that management made it out to be, whether it kept its promises to employees and honored its contracts with policyholders. Satisfied on these two points, he aspired to become the company's president through hard work, honest effort, and results.

Earning quick promotions to assistant manager, chief assistant manager and, ultimately, manager of the St. Louis office, Rock's leadership brought him to the attention of the home office. In 1924 he was assigned to Cleveland, which had been a company trouble spot since it opened in 1919. Within a few years, the office had such an outstanding record that President Paul Burnett selected Rock to chair the 1925 sales convention in New Orleans.

Appointed vice president of Field Services in 1930, Rock accepted responsibility for motivating the company's agents and offices in the depths of the Depression. His knowledge of the practical end of the business equipped him to handle the company's agency force. In 1936, at the young age of thirty-seven, his success in that role earned him the position he had worked so hard to achieve— presidency of the eighth largest Industrial-Ordinary life insurance company in the United States.

Leo Rock served as Monumental Life's president through World War II and into the peaceful, prosperous decade of the 1950s. Before his own death in 1944, Chairman Paul Burnett urged Rock to stay on as president, noting that "no other company I know anything about has as capable and thoroughly intelligent and practical president as Monumental Life."

Leo Rock retired with thirty-one years' service in 1953, knowing from firsthand experience that the company he headed kept its promises and was everything he had hoped it would be so many years before.

He aspired to become the company's president through hard work, honest effort, and results.

ABOVE: *The 1939 home office addition—including an ornate iron fence, lighted fence posts and plantings—increased Monumental Life's visibility and presence on North Charles Street.*

NEW BUILDING

With the economy still depressed and the cost of real estate and construction at its lowest point in many years, the company's directors took advantage of conditions to expand Monumental Life's home office building. Since the move to Charles and Chase Streets in 1926, the company had grown considerably. In 1938 close to two hundred home office employees served approximately 1,250 agents, managers and administrative personnel in fifty-four field offices in twelve states. Clearly, more space would be needed soon if the company continued on its positive course.

When the properties adjoining Monumental Life at 1109–1111 North Charles Street and 1112 Lovegrove Alley were offered for sale in 1938, directors approved the purchase price of $32,500 and authorized Paul Burnett to proceed with plans for a six-story addition facing on Charles Street.

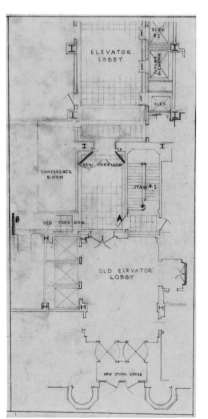

LEFT: *Hand-drawn blueprints define new lobby space included in the 1939 addition.*

Under Lock and Key . . .

Assets Secure behind Tons of Steel

BURIED DEEP beneath the 1100 block of Baltimore's Charles Street is a vault as big as any in the city's largest national bank. Few people, including company employees, know it exists, and even fewer have passed through its steel gate and three-foot-thick, solid steel door to see what's inside. Only Monumental Life's treasurer and one other person hold its keys and have committed to memory the combinations that open its locks.

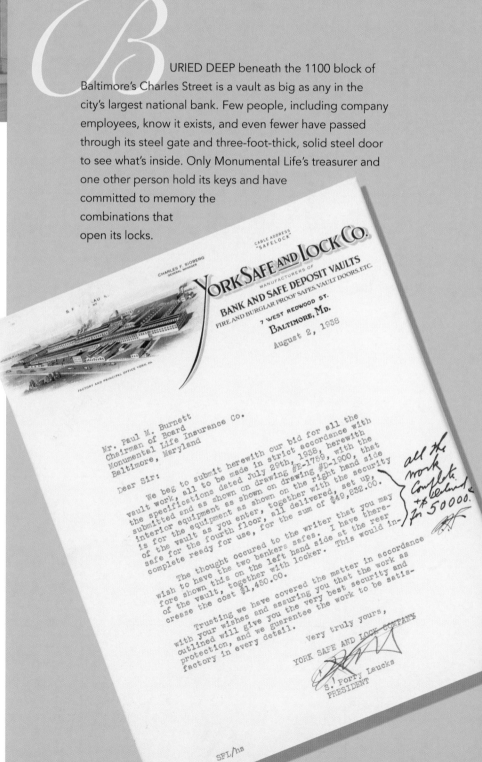

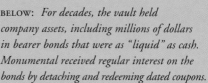

Monumental Life's large vault, buried deep beneath the 1939 building and built by the York Safe and Lock Company for $50,000, is protected by a solid steel door, three-feet thick.

BELOW: *For decades, the vault held company assets, including millions of dollars in bearer bonds that were as "liquid" as cash. Monumental received regular interest on the bonds by detaching and redeeming dated coupons.*

In planning the home office addition in 1938, President Paul Burnett instructed architects to include a vault large and secure enough to protect all of Monumental Life's invested assets. Their solution was to bury the vault, manufactured by the York Safe & Lock Company, deep underground and build the new addition over and around it. No one can dig through the vault's walls because they are surrounded on all sides by tightly packed, factory-hardened railroad ties. When closed, its thirty-five-ton door creates an airtight seal. The vault is so secure that officers in 1939 agreed that insurance to protect its contents would be an unnecessary expense.

Since 1926, the company's assets had been stored in a vault with four safes, owned by the Real Estate Trust Company, in Monumental's own building. Even so, Burnett was still concerned about security. Access to the $50,000 fire- and heat-proof vault and vault room under the new Treasury Department was tightly controlled and protected by alarms, armed security guards, a series of locked doors, and mandatory sign-in and sign-out procedures.

Was Burnett paranoid? Bonnie and Clyde were robbing banks, Al Capone was creating mayhem in Chicago, and Depression-era Baltimore was full of desperate men. Several banks had failed, and people assumed that successful life insurance companies could have on hand millions of dollars in cash, stocks and bonds and other liquid assets. In Monumental Life's case, they were correct.

Between June and December 1938, the company had immediate access to just over $1.3 million in cash on hand. With hostilities escalating in Europe, directors feared that a financial crisis might close even more banks and disrupt the company's business. In addition, for as long as home office employees were paid in cash, up to $35,000 was always in the vault to cover one month's payroll.

For many years, the vault also held millions of dollars in bearer bonds, which could be cashed by the bearer at any time. Monumental Life received regular interest on its bonds by redeeming attached coupons. "Clipping coupons" was a tedious, time-consuming process, and none of the loyal, trusted employees selected regularly as "clippers" looked forward to the long, stressful days in the windowless vault. They were not permitted to leave until the job was finished, and cuffs and pockets were checked before they returned to their departments.

LEFT: *The foundation of the 1939 building included tightly packed, factory-hardened railroad ties around the vault to make it impregnable from any side.*

Until 1990, when assets were removed and filed electronically, the vault often held stocks and bonds valued at more than $280 million. As assistant treasurer in the 1980s, Walter Weiss was responsible for their physical security. He remembers having to memorize the combinations for eighty-eight different vault locks. Whenever stock was bought or sold, Weiss had to physically remove an asset from a vault drawer and complete a vault entry record before sending the asset or check to the company's broker.

Entering the vault during those years always required two officers—one from inside Treasury, and one from another department—for additional protection and control. "It was stressful," Weiss recalls, "knowing we were responsible for so much of the company's wealth."

To enter the vault today is to walk back in time—to a simpler era before computers, cell phones, passwords, viruses, voice-activated alarms or network-wide security systems.

When the vault was installed in 1939, the company's assets could be secured with locks, keys, reinforced walls, and doors of solid steel. Today, no electronic gadgetry provides the same level of protection or security that Paul Burnett achieved when he closed the vault's door and pocketed the key.

BACKGROUND: *By mid-year 1939, construction crews had reached the roof!*

Construction costs, estimated at $500,000, included an underground vault as large and secure as any bank's in the city. Also planned was a Treasury Department protected by bronze doors, bulletproof glass windows, and gun "ports" through which security guards, if necessary, could shoot robbers. Just outside Treasury, a second and larger bronze "Wheel of Progress" was inlaid in the marble floor. This one contained a spoke for each of the thirty-eight cities in which Monumental Life had offices in 1938. During construction, ductwork was added so that the entire home office complex could be air-conditioned later.

Completed in the summer of 1939, the new addition added significantly to the company's prominence on Baltimore's "Fifth Avenue." Featuring the words "MONUMENTAL LIFE" in gold letters several feet tall above an imposing new entrance, the building was separated from the Charles Street sidewalk by an ornate iron fence, lighted fence posts and plantings. The completed structure presented an image of strength, stability and success to all who passed by.

BELOW: *The new addition included a second "Wheel of Progress," updated to include all Monumental Life field offices in 1939, inlaid in the marble floor outside Treasury.*

CONGRESS INVESTIGATES INSURANCE INDUSTRY

Between 1906 and 1938, the assets of the country's life insurance companies increased by more than 800 percent, a rate twenty-five times faster than the country's population. As assets grew, so did the insurance industry's influence, power and role in the national economy.

At year-end 1937, U.S. life insurance companies reported $28 billion in assets—twice the total savings on deposit in state and national commercial banks—and over $111 billion of life insurance in force. The following year, the industry reported annual income of $5 billion—just slightly less than that reported by the federal government. With billions of dollars in premium income and liquid assets at their disposal, the country's twenty-six largest, most successful life insurance companies held large blocks of government bonds, invested sizable sums in farm and urban mortgages, and purchased 47.7 percent of all corporate bonds and notes issued in 1938.

Such prosperity during a decade of severe national economic depression brought Monumental Life and many of its competitors to the attention of Congress. Legislators expressed concern that so many of the nation's resources were concentrated in the hands of a few dozen companies within the same industry.

On July 7, 1938, the Temporary National Economic Committee requested that the Insurance Section of the Securities and Exchange Commission (SEC) investigate the economic power and practices of the life insurance industry. The committee's request focused on three specific areas: the industry's concentration of control and competition; the effect of the industry's pricing system and policies on consumption, trade, employment and long-term profits; and the effect of existing tax, patent and government policies on competition, pricing, unemployment and insurance industry profits. Additionally, the commission examined why more than one hundred smaller life insurance companies had failed

during the Depression and focused on the increasing amount of Industrial insurance being written by 138 of the country's life insurers.

Between 1927 and 1937, life insurance agents sold 6.7 million small, paid-weekly Industrial policies to America's lower income families. Accounting for $20 billion of the $111 billion total of U.S. life insurance in force at year-end 1937, the number of Industrial policies had grown from 82.2 to 88.9 million policies in just ten years. In some states, like Maryland, which reported 1.5 policies per person, the number of in-force Industrial policies actually exceeded the state's population.

During public hearings conducted in Washington from August 24 to September 8, 1939, the commission headed by Gerhard Gesell, special counsel for the SEC's Insurance Section, interviewed dozens of officers from both Ordinary and Industrial life insurance companies. Monumental Life's Paul Burnett, Milton Roberts and Harold Loweree were among those called to testify. "Had it not been for the war news breaking and taking precedence," wrote President Leo Rock in the *Old Black Hen*, "it is a safe assumption these hearings would have been more widely publicized."

The commission's report documented that Monumental Life executives answered questions regarding the company's conversion from a mutual to a stock company, the allocation of shares to its stockholders, its investment practices, collateral loans made to company directors, product pricing, and sales techniques used to increase sales of the company's policies.

On returning from Washington, Chairman Burnett reported to the company's directors:

> [I]t was apparent early in the hearings that [examiners desired] to make sensational reading [by] discrediting Company executives, and to destroy public confidence in the institution with the

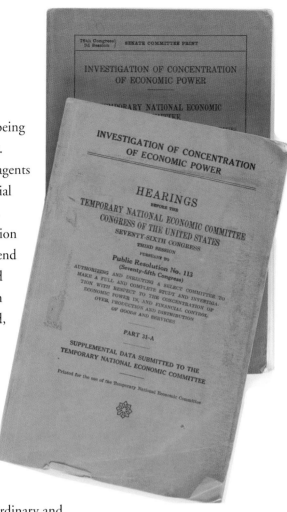

ABOVE: *Testimony from Monumental Life officers was included in final reports distributed by the Temporary National Economic Committee following the Securities and Exchange Commission's 1939 investigation of the insurance industry.*

objective being Federal control and regulation of [our] business.

As applying to the Industrial business particularly, Mr. Gesell evidently feels that the soliciting Agent is of little social value, that Industrial life insurance is primarily 'burial insurance' (usually being issued in average amounts of $250 per person), that the rates on Industrial insurance are very much in excess of those on Ordinary, that lapsation is excessive and that such lapsation is due to pressure selling, that agency turnover is high, and that companies are making tremendous profits out of the business.

We anticipate that Mr. Gesell will recommend that either the Social Security Act be broadened to provide a death benefit of $250 for every man, woman and child in the country . . . or that the mutual savings banks throughout the country actively undertake the writing of Industrial life insurance, or that the government itself, separate and apart from the proposed broadening of the Social Security Act, undertake the writing of Industrial life insurance through the Postal Department.

The company's agents and managers received "Monumental Honor Men" pins to commemorate significant years of service in the field.

In 1939, Congress did in fact amend the Social Security Act to provide "survivor's insurance" for dependent widows, children and parents. The amendment resulted in the government's underwriting approximately $50 billion of life insurance.

Though critical of Industrial insurance, the SEC Commission's final report to the Temporary National Economic Committee, distributed in 1940, recognized the industry's strengths and contributions to the national economy. In his introduction to the report, commission chairman Gesell wrote that the development of the life insurance business represented an "outstanding achievement" and provided the channel by which millions of Americans could save and thereby "gain for themselves and their families a larger measure of security and financial

independence." That Americans had confidence in the industry was evident in "the continually increasing numbers of people who take out life insurance policies."

Between 1933 and mid-1940, U.S. life insurers paid $19.6 billion in benefits. As a point of comparison, during the same period federal, state and municipal agencies paid $21.1 billion to people in need.

During the many decades when the federal government was unwilling or unable to intervene, insurers like Prudential, Metropolitan Life, John Hancock and Mutual Life of Baltimore helped the working poor protect themselves through the purchase of small face amounts of Industrial life insurance. Paying premiums weekly was the only way many breadwinners could afford to protect their families. Agent salesmanship and collection of premiums in their customers' homes was often necessary to keep their coverage in force.

Monumental Life's agents continued to meet needs through the sale of weekly premium Industrial insurance until the 1970s. For more than one hundred years, Industrial insurance formed the strong foundation on which both the company and its policyholders built their financial security and futures.

During its regular examination of Monumental Life's statements and records in 1934, the Maryland State Insurance Department reported: "The affairs of the company are efficiently managed and the business is being conservatively underwritten and steadily increasing."

Five years later, as war raged in Europe, examiners noted: "Death claims are paid promptly upon receipt of necessary documentary proof. Payment is resisted only when the company feels that it has reasonable grounds for refusal of payment." Examiners in 1939 did, however, question why the company was holding over $1.3 million in cash in the company vault. Officers explained that it was there "in order that the company might be able to carry on its business even through a banking moratorium or other financial crisis might be brought about by the outbreak of hostilities abroad."

James D. Iglehart, MD organized Baltimore's first lacrosse team.

Dr. James D. Iglehart . . .

Athlete,
Medical Director,
Lacrosse Pioneer

WHEN HE PASSED AWAY in 1934 at age eighty-four, Dr. James Iglehart, Mutual Life's "grand old man," was remembered as one of the few surviving "Southern gentlemen" who had lived through the Civil War. Born in 1850, Dr. Iglehart joined Mutual Life's board of directors in 1901 and was elected the company's medical director in 1918. He was known and respected not only as a physician but also as a veteran of the Spanish-American War and as the man who brought lacrosse to the city of Baltimore.

Dr. Iglehart received his B.A. degree from St. John's College in Annapolis in 1872. While there, he was captain of cadets, captain of the baseball team, and "stroke" on the college's crew team. After completing his medical degree at the University of Pennsylvania in 1875, he returned to St. John's and earned an M.A. degree in 1878.

That same year, Dr. Iglehart organized the Baltimore Athletic Club's lacrosse team—the first in the city—and was its captain and goalie. The team played its first game in Baltimore on November 23, 1878. Between 1879 and 1891, it challenged club teams from New York, Boston, Brooklyn, Philadelphia, and Montreal. Dr. Iglehart himself refereed many of the games. Elected the first vice president of the U.S.

National Lacrosse Association in 1880, he served as the association's president in 1881. Two years later, because of Dr. Iglehart's influence, the Johns Hopkins University fielded its first lacrosse team.

An avid cyclist, Dr. Iglehart was also a member of the Century Cycling Club of Maryland. At the age of forty-six in October 1896, he won the club's Fourth Annual Cycling Run.

Dr. Iglehart began his distinguished medical career in Baltimore in 1876. His letters and papers, archived at the Maryland Historical Society, provide a record of illnesses and medical problems commonly diagnosed and treated in the early 1900s. In addition to serving as Mutual Life's medical director for sixteen years, Dr. Iglehart was a surgeon for the Fifth Regiment of the Maryland National Guard and the B&O Railroad for more than fifty years. He belonged to the Medical-Chirurgical Faculty of Maryland, the Maryland Historical Society, the War of 1812 Society, and the Association of Railroad Surgeons. As a member of the Sons of the American Revolution and the Association of Veterans of the Spanish-American War, he raised money to build a monument to recognize Marylanders who died in the Mexican War.

In 1968 the National Lacrosse Hall of Fame, located in Baltimore, named Dr. Iglehart to its list of distinguished members and honorees.

In 1968, the National Lacrosse Hall of Fame, located in Baltimore, named Dr. Iglehart to its list of distinguished members and honorees.

CHAPTER 7

Bombs, War Bonds, Economic Boom

(1940–1945)

ABOVE: *Albert E. Bouthot was commissioned as a second lieutenant in the U.S. Army Transportation Corps on January 3, 1943.*

IN DECEMBER 1941, Japan bombs Pearl Harbor, Germany declares war on the U.S. and thirty-one-year-old Albert is one of hundreds of thousands of young men who volunteer to enlist. Though he had dreamed of going to West Point after high school to follow his older brother, a World War I veteran, into the armed forces, the Depression derailed his plans. He is working as a meter reader for the gas and electric company when the U.S. enters the war. Albert celebrates his thirty-second birthday in Officer Candidate School at Mississippi State University. On January 6, 1943, he graduates as a second lieutenant in the U.S. Army Transportation Corps, the army's smallest branch, responsible for moving men and materiel by truck, rail, air and sea.

LEFT: *Eight-year-old Albert played "soldier" during WWI in a uniform made by his mother to match one worn by his older brother, serving in France.*

Three days after receiving his commission, Albert returns home to marry his sweetheart. Like most weddings these days, it is a small one. Frances wears a white gown and veil, Albert his officer's uniform. After a weekend together in New York City, he ships out immediately. They will not see each other again for almost three years.

Though older than most GIs serving in World War II, Albert is typical of "The Greatest Generation" of American men and women profiled by journalist Tom Brokaw in his book of the same name. His life is also similar to the lives of many Monumental Life employees and middle-income policyholders who went off to war in the 1940s.

Albert's orders send him to North Africa. Fluent in French, his second language is an asset on the docks in Morocco and Algeria where he is responsible for unloading troops and supplies. When he arrives in late January 1943, the Axis still controls all Mediterranean ports in Spain, France and Italy, but that soon changes. From July 1943 through May 1944, Albert's unit takes part in the Allied invasion of Sicily and the Italian peninsula. Promoted to first lieutenant, he is working in the port of Naples when Mount Vesuvius erupts, opening tombs and spewing molten lava down the mountainside. The volcano rests only after burying many village streets. Before leaving Italy, Albert buys his bride a cameo carved from the lava's hardened residue.

As Allied forces land on the Normandy beaches in June 1944, push across France, liberate Paris, fight the Battle of the Bulge, and begin to liberate German concentration camps, Albert's unit continues to provide support along the Mediterranean coast.

Notified by the Red Cross of his father's death in March 1945, he is unable to get leave or return home. V-mails from his wife and sister are reassuring. "Don't worry," they say. "We will take Dad's body home to Maine." The funeral will be paid for, in part, by the Société de St. Jean Baptiste, a fraternal organization to which this U.S. citizen of French-Canadian descent has contributed one dollar per month for over thirty years.

ABOVE: *After the Germans were defeated in Italy, Albert located his cousin's mother-in-law and family, thought dead, in the liberated village of Barga.*

On a personal mission of his own, the young lieutenant looks for and finds his cousin's mother-in-law, thought dead, in the liberated Italian village of Barga. When he notifies relatives that she is alive, local papers back home feature the story. The lieutenant is a hero! As Albert tells it:

They had it a little rough under the Nazis as far as food was concerned. . . . I knew where they were but didn't know whether it was still in Nazi hands until recently. When I got to the town, I stopped the first person I saw. Then a few more gathered. Between them and the little Italian I know, we managed to find someone who knew the family. A villager on a bicycle took me directly to the house. I gave him a pack of cigarettes for his trouble.

On the home front, Frances buys war bonds through her job at Prudential Life Insurance Company in Newark, New Jersey, where she has worked since graduating from secretarial school in 1938. In June 1945, one month after Germany surrenders, she writes to Al: "I continue to purchase one bond a month through the payroll savings plan and will continue to do so until I leave this place." From Albert's military allotment pay, she also continues to pay premiums on his life insurance policy.

Later that summer, just days after the U.S. drops atomic bombs on Hiroshima and Nagasaki, Albert receives word that an older sister is dying. This time, with the war in Europe over, the Army agrees to send him home. Albert arrives at New York's LaGuardia Airport on August 25, 1945, a week before Japan surrenders. The young officer is finally discharged from active duty in mid-September.

From his military training, Albert learns self-discipline, resourcefulness and a healthy respect for authority. Patriotic and proud to put on a uniform and go off to war, he believes passionately in what he fought for and returns home a hero. Touched by the Depression, he understands sacrifice. Having experienced separation and death firsthand, his priorities become family, home, work and church . . . in that order.

When he passed away at ninety-two in 2003, Albert's children buried him in his army officer's uniform (it still fit!), *using benefits received from the $10,000 life insurance policy he'd purchased before shipping out for Europe in 1943. Representatives from the U.S. Army played "Taps" at his gravesite.*

The years he spent overseas were among the highlights of his life. As was typical of many World War II veterans, they also helped shape his life.

AMERICA GEARS UP FOR WAR

Still recovering from the Depression in 1940, the United States faced the possibility of involvement in the growing European conflict. By the time Americans reelected Franklin D. Roosevelt for a third term in November, Norway, Holland and Belgium had surrendered to the Nazis; Hitler had signed an armistice with France and begun massive air strikes against England; Italy had invaded Greece; the Russians controlled Lithuania, Latvia and Estonia; German U-boats had attacked merchant ships in the North Atlantic; and Germany, Italy and Japan had signed the Axis Pact.

Congress passed several pieces of legislation that signaled important changes in American life. The Selective Compulsory Military Training and Service Act required all young men between the ages of twenty-one and thirty to register with their local draft boards. This first peacetime conscription in U.S. history was later expanded to include men ages eighteen to forty-five. The Revenue Act of 1940 included a provision for National Service Life Insurance, which made all persons serving in the U.S. armed forces eligible to purchase up to $10,000 of life insurance.

The Lend-Lease Act signed by President Roosevelt in March 1941 committed U.S. financial, industrial and manufacturing resources to support Great Britain and its Allies. It also gave the president unlimited authority to direct ammunition, tanks, airplanes, trucks and food to the war in Europe without violating the nation's official position of neutrality.

As U.S. factories retooled for wartime production, unemployment disappeared. Companies hired thousands of additional workers to meet the increased demand for iron, steel, machinery, railroad equipment, ships, airplanes, and land vehicles—including the new "jeep" and "B-29" bomber. Across the United States, war-related industries offered employment and training. Eager to make money in the booming economy, workers relocated to find jobs, and depressed areas of the country sprang back to life.

Because of its location on the East Coast near Washington, Baltimore benefited greatly from defense contracts, war-related jobs and spending. In the early 1940s, the state ranked twenty-eighth by population, but twelfth in government contracts. More than six hundred Maryland firms were engaged in war work, but six large companies—Bethlehem Steel, Glenn L. Martin Aircraft, General Motors, Westinghouse, Western Electric and Bendix Corporation—formed the backbone of the state's war economy. Manufacturing ships, aircraft, ammunition and communications equipment, they accounted for 60 percent of Baltimore-area jobs.

LEFT: *As U.S. manufacturing firms geared up for war, President Roosevelt toured the Glenn L. Martin Aircraft plant in Baltimore.*

(Courtesy of the Maryland Historical Society)

PEARL HARBOR CHANGES LIVES

BELOW: *The July 1942 cover of Monumental's Old Black Hen reflected the country's determination. Americans everywhere were united in their support of U.S. entry into World War II.*

Japan's unexpected attack on Pearl Harbor on December 7, 1941, galvanized the country in support of U.S. entry into the war. Never before had there been such united support and unparalleled national "connection" and commitment to a cause. Four days later, when Germany declared war on the United States, Americans were ready to fight on two fronts to protect and preserve their freedoms.

Early in 1942, Monumental Life president Leo P. Rock wrote to employees in the company publication, the *Old Black Hen*:

> Prior to Pearl Harbor, . . . we realized there was a WAR, but there was little thought about being in the thick of it, fighting not just for "our way of life" but . . . for our very existence. We were caught flat-footed and unprepared, and we are now going through the transition from normal peacetime pursuits to an all-out war effort. . . . The battle front is no longer confined to the Armies facing each other on land or the Navies on the seas; it . . . reaches into every city, every hamlet, every countryside and every home.

Hundreds of thousands of young men immediately volunteered or were drafted into the armed forces. Lives, weddings, educations and careers were put on hold, postponed or accelerated as America's healthiest young men left for basic training and Officer Candidate School. Almost overnight, tent cities arose to train new recruits. When gas, tires, sugar and meat were rationed, few complained. Before long, the entire country was committed to the war effort.

Writing from the company's Salisbury District Office on Maryland's Eastern Shore, Cashier Elizabeth Williams noted what many Americans no doubt were thinking:

> Situated just thirty miles from the Atlantic Coast, our office seems to be right in the thick of things. We sometimes wonder if you out in Louisville, Chicago and Saginaw know there is a war going on! Your cities might be crowded with industrial workers and the tempo of your lives might be changed, but do you—as you sit at your work—become accustomed to the frequent roar of airplanes overhead or, if you have time, count the number of Army trucks and jeeps that roll by? Do you notice that approximately five out of every ten men you pass are in uniform? It really is gratifying to see how our country has mobilized so rapidly to defend itself.

WOMEN ACCEPT NEW ROLES

As men left for basic training and shipped overseas, women took over many responsibilities at home. Like "Rosie, the Riveter," women put on pants, went to work, learned to drive trucks, handled welding torches, manned assembly lines or ferried aircraft across the country to free male pilots for duty overseas. Secretaries and clerks moved into corporate accounting and administrative positions. In the previously male-dominated life insurance industry, women assumed sales and management roles.

At Monumental, bookkeeper Emily Limke—the first woman hired for a home office position in 1918—assumed responsibility for filing the company's annual statements in the 1940s, while Florence Watts managed the Actuarial Department and Ruth Granger headed the company's first "all-girl" Records Department. In the field, wives picked up their drafted husbands' debit books and began making calls as managers recruited female agents.

Describing changes in her field office in early 1943, a Commonwealth Life cashier in Fort Wayne, Indiana, wrote in their employee magazine:

Gone are the days when smoke hung like a pea soup fog in the agents' room and when a boisterous comradeship prevailed in that sanctum. . . . Gone are the metal cuspidors. A large mirror now hangs on the wall in the cloak closet. There may be a box of powder or a jar of face cream in the lady's briefcase among the applications. She may use the feminine touch in her approach to applicants, and she has a technique of selling all her own; but, in her well fitting slacks, she walks her debit in the snow, where her predecessor drove his car, and she gets results. Nothing remains the same but the standardized greeting of the insurance agent: "How much business have YOU got today?"

For Rose Miller in Gary, Indiana, becoming a Monumental Life agent was a real education:

Accustomed to being mistress of my home, I now find that work is my mistress. . . . There is always "one more thing" that demands my attention, but I am slowly and surely overcoming that obstacle. . . . It would behoove any housewife to become a life insurance agent if the opportunity presented itself. It has taught me, . . . appreciation of our home life and family, and I have acquired more tolerance, perseverance and adaptability since engaging in life insurance service and selling.

ABOVE: *During World War II, more and more women took over men's roles and responsibilities in the home office. Esther Murray (seated, center front) managed the "all girl" Policy Writing Department.*

Women put on pants and replaced men on assembly lines and as machine operators. Fairchild Aircraft in Hagerstown, Maryland, hired many women to help meet wartime contracts and quotas.
(Courtesy of the Maryland Historical Society)

LEFT: *Women also staffed the entire Records Department, managed by Ruth Granger (seated, center front).*

Agent Margaret Conner . . .
Monumental 'First Lady' and Role Model

HIRED DURING World War I as the company's first female agent, Cumberland's Margaret ("Marge") Conner remained Monumental Life's *only* female agent until World War II, when the company again needed women to help out on the sales front. "Not since the last World War have women invaded the Industrial Insurance field," wrote one manager in 1943. "Once again, the women of America have answered the call in unexpected numbers."

ABOVE: *Cumberland agent Margaret Conner during World War II.* ABOVE RIGHT: *Margaret Conner at her December 1952 retirement.*

When Marge became an agent in 1918, a woman's place was in the home. Few females were employed in the business world, especially in western Maryland, but she had already crossed that threshold. She had been a saleswoman in a local department store, and, when the local mail carrier was called to serve in World War I, she had taken over his twenty-six mile route—on horseback when weather closed the roads.

Working her rural territory when the company was still called Mutual Life of Baltimore, Marge was one of five agents in the Cumberland office. For five years, she caught a local train every morning to the farthest point on her debit, eight miles away, then walked home in the afternoon. She found the work to be "healthful, enjoyable, profitable and pleasant" and continued to cover her debit on foot until 1923, when she bought her first Ford roadster. Many of her policyholders became her friends.

At first, Marge was doubtful about how the public would regard a woman entering what, until then, had been a man's world. In 1943, during her twenty-fifth year of service with Monumental, she wrote:

> After the first few months on my debit, people did not think it strange at all to have a woman agent. In fact, I think I had an advantage over the men since most Industrial insurance contacts are with housewives. Being a woman, I was often more successful than the men in getting into a home to write new insurance. . . . I never had a door slammed in my face.

I wish I could talk personally to all the women making connections today with Monumental. I would heartily commend them for their wise decisions to enter life insurance work and their good fortune in being connected with the best company on earth. I look forward with pleasure to the coming years, knowing that under my company's generous service and retirement policy, I shall be taken care of when I am no longer physically able to sell and service life insurance.

Throughout World War II, Marge was an encouraging role model for the many women who, out of necessity or a sense of adventure, joined Monumental Life's field force to replace a man. A few, like herself, remained in the field to build long and successful careers of their own.

In 1950, Margaret Conner was still selling life insurance in the Cumberland area. She often said: "An insurance agent can do a lot of good work if he [or she!] keeps his eyes open. The job offers an opportunity to help a lot of families." When she retired in December 1952 after thirty-four years of service, she received a wrist watch inscribed: "Margaret L. Conner, 1918–1952, Loyalty & Service. M.L.I.C." In making the presentation, agency executive Thomas O. Carroll remarked that the inscription symbolized Marge's life. During her career, he said, she had "contributed more to the life insurance industry in Cumberland than any other single individual. Her sales methods, her character and her influence in the homes of her customers had helped give people a kindly feeling toward life insurance."

Margaret Conner remained an independent, single women and advocate for life insurance until her death on October 22, 1982, at age ninety-five.

World War II raised women's role in the work force to new heights and changed forever their contribution to the American economy. In just five years, U.S. employment increased by nineteen million jobs, and women were doing 35 percent of them.

Monumental Life retiree Lillian Rogowski remembers being approached by the Navy to join the WAVES (Women Accepted for Volunteer Emergency Service) in 1941. She was working in Gutman's Department Store in Baltimore for nine dollars a week and wanted to enlist, but her mother refused to let her go. Instead, she found a job earning twelve dollars a week as a "checker" in Monumental's Underwriting Department. Though retired since 1983, Lillian will never forget those years:

> There were so many applications that everyone worked Saturdays and evenings until 8:00 or 9:00 p.m. Women hired as clerks, typists and stenographers often helped with underwriting, even if they couldn't approve applications. But no one received overtime pay—just fifty cents supper money.

> Until the war, the company wouldn't hire married women. Management believed if you had a husband, you didn't need a job. If a woman got married, she used to keep it a secret and used her maiden name. World War II changed some of that.

Still single, Lillian and her friends went to the USO Club—the United Service Organizations' entertainment center for soldiers and sailors. They also brought GIs home to family dinner and attended chaperoned dances at Maryland's Fort Meade, Fort Holabird, Edgewood Arsenal and Aberdeen Proving Ground. As "dates" for the "ninety day wonders" completing Officer Candidate School, they listened to Glenn Miller, Benny Goodman and Woody Guthrie and watched Clark Gable, Bette Davis, Fred Astaire and Ginger Rogers on the silver screen. When the company held dances for employees and servicemen stationed in the Baltimore area, Lillian's supervisor, Al

LEFT: *Lillian Rogowski (far right, front) and friends outside Monumental's Charles Street entrance during the 1940s.*

Huegelmeyer, "stood on Charles and Chase Streets and dragged in uniformed men to be our dance partners."

In cities throughout the country, women worked their day jobs, and then spent extra hours volunteering at USOs, donating blood, driving for the Red Cross, and training to become air raid wardens, auxiliary firemen and policemen. With fathers, sons, brothers and husbands in the service, everyone at home wanted to do his—and her—part.

"Nobody has any spare time," noted Toledo, Ohio, cashier Florence O'Connor in a letter to the *Old Black Hen*. "There are more jobs to do than hands to do them. Women's role in maintaining morale is as important as manufacturing munitions." She reminded the company's female employees to follow the example of British women, who "kept their chins up, clung to their lipsticks, and did their jobs."

O'Connor saluted those who displayed initiative, resourcefulness and a willingness to share, make do, and do without. Clerks saved rubber bands, paper clips, erasers and carbon paper. Typists dusted, oiled and repaired typewriters because they could not be replaced. Cashiers rewound adding machine tape and used both sides. The company's "working girls" saved time and energy as well as supplies. They took care of their health because America needed them on the job.

BELOW: *Throughout World War II, many Baltimore women worked, but many also retained more traditional roles . . . such as scrubbing Baltimore's famous "white marble steps."*
(Courtesy of the Maryland Historical Society)

Florence O'Connor (above) joined the WAVES, and Pvt. Ruth Frye (below) enlisted in the Marines.

After five years as a Monumental cashier, Florence O'Connor enlisted in the WAVES. The next year, Ruth Frye, a cashier in Lansing, Michigan, joined the Marine Corps. From Parris Island, Private Frye wrote that "boot camp was really rugged," but that she had "never been healthier." One of her proudest moments was her first review. "We stood just a little straighter and held our heads a little higher . . . when the band started playing the Marine Corps hymn." Working as a payroll clerk, she noted: "There are four women and four men in our office. Three of the men will be shoving off for active duty before too long. [That's when] we will really be accomplishing the reason we joined the Corps . . . to free a Marine to fight."

By 1944 twelve million American men and women were serving in the armed forces, war spending totaled more than 20 percent of the U.S. budget, and war production accounted for 44 percent of the gross national product.

Realizing that many male employees would be drafted, the company agreed that years of company service would continue to accumulate while an employee was in the armed forces. Officers also voted to give all draftees from the field and home office up to three months' bonus pay, based on years of company service. "Voluntary payments" totaling $20,000 in 1942 averaged $35 per draftee per month. Two years later, the payments topped $60,000.

"My wife received a month's pay several weeks ago and was informed she would receive another month's pay divided over the next twelve months," wrote Private James Sorrentino from basic training. "There aren't enough words to express my thanks." Another draftee noted: "It means a lot to a man to know his company is behind him 100%." After talking with other former insurance men on his base, Private Paul A. Mueller reported proudly: "When I outline the Voluntary Monthly Income Plan that Monumental so generously gives its men in the service, they look at me in astonishment."

DOING OUR PATRIOTIC DUTY

Even before Pearl Harbor, Monumental Life was doing its part to support the war effort. In 1940 the board of directors approved investing $2.9 million in U.S. Treasury Bills. The following January, directors agreed to invest $4.5 million in bonds of corporations engaged in war-related manufacturing, chiefly Firestone Tire & Rubber, General Electric, General Motors, Phillips Petroleum, Timkin Roller Bearing, Vick Chemical, and Westinghouse Electric & Manufacturing.

LEFT: *Cities like Baltimore along the U.S. East Coast took extra precautions during the war to protect citizens and businesses from German saboteurs and submarine attacks.*
(Courtesy of the Maryland Historical Society)

On hearing reports that German submarines had been spotted off the Atlantic coast, the company installed an air raid warning system in the home office. Management also scheduled first aid training, appointed fire and roof wardens, purchased war damage coverage on all company-owned property, and agreed that the home office basement could be designated an air raid shelter for its Baltimore neighborhood. By 1941, Monumental Life was also contributing to the Baltimore Safety Council, the Maryland Public Expenditure Council, and the United Service Organization for National Defense.

As rationing increased in 1942, President Rock announced that Monumental Life's field agents would be "on foot" for the duration of the war. "The rubber situation is serious," he wrote, "and automobile tires are not available for civilian use." He urged field managers to consolidate agent territories and advise customers in areas inaccessible by bicycle or public transportation to mail in their payments to Baltimore or their local field office. Acknowledging that policyholders, agents and the company would all be inconvenienced, Rock reminded employees: "This is just one of the many sacrifices and hardships that will be imposed on us during this emergency."

Servicing policyholders became even more difficult later that year. In October 1942, Rock reported to directors that more than 360 agents had been drafted, enlisted voluntarily, or left the company to take positions in war-related industries. By year-end, sixty-five women also resigned from the home office to take higher-paying positions at Westinghouse and other manufacturing companies. With fewer workers, management focused on efficiency and eliminating unnecessary forms and reports. To retain and attract employees, directors drafted the company's first retirement and disability plan and raised home office wages by 10 percent—an average $3.75 a week—to cover rising "cost of living" expenses and Social Security taxes. When the government restricted salary increases in non-war related industries in 1943, Monumental directors also agreed to provide a new benefit—FREE lunch in the company cafeteria!

LEFT: *Air raid sirens were placed on strategic downtown corners to alert Baltimore's citizens to an airborne attack.*
(Courtesy of the Maryland Historical Society)

LIFE INSURANCE 'ESSENTIAL' TO SECURITY

Though not included on the government's list of "essential" industries, the nation's life insurers provided much of the financial support needed to fight the war. Through the investment of premium dollars, the industry continued to build the energy, transportation, communication, industrial and agricultural infrastructures on which the country and its armed forces depended. By 1944, U.S. life insurance companies had invested 40 percent of their assets—$16.5 billion—in government securities. Seventy-nine cents of every invested dollar flowed directly into financing the purchase or manufacture of war materials.

Premium dollars also protected Americans on the home front. The country's defense depended on the financial security and sacrifice of its citizens. By providing life insurance, America's insurers helped families preserve their economic independence and the quality of their lives. Speaking on the importance of life insurance in wartime, Gen. Hugh A. Drum advised life insurance agents to "Take pride in the contribution you are making directly and indirectly to the national war effort. . . . Your daily work means the comfort and welfare of our people." Throughout the war, agents helped families protect themselves, and every sale of life insurance helped stabilize the national economy by encouraging savings and thrift.

When the U.S. entered the war in December 1941, Monumental Life and many of its competitors announced that new life insurance policies would include restrictive war clauses. Eager to beat the 1942 effective date, thousands of Monumental policyholders and prospects applied for coverage that January. In doing so they created an "avalanche of applications" and a record-breaking month for Industrial increase. With troop counts escalating in July 1943, the National Association of Insurance Commissioners (NAIC) recommended that companies disregard their contracts' war restrictions and exclusions when the death of a policyholder occurred

within the "home area" that included the forty-eight states, Washington, D.C., and Newfoundland, Canada.

The war years provided unanticipated opportunities for U.S. life insurers. High employment, higher wages and taxes, restrictions on installment buying, and a shrinking supply of consumer goods—including everything from gasoline, cars, cigarettes and beef to radios, refrigerators, long underwear and nylon stockings—all converged, forcing Americans to save rather than spend, and life insurance offered an attractive way to save. By diverting funds from the consumer markets, the dollars used for life insurance premiums also decreased the demand for non-essential goods and reduced inflationary pressures. Invested, they helped finance the war.

According to the Institute of Life Insurance, now called the American Council of Life Insurance (ACLI), American families increased their life insurance holdings by $8.7 billion during 1943 alone. It was the largest gain in family protection in a single year recorded to date by the industry. Monumental Life contributed $35.5 million to that gain, reporting $5 million more increase in 1943 than it had in 1942. By year-end 1944, sixty-eight million U.S. policyholders owned $139 billion of life insurance—$14 billion more than when the U.S. entered the war.

Operating with nearly a third fewer employees during the war years, the company's life insurance in force and assets nonetheless grew steadily, from $323.4 million and $37.2 million, respectively in 1940 to $475.4 million and $71.5 million at year-end 1945. As expected, death claims and benefit payments also multiplied dramatically. Even with war clauses on new policies, war-related death claims jumped from $38,602 in 1942, to $161,449 in 1943, to $298,762 in 1944, to almost $600,000 in 1945.

Equally striking during those years were Monumental Life's low lapse and high collection rates on its Weekly Premium Industrial and Monthly Ordinary business. Earning more money than they had in many years, the company's working-class customers could afford to buy additional coverage and pay their premiums.

As the war continued, more and more battle-related images and language appeared in company publications.

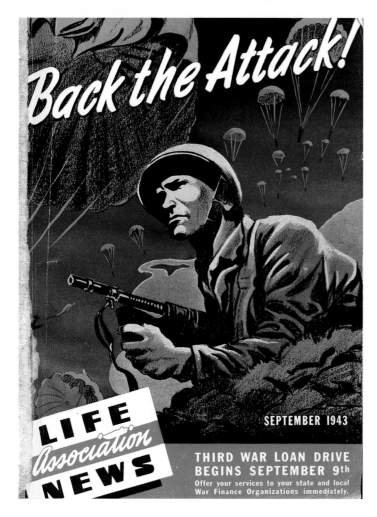

Back the Attack!

SEPTEMBER 1943

LIFE *Association* **NEWS**

THIRD WAR LOAN DRIVE
BEGINS SEPTEMBER 9th
Offer your services to your state and local
War Finance Organizations immediately.

AGENTS 'BACK THE ATTACK'

As early as 1942, war images and "fighting" language began to appear in the *Old Black Hen*. Articles, letters, cartoons and cover art encouraged the company's agents to "retool" their sales presentations, "defend" their positions, prepare for "counter attacks," and "fight" for the financial security of American families. "Do you think U.S. bomber pilots would head for Nazi targets without first making a reconnaissance trip?" one manager asked readers. "If strikes aren't well planned before take off—including selecting the most opportune time and sites, and going over every detail carefully—do you think pilots would have any chance of successfully completing their mission?"

In sales, as in war, life insurance executives advised their frontline "troops" to remember their mission and select the most appropriate tools and targets to achieve their objectives. Promoting a "Thrift and Protection Campaign" in 1942, Monumental Life's sales promotion materials reminded agents that "Protection has always been our watchword. Today, more than ever, you have a

responsibility to extend the mantle of protection to the greatest possible number of families. Sell Protection! Win War Bonds!"

In a nationwide broadcast over the CBS radio network in April 1942, Grant Taggart, president of the National Association of Life Underwriters (NALU), outlined the industry's strategy for supporting the war and urged America's life insurance agents to sell insurance and promote the sale of war bonds. Life insurance, especially National Service Life Insurance, and war bonds became two of the nation's most powerful weapons.

Though they did not actually sell war bonds during World War II, agents contributed to the war effort by providing information and assisting individuals and groups in purchasing bonds through employer-sponsored payroll deduction plans. "The salary savings idea proved popular with American workers," announced *Life Association News* (LAN) editors in August 1942. NALU volunteers enrolled 8.5 million employees from 46,000 firms, reaching their first goal two weeks ahead of schedule with bond sales totaling $1 billion.

Monumental Life's field and home office employees were among those who contributed to this first successful war bond drive. On April 9, 1942, President Leo Rock announced $140,000 in voluntary sales and congratulated employees on their "splendid spirit of patriotism." In late December 1945— with victory declared on both fighting fronts—the company recognized eighty-seven employees who had purchased war bonds every week since January 1942. Throughout four years of war, they helped provide critical support for the country's servicemen and women.

"you buy ém we'll fly ém!

DEFENSE
BONDS
STAMPS

ABOVE: *Drafted in February 1941, Master Sgt. Donald Weeks served in a Military Police battalion stationed in the North Atlantic.*

Both Charles Coale (above) and Rosendo A. Gomez (right) were drafted out of the home office before Pearl Harbor.

FAR RIGHT: *Baltimore agent Benjamin Weinraub served in the U.S. Army Air Corps.*

EMPLOYEES SEE ACTION OVERSEES

The first "Monumental man" to be called into the armed forces was Donald Weeks. Hired in 1923, he was drafted on February 15, 1941, and assigned to a military police battalion. Though forbidden to disclose his exact location, Master Sergeant Weeks served in Scotland, England and Iceland, where he experienced bombing raids, invasion threats, and close calls with German submarines. Home on furlough in 1943, he married his home office sweetheart. Two days after being discharged in 1945, he returned to a position in the Claims Department.

Also drafted in 1941—and entitled to wear a yellow service ribbon indicating their status as pre-Pearl Harbor draftees—were Underwriting's Charles Coale and Actuary Rosendo A. Gomez. Staff Sergeant Coale was assigned to the coast artillery stationed in our nation's capital. As one of "Washington's Own" defenders against enemy aerial attack, he trained army personnel in the use of radar-controlled anti-aircraft guns. In Dutch New Guinea, Gomez was promoted to captain of the 595th Field Artillery before being discharged in 1945. His mother carried on his work in the Actuarial Department while he was away.

Chicago Agent Herbert Meyer was one of the first field agents to be drafted. During basic training in San Diego, he wrote to Agency Manager William J. Biehl in Baltimore:

> I thought I'd let you know what's really going on in Uncle Sam's drafted forces. I'm working in the kitchen as a student cook. I also go to school part-time taking a course in cooking and mess at Sergeants Specialists School. It seems kind of funny, but almost every night I have some sort of dream about my debit. Army life is OK except I wish I were back in my car collecting a debit for fifty or sixty [dollars] per week instead of the huge sum of twenty-one per month, which we will receive for four months."

Writing from Fort Riley, Kansas, early in the war, Rockford agent Kenneth Stokes noted: "It straightens a man up when Old Glory is waving in the breeze and the strains of the National Anthem tickle your spine." He added: "I am in the Cavalry, learning horsemanship and use of weapons such as a rifle, pistol, and machine gun; also combat training, chemical warfare, and map-reading. There is much to learn." Indeed there was.

Baltimore agent Benjamin Weinraub, at Drew Field in Florida, explained that since his induction into the air corps, "I am engaged in doing my part to learn how to fight [to insure] the sort of life we Americans believe in. . . . I am being readied for an important task. . . . [and will] carry

into my new job the same perseverance and fortitude which characterized my efforts at Monumental."

Many men were naively anxious to see action. "I'm a radar operator on a B-29 bomber and have been flying extensively," wrote Norman J. Stephen, 678th Bomber Squadron, from his Kansas army air base in April 1944. "In the midst of a very thorough overseas training program, I expect my stay in the States to be a brief one. I believe firmly in our military leaders and feel certain that I shall return as soon as possible, physically and mentally fit."

During the heaviest fighting in 1945, the company's "Honor Roll of Those in Service," published monthly in the *Old Black Hen*, listed 270 names, including a few women.

RIGHT: *Monumental's Service Honor Roll in the home office lobby preserves in bronze the names of employees who served in World War II, including three, marked with a star, who were killed in action.*

IN HONOR OF OUR EMPLOYEES
WHO SERVED IN THE ARMED FORCES IN
WORLD WAR II

BRENTON T. AARON	MILTON K. COOPER	JAMES C. HUGHES	PAUL MILEY, JR.	WILLIAM O. SCHULLER
WILLIAM AHRENS	JAMES A. CORUM	JOHN V. HULING	BENJAMIN MILLER	HERMAN SCHWARTZ
GEORGE P. ALDOM	FRANK COTTONARO	HENRY H. HURST	CARROLL MILLER	WILLIAM F. SCIBLE
ULMONT H. ANDREWS	DALE L. COUNCILMAN	STEWART HUSSEY	ELMER MILLER	ANTHONY SCIORTINO
WALTER ARATA	JACK K. CUNDIFF	GASTON C. HYDE	ROBERT R. MILLER	GEORGE V. SENG
JOHN L. ARNOLD	GLENN CUNNINGHAM	PAUL M. ISBELL	LOUIS MIRABELLA	ROBERT L. SHAW
HENRY ARTES	ELMER B. DALBY	WILLIAM C. JACKSON	STEPHEN MISKIN	VINCENT SIMMONS
JOHN J. ATKINSON	WILLIAM J. DAVIS	GEORGE F. JONES	ALBERT MONFERRATO	FRANK SIMONIE
WILLIAM AUSTIN	THOMAS W. DAVISSON	LESTER JONES	VERNON W. MOORE	WILLIAM SLEITZER
FRANK BAKER, JR.	S. EMIL DeGREGORIO	LINWOOD S. JONES	JOHN E. MORSE, JR.	PAUL L. SMITH
JAMES E. BAKER	WILLIAM E. DeLANEY	NATALIE JONES	PAUL A. MUELLER	RAYMOND SMITH, JR.
JOSEPH T. BALL	CHARLES H. DENNISON	ROBERT JONES	MYRON C. MULLEN	ROBERT SMITH
FRANKLIN E. BARBOUR	CHARLES DePASQUALE	SAID S. KABALAN	PATRICK MULLEN	JULIAN SOBEL
EDMUND S. BARRETT	FRANK M. DERENDAL	ALBERT KAIMAN	EMIL J. MUNSON	JAMES SORRENTINO
KENNETH BAYNARD	HARRY DUGAN	ROBERT F. KEATLEY	EDWARD C. MURRAY	JAMES SPRINKLE
TRUMAN K. BENNETSEN	BETTY MOCK DUPLER	CARLOS KEENE	THURMAN S. MUSTAINE	NORMAN STEPHAN
ANDREW BENNETT	IRA EASTER	GEORGE E. KERR	JESTON A. MYERS	CARROLL STINE
GERARD T. BENNETT	GUY S. ERWAY	EMIL KINDERMAN	THOMAS V. NICHOLSON	KENNETH STOKES
CHARLES H. BIRELY	H. FRED EUBANK	RICHARD R. KIRKPATRICK	FREDERICK NIEMEYER	RALPH H. STROUP
JOHN A. BLANDFORD	ANTHONY F. FACCIOLO	FRANK KLAUS	CONRAD NOONAN	M. CLAUDE SUTTON
JAMES S. BLINCOE	RAYMOND FANNON	GEORGE KROMREY	FLORENCE O'CONNOR	ROBERT R. TATE, JR.
FRANK BOLOGNA	FRANK FASTRING	RALPH KUHN	JOHN G. O'HARA	BENJAMIN TAYLOE
KENARD BOORD	ARTHUR FELTER	HERMAN T. LaFORCE	JAMES F. OJILE	ROBERT J. TAYLOR
CLYDE BORING	JAMES FEMRITE	CHARLES LANE	JAMES OLESICK	WILMER B. TAYLOR
C. BROOKS BOSLEY, JR.	JAMES C. FIFER	HERBERT T. LANE	JOSEPH OTTO	FREEMAN THOMAS
KENNETH BOWARD	ANTHONY FILIP	ALFRED LANG	RICHARD OWEN	MITCHELL THOMAS
EARL BRADLEY	GILBERT FISHER	★ WILLIAM A. LANZELOTTI	ALEXANDER PARHAM	LEWIS S. TILGHMAN
CHARLES H. BREITLING	GREGORY FISHER	DELBERT H. LEATHERBERRY	FRED PARKER	RICHARD J. TOMMEY
JOHN J. BRISTOW	JOHN H. FISHER	JAMES B. LEDDY	ANDREW PARR, M.D.	★ VERNON TOWNER
HAROLD E. BROWN	VINCENT FISHER	ARTHUR H. LEHMANN	FLOYD PARSH	WILLIAM P. UHLER
THOMAS BRYANT	RAYMOND S. FOX	ANTHONY J. LIBERI	CARL J. PASCHEK	MICHAEL VETRONE
CHARLES E. BUCHANAN	GEORGE FRANCE	★ EDWARD LINDAU	CHARLES W. PATTON	JOSEPH VICARI
MAX BUCHOLTZ	LOUIS R. FRANZINI	LEON G. LIGON	THOMAS J. PHENEY	SNOWDEN WAGNER
HENRY F. BUETTNER, M.D.	ANTHONY FRANZOLINO	DANIEL B. LIPSITZ	CLAUDE PITTARD, JR.	HARRY WALKER
EDWARD L. BULGER	RUTH FRYE	HAROLD M. LONG	FOREST PLACE	JOHN J. WALKER
J. EDWARD BULLEN	DOMINEC FUSCO	WILLIS B. LORD	BEN PLASKIE	HARRY S. WALLACE
BRUCE BURGESS	ELLIS GLIME	ROBERT E. LOVE	STEPHEN J. PODOLSKY	EDMUND T. WALSH
RAYMOND BURGESS	ELMO GLIMPSE	JOHN A. LOY	JAMES RAMSAY	STANLEY WARREN
GEORGE BURNELL	ROSENDO A. GOMEZ	RAYMOND E. LUST	FORREST H. RANS	DONALD WEEKS
GILBERT L. BURT	ARMANDE GRAY	EDWIN J. McCLASKEY	WILLIAM RAPP	CLARENCE WEIDMAN
WALTER L. BUSH	WILBERT GRIES	ROBERT J. McGIBENY	JAMES F. REID	BENJAMIN WEINRAUB
PAUL V. CARROLL	MILTON GUITTERREZ	HAROLD V. McINTIRE	JESSE M. RHODES	WILLIAM WHALEN
OMER R. CARTER	RALPH B. HALE	ORVILLE McKELVY	WILBER T. RICHARDSON, JR.	DARWIN N. WHITE
KEATH B. CASHNER	WILBURN C. HALE, JR.	LeROY McMILLEN	JOHN RODMAN	ANDREW WILLEY
HUGH R. CAVOLI	ROSS HAMLIN	EDWARD McPARTLAND	PAUL ROEDER	ELIZABETH WILLIAMS
WALDO J. CHAPMAN	SOTHERN C. HAMMETT, JR.	FRED A. McSHERRY	PATRICK L. ROGERS	ROBERT WILLS
JOSEPH G. CHARLEY	G. EARL HANCOCK	EDDIE F. MALLORY	GEORGE RUGGIERO	JEROME WILSON
JOSEPH F. CHEMES	CHANNING J. HANLEY	BERNARD K. MARSH	MICHAEL J. RUSNAK	PRINCE N. WINDSOR
FRANK CHRISTIAN	PETER HANSEN	MILLARD M. MARTIN	DAVID H. RUSSELL	FLOYD E. WINEBRENNER
FRED J. CLATENBAUGH	JAMES HARTMAN	LEO J. MATHEW	CHARLES K. RYAN	GEORGE WINTERSTEIN
GROVER S. CLAY	HENRY HATTEMER	CARL S. MATTHEWS	LOUIS A. SAHLEY	BERNARD F. WOLF
CHARLES COALE	RUDOLPH HAVLIK	HAROLD T. MAXWELL	NICHOLAS SANTOIEMMA	OLIVER W. YANDA
CLARENCE COLLINS	RAYMOND E. HAWKINS	WALTER E. MEANS JR.	MELVIN M. SAUERHAMMER	EDWARD YOUNGER
FRANK COLLINS	DAVID HAZLETT	MICHAEL E. MEENACH	EDWARD W. SCHELLHAS	JUSTIN ZAGAME
HARRY L. COOKE, JR.	HARVEY E. HICKSON	THOMAS MELTON	ELBERT R. SCHIMMEL	CHARLES ZENTGRAF
	WILLIAM V. HILL	HERBERT MEYER	HAROLD E. SCHNEIDER	

MONUMENTAL LIFE INSURANCE COMPANY

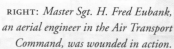

With eighteen years of Monumental service in 1943, William A. Ahrens, assistant manager, Auditing, was drafted into the navy and sent to the Pacific. He later became the company's assistant treasurer. Edmund S. Barrett, an infantry private, was drafted out of the Akron District Office. Promoted to assistant manager in Philadelphia when he returned, he retired decades later as vice president of District Agencies.

Frank Baker, Jr., the company's assistant secretary, returned from naval service and rose through the ranks to become Monumental Life's chairman of the board and CEO in 1967. James E. Baker, Frank's brother, worked ten years in Auditing before joining the army. A technical sergeant, he shipped out for North Africa in January 1943 and served in Italy, Britain, France, Belgium, Holland and Germany. Claims Department manager Leroy G. Patton completed his tour of duty in the army, then enlisted in the Coast Guard Auxiliary. He continued to volunteer as a signalman directing ships in and out of Baltimore Harbor after the war ended and he was back at Monumental.

All but three employees returned home safely. U.S. Navy seaman William A. Lanzelotti from Philadelphia was killed in action aboard the U.S.S. *Houston* in the Philippines. Air Corps sergeant Edward W. Lindau from Chicago was killed during a bombing mission. Army sergeant Vernon E. Tower from Flint, Michigan, died in an accident in Italy after earning five combat ribbons.

Among those wounded in action was Agent Robert L. Jones from southern Maryland. Drafted in 1942 at twenty-seven, Jones left a wife and two children at home when he went overseas. He participated in the invasions of North Africa, Italy, and southern France, experienced hand-to-hand combat, and received a Purple Heart "for stopping a bullet" while serving with the 5th Infantry in Italy. Jones retired in 1979 with thirty-eight years' service. "I was glad to come back alive and find my job waiting for me," said the decorated veteran when interviewed at age ninety-two.

Master Sergeant H. Fred Eubank from Atlanta, an aerial engineer in the Air Transport Command, was also wounded in action when the Japanese attacked his B-24 bomber during a flight from India to China.

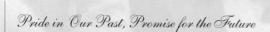

Whether stationed in Europe, in the Pacific or on bases in the United States, Monumental employees looked forward to receiving their monthly copy of the *Old Black Hen*, which kept soldiers and sailors in touch with friends back home. Drafted agents could also see who was producing sales in their absence and what they would be facing on the sales front when they returned. By printing letters and stories from overseas, the company's popular publication also enabled servicemen and women to share their wartime experiences.

From a U.S. Navy ship near the Philippines in March 1945, James S. Blincoe sent home the following update:

> I've been through hell and high water since the last time I wrote. Our outfit has been in all the excitement over here in the last three months. We have [been part of] five invasions and half a dozen lesser operations. My heart was in my mouth many times as we left our snug little harbor. My job is keeping supplies aboard the ship. My sales training has come in handy many times in obtaining supplies. This week I needed provisions, and we were just about out. A convoy wasn't expected for several days . . . so I went to the Army. After waiting about an hour to see the colonel in charge, I got what I went after!

Writing from Italy in May 1945, one month after the death of President Franklin D. Roosevelt and four days before V-E (Victory in Europe) Day, Baltimore agent Raymond P. Smith, Jr., shed light on what it was like on the front lines:

> Well, we finally stopped long enough for me to write. It's eight o'clock in the morning. It looks like things are pretty well finished in Italy. We've been on the go day and night since the 5th Army started the push. Our division was the first to enter Bologna. The Germans are surrendering right and left.
>
> I had quite an experience myself. We sent out three patrols on three different roads leading into a small town called Caruso. The town was supposed to be clear of Germans. As we got into town, church bells rang seven times. A few minutes later, all hell broke loose. We grabbed our rifles, two light machine guns, and ran for the buildings. Thirty of us were on one side of the street and "Jerry" was in buildings on the other. We shot it out for about an hour, and "Jerry" raised the white flag. We told them to come out. Sixty Germans appeared.

Later that same day, Smith witnessed a surrender following a bitter tank battle. "Eight hundred Germans marched into town with the Colonel and his aide riding two horses in front," he wrote. "You could see the Germans were tired and beaten, but they marched like real soldiers. It was really a sight."

War Experiences Become Stepping Stones

N THE AFTERMATH of World War II, as Monumental Life employees who had traded debit books, pens and adding machines for rifles returned to their jobs, the ranks of employees in the company's home office and sales offices across the country also swelled with new hires. Among the new postwar hires were former soldiers, sailors, marines and airmen anxious to pursue dreams and enjoy the freedoms they had fought so valiantly to preserve. Tested by war, mature and focused beyond their years, one can only imagine their thoughts when asked to detail their "experience" on job applications.

The experiences of two Monumental Life employees—now retired after thirty-plus years of service—touched pivotal moments in the era and underscored the profound changes still to follow as nation, industry and Monumental Life transitioned to the future.

John Bosley Ensor . . .
Action on Okinawa

John B. ("Bos") Ensor on Okinawa in 1945.

When the Japanese struck Pearl Harbor on December 7, 1941, the call to arms affected everyone—including Baltimore-born John Bosley ("Bos") Ensor, then in his second year of business studies at Northwestern University. Ensor was drafted into the army in April 1943 and sent to Camp McCoy in Wisconsin for basic training. Boot camp was followed by eight months of accelerated engineering training at Kalamazoo College in Michigan. When the government unexpectedly shut down that program, Ensor and others—nicknamed the "cross-eyed commandos" because so many wore glasses—were reassigned as riflemen to different companies in the 96th Infantry Division.

By July 1944, Ensor's division, under Admiral Chester Nimitz's control, was in Hawaii preparing for a September landing on the island of Yap. That attack never took place, thanks to bloody U.S. victories elsewhere in the Pacific, and Ensor and 17,000 other soldiers of the 96th were

reassigned to the Sixth Army under Gen. Douglas MacArthur. Ensor took part in the landing on the island of Leyte in the Philippines on October 20, 1944, when MacArthur famously proclaimed, "I have returned." The intensive campaign— which marked Ensor's first time under fire—would last until Christmas Day.

"I remember an eerie feeling that night seeing hundreds of ships in a line that curved back and forth," says Ensor. "Up to that point it was the biggest invasion of the Pacific."

But it was only a prelude to the even greater Okinawa Campaign, which began April 1, 1945, and lasted until June 14. Still recovering from wounds received on Leyte, Ensor rejoined his company two weeks after the initial landing and saw extensive combat—first as a BAR ammunition bearer and later as a radio operator. Six of his company (four in his platoon) of 225 were killed on Leyte. Another sixty died on Okinawa. Almost 119,000 U.S. troops participated in the invasion of Okinawa, of which 12,500 were killed and another 35,500 wounded.

When the atomic bombing of Hiroshima effectively signaled the war's end, Ensor was back on Leyte, preparing for another and far more terrible invasion that was never needed. Only twenty-two years old, the young corporal was discharged in January 1946 and returned to Baltimore, where he took a part-time job working in Monumental Life's Agency Department.

Left behind in the Pacific was a helmet with a hole in it. The enemy "was six feet away and a terrible shot." Ensor returned with memories, medals, a Presidential Unit Citation awarded to the 96th Infantry Division, of which he is most proud, and a Japanese flag covered with names and writing. Recovered on Leyte, the flag was returned to a Japanese family in an unusually emotional presentation in 1994. "It belonged to a 19-year old soldier (my age) whose body was never found," explains Ensor. "It was added to his grave and the family was finally at peace with his death."

Ensor's brief postwar experience at Monumental, which ended when he returned to Northwestern to complete his degree, left him with more than good feelings. By 1952 he was married to Betty Smith, an Actuarial Department employee, and back at Monumental working full-time in Underwriting. He retired in 1984, after rising to the rank of senior vice president.

James O'C. Gentry . . .
War's Bitter Reminders

In another time, another place, being an eighteen-year-old high school graduate and a draftee might have been viewed negatively, but not then, and surely not for James Gentry and many of his Baltimore classmates. "It was July of 1944, right after D-Day," Gentry recalls, "and it was a war we kids wanted to participate in. We were patriotic."

In the service by September, Gentry completed basic training and was shipped overseas as a rifleman in the 317th Infantry Regiment of the 80th Division. Arriving in France a few days after Christmas, he found himself thrown into the Battle of the Bulge (also called the Battle of the Ardennes). For six weeks ending on January 25, 1945, over a million men fought bitterly on the snow-covered slopes and forests near the German/Belgium/Luxembourg border. Gentry participated in a key breakthrough to relieve the 101st Airborne, which had been surrounded at Bastogne. That was his first taste of

battle. His worst battlefield experience—crossing the Rhine River by paddle boat under fire, landing, taking prisoners and moving forward with his regiment—came later.

His most unforgettable experience came near the war's end in 1945. "We were the first ones to liberate Dachau. I'll never forget entering the concentration camps and seeing the emaciated Jewish prisoners. So thin, just walking skeletons . . . horrible."

From there, Gentry's division continued on to Austria, where he served as part of the occupation forces. Discharged with the rank of staff sergeant in August 1946, he earned a Bronze Star and Combat Infantryman's Badge in service to his country.

But duty would call one more time. After returning home, going to college on the GI Bill and then to law school, Gentry was among tens of thousands of veterans recalled to active duty in Korea. This time, he did not see combat.

Although still patriotic, the thrill of "John Wayne shoot-'em-up movies" that had so excited him as a teenager had been tempered by wartime realities and the waiting world of marriage, family, and adult responsibilities. Following law school, Gentry worked in both public and private law practice before joining Monumental Life in 1960. He retired from his position as Monumental vice president, general counsel, and corporate secretary in 1993 after thirty-three years' service. He still does consulting work and lobbies in Annapolis on the company's behalf.

ABOVE: *Now in his eighties, Gentry is still proud to have served his country in World War II.*

LEFT: *Jim Gentry was just eighteen years old when he was drafted, trained as a rifleman, and sent to France in December 1944.*

WELCOME HOME!

World War II ended more abruptly than most Americans expected. Germany surrendered in May 1945. The destruction of Hiroshima and Nagasaki three months later broke Japan's fighting spirit and brought the war in the Pacific to a calamitous end.

On the home front, the Supreme Court had dropped a bomb of its own in June 1944, when it declared that insurance transactions conducted across state lines could be considered "interstate commerce" and thus were subject to federal antitrust regulations. Within a year, Congress enacted the McCarran-Ferguson Act, protecting the states' broad authority to regulate the business of insurance within their boundaries.

By the fall of 1945 the army was discharging GIs at a rate of a million per month. Over the next year or so, millions of servicemen on both fighting fronts packed up their duffel bags, boarded military transports, and headed home.

America welcomed its returning heroes with hugs and ticker tape parades. Waiting at home, proud wives and sweethearts were also proud of themselves. Many had worked during the war, moved in with family, deposited military allotment checks, and accumulated sizable bank accounts. Between 1942 and 1945, Americans saved $132 billion. Families and individuals earning less than $5,000 annually—including many Monumental employees and the company's lower- and middle-income target market —saved 45 percent ($59 billion) of that total.

During the same period, American families increased their life insurance holdings by $40 billion—about $1,000 per family. By war's end, Americans owned two-thirds of the world's life insurance and averaged $4,500 of coverage per family. With life insurance ranking fourth or fifth in most family budgets, the United States definitely earned its much-deserved reputation in those years as a "nation of savers."

Reunited with loved ones in 1945 and 1946, returning GIs were eager to begin families and buy houses, cars, radios and appliances. Before retaking their places in civilian life, however, thousands of veterans—including young men who had been drafted or who had enlisted right out of high school—had to find jobs.

In July 1943, President Roosevelt had recommended a six-point program to take care of men and women honorably discharged from the armed forces. The Servicemen's Readjustment Act of 1944 (better known as the "GI Bill") provided for free college or vocational training at the government's expense, up to fifty-two weeks of unemployment compensation at $20 per week, and low-interest zero-down payment loans to purchase homes and businesses.

Though the country experienced temporary unemployment and upheaval as industries scaled down production and released workers, the legislation helped prevent a much-feared depression. The majority of discharged servicemen found jobs or pursued higher education. So few veterans applied for the "52-20" mustering-out pay that less than 20 percent of the allocated budget was actually used. Even more important, by providing funds for education, home and business ownership, the GI Bill helped democratize the "American Dream" and enabled it to become a reality for a whole generation of veterans.

NATIONAL SERVICE LIFE INSURANCE

Before shipping overseas, more than 98 percent of enlisted men and 99 percent of officers had heeded the government's advice to purchase National Service Life Insurance (NSLI). By January 1944, 90 percent of all servicemen owned the maximum $10,000 of coverage, accounting for $100 billion of life insurance in force.

As buddies died beside them, America's GIs—whether young and single, or fathers with families back home—began to understand the purpose of life insurance. To a man, they also appreciated life, home and family more than their peers who had not gone off to war.

Even so, once back in the States, many veterans let their NSLI policies lapse or failed to convert them to permanent coverage. Anxious to get home after three or four years overseas, few paid attention to the options explained at their discharge centers.

In December 1945, more than 1,300 life insurance agents and managers gathered at the National Association of Life Underwriters (NALU) annual meeting in New York City to hear Gen. Omar Bradley explain why the government needed their help. "Despite counseling, speeches and booklets," he said, "early lapse rates show that the government alone is limited in its efforts to convince veterans of the peacetime advantages of lifetime protection by the insurance they held in service." Over the next year, receiving no commission and working only for "the public good," the nation's life insurance agents educated thousands of GIs and prevented the potential lapse of millions of dollars of NSLI. "To their credit, most of the old line life insurance companies have been urging veterans to keep their GI insurance and to reinstate policies which have lapsed," one reporter commented. "This enlightened attitude is especially encouraging at a time when self-interest seems to be the all-powerful influence in so many lines of endeavor."

Reminding employees in 1945 that "policyholder service is essential, fifty-two weeks a year," President Rock urged Monumental agents to focus on educating GIs and reestablishing contacts and relationships with families dislocated by the war. Sales teams returned to their assigned neighborhoods in full force to provide the face-to-face advice and service customers had come to expect.

ABOVE: *Ninety-eight percent of the U.S. armed forces serving in World War II purchased National Service Life Insurance before shipping overseas to Europe or the Pacific. Many kept their coverage for decades.*
(Courtesy of the National Association of Insurance and Financial Advisors)

JOB SECURITY

Before the first employee had left for basic training, Rock promised draftees they would have jobs after they were discharged. The company kept its promise. Despite the growing national concern about postwar cutbacks, wages, and unemployment, Monumental Life welcomed back all veterans. Many resumed their old jobs in the home office. Others took positions with equivalent responsibility and pay.

In 1946, approximately one hundred discharged veterans also returned to Monumental Life field offices. Remembering combat at sea and round-the-clock shifts on the front lines, they were thankful to be home and have jobs. Most were anxious to get back to work helping people. Mature, responsible and "seasoned" by the war, they could speak candidly and with conviction about life, death and the importance of protecting families, incomes and futures with life insurance.

Agent Robert Jones's son, Ron, remembers sitting in the car while his father called on customers in southern Maryland after the war. "It was hard work and Dad was very dedicated. Everyone paid weekly. Sometimes, people weren't home. Sometimes, they just didn't answer the door. We had to go back a few times to collect those premiums."

With no shortage of available manpower, managers who needed to fill open positions had many well-trained GIs and former military officers from which to choose. Perhaps feeling threatened by the growing numbers of returning veterans and eager young recruits, the company's less successful, lower-paid producers began to look to union representation as the answer to job security, better pay and guaranteed benefits.

AGENTS VOTE FOR UNIONS

Company-wide, the average Monumental agent earned $3,640 a year during the war. In more established, successful offices in Baltimore and other cities, agent pay

averaged closer to $4,500 a year. The company's sixty-one highest-paid agents earned $5,000 to $6,000.

Agent pay had created challenges for Monumental management for many years. The agent contract, though uniform from state to state, left room for interpretation. Agent earnings also depended on commission rates, which varied by product sold and mode of premium payment. Despite the company's effort to stabilize pay and standardize reports, routines and expectations, many agents resented the sales pressure put on them by managers whose pay was tied to their production.

As talk of agent "unionization" began in 1944, Monumental officers entered into negotiations with the American Federation of Labor (AFL) in Baltimore City and the Congress of Industrial Organizations (CIO) in Missouri. Insisting that efficient management in the field demanded uniformity, the company said it would not agree to any contract that provided a "favored situation" for any group, regardless of conditions or circumstances.

On September 4, 1944, Monumental Life's Baltimore agents selected the AFL as their bargaining agent by a vote of 55 to 52. On March 8, 1945, by a vote of 35 to 32, the agents in Missouri selected the CIO to represent their interests in negotiating working conditions, work hours and rates of pay. That summer, Ohio agents voted against joining the United Office and Professional Workers of America by a vote of 78 to 55.

Speaking for Monumental Life's officers and managers in August 1945, President Rock reported his belief that a union was "neither necessary, desirable nor beneficial" to agents, who could be better served by the Agency Force within the company. Moreover, Monumental had consistently worked to improve working conditions and compensation. The company was, he added, "vitally interested in the success and welfare" of each agent, because on them rested the future of the company. "It would be impossible for the company to climb to success upon the back of an underpaid, dissatisfied, inefficient field force."

By the 1940s, Baltimore Northeast agent Frank Deegan had walked city blocks for more than thirty years, carrying his debit book to collect weekly premiums and deliver "service with a smile."

By April 1946, a new commission contract had stabilized agent earnings and improved morale. With close to eight hundred agents, less than twelve "open" (unassigned) agent books of business, and fifty-eight field managers who averaged fifteen years of service each, Monumental Life's field force was stronger than ever. Management reported $42.6 million of increase for the first nine months of 1946—the best three quarters to date in the company's history—thanks to a record number of marriages in 1945 and the birth of America's first "Baby Boomers" in 1946. Since 1941 the company's agents had collected approximately $60 million in premiums—$16 million in 1946 alone.

Though agents in Philadelphia and Indiana also voted to unionize in 1946—and a significant number of agents would join unions and engage in a month-long paralyzing strike in 1947—union issues were overshadowed by President Rock's announcement in mid-1946 that the company had achieved a major milestone—$504,503,623 of life insurance in force!

HALF-BILLION DOLLAR CELEBRATION!

Having celebrated victory in 1945, Monumental Life employees were soon ready to celebrate again. May 1946 marked President Rock's twenty-fifth year with the company, his tenth as president. Since 1921, Monumental Life had grown from a small Maryland company to a large organization with fifty-eight branch offices in fourteen states. During those twenty-five years, the company's life insurance in force had also grown dramatically—from $35.2 million at the end of 1920 to just over a half-billion dollars on June 30, 1946.

To mark the milestone, the company scheduled a "Half-Billion Celebration" in Baltimore for the weekend of October 10–12, 1946. The festivities included a males-only "stag party," a dinner dance, tours of Annapolis and Washington, D.C., a football game, and a presentation announcing the company's new Retirement Program.

Attaining one-half billion of life insurance in force was primarily a "field man's triumph," wrote the *Old Black Hen* editors, but "management and all home office departments had their part to play." The celebration recognized everyone's contributions, helped build goodwill, and cemented relationships between the home office and the field. For one agent, a weekend highlight was examining the home office's exact duplicate of his collection book. For others, it was meeting face-to-face with people who previously had been only "names on a piece of paper."

Among those invited for the weekend were a number of "old timers" whose efforts, loyalty and perseverance over many years had contributed to the company's expansion and success. Also attending were many "young ones" on whose shoulders rested responsibility for the company's future growth. As field men left for home, an employee in the Controller's Department voiced what others may have been thinking. "Those of the new generation that we had the pleasure to meet left no doubt . . . that they could or would carry on in the tradition of the builders of the past."

BELOW: *Monumental Life celebrated a half-billion dollars of life insurance in force and President Leo Rock's twenty-fifth year of company service in 1946 with a celebration in Baltimore. A special sales campaign, planned by Agency Manager William H. Keidel (left) contributed to reaching the half-billion dollar goal.*

CHAPTER 8

Postwar Prosperity, Growth, Opportunity
(1946–1959)

FACING PAGE: *Peace, prosperity and patriotism reigned in the years immediately following World War II, which also saw the first wave of the "Baby Boom."*

ALBERT is more fortunate than many GIs who served overseas during World War II. Uninjured in combat, he arrives home knowing his job at the gas and electric company is waiting for him. He returns to work, but not before he and his wife take a much delayed honeymoon. Their first child, a daughter, is conceived during that month-long, cross-country drive. She is the first of the couple's four "Baby Boomer" children born between 1946 and 1954.

In 1949, Al and Fran buy a two-story colonial house in a new place, called the suburbs. Cutting the pickets for a white wooden fence himself, the proud new homeowner encloses his prized quarter-acre. He plants vegetables and fruit trees, builds a grape arbor, and puts in a concrete patio. Wearing an apron and "housedress," Fran cans and freezes what they grow in their garden.

Growing up in the Fifties, Al and Fran's children wear cowboy outfits, take ballet and piano lessons, listen to rock 'n roll, and join Little League teams coached by their dad. On hot summer days they run through the sprinkler, play "hide 'n seek," buy ice cream from the Good Humor man, and ride bicycles on traffic-free streets. The development is called Ridgewood Acres by its builder, but the neighborhood's young homeowners appropriately nickname it "Bunny Hollow." During the school year, dozens of children catch the yellow school bus on the corner. In overcrowded classrooms, they learn to read with "Dick and Jane."

After homework and dinner, which they all eat together, the family gathers in front of a small, seven-inch black and white TV screen to watch their favorite shows—Howdy Doody, I Love Lucy, Father Knows Best, Leave it to Beaver, the Mickey Mouse Club, Gunsmoke and the Ed Sullivan Show. Fran is shocked when a hip-swiveling Elvis appears before screaming teenage fans during "family" viewing time one Sunday evening in 1957.

Life is good. Albert and his family don't want for much, but he watches every penny. He rarely calls in a repairman to fix what he can do himself. Equally resourceful, Fran sews clothes for the girls and darns Al's socks. The family's first new car is a Plymouth station wagon. On summer evenings, getting "take out" and going to "drive-in" movies are special treats. So is staying in a motel when they travel. To save money, at least two of the kids always curl up in sleeping bags on the floor.

ABOVE: *Like many children growing up just after the war, Walter Weiss, future Monumental Life treasurer, enjoyed playing "cowboy."*

ABOVE: *Fran and Al moved into their new suburban home in 1949, shortly before their third "Boomer" baby was born.*

Every Tuesday evening, Albert puts on his officer's uniform and drives to weekly meetings of his Army Reserve unit. For almost twenty years, he attends camp for two weeks every summer. Asked why by co-workers and friends, he replies: "It's my second career . . . extra money today and income for the future." When Albert retires with the rank of captain in 1965, his military pension is larger than the one he will eventually receive from the gas and electric company.

As a "meter reader" in the Fifties, Albert walks city and suburban streets and enters hundreds of lower and middle-class homes. Like Monumental's career agents, he sees a cross-section of American life every day. He empathizes with young families struggling to qualify for mortgages, buy homes, pay bills, and keep their kids in clothes and shoes. From his years in the army, he has seen a lot of the world and knows how to deal with all kinds of people. In civilian life, he appreciates what he has and does all he can to protect it. He continues to "give back"—as a member of the Veterans of Foreign Wars, as a neighborhood association board member, and as a church usher and volunteer.

Like many men back from the war, Albert expects no handouts. He "likes Ike" and votes for General Dwight D. Eisenhower, his World War II hero, in the 1952 and 1956 presidential elections. He takes advantage of the peacetime prosperity of the 1950s to create a better life for himself and his young family. Though he never uses the GI Bill or graduates from college himself, Albert completes dozens of scholarship forms for his children, and all four go to college. Even after he retires in 1975, he continues to save. When his grandchildren leave for college in the 1990s, he helps pay their tuition bills.

At his death in 2003 at age ninety-two, Albert leaves his lifetime savings and the house he bought for $13,000 in 1949 to his four children, who are thankful for a father whose resourcefulness and sense of responsibility gave them a good life and helped secure their own futures. Albert's oldest daughter became a Monumental Life policyholder in 1985. His oldest granddaughter and her husband married in 1994 and bought their first policy from a Monumental Life agent in 1995.

BOOMERS BORN, SUBURBS GROW

Returning World War II veterans wasted no time getting on with their lives. Beginning in 1946 they married, had babies (in that order!), and bought homes in unprecedented numbers. In 1947 alone, the U.S. population grew by 3.75 million, as new mothers gave birth to ten thousand "Baby Boomers" every twenty-four hours. Between 1950 and 1959, twenty-nine million more babies were born.

"Think of it!" wrote the editor of Monumental Life's *Old Black Hen* in 1954: "By this time tomorrow, there will be 11,000 more crying needs for a future with security. . . . New families, new homes, new babies—a natural combination and market for the alert life insurance field man."

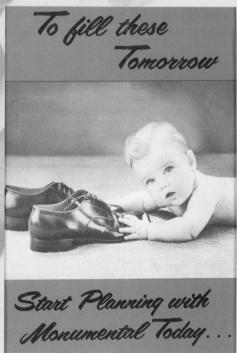

To fill these Tomorrow

Start Planning with Monumental Today . . .

Monumental aimed this ad at "Boomer" parents.

Construction boomed along with birth rates in the postwar years. Couples dreamed of raising kids on tree-lined streets in the suburbs. Houses replaced farms and open fields. As suburban neighborhoods grew, so did the need for roads and highways, schools, churches, shopping centers, suburban businesses and industrial parks.

Rationing was over, and a new generation of American middle-class "commuters" bought cars to drive to work and TVs, radios, washing machines, refrigerators, and other appliances to furnish their new homes. The economy grew to keep pace with increasing consumer demand. Although the U.S. accounted for just 6 percent of the world's population during the 1950s, Americans produced and consumed a third of the planet's goods and services.

In Baltimore and around the country, most Americans had jobs and steady incomes. Thanks to the GI Bill, veterans could complete technical training, earn college degrees and move into higher-paying positions. During the 1948–49 academic year, for example, 70 percent of all undergraduates at the Johns Hopkins University in Baltimore were ex-servicemen. The conversion from coal and oil to gas and electric-powered heat and air-conditioning increased the demand for home heating and plumbing contractors, but opportunities were endless in all walks of life. By 1956, one-third of U.S. workers were women. Even so, 90 percent of the "Baby Boomers" born between 1946 and 1959 had stay-at-home moms.

In September 1956 the Institute of Life Insurance reported that more than 18.9 million of the 52.2 million American households earned between $5,000 and $10,000 a year. Another 14.7 million had household income in the $3,000 to $5,000 range. Buying, but still not extravagantly, these children of the Depression managed their hard-won

prosperity carefully. They seemed to have a "natural resistance to conspicuous consumption," wrote journalist Tom Brokaw in *The Greatest Generation.* "Moderation was as important as faithful marriages, well-behaved kids, and going to church."

Couples used wartime savings to pay cash or "charged" their purchases using the country's first multi-vendor "credit cards," introduced in 1950. With twice as much spending power as they had in 1940—and influenced by television ads that promoted all kinds of new products—young mothers bought "Speedy" Alka Seltzer to sooth upset stomachs, Campbell Soup because it was "mm . . . mm . . . good," frozen TV dinners and Pillsbury "Doughboy" biscuits to simplify their lives.

On May 7, 1947, the first stand-alone suburban shopping center on the East Coast opened on Baltimore's west side, near the Baltimore County line. Built by Joseph Meyerhoff and his brother Jacob, Edmondson Village Shopping Center was clearly a sign of the times. By 1949 it included off-street parking for dozens of cars, a department store, twenty-nine smaller shops, a movie theater, a bowling alley, and a clubhouse for community activities.

ABOVE LEFT: *World War II veterans got married, began families, purchased homes and bought furniture and household appliances.*
(Courtesy of the National Association of Insurance and Financial Advisors)

ABOVE RIGHT: *Edmondson Village, built in 1947 by the Meyerhoff family on Baltimore's west side, was a sign of the times.*
(Courtesy of the Maryland Historical Society)

BELOW: *Parents in the 1950s expected their children to be well-behaved. Families still ate dinner together and dressed in their "Sunday best" for church services.*

Families could make bank deposits, shop for groceries, get haircuts, be entertained, meet friends, and buy shoes for their children, all in one place.

During the 1950s, the Meyerhoffs also built Eastpoint Shopping Center on Baltimore's east side, Hillendale Shopping Center in north Baltimore, and Westview Mall—anchored by Hutzler's and Stewart's department stores. The drive from the suburbs to these shopping centers became even easier as the state opened the Harbor Tunnel, the Baltimore "Beltway" (Interstate 695), the Chesapeake Bay Bridge, the Baltimore-Washington Parkway, and sections of Interstate 95. These projects were completed just in time to handle the thousands of cars filled with football and baseball fans headed to Baltimore's Memorial Stadium beginning in 1953 and 1954 to cheer for the Colts and Orioles. In many ways, both major league teams gave the local economy a bigger boost than any building project.

SPLIT LEVELS AND "SLABS"

BELOW: The opening of the Chesapeake Bay Bridge shortened the drive between Baltimore and Maryland's Eastern Shore and beaches.

Builders like Joseph Meyerhoff and the James Keelty Company made significant contributions to the growth of Baltimore's suburbs. By the 1950s, both had strong track records in the construction business.

RIGHT: The Meyerhoffs built and sold hundreds of small "slab-on-grade" homes, like this one in Woodcroft, to young Baltimore couples in the 1950s.

Keelty began building Baltimore rowhouses at the end of the nineteenth century when the electrification of streetcars brought potential homebuyers to the western edge of the city. He developed most of the rowhouse communities on the west side between the two world wars.

After he died in 1948, the Keelty Company expanded into Baltimore County, where it built rowhouse and detached-house neighborhoods in suburban Catonsville and Towson.

The Meyerhoff family had begun building rowhouses and apartments in northeast and northwest Baltimore in the 1920s and 1930s. After World War II, they focused on large-scale residential developments in the Dundalk-Essex

area on Baltimore's east side. Their first detached, single-family houses appeared in 1954. One model, called a "slab-on-grade," had no basement. "You could build it faster and at less cost," explained Harvey M. ("Bud") Meyerhoff, Joseph's son. These were "important considerations in those house-hungry, postwar years. Within six weeks we sold 180 of them!" A typical three-bedroom, slab-on-grade house sold for $8,600 plus ground rent.*

The Meyerhoffs, explains Bud, also built some of the area's first split-level houses:

> We bought a big tract of land on the west side of town, named it Westview Park, and put up split-level houses as well as slab-on-grades. Split-levels were all the rage in the '50s; we had phenomenal success with them. . . . The question was, could we produce enough to satisfy all the customers? It was a challenging but wonderful time in terms of sales and fighting to keep up production.

Many builders and realtors throughout the country no doubt experienced similar success in those postwar years as returning veterans looked for safe, less congested neighborhoods in which to raise their kids.

Bud Meyerhoff had joined the family business in 1948 after being discharged from the U.S. Navy and graduating from college. Married the same year, he and his wife, Lyn, had four children in the 1950s. When they were ready to build a home in 1953, Bud came to Monumental Life for a mortgage loan. The Meyerhoffs knew Monumental

---

* "Ground rent" refers to the money some Baltimore and Maryland homeowners pay to lease the land beneath their houses from a person, charity or business. Leases are written for terms of ninety-nine years, renewable forever, though homeowners can buy out most ground rents at the time they purchase their houses under terms specified in a state law. The concept of ground rent dates back to 1632, when King Charles I of England gave the second Lord Baltimore all the land that is now Maryland. Lord Baltimore charged rent to colonists who wanted to build on his land. After the American Revolution, the Maryland legislature empowered landholders to demand rent. In the late nineteenth century, developers created ground rents to make the purchase of rowhouses more affordable for working people. Homeowners who pay ground rent own their houses but not the land.

well because the life insurer had purchased many of the Meyerhoff's ground rents* for its investment portfolio. From these early contacts grew a prosperous partnership between Monumental Life and the Meyerhoff family.

MORTGAGES IN THE INVESTMENT 'MIX'

In 1946, the best sales year to date in Monumental Life's history, total admitted assets increased $7.4 million—to $78.9 million. Though the war was over, government securities still constituted 73.7 percent of the company's investment portfolio. Another 10.4 percent was invested in railroad, utility and industrial bonds. That same year, the company's mortgage loans also increased dramatically—from $3,396,000 to $9,295,000—to reach 12.8 percent of invested assets.

Even so, Monumental's directors wanted to increase the portfolio's yield—then just 2.5 percent and .4 percent below the industry average—and capture a larger share of the mortgages guaranteed by the Servicemen's Readjustment Act of 1944. In 1946 they authorized the Investment Committee to appoint mortgage correspondents in Maryland and other states. Representing the company, the correspondents acquired and serviced loans and signed forms required by the Federal Housing Administration (FHA) and the Veterans Administration (VA) to secure the government's home mortgage guarantee and insurance for returning veterans.

This initiative increased mortgage loans to $13.3 million—15.4 percent of

BELOW: *During the prosperous post-war building boom, Monumental's investment in home mortgages also boomed.*

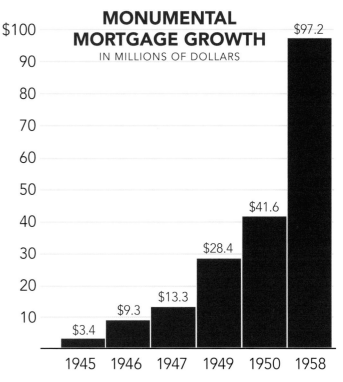

MONUMENTAL MORTGAGE GROWTH
IN MILLIONS OF DOLLARS

1945	$3.4
1946	$9.3
1947	$13.3
1949	$28.4
1950	$41.6
1958	$97.2

the company's invested assets—during 1947. One loan, for $8,500 at 4 percent interest, was approved for Monumental Secretary Frank Baker, Jr., and his wife Miriam. Having served in the navy during World War II, Baker was eligible for a home mortgage under the GI Bill. The VA appraised the land and house at $10,450 and guaranteed the mortgage for $4,000.

As the suburbs grew, so did the company's investment in home mortgage and construction loans. By the end of 1949, the value of mortgages held by Monumental Life had more than doubled to $28.4 million and included one $285,000 loan for the construction of the Tidewater Inn in Easton, Maryland. The mortgage portfolio accounted for 38 percent of the company's invested assets on March 31, 1951, and by 1954 was large enough to justify creating a separate Mortgage Loan Department that reported to Executive Vice President Fred Wehr and the Investment Committee. By 1958, the portfolio had grown to $97.2 million with ten thousand loans averaging $9,700.

It is interesting to note that, although Monumental Life operated in fourteen states during those years, 50 percent of its mortgages were in the Baltimore area. The city and its surrounding suburbs were home to many diversified and expanding industries—including the federal government, the largest single "industry" in the state. Jobs were plentiful, houses were affordable and contractors were building neighborhoods to meet the growing demand. Investing in the suburban building boom made good sense.

A 'COLD WAR' TURNS HOT

As young couples built homes and moved to the suburbs, the U.S. government was helping its former enemies in Europe rebuild cities, towns and economies destroyed by the war.

In a speech to Congress on March 12, 1947, President Harry S Truman outlined the Truman Doctrine, which committed the U.S. to protect nations threatened by communism. Three months later, Secretary of State George C. Marshall called for an American plan to begin recovery efforts in Europe. The resulting Marshall Plan, sent more than $13 billion in aid to war-torn Europe between 1948 and 1951.

In 1948 a Soviet-backed Communist coup in Czechoslovakia signaled the start of a "Cold War" between communism and the free world that would demand international attention for four decades. Just four months later, the Soviets triggered a crisis in Berlin by closing off that divided city from the West. On June 29, 1948, Truman approved a British request for joint military planning of an airlift to provide relief. The ultimately successful "Berlin Airlift" was born. For 318 days, U.S. and British cargo planes and pilots, based in England and averaging 625 flights per day, delivered millions of tons of much-needed food and supplies to the city.

But the first real test of the Truman Doctrine would come nearly half a world away from Berlin. On June 25, 1950, Communist-backed North Korea invaded South Korea in an attempt to force reunification of that country, which had been divided along the 38th parallel since 1945. The invasion caught the U.S. by surprise and triggered an immediate response from the United Nations. Initiating a "police action" against the aggressors, military units from the U.S. and other western countries scrambled to contain North Korea's fast-moving army and answer a threat viewed globally as a Communist challenge to the world.

Once again, Americans quickly mobilized to respond. World War II ships, aircraft and military equipment were pulled out of "mothballs," put back into service, and sent to Korea. American industry retooled and increased production to meet military needs. Reserve units recalled or put on alert tens of thousands of eligible, well-trained men.

The first U.S. servicemen sent to Korea arrived from Japan under the command of Gen. Douglas MacArthur. Over the next three years, the U.S. committed 480,000 soldiers, sailors, airmen, and marines to the conflict. By July 1953, 33,686 had been killed in battle, 103,000 had been wounded, and 8,142 had been reported missing in action.

Meredith Darlington . . .
Flying the Berlin Airlift

Airman Meredith Darlington participated in the 1948 Berlin Airlift.

As World War II ended and millions of Americans enjoyed peacetime wealth and prosperity, trouble appeared again on the global horizon. A new war, a Cold War, was heating up as two superpowers, the United States and the Soviet Union, threatened one another over the city of Berlin. For some historians, the defining start in the Cold War was the Berlin Airlift, which began on June 27, 1948 and did not end until May 12, 1949.

Future Monumental Life employee Meredith Darlington remembers. He was there.

Joining the air force in 1947 at age seventeen, Darlington completed basic training, went to radio operators school, and was assigned to a little airfield in Correopolis, Pennsylvania, for ROTC pilot training. "I remember being awakened at 5 a.m. one morning," recalls the former airman. "I was told to pack my bags because the Russians had blocked off the city of Berlin and I was going to Germany that same day."

Another world war was looming and radio operators, especially those with their Class 1 certification like Darlington, were needed on flights in and out of Germany. He remembers exciting times flying C-47s in the early days of the massive airlift and later the larger C-54 cargo planes. Still later, he was assigned to USAFE (U.S. Air Force in Europe) headquarters in Wiesbaden, Germany. From there, he traveled to Europe and North Africa. "You never knew where your daily assignments would take you," he says, recalling one bumpy landing in a field in the Italian Alps when a C-47's engine caught fire. He also fondly remembers his elation when first assigned to fly on a C-82, the famous "Flying Boxcars" built in Hagerstown, his hometown, by Fairchild Engine and Airplane Corporation. He would later return to Hagerstown to work at Fairchild, one of several jobs that preceded the start of his long career at Monumental Life.

A year after first landing in Europe, Darlington returned home to Wright-Patterson Air Force Base near Dayton, Ohio. Pending reassignment, the young lieutenant hitchhiked home to Hagerstown every weekend to see his sweetheart until he was reassigned to an Air Force base in Riverside, California. After six months there, he was discharged.

"I called Doris, got on a bus and crossed the country to come home," he says. "We were married on November 18, 1950."

Proud to have served his country during a major world crisis—"we backed the Russians down in Berlin"—Darlington returned to civilian life with strong feelings of patriotism. He served Monumental Life as a successful agent and field investigator in the Auditing Department for thirty years.

LEFT: *The U.S. sent 480,000 troops to Korea in the early 1950s to halt the spread of communism.* (Courtesy of the Truman Library)

In January 1951, William G. Barrett, Jr., Monumental Life's first Korean War "draftee" and an employee in the home office Supply Department, received his notice to report to Fort Meade, Maryland, where he was assigned to the Quartermaster Corps. One month later, Ernest "Bud" Mayr, a data processing specialist and army reservist, was called into active duty. His Monumental softball teammates would miss his .571 batting average that season.

Leo Gugerty, a security analyst in the Investment Department, left on May 23, 1952, for a two-year hitch. After nine months in the navy during World War II, Gugerty had returned home, attended the Johns Hopkins University, and signed up for the Reserve Officers Training Corps (ROTC). He graduated in 1950 with both a degree and his commission as a second lieutenant in the air force. Because of his limited active duty in World War II, he was still eligible for additional service in Korea when war broke out.

Duty also beckoned again for Wylie Hopkins. Drafted immediately after college graduation in 1942, Hopkins completed Officer Candidate School, was commissioned into the Quartermaster Corps as a second lieutenant, and spent much of the next four years on cargo ships crossing oceans. Recalled from the army reserves in 1951, he pinned his first lieutenant's bars and Transportation Corps "Wheel" onto his officer's uniform and returned to active duty.

After a year stateside, Hopkins found himself flying to Puson, where he would serve as a Cargo Accountability Officer. Ensuring the safety of vitally needed supplies was hard work, important work. He was thankful, however, that he was twenty-five miles and one mountain range removed from the bitter cold and snow that was then making the lives of frontline combat troops miserable.

Hopkins returned home in 1953. Already a CPA, he worked for an accounting firm for a year, then joined the company's Investment Department. He retired from Monumental Life with twenty-seven years' service in 1981.

Between 1950 and 1952, U.S. life insurance companies

ABOVE: *World War II veteran Wylie Hopkins also served in Korea before joining Monumental's Investment Department in 1954.*

paid $16 million in Korean War death claims on approximately 13,000 life insurance policies. The figure represented just one-half of one percent of the total death benefits paid by the industry for that two-year period. The death toll in Korea would have been much higher had it not been for advances in battlefield medical services such as the Mobile Army Surgical Hospital, popularized in the movie and TV show M*A*S*H, and the use of helicopters to transport the wounded. Only 2.6 patients of every hundred who reached hospital units close to the front subsequently died.

BLOOD FOR OUR BOYS

As fighting escalated in Korea, President Truman designated the American Red Cross as the nation's official blood collection agency and called upon the American people to help the Red Cross meet wartime needs. During some of the heaviest fighting in 1952, the Red Cross collected and processed 300,000 pints of blood and blood plasma every month. Between 1950 and 1953 the American people donated five million pints of blood, which the Red Cross shipped to U.S. armed forces overseas.

Responding to the president's call for help, Monumental Life's officers invited the Red Cross to conduct "Blood for Our Boys" donation drives at the company's home office. Volunteers hung Red Cross banners and parked a Red Cross mobile unit on Chase Street. One employee vividly remembered the first of these blood donor days:

> Promptly at 8:30 a.m. on September 5th the Baltimore Chapter of the American Red Cross moved its mobile unit to the Home Office and set up its equipment in the auditorium. By 9:30 they were ready to take donations from the many Monumental employees who had signed up to give blood for the high purpose of "saving a soldier's life." The unit was complete with supervising physicians and nurses in attendance who were kept on the job until late in the afternoon.

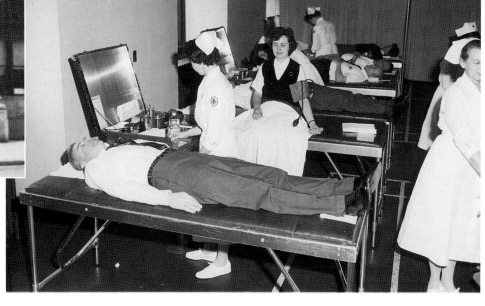

Vice President Fred Wehr, chairman of Baltimore City's 1953 Red Cross Fund Appeal, got busy and enthusiastically went around the neighborhood calling attention to the fact that the unit was at Monumental for the day. His efforts brought in donors from a number of our neighbors.

One hundred and ten Monumental home office and Baltimore branch office employees, plus forty-one neighborhood employees, rolled up their sleeves that day and donated 151 pints of blood. Earlier that year, employees had also participated in First Aid training conducted by the Red Cross and had responded generously to the company's annual fund-raising drive. With a total donation of $2,360 they achieved 105 percent of that year's goal.

In 1952 alone, the American Red Cross used $38.4 million in donated funds to provide emergency flights home, battlefield counseling, and delivery of messages, food, and supplies to U.S. servicemen and their families. When the fighting in Korea ended in 1953, the Red Cross also helped secure the smooth release and exchange of nearly 12,000 prisoners of war held by the Communists.

Since its founding by Clara Barton in 1881, the American Red Cross had provided national and international disaster relief and served as the intermediary between members of the armed forces and their families in time of war. It more than proved its value at home and overseas during World War II and the Korean Conflict. As a result, in 1952, one of every four U.S. citizens—including hundreds of Monumental employees—were card-carrying Red Cross members, and one of every ninety citizens was an active volunteer.

GIVING BACK

The American Red Cross was just one of many civic and charitable organizations that Monumental Life and its employees supported during the postwar years. Early in the decade the company's stockholders had authorized the board of directors to make "reasonable gifts or contributions out of profits to or for the use of any corporation, trust, community chest, fund, foundation, society or other organization for religious, charitable, civic, scientific, literary or educational purposes."

By 1952—when the Executive Committee approved its first official "contributions" budget of $11,780—the list of recipients included the American Cancer Society, the Associated Jewish Charities of Baltimore, Catholic Charities, the Community Chest of Baltimore, the Heart Association of Maryland, the March of Dimes, the Mental Health Fund, and United Fund appeals in many of the cities where we had field offices. In 1956 additional health-focused organizations such as the Arthritis and Rheumatism Foundation, the Maryland Tuberculosis Society, the National Multiple Sclerosis Society, and the Maryland Children's Aid Society were added to the growing list.

ABOVE: *Monumental responded to President Truman's call for "Blood for Our Boys" fighting in Korea by inviting the Red Cross to conduct its first on-site blood drive at the home office.*

Americans liked Ike, but they loved Lucy!! TV personalities Lucille Ball and Desi Arnaz were so popular in the Fifties that they became spokespersons for the decade's March of Dimes campaigns, to which Monumental employees contributed generously.

These corporate gifts were often supplemented by individual donations from employees. During the 1959 Community Chest–Red Cross United Appeal, for example, the corporate contribution of $19,335 included $930 from home office clerical employees, $4,048 from managers and officers, $1,481 from district offices, and $12,875 from the company.

Directors also approved significant contributions to the Baltimore Symphony Orchestra, the Baltimore Museum of Art, the Johns Hopkins University, Goucher College, Loyola College, the College of Notre Dame of Maryland, area hospitals and their building funds, and such efforts as Junior Achievement and the Baltimore YWCA's "Building for Youth" Program.

The Depression and World War II had taught the company, its employees and all Americans important lessons about sacrifice, giving, volunteering and working together to help those in need. Thankful for jobs and decent wages in the prosperous postwar economy, the men and women who lived through the war also became the country's first generation of real givers and "joiners."

Veterans signed up for the reserves, marched proudly in parades, and met regularly with buddies at V.F.W. and American Legion halls in their communities. Looking to "give back" to the folks back home who had kept life going while they were away, GIs joined church and service organizations in unprecedented numbers. As members of the Kiwanis, the Rotary, the Elks, the Lions, the Knights of Columbus, the Masons, and their local Chambers of Commerce, they helped and supported small businessmen, disabled veterans, school children and the elderly.

Women also met in church basements to roll bandages for the Red Cross and dressings for the American Cancer Society. Men and women joined volunteer fire and ambulance units in the suburbs. New homeowners attended social events planned by their neighborhood associations. More than ever before, parents also got involved in their children's schools through local Parent-Teacher Associations and organized the country's first Little League teams.

Like America's "Greatest Generation" . . .

Monumental Life Became a Joiner

DURING THE PROSPERITY of the postwar 1940s and 1950s, Monumental Life's officers and executives copied the behavior of many returning veterans by becoming dues-paying members of many new and established civic, professional, and insurance industry organizations. As "joiners," they benefited from these memberships and gave back to the following organizations by contributing ideas and sharing their expertise:

American Arbitration Society
American College of Life Underwriters
American Institute of Management
American Life Convention
Association of Life Insurance Medical Directors
Baltimore Association of Commerce
Baltimore Life Underwriters Association
Baltimore Safety Council
Better Business Bureau
Chamber of Commerce of the U.S.
Citizens Planning and Housing Association of Baltimore
Cooperative Fund for Underwriter Training
Greater Baltimore Committee
Home Builders Association of Maryland
Institute of Home Office Underwriters
Institute of Life Insurance
International Claim Association
Life Insurance Agency Management Association
Life Insurance Association of America
Life Insurers Conference
Life Office Management Association
Life Insurance Medical Research Fund
Middle Atlantic Life Insurance Medical Directors Club
Mortgage Bankers Association of America
Real Estate Board of Baltimore
S. S. Huebner Foundation for Life Insurance Education
Society of Actuaries

LEFT: *The company's Rocklowe Social Club organized badminton tournaments for employees during the 1940s and 1950s. Played in the company's all-purpose auditorium, the matches attracted male and female players and spectators.*

BADMINTON . . . BOWLING . . . BARN DANCES . . . BINGO!

The desire to belong also carried into the workplace. At the height of World War II, when so many men were overseas, Monumental Life's board of directors created the Rocklowe Social Club—named after President Leo Rock and Vice President F. Harold Loweree—to plan and support social and athletic activities that would bring employees together and take their minds off the war. Families were dislocated, life was disrupted, and money was scarce. Officers decided to give everyone the benefit of a little fun!

When the club organized a duckpin bowling league in 1944, fifty home office and local field employees signed up. "Duckpins"—played with a smaller ball and shorter, fatter targets than "ten pins"—had been born in Baltimore at the turn of the century. With 75,000 people playing on duckpin teams in the 1940s, it was one of the city's most popular pastimes. A few months later, officers announced "the badminton courts are in and ready for play!" Retiree Mary Rose Miller, hired in 1958, remembers that employees were still playing badminton when she arrived. Before and after work hours, men and women, managers and clerks—including twelve to fifteen "regulars"—put on tennis shoes and shorts to play in mixed doubles tournaments before cheering co-workers in the fifth floor auditorium. Stopping by one evening, President Rock noted that there seemed to be "considerable interest in both activities."

LOWER LEFT: *One of Monumental's "all girl" duckpin bowling teams in 1946.*

LOWER RIGHT: *In 1957, more than forty employees bowled regularly with Monumental's bowling league.*

RIGHT: *Employees also played on the company's softball teams for more than thirty years. Pictured are the men's team from the late 1950s and the women's team in 1964.*

Clare Nardini, hired as Fred Wehr's secretary in 1935, had an important role on the badminton courts. "I was exactly five feet tall," she remembers, "and they called me to measure the net height before every tournament!"

The men's softball team played regularly on spring and summer evenings beginning in the 1950s. Employees also signed up for ping-pong, card parties, bingo and boat trips. They looked forward to annual holiday dances, spring barn dances, and summer picnics—all funded by the Rocklowe Social Club. The summer picnic, which included swimming, food, games and prizes for children as well as adults, was one of the highlights of the year.

The spring dance was also popular. In 1951 it marked the first performance of the Monumental Glee Club.

"Only recently organized," noted the *Old Black Hen*, "the group has made splendid progress under the capable leadership of Frank Baker, Jr. and Donald Weeks." The same evening, Baker joined Bill Ahrens, Tom Carroll, and Actuary George Immerwahr for a barbershop quartet medley that included "Let Me Call You Sweetheart" and "On Top of Old Smoky." The Rocklowe Ridge Runners square dance group also performed, "dressed in hillbilly costumes . . . and not missing a step." The group included Underwriting Manager Al Huegelmeyer and "represented almost every Home Office position from clerk up to vice president."

RIGHT & LOWER LEFT: *Company dances, bingo and card parties were well-attended throughout the 1950s and 1960s.*

RIGHT: *The spring dance in 1951 marked the debut of the Monumental Glee Club.*

LIKE A FAMILY

Company-sponsored social events and athletic activities helped solidify the sense of "family" that developed at Monumental Life during the 1950s. Employees worked together during the day and frequently got together to socialize in the evening. One group of female friends, for example, dressed up and went "downtown" after work every Thursday for dinner and an evening of shopping.

Officers actively participated in social events and knew most employees by their first names. Many managers had progressed through the ranks and worked side-by-side with the same group of employees for decades. Even so, titles, appearances and position mattered, and every employee knew his or her place.

Like most families in those days, the men were clearly in charge, and it was still very much a man's world. The officers, all men, ate together in the executive dining room and were always referred to as "Mr. Rock," "Mr. Loweree," and "Mr. Wehr." Men over fifty were encouraged to take daily afternoon naps to reduce stress and become rejuvenated for the rest of the day. Interestingly, their "girls" kept working, at less than half the pay. The company even provided a quiet "nap room," complete with reclining lounge chairs. Managers signed up for regular half-hour slots and instructed secretaries not to make any appointments at these times. Missed naps could not be made up!

The atmosphere in the office was precise, professional, cautious and quite paternalistic. Like fathers, management made all the decisions, tightly controlled the purse strings, and watched expenses closely. Employees in clerical and administrative positions were paid weekly in cash—similar to children receiving an allowance—while managers and officers, who presumably knew better how to manage their money, were paid monthly.

ABOVE: *Underwriting manager Al Huegelmeyer (at left) leads the Rocklowe Ridge Runners in a lively square dance. Groups of employees, like these costumed couples, also entertained at spring dances. (Note the badminton court painted on the all-purpose auditorium floor in all photos.)*

BELOW: *In the decade following World War II, Actuarial Department employees worked side-by-side, each with his or her own adding machine.*

RIGHT: *F. Harold Loweree was elected president of Monumental Life in 1953.*

When a 1941 survey of telephone usage revealed that 44 percent of incoming and 37 percent of outgoing home office calls were personal—38 percent of them to drug stores and restaurants—management put a pay phone on the first floor, charged five cents per call for personal calls, and restricted long distance dialing.

ABOVE: *For decades, many departments were set up like classrooms, with managers seated at desks facing their "classes."*

Margaret Curran managed her Weekly Premium Accounting Department of thirty-five or more employees like a "tight ship," remembers retiree Ann Moreland. "She timed rest room breaks and handed out new pencils only when an old one was turned in!" Walking into many departments in those years, visitors might have thought they were back in school. Metal desks were arranged in rows with the department manager sitting, like a teacher, near the front of his or her "class."

Even so, employees, especially those in the home office, remember feeling cared about and well cared for in those years. Few considered leaving the company, and it was not unusual for employees to work in the same department for thirty, forty or more years. "If you did your job and kept your nose clean," said one retiree, "your career was secure, and you received regular raises and promotions."

ROCK RETIRES, LOWEREE ELECTED TO LEAD MONUMENTAL

President Leo Rock was one of many Monumental Life employees to prove himself, rise through the ranks, and stay with the company for more than thirty years. His leadership was based on firsthand knowledge and experience gained as an agent, district manager, home office manager, and corporate vice president. When he retired in 1953, Rock turned over responsibility for the company's future success to another company veteran, F. Harold Loweree, who had joined the company in 1927.

An "expert accountant," Loweree had no knowledge of life insurance when he arrived at Monumental Life. During the 1930s, he learned the business through hard work, study and frequent visits to the field. Promoted to assistant secretary, with total responsibility for the company's accounting system, he revamped home office and field accounting practices, eliminated unnecessary overhead expenses, and set up an efficient accounting system that was used for decades.

A conscientious officer, Loweree nonetheless did not believe in "all work and no play." He was an avid sailor and sailboat racer who spent many weekends on the Chesapeake Bay with his family and friends. Loweree and Leo Rock, partners in founding the company's Rocklowe Social Club, also co-owned a sailboat named *Pabineau.*

Shortly after being elected president and chairman of the board on March 16, 1953, Loweree noted his responsibilities and obligations to the hundreds of dedicated men and women who then composed "the fine organization which we call the "Monumental Family":

It is a successful family, and a happy one. My obligation to you is to keep it so, and that I intend to do. Our company as it is today is not the result of the efforts of just one or two individuals, or even of a small group, but rather it is the sum total of the efforts of each and every one of you in the entire organization. Our present position of importance in the field of life insurance is the result of your combined efforts, your loyalty, and, during your years of service, the contributions you have made to our progress, each according to your ability.

Because this is true, there is no necessity for any sweeping reforms or major changes in our ways of doing business. We shall carry on as usual. I am confident that a continuation of the spirit of cooperation and team work which is so characteristic of our company, is all that is needed to insure our continued progress, and a happy and successful future.

As a director and member of the Executive Committee, Loweree had helped secure for employees many valuable benefits that tied them tightly to the company and gave them reasons to continue contributing to its success.

BENEFITS

The days when directors approved employee medical expenses and retirement stipends individually for each employee—based on perceived loyalty, contributions and years of service—were definitely over by the end of the war. Starting in 1941, the company began to introduce defined benefit programs that applied to entire groups of home office and field employees.

All home office employees with fifteen or more years of service received an extra week of "winter vacation" in 1941. The same year, the company introduced its first retirement plan, followed by free lunch in 1943 and Muzak piped into home office departments in 1945. By the time most World War II veterans were back on the job in January 1947, the company had a comprehensive retirement program provided by the Equitable Life Assurance Society of the United States. From a cost and benefits perspective, directors agreed that it offered the best value for the money for both the company and employees.

The first employee to benefit from the new retirement program was William J. Leimkuhler, who had joined the company as a clerk in 1896 at the age of thirteen. In his earliest years in the business, the home office staff consisted of seven people—the president, secretary, cashier, three clerks, and a superintendent who managed the field force of thirty-five or forty agents, handled actuarial work, adjusted claims and did some underwriting. Their working conditions were primitive at best. The office had no gas or electric lights, no adding machines, no typewriters and no telephones. Quitting time was 4:00 p.m. (before dark!) except on Wednesdays, when the clerks refilled oil lamps in preparation for a long night writing policies by hand. By the time he retired from the Claims Department in 1948, Liemkuhler had spent half his career in the home office and half in the field. With fifty-two years' service, he had certainly earned his pension.

In 1951 directors approved a base salary of $100 per week for all field managers and began providing group life insurance, equal to one year's salary, for all employees. The same year, a survey by the Life Office Management Association (LOMA) revealed that Monumental Life's retirement program did not provide benefits comparable to those given by seventy-four other stock life insurance companies. Directors immediately voted to amend the contract to provide additional benefits for eligible employees electing to participate.

ABOVE: *William J. Leimkuhler joined the company in 1896 and retired with fifty-two years' service in 1948. He was the first employee to benefit from Monumental's comprehensive retirement program.*

In the summer of 1952, the company beat the city's oppressive heat and humidity by installing Westinghouse air-conditioning units in all home office work areas. The result was well worth the $111,646 expense. "Gone are the fans that blew papers around," noted one employee. "Gone is the dust blowing in the windows. With filtered cool fresh air circulated through the office we have ideal working conditions without heat, dust and street noise."

Medical insurance came next, in 1957. For fifty cents per week, full-time home office employees could purchase medical-hospitalization insurance coverage. Part-time employees could participate in the plan for twenty-five cents a week. And, thanks to the company's significant support of the Red Cross, all employees who enrolled in the Blood Assurance Program were assured that their family would receive blood should a need ever occur.

In 1957 directors also approved a contributory group life insurance plan and reduced eligibility requirements for retirement plan entry from five to two years' service and age thirty. The retirement plan was amended again in January 1958 to allow retirement at age fifty-five after thirty years' service.

BOOM IN INSURANCE SALES

Such growth in employee benefits contributed to and benefited from a remarkable postwar growth in life insurance sales. By 1956, with the birth rate showing no signs of slackening, life insurance was the most widely used means of establishing family protection and savings. Fifty-eight percent of Americans owned individual life insurance policies. Another 14 percent had group coverage through their employers, and 12 percent had coverage through fraternal organizations and other associations. Additionally, no less than six million Americans—4 percent of the U.S. population—still held veterans policies issued during the war. On average, American families carried $7,600 of life insurance protection in 1956, up from $4,500 per family in 1946.

Monumental Life's lower and middle-income policyholders owned less coverage but continued to buy in record numbers. Since the end of World War II, the company's insurance in force had grown steadily from $528.4 million (1,287,073 policies) in 1946, to $658.9 million (1,368,761 policies) in 1950, to almost $930.7 million (1,487,488 policies) in 1956. Weekly premium industrial insurance accounted for 46 percent of that $930.7 million total; ordinary insurance—larger face amount policies with premiums paid monthly, quarterly or annually—made up the balance.

The boom in life insurance sales was fueled by the booming birth rate and postwar prosperity. Growing families had more to protect, but also more disposable income with which to purchase coverage.

Two additional factors also played a role in the life insurance industry's unprecedented growth during these years. One was the increasingly positive perception of the life insurance agent as an indispensable friend and family advisor. Like one's doctor, lawyer or accountant, the professional "Insurance Man" of the 1950s was respected for his knowledge and was welcomed by families into their homes.

The other factor was the tremendous increase in the variety of life insurance policies. By the mid-1950s, the nation's life insurers were selling regular term insurance, straight life insurance, limited payment life insurance, endowment insurance, family income and other term/permanent combination coverage, retirement protection, credit life insurance, and decreasing term insurance. Companies introduced new products to meet just about every family's need and budget.

"Selecting the right type of insurance in the right amount at the right time is obviously neither an easy or a static matter," Wisconsin Senator Alexander Wiley stated in 1956. "The average American . . . knows that his social security coverage is not going to be enough to meet his needs. He wants to help provide for his own and his family's protection, through his own foresight and initiative."

INSURING 'DICK AND JANE'

Monumental Life introduced a new rate book during the 1950s as well as a dozen or more new life insurance policies and riders to meet the growing needs of "Baby Boomer" families. By far, two of the most profitable and popular plans were weekly premium Juvenile Insurance, paid up in ten years, for children aged "0" to nine, and the new Family Income Benefit. "Every time the stork makes his trip," noted the *Old Black Hen* in 1954, "it means Daddy has one more responsibility . . . and needs additional protection on his life."

The Family Income Benefit—a combination of term and permanent coverage—built cash value and provided an increased amount of coverage and income for a specific period of time—until all children reached eighteen or twenty years of age, for example. Ten-Pay Life and the Endowment at Age 18 "educational policy" were also popular.

With countless opportunities for sales, Monumental Life's 854 agents in more than sixty locations were urged to become "part of America's future" by insuring every family, every new baby and every school-age "Dick and Jane." (The characters and their dog "Spot," popularized in the era's elementary school readers, symbolized an entire generation of suburban children.)

Infant mortality was on the decline, with less than thirty deaths per thousand during the first year of life in 1957 compared to 160 deaths per thousand fifty years earlier. Since 1900 the health of older children had also improved. In 1957 less than one child in a thousand died between the ages of five and fourteen compared to four per thousand in 1900. Patch tests and chest X-rays helped doctors diagnose tuberculosis before it became debilitating. By the end of the decade, Dr. Jonas Salk's polio vaccine had nearly eradicated infantile paralysis. Children and young adults would no longer fall victim to a cruel disease that had disabled more than 50,000 lives during one epidemic in 1952.

"Every school age youngster is looking forward to a better education and a healthy, safe and secure future," wrote the *Old Black Hen* editor. "They are going places, and you can plan a financial program that will help them along the way." Providing coverage at a young age guaranteed insurability and gave children the lifelong benefit of low rates. Juvenile policies also provided growing cash values that could be used later in life to help pay college tuition or start a business.

During those teen-focused years in the late 1950s—when adolescents were already eating McDonald's fast-food fries and hamburgers in California and dancing on *Dick Clark's American Bandstand* in Philadelphia—many American parents worried about their children's futures. One enterprising young staff manager, Chicago's Rocco ("Rocky") Gaetano did very well with a $5,000 level-premium whole life policy, which he promoted as an "Estate Plan for Teenagers." Gaetano went through his debit book, identified all of his teenage policyholders—a total of thirty, all boys—and started scheduling appointments.

I spent many evenings with the heads of households, explaining my proposals and what they could do for their sons by taking out this plan now. I then asked the fathers if they would like to have the chance to purchase this plan at

763-55

Congratulations

CF043 NL PD=FAX BALTIMORE MD JAN 10=
ROCCO J GAETANO, DLR DONT PHONE=
    4533 WEST MONROE ST=

YOU HAVE QUALIFIED AS AN HONOR MEMBER OF THE PRESIDENT'S CLUB
FOR 1956. THIS SPLENDID ACHIEVEMENT RANKS YOU AS ONE OF OUR
MOST OUTSTANDING FIELD MEN, AND I OFFER YOU MY MOST HEARTY
CONGRATULATIONS.
WITH EVERY GOOD WISH FOR YOUR HAPPINESS AND CONTINUED SUCCESS
THROUGHOUT THE NEW YEAR, I AM,
SINCERELY=
        F H LOWEREE PRESIDENT=
    B Y   W E S T E R N   U N I O N

their son's rate. They all said they would jump at the chance, [considering] their current age, but I told them in the insurance business there is no second chance.

I sold 22 cases from my 30 proposals. Within a six-week period I wrote and placed $100,000 in Teenage Estate Plans, all minimum $5,000.

Gaetano, a sales leader, was just one of many dedicated Monumental Life career agents and managers who contributed to the company's success over several decades.

GENERAL AGENTS, GROUP INSURANCE, GROWTH

In October 1957, President Loweree announced to directors that the company would open a new distribution channel and have nineteen licensed general agents

(GAs) selling Monumental's life insurance products in North Carolina, Pennsylvania and Virginia by year-end. Marketing ordinary products with a higher face amount, their goal was to broaden the company's "reach" in that marketplace.

At the same meeting, President Loweree proposed establishing a Group Department to enter the highly competitive group insurance field. He noted that product offerings could include group life, credit life, annuities, accident, disability and health insurance, including plans with hospitalization, medical and surgical expense coverage. Directors liked the idea and instructed Loweree to get leads on experienced specialists to fill Group

Department positions, at salaries in excess of $10,000, if necessary. By July 1958 four managers—G. Rick O'Shea, Manager of Group Sales; Charles M. Ramsey, Group Administrator; Ian Charlton, Group Actuary; and Thomas B. Ambrose, Group Accounting—were in place and anxious to get started.

In 1954 the company had also appointed Frank J. Doetzer, a Monumental veteran with thirty-three years of field and home office experience, as agency director and opened traditional field offices in several new locations. In Hagerstown, Salisbury and Cumberland, Maryland, and in Detroit, Michigan, where Monumental Life already had successful field operations, the company purchased land and built new stand-alone office buildings. These were the first Monumental-owned field offices designed and built to meet the company's field office needs and specifications.

But even bigger building challenges were being undertaken right outside the home office windows in Baltimore. Business was booming. The Mercantile Bank and Trust Company still leased and occupied significant first-floor space in the building's Charles-Chase Street corner, and Monumental needed more room for its growing, extended family.

In late fall 1957 construction workers broke ground for a 6,500-square-foot, three-story home office addition facing Lovegrove Alley. Built using the latest construction techniques, it included movable partitions, bright fluorescent lighting, and ceilings covered with acoustic tiles. Though a harsh winter caused annoying delays, the addition was completed in 1958, just in time to celebrate two important Monumental milestones— the company's 100th Anniversary and its One Billion Dollar Year.

ONE HUNDRED YEARS
ONE BILLION DOLLARS INSURANCE IN FORCE

On March 5, 1958, the company celebrated the centennial of its founding with simultaneous parties, cake cuttings and rousing renditions of "Happy Birthday!" in Baltimore and sixty field offices around the country. In all, 1,611 members of the field force and their guests participated in events that included dinners, dancing, and messages from President Loweree to all employees.

In Baltimore the celebration was held at the Lord Baltimore Hotel. Serving as the evening's toastmaster, Executive Vice President Fred Wehr traced the company's history; introduced directors, retirees and special guests; thanked everyone on behalf of President Loweree and the board of directors for their loyalty and dedication; and dedicated a bronze commemorative plaque that would

ABOVE: *Every employee received a brass coaster with Monumental's 100th anniversary seal as part of the company's Centennial Celebration in 1958. The seal appeared over the home office entrances on Charles and Chase Streets.*

BELOW: *A bronze Centennial Tribute plaque was placed outside the Treasury Department, where it remains today.*

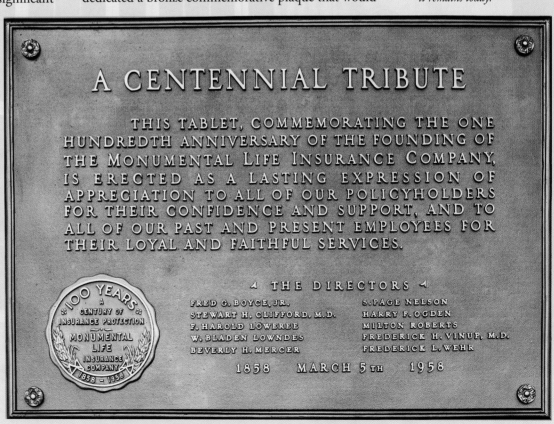

A CENTENNIAL TRIBUTE

THIS TABLET, COMMEMORATING THE ONE HUNDREDTH ANNIVERSARY OF THE FOUNDING OF THE MONUMENTAL LIFE INSURANCE COMPANY, IS ERECTED AS A LASTING EXPRESSION OF APPRECIATION TO ALL OF OUR POLICYHOLDERS FOR THEIR CONFIDENCE AND SUPPORT, AND TO ALL OF OUR PAST AND PRESENT EMPLOYEES FOR THEIR LOYAL AND FAITHFUL SERVICES.

◢ THE DIRECTORS ◣

FRED G. BOYCE, JR.   S. PAGE NELSON
STEWART H. CLIFFORD, M.D.   HARRY F. OGDEN
F. HAROLD LOWEREE   MILTON ROBERTS
W. BLADEN LOWNDES   FREDERICK H. VINUP, M.D.
BEVERLY H. MERCER   FREDERICK L. WEHR

1858   MARCH 5TH   1958

earth-orbiting "Sputnik" in 1957, and the start of the "space race" with Explorer 1 on January 31, 1958, no one could have imagined how swiftly technology would change their industry and the company beginning the next year.

ENTERING THE ELECTRONIC AGE

For a company that started out writing policies in longhand by the light of oil lamps, change had come steadily but slowly since 1900. Electric lights, telephones, typewriters and adding machines appeared first. Then secure vaults, time locks, and company-wide accounting systems. Electric typewriters and Dictaphones were next, followed by addressograph plates in 1956. Both simplified sending an estimated 400,000 premium notices that year. Another innovation, premium payment through Monumental Life's "Mon-U-Matic" bank draft system in early 1958, saved policyholders the cost of postage and further reduced the number of mailings and agent collections.

be displayed outside Treasury in the home office. The highlight of the evening was a parade of flaming birthday cakes. Servers delivered identical cakes to each table! Every employee also received a set of bronze coasters with the 100th Anniversary logo.

Earlier in the day, Loweree had marked the occasion by participating in a statewide radio broadcast during which he was interviewed on air by one of the station's personalities. With $1 billion of insurance in force and a hundred-year tradition of serving Maryland policyholders, he and Monumental Life had every reason to publicize their success. In 1958 the company was the eighteenth largest life insurer doing business in the United States. It was also the first and only life insurance company founded in Baltimore to reach its centennial.

When employees returned to their desks the next day, they all might have wondered: "What changes will employees see in the next fifty to one hundred years?" Even in their wildest dreams—having watched the first U.S. satellite launch and Russia's

But the biggest changes—punch cards and electronic data processing—like the space race's booster rockets (and most innovations at Monumental Life) were introduced in stages.

Early in the 1950s the company's actuarial and accounting employees still kept records and accumulated statistics much as they had for several decades—by writing data on cards or in ledger books, then typing final reports to meet board needs and the insurance industry's state regulatory requirements. As a stock life insurance company, Monumental Life also had to submit annual reports to stockholders and the Securities and Exchange Commission.

As sales increased in the postwar years, along with the number of policyholders and policies, Monumental Life's actuaries realized that it was no longer possible to keep accurate manual records. In July 1957 the company's first computer was installed in the Actuarial Department, headed by George E. Immerwahr.

A graduate of Princeton University and a Fellow of the Society of Actuaries, Immerwahr had come to Monumental Life in 1949 after having served as an actuary for New York Life Insurance Company, the U.S. Bureau of Old Age and Survivors Insurance, and the Pension Trust Division of the Internal Revenue Service. He understood the importance of accurate records and, with Frank Baker, co-chaired the Electronics Committee that worked with IBM to select and install the company's first data processing equipment.

Though the process seems archaic today, employees keyed-in data that was punched onto cards. To tabulate data and produce reports, the cards were "read" by the data processing equipment. The system was first used to create policy-driven reports for sales conferences, vacation schedules, savings bond purchase data and bills for non-serviced mortgage loans.

With the installation of a leased IBM tape 650 Electronic Data Processing Machine in April 1959, capabilities and uses increased. Equipped with both magnetic tape and punch card input and output, the IBM 650 could add and subtract at a rate of 78,000 calculations per minute. Records were stored on reels of magnetic tape, two hundred characters per inch, and processed at a rate of seventy-five inches per minute.

Weekly premium policy records were the first to be converted to the new electronic system, at an initial cost of $250,000 and an estimated future savings of $40,000 per year. Key punchers copied all accounting records from agent debit books onto punch cards. Information from punched cards was uploaded to tape, and the tapes were posted for collections, issues, revivals, lapses and transfers. The information for one policy fit on one-half inch of tape; the records for fifteen average-sized debits fit on one reel of magnetic tape. The data for six debits could be processed in nine minutes.

"The Weekly Premium accounting program will replace, in its entirety, the work once performed by the Record Department and also the retyping of [agent] collection books which has been performed by the Policywriting Department's Weekly Premium Section," reported the *Old Black Hen*. "The conversion of all districts will require approximately nine months to one year."

In a meeting with employees, Frank Baker stated that the installation of the new equipment was "another step forward being taken by the company to eliminate voluminous and repetitive jobs now being performed on a manual basis." He then quoted an article from *US News and World Report* entitled "Revolution in Office Work," as follows:

> In offices all across the country, a whole army of ingenious new machines is helping fight a rising tide of paper work. Electronic computers, calculating machines, all sorts of devices to speed clerical tasks—now are doing jobs that once demanded human effort. Is all this throwing a great many office employees out of jobs? Just the opposite is happening. The mountain of paper keeps piling up faster than machines can handle it.

Despite mechanization of manual operations, added Baker, eighty-five home office positions were added during the decade to meet the company's growing needs and distribution systems. "At no time will we have a surplus of personnel. And no one need fear losing his or her job because of the new equipment."

ABOVE: *George E. Immerwahr, head of the Actuarial Department, co-chaired the Electronics Committee that selected and installed Monumental's first data processing equipment.*

OLD GUARD RETIRES, PASSES ON

Howard M. Emmons . . .
Old Black Hen Editor

In announcing the death of Howard Emmons on March 11, 1949, Monumental Life's board of directors noted: "We have lost a most valued member, an associate and friend, a wise counselor and one who gave himself unstintingly in the interest and service of our company."

Born in Baltimore in 1865, Emmons graduated from public high school, received his law degree from the University of Maryland in 1889, and practiced law with his father for several years before joining the company in the late 1890s as assistant counsel. Elected to the board of directors in 1909, Emmons became counsel in 1919 and was elected vice president and counsel in 1922. He remained in that position until his death.

Though Emmons played a role in many of the company's landmark decisions during his fifty years of service, two personal achievements stand out above the rest.

In 1923, when officers were looking to expand the company's scope and services beyond its existing Weekly Premium business, they appointed Emmons to organize the Regular Ordinary Department. He worked diligently over the next twenty-five years to increase sales and educate agents about the benefits of working in the higher-income Ordinary marketplace.

On March 31, 1949, three weeks after Emmons's death, Monumental Life reported $158.9 million of Regular Ordinary life insurance and $120.3 million of Monthly Ordinary life insurance in force. Though still not equal to the company's $329.9 million of in-force Weekly Premium life insurance, the department, said directors, "stands as a monument to the efficiency and thoroughness with which he accomplished his assignment."

Despite this achievement, Emmons had been better known to employees in both the home office and field as the editor of *The Old Black Hen*, since it first appeared in 1922. The counselor had both an interest in journalism and a way with words. He could write about industry issues, report on company social events, motivate agents, direct artists to create cartoons, and edit articles and sales tips sent in by district managers—all with equal ease.

Thanks to his untiring efforts to educate and entertain, *The Old Black Hen* was one of the industry's most interesting and worthwhile employee publications for many decades. From 1922 through 1949, Emmons established a level of excellence that continued with his successor. For almost fifty years the publication documented, in unbelievable detail, the company's traditions, personalities, achievements and growth.

Without Howard Emmons, very little of the company's unique history would have been preserved. Without *The Old Black Hen*, the author of *this* history of Monumental Life would not have found many of the employee comments and stories we are able to share.

ABOVE: *Howard M. Emmons was general counsel and editor of the Old Black Hen from 1922 until his death in 1949.*

Harry C. Roth . . .
Treasury 'Watchdog' and Controller

HARRY C. ROTH joined the company in May 1899 as one of three home office clerks who worked by the light of oil lamps. He retired on March 1, 1948, having been absent due to illness only seven days during his forty-nine years of service to Monumental Life. Whether this achievement was attributed to excellent health, discipline, dedication or simply dogged determination to be at his desk every day no one can say for certain. At his retirement, directors simply saluted the "Watchdog of the Treasury" for his remarkable attendance record and five decades of loyal, faithful service.

Roth followed his father, Henry Roth, the company's secretary from 1888 to 1928, into the life insurance business. The young Roth's ability to focus on the details and keep accurate records, without the benefit of an adding machine, earned him positions of increasing responsibility early in his career. When he was finally promoted to treasurer and controller, officers and employees agreed no one was better suited to the job of taking care of the company funds.

Roth spent his retirement years working with his hands instead of with figures in his head. Before passing away in 1954, he enjoyed taking care of his garden and two-acre apple orchard in the Baltimore suburbs. We wonder if he kept track of each tree's productivity!

Milton Roberts . . .
Monumental Life Director, President of the Real Estate Trust

For thirty-six years, Milton Roberts played a critical role in the company's growth and financial success. First elected to the board of directors in 1923, he became the company's secretary in 1928, the same year it changed from a mutual to a stock life insurance company. Elected vice president in 1934, Roberts served as a member of the Investment Committee for all of his remaining years on the company's board. His knowledge and advice on mortgages and securities contributed substantially to the excellent quality of Monumental Life's investment portfolio.

Born in Baltimore in 1881, Roberts attended Baltimore public schools, graduated from Baltimore City College in 1901, and earned his law degree from the University of Maryland in 1904. Although he was a practicing attorney who served in the legal department of Baltimore's Merchants and Miners Transportation Company for several years, Roberts seemed more interested in real estate, banking and investments than law.

He was one of the founders of the Real Estate Trust Company, a mortgage banking company that leased office space on the first floor of Monumental Life's home office beginning in 1926. The two companies shared a director or two and used the same building sketch on their letterheads. Until Monumental Life built its own solid steel Treasury vault in 1939, many of the company's securities were safeguarded in Real Estate Trust Company vaults.

In 1939, Roberts joined President Paul Burnett of Monumental Life, Secretary F. Harold Loweree and other industry executives in testifying before the Temporary National Economic Committee investigating the economic power and practices of the life insurance industry. Their testimony became part of the permanent congressional records.

Still president of the Real Estate Trust when it was acquired by Baltimore's Mercantile Trust Company in 1943, Roberts renewed the company's lease with Monumental in 1944 for another twelve years at $6,000 rent per year. Mercantile maintained a branch in Monumental Life's building until the 1990s, when the bank constructed its own building directly across from Monumental, on the west side of Charles Street.

Roberts continued to serve as a director of both Monumental Life and the Mercantile Safe Deposit and Trust Company until his death in 1959.

Dr. Fred H. Vinup . . .
Medical Director Set Underwriting Milestones

Dr. Fred H. Vinup earned the money needed to pay his way through medical school by working as an agent for the Mutual Life Insurance Company of Baltimore in the early 1900s. Twenty years later, in 1924, he had the unusual distinction of being appointed medical director for the company whose policies he once sold. Elected a company director in 1928, he remained Monumental Life's medical director until his retirement in 1958. He continued to serve as a director until his death in 1960.

Dr. Vinup graduated from the University of Maryland, School of Medicine, in 1909. When he joined the company in 1924, he brought with him a wealth of medical knowledge gained from fifteen years' experience as a successful practicing physician and from service overseas during World War I at the U.S. Army base hospital in Tours, France. He retired from active service in the 104th Medical Regiment of the Maryland National Guard with the rank of colonel in 1951 and was promoted to brigadier general, retired, in 1957.

A member of the American Medical Association, the Radiological Society of America, the Medical and Chirurgical Faculty of Maryland and the American Industrial Association of Physicians and Surgeons throughout his medical career, Dr. Vinup also served on the Baltimore City Health Department and the Board of Welfare and was president of the Board of Police Examiners.

Under Dr. Vinup's supervision for more than thirty years, the Underwriting Department made enviable strides in managing risk and maintaining excellent mortality experience. The changes he instituted and the results achieved contributed to the company's growth, progress and financial success from the 1920s through the 1950s. Following Vinup's retirement, Monumental Life's directors appointed Dr. Francis Gluck as the company's medical director.

Fred H. Vinup, M.D., served as medical director for more than thirty years.

ABOVE: *In still segregated, pre–Civil Rights era Baltimore, the races did not mix at social functions. The company's African American cafeteria and maintenance workers and family members attended separate picnics and holiday parties throughout the 1950s.*

"Desegregating Public Schools"
© 1999 U.S. Postal Service. All Rights Reserved.
Used with Permission.

Hundreds of employees and their families attended the annual company picnic, which included food, swimming, boat rides and games for adults and children.

CHANGE IN THE AIR

Remembered as an era of peace, prosperity, opportunity, and order—and, on the surface, it was—the 1950s were also a time of fear and growing resentment for many Americans. Communism and the Cold War were real threats that prompted East Coast businesses and school systems to construct air raid shelters and hold regular safety drills. The Ku Klux Klan in hooded white robes had reappeared in the South.

In many areas of the country, the 1950s presaged a more turbulent decade of dissent and civil disobedience. Following World War II, wrote journalist Tom Brokaw, America was forced to "confront its hypocrisy concerning equality under the law. The war started the country on the road to long-overdue changes that finally came in the Sixties for women and blacks."

The post–World War II years were especially difficult for America's working women. Thousands had done men's work during the war and felt cheated at being pushed back into more traditional female roles when the men returned. Some married and pregnant women lost their jobs. Others who had been promoted to management positions resented being paid half the salaries of men with similar responsibilities.

Having proven they could take care of themselves, their children and their households while their husbands were fighting overseas, many hard-working, educated housewives also began to speak up for themselves. Not all stay-at-home moms in the Fifties believed that "Father Knows Best." Many wanted to be heard and to have some say in the decisions that influenced their lives.

By 1954, when the U.S. Supreme Court declared segregation unconstitutional, change was also on the minds of many African American citizens. During World War II, black men and women had found less menial, better paying jobs as defense and factory workers, clerks, bus drivers, and fire and police officers. Black veterans had enrolled in colleges and training programs through the GI Bill. During the Korean War, black men had served in the armed forces' first integrated units. Yet on returning to their southern home towns, they found they were still not permitted to sit next to whites on buses, eat in many restaurants, or use "Whites Only" water fountains and rest rooms.

Though employees hesitate to discuss it, no history of Monumental Life would be accurate or complete without noting that in still-segregated, pre–Civil Rights era Baltimore, the races did not mix during the 1950s. The company's maintenance and cafeteria employees—all African American, some with fifteen to twenty years' service—attended separate social events. Photos in the *Old Black Hen* document that their well-attended parties and picnics often

included family members. But during those years not one African American face appears in photos showing employees at work in departments that provided administrative or professional support and service to the company's field offices and policyholders. And the company's agents still did not venture to make sales in predominantly African American neighborhoods.

The Supreme Court ruling ended neither segregation nor racism in the United States. In 1955, Rosa Parks refused to give up her bus seat to a white man in Montgomery, Alabama. In September 1957 nine African American students defied convention and walked into a previously all-white high school in Little Rock, Arkansas. By the end of the decade, Dr. Martin Luther King had become an outspoken leader and spokesperson for civil rights.

As the reins of leadership once more passed into new hands at Monumental Life, the winds of change were gaining force throughout the country. By the time the company's directors elected Frederick L. Wehr president and F. Harold Loweree chairman of the board on January 21, 1960, John F. Kennedy, a Catholic, was campaigning for the presidency, women could buy birth control pills, and a growing group of Dr. King's followers had demonstrated, non-violently, in the South.

Teenager John Sankonis (center, white shirt) danced on Baltimore's popular Buddy Deane TV Show beginning in 1959.

John and Concetta Sankonis . . .

Dancing Teens on Buddy Deane!

Sankonis and his wife, Concetta, pictured here in Venice in 1997, attended Monumental conferences for more than twenty years.

THE rock 'n' roll "teen scene" in Baltimore can be neatly summed up in four words—*The Buddy Deane Show*. The legendary teen dance show, airing on WJZ-TV, was the undisputed local king of afternoon dance. Six days a week it featured top rock 'n' roll acts and a core group of teens, called the "Committee," who twisted and "Madisoned" their way into the hearts and homes of teenagers everywhere.

For a time it was the most popular local dance show in America and, says retired Monumental Life agent John Sankonis, "the only show in Maryland that ever pre-empted Dick Clark's *American Bandstand*. Sankonis remembers it well—he danced on camera every day!

Following an audition in late 1959, the fourteen-year-old Brooklyn Park high school student was invited to become a "Committee" member. He remained a regular until the show's demise five years later. It was a heady time for young Sankonis, who became a professional musician before starting his insurance career with Monumental Life. He recalls hurrying to the studio after school, playing drums on the air, spending long hours learning new dance steps, and being pressed for autographs at local record hops.

On the show, he also met his wife Concetta, another "Committee" member. "We met all the stars," says Sankonis, "and it was kind of neat being so popular. But there were also a lot of rules and regulations. Through the show we also learned a lot of things that really helped us in life."

The *Buddy Deane Show* phenomenon is the subject of the John Waters movie and Tony award–winning musical *Hairspray*. "He [Waters] did it about us," explains Sankonis, "even though he did it his way."

Looking back, Sankonis acknowledges that one reason for the show's cancellation was its reluctance to integrate. Many well-known black and white singing stars were showcased, but all the kids who danced on camera were white. "It [the prejudice] didn't really touch us kids," says Sankonis. "Neither Concetta nor I were ever asked how we felt about it."

Perhaps music was the great leveler. Four years later, when riots broke out in Baltimore following Martin Luther King's assassination, Sankonis recalls being the only white member of a band performing in a predominantly African American neighborhood. "There was a TV on in the middle of the dance floor showing the riots," he says, "but it wasn't a problem for me."

Sankonis rarely missed a show taping, and when he became a Monumental Life agent in 1976, he brought with him that sense of responsibility, rarely missing an opportunity to talk to people about their insurance needs. In 1996 the company recognized Sankonis for a record which few successful life insurance agents ever achieve. He had made at least one sale *every* week of *every* year for twenty years!

Though Buddy Deane died in 2003, his memory lives on in Baltimore. Today, Sankonis not only still listens to the old songs—he still plays them.

CHAPTER 9

Civil Rights. Civic Responsibility
(1960–1969)

S IRENS. The crash of breaking glass. Fire and smoke wherever I turn. Men, women and children run in every direction, pushing and stumbling over those in their way. I don't see anyone I know. Can't find my family or friends. How do I get out of here? Is any place safe? Scared and all alone, I finally hear a familiar voice.

"Alisha, it's time to get up."

Thursday, April 11, 1968. I open my eyes and hear my mother calling me to come downstairs for breakfast. I lie in bed a moment, thinking about the events that have led up to this day. My dream was terrifying. My mother calls my name again. This time I get up, wondering apprehensively what will happen next.

Dr. Martin Luther King is dead, killed last week in Memphis. In cities across America, black people have taken to the streets in violent protest. Here in Baltimore, we had three days of rioting and looting. Six people were killed. Seven hundred injured. Fifty-three hundred arrested as firefighters extinguished over a thousand fires. The curfew has been lifted, but schools and many businesses are still closed. I haven't been outside since more than five thousand armed soldiers arrived to patrol the streets.

I look in the mirror, check my hair and clothes, and go downstairs knowing that today will be tough for me. I have an interview at Monumental Life Insurance Company on North Charles Street. With high school graduation just six weeks away, I need to find a job, and Momma heard that

Monumental Life was hiring. She wants more for me than the hard life she's had, cooking and cleaning other peoples' homes. She looks at my skirt, sweater, heels and stockings and nods approvingly.

Too nervous to eat, I head for the door, but Momma calls me back.

"Are you sure this is a good idea?" she asks. "Is Monumental Life even open today?" Their building is south of North Avenue, a few blocks west of Greenmount, where some of the worst rioting occurred. "Do you know if the buses are running? I'm worried about you going downtown by yourself."

I assure her I will be okay. I called the personnel office. They are expecting me. I have to walk an extra block to catch the bus, I explain, but the bus line I need is running. I give Momma a quick kiss. It's time to go.

I can hardly believe how unfamiliar my own neighborhood looks. Whole blocks of shops and businesses have been burned out. Charred wood, bricks and rubble litter curbs and sidewalks. Store owners have boarded up shop windows and doors to prevent further looting. Many

FACING PAGE: *Armed National Guard troops marched down Greenmount Avenue, a few blocks east of Monumental's home office, during violent riots following the April 4, 1968, death of Dr. Martin Luther King.*

will never open again. *Neighbors gather on corners and front steps, waiting for the release of sons and daughters who were handcuffed and taken to holding stations by police and National Guardsmen in riot gear.*

Why these riots and random acts of violence? Mobs of our own people have destroyed communities, homes and businesses! I know they are angry and upset about Dr. King's death. So am I. But this craziness will not bring him back. I arrive at the corner just as my bus pulls up.

Twenty minutes later the bus stops. I get off and walk the few blocks to Charles and Chase Streets. At Monumental Life's front door, I stop and look around. The building fills the whole block! Hundreds of people work here, Momma said, including a dozen or so young black women just like me. We all want the same thing really—better lives for ourselves than our mothers had. Momma never had the chance to work in an office. But I know I can do more than scrub floors and wash clothes. I can sort mail, file letters and take phone messages as well as any white girl.

I really need this job. If I make a good impression and show them what I can do, maybe they'll give me a chance. Maybe I can even go to college some day. I take a deep breath, walk into the lobby and think positive thoughts. "Today's my day, I can feel it. I feel good and I'm going to get this job!"

Many young black women, just like Alisha, were employed by Monumental following high school graduation in the late Sixties. Like Alisha, some of them dreamed of going to college and did so with the help of Monumental's Tuition Reimbursement Program. Others began decades-long insurance careers that provided benefits, regular paychecks, pensions and retirement plans still unavailable to many of their less determined and resourceful peers.

JFK . . . RFK . . . MLK . . . KKK. Khrushchev . . . Castro . . . Cuban Missile Crisis. Bay of Pigs . . . Berlin Wall . . . "Ich bin ein Berliner." Sit-Ins . . . Selma . . . Riots in the Street . . . March on Washington . . . "Ole Miss" . . . Memphis . . . Motown. Dissent . . . Demonstrations . . . Draft Dodgers. Counter Culture . . . College Campuses . . .

Americans elected John F. Kennedy president in November 1960.

Kent State . . . Canada? Protests . . . Peace Symbols . . . Peace Corps . . . Flower Power.

Peter, Paul and Mary . . . Potheads . . . "Puff the Magic Dragon." Barbie . . . Birth Control . . . Beehives . . . *Hair.* Barbra . . . Baez . . . Beatles . . . Beach Boys . . . Buddy Deane in Baltimore. Friedan . . . Free Love . . . *The Feminine Mystique.* NAACP . . . NOW . . . NASA. Astronauts . . . Armstrong . . . Apollo 7. Women's Lib . . . Woodstock . . . Watts . . . "We shall overcome."

DREAMS DASHED

For those who grew up or raised children during the 1960s, these words bring back unforgettable images of a turbulent era that forever changed the United States.

The dream of an idyllic "Camelot" with President John F. Kennedy as our elected king died in a Dallas motorcade on November 22, 1963. His death, like Franklin D. Roosevelt's in 1945, drew the country together in mourning. But instead of standing at train stations waiting to see FDR's cortege, American families in 1963 interrupted their Thanksgiving dinners to watch JFK's funeral procession on television.

During the Sixties, TV cameras brought images of a chaotic, Cold War–era world into our living rooms in ways we'd never experienced. For two weeks in October 1962, we watched in stunned disbelief as aerial reconnaissance photos revealed Soviet nuclear missile sites in Cuba. We held our collective breath as Russian ships approached a U.S. naval blockade. Seeing the Soviets turn back to avoid armed confrontation, Secretary of State Dean Rusk commented: "We're eyeball to eyeball, and I think the other fellow just blinked." The news footage dispelled any illusions Americans might have had about peace between the two superpowers and created a fear few will ever forget.

Without television, the country could not have witnessed such historic milestones as the March on Washington, Dr. King's "I Have a Dream" speech, the

Beatles' arrival in America, weightless walks in space, and man's first footsteps on the moon. Without it, we would have paid far less attention to peace symbols, flower children, civil rights sit-ins and student protests on college campuses. By the time television showed U.S. Marines landing in Danang in 1965, American women were shedding bras and fighting for their freedom as dismayed husbands asked: "What has happened to my wife?"

Later in the decade, television also showed many things we did *not* want to see—flag and draft card burnings, Robert Kennedy's assassination, wounded soldiers and bloody massacres in Vietnam, army tanks in U.S. cities, National Guardsmen in riot gear, tear gas clouds, and college students lying dead on a Kent State street.

Parents who had lived through World War II could not understand how their once obedient and agreeable children could shun patriotism and refuse to register for the draft. What, they wondered, would cause college students from "good homes" to drop out, join communes, dress in rags, chant on street corners, and flee to Canada?

After decades of living with discrimination, many black Americans were especially angry. They protested, peaceably at first, with sit-ins in the South. As the Black Power movement grew and peaceful demonstrations produced few concrete results, many young black men and women began to doubt they would ever experience Dr. King's dream. When he was murdered on April 4, 1968 in Memphis,

their pent-up anger and frustration erupted in violence, looting and destruction on the streets of Baltimore, Washington, Los Angeles, Chicago and more than a hundred other U.S. cities.

Television news documented the decade's events in graphic detail. Americans reacted with fear and apprehension. Some families built and stocked fallout shelters to protect themselves from nuclear attack and radiation. Others bought life insurance in record numbers.

ABOVE: *Fathers Daniel and Philip Berrigan, both Jesuit priests, and seven of their followers were arrested in Catonsville, Maryland, for seizing and burning Selective Service records outside the local draft board in May 1968.*

(Courtesy of Herman Heyn, Baltimore)

Dr. Martin Luther King.

Prototype of a 1960s vintage fallout shelter.

ABOVE LEFT: *Peace march on South Gay Street, Baltimore, in 1969.*
(Courtesy of Herman Heyn, Baltimore)

ABOVE RIGHT: *Vietnam War protestors and college students gather on North Charles Street, just south of Baltimore's Penn Station, in the late 1960s.*
(Courtesy of the University of Baltimore)

BELOW: *Senior Girl Scouts in Cedar Grove, New Jersey, were trained by local Civil Defense officials to read radiation levels and help residents in case of a nuclear attack.*

DAWN OF A DIFFERENT DAY

How did the decade's turmoil play out in corporate boardrooms across the country? If Monumental Life was typical, and we cannot say that it was, company publications barely acknowledged what was happening on the streets and appearing almost nightly on the evening news. In 1961 board members discussed the company's Nuclear Warfare Emergency Preparedness Committees. In 1964 they reviewed language in policy war risk clauses. In 1967 officers gave one-sentence updates on Vietnam death claims and the Detroit riots. But few other social issues were included on meeting agendas. That's not to say, however, that industry executives were unconcerned or believed that business in the 1960s would be a rerun of past decades. In fact, just the opposite was true.

Since the end of World War II, the life insurance business had become increasingly competitive, with innovative products, electronic data processing and professionally trained management teams playing a larger and larger role in every company's success. Carrol M. Shanks, president of the Prudential Life Insurance Company, summed up the situation well when he predicted early in 1960 that the "soaring sixties" would bring more change to the life insurance business than had been seen in the previous one hundred years.

Writing to employees early in 1960, Fred Wehr, Monumental Life's newly elected president, looked forward to the decade's challenges with confidence and optimism:

I am taking office at the start of what many economists believe to be a decade of great promise—a decade, provided it is not interrupted by a major war, which gives every indication of being one of outstanding growth in production of both capital and consumer goods, family units, homes and, of course, babies. Logically, life insurance sales should rise to unprecedented heights.

Logically, Wehr was right. At the time, who would have thought otherwise? The Sixties dawned bright for our business. Thanks to the efforts of thousands of agents talking to families about their insurance needs, Americans were buying life insurance products as never before. During the 1950s the number of policyholders had increased by thirty million as the amount of life insurance in force more than doubled to $534 billion. During 1959 alone—a record-breaking year for the industry—American families purchased $69.5 billion of life insurance. By 1960 the average family owned $11,900 of coverage versus $5,000 in 1950.

As the U.S. population exploded—especially with children under age fifteen—better educated parents bought life insurance to help secure futures, protect family incomes, cover home mortgages, and fund college educations for the kids. Insurance companies like Monumental Life continued to fund suburban growth as they had throughout the 1950s by investing policy premiums in building residential neighborhoods, shopping centers, industrial parks and apartment complexes.

In 1960 social change was sweeping the country, but no one could have predicted how violent and destructive it would become. Within the decade, "block busting" and "white flight" to the suburbs would cause families, established neighborhoods and communities to become unglued.

As the demographic fabric of cities like Baltimore changed color, so did the faces of the people employed and insured by Monumental Life and other companies. The passage of the Civil Rights Act of 1964 put an end to discriminatory practices long accepted as the "status quo." Corporate decision-makers were forced to look differently at products, rates, employee benefit programs, how to attract customers, and how to conduct their businesses. Educationally, professionally, socially, culturally and economically, much of what the nation had taken for granted would never be the same.

Dr. Gluck in his rose garden.

LEADERSHIP, LOYALTY, LONG-TERM SERVICE

When he assumed the presidency of Monumental Life in 1960, Fred Wehr continued a legacy of leadership, loyalty and long years of service begun by company officers in the late nineteenth century. Like several of his more immediate predecessors, Wehr was a "home grown" Monumental man and industry veteran. He valued the company's culture and traditions and had climbed the corporate ladder to success by following many of the "old school" rules.

Joining Wehr in leading Monumental Life into the 1960s were several men who had also spent most of their careers working for the company. Frank J. Doetzer, vice president of District Agencies, had joined the home office as an office boy in 1921 and risen through the ranks. Treasurer James Lehane would celebrate thirty-five years of service in 1961. Chairman of the Board F. Harold Loweree had been with the company since 1927. Vice President and Secretary Frank Baker, Jr. had been hired in 1932 as an Auditing Department clerk.

In comparison, Vice President and Counsel Allen A. Davis, Jr., Vice President Donald H. Wilson, Jr., Dr. Francis W. Gluck; and Charles L. Hayes, elected secretary in 1961, could still be considered relative newcomers. Davis had joined Monumental Life in 1946. Wilson, a certified public accountant (CPA) and Chartered Life Underwriter (CLU), became part of the Securities Investment Department in 1947 after teaching accounting for four years at the Johns Hopkins University, his alma mater. Hayes, a CPA and the company's first FLMI (Fellow, Life Management Institute), had begun his insurance career in the Actuarial Department in 1949. Dr. Gluck became Monumental's medical director in 1958. (Every day from June through September until he retired in 1971, Dr. Gluck selected a rose from his home garden and wore it in his lapel!)

Frank J. Doetzer

Frank Baker, Jr.

Donald H. Wilson, Jr.

Charles L. Hayes.

"Mus" and "Mr. Wehr"

ABOVE LEFT: Clare Nardini, executive secretary

ABOVE RIGHT: Frederick L. Wehr, Monumental Life president in the 1960s.

LOWER RIGHT: Clare Nardini served as a Red Cross volunteer for more than two decades.

BELOW: In 1965, Wehr was recognized as an honorary "Colonel" of the Fort McHenry Guard.

HE called him "Mr. Wehr." He called her "Mus." For thirty-two years, they worked together as a team. The red-haired Monumental Life senior officer was outgoing, polite, gracious, appreciative, and a stickler for accuracy. His dark-haired secretary was "mousy" and shy, as different in personality as one could imagine from the Italian dictator after whom she'd been nicknamed. When he was promoted, she moved up with him. After he retired as chairman of the board and CEO in 1967, she had a series of new bosses over the next ten years. It was a big "come down," she says, to no longer have employees drop everything every time she called.

Frederick L. Wehr graduated from the Baltimore Polytechnic Institute in 1921 and the University of Pennsylvania's School of Finance in 1925. He joined the company as assistant secretary in August 1934 and was elected Monumental Life secretary in 1941, a director in 1944, vice president in 1947, and president in 1960.

Clare Nardini was a 1930 "commercial course" graduate from Baltimore's Seton High School. She joined Monumental as Mr. Wehr's secretary in 1935. Though her brother thought his smart, never married sister could earn more money elsewhere, Clare stayed for forty-two years because she had made many good friends and was happy working for Mr. Wehr.

"Our personalities clicked," she says. "We understood one another." Clare not only did Wehr's clerical work, she also ran his personal errands and picked up gifts for his wife. One day, she remembers, "Mr. Wehr had to take an unexpected business trip. He had not packed and needed to take clean clothes with him. He called his men's store, ordered necessities like 'garters and drawers,' and asked me to pick them up. Of course, they were wrapped when I got there!"

Clare remembers proudly that Wehr was very active in the community. He started Baltimore's Blood Bank, was president of the Board of the Children's Hospital and served as a director of the Equitable Society, the First National Bank, and the Baltimore Gas & Electric Company. He also served as president of the Chamber of Commerce of Metropolitan Baltimore. When he turned over his gavel in January 1965, the State of Maryland recognized him as an honorary "Admiral of the Chesapeake" and honorary "Colonel" of the Fort McHenry Guard.

Following his retirement in 1967, Wehr continued to serve as chairman of Monumental Life's Executive Committee. In 1970, the Maryland Region of the National Conference of Christians and Jews honored him with its Brotherhood Award "for distinguished and devoted service to his fellowmen and community in the field of human relations."

Clare learned a lot about community service from helping Mr. Wehr. She was a Red Cross volunteer for more than two decades. And though she can no longer walk without a walker, she continues to volunteer every week at Baltimore County's Calvert Hall High School, as she has done for almost thirty years. At age ninety-four in 2006, she was interviewed and recognized as her own high school's oldest living graduate. Asked what advice she would give to young women graduating today, she thought a minute—perhaps remembering her own "mousy" days—and replied: "Be more assertive. Speak up and ask for what you think you deserve."

All talented, well-educated professionals, every member of the senior management team was committed to the company, its stockholders, and to the Baltimore community. Under their leadership, Monumental Life had earned a reputation within the industry as a traditional, no-frills, low-cost home service company and a model among its peers. And like many of their peers, Monumental's officers realized they would have to find new ways to keep their century-old company profitable, competitive, and in step with the times.

MONUMENTAL . . . IN A NEW LIGHT

On April 21, 1960, Wehr reported to directors that he had engaged the H. W. Buddemeier Company as Monumental Life's advertising agency. "The agency," he explained, "will work with us to develop sales materials, sales promotion ideas, employee and policyholder communication aids, and advertising for newspapers and magazines." Though the company had occasionally run ads in a few industry and trade publications, it had never before attempted an advertising and image-building campaign of such size and scope. A new logo—featuring a lighted candle protected by a strong hand and the words "*PROTECTION in a new light!*"—debuted in the September 1960 issue of *The Old Black Hen.* In the same issue, management proudly introduced a new product line, a new rate book, and totally redesigned sales proposals, forms and customer service materials. Every piece included the new logo and the Monumental Life name in a bold, modern typeface.

The new Multiple Coverage product line for middle-income consumers included Waiver of Premium, Accidental Death and Dismemberment benefits on all policies. "These policies have everything—and all in one package!" announced Wehr. "They offer the utmost in life insurance protection. To our knowledge, they are without equal in the industry today."

Later that year, the company also introduced a one-year plan of insurance, covering school children, followed in 1961 by a Triple Benefit weekly premium policy and a new Family Protection Check-Up Program. As hoped, the lower rates and broader coverage generated $70.6 million of life insurance, making 1961 the best sales year to date in Monumental's history.

Monumental ads (left) and brochures (above) in the 1960s featured the company's new "Protection in a new light" tag line and symbol.

BELOW: *Policies introduced in the Sixties appealed to couples with young children, including Jack Brandt, the Baltimore Orioles' leading hitter in 1961, who bought a Monumental policy from agent Russ Phillips.*

ACTIVITY, KEY TO PRODUCTIVITY

To keep agents focused on productivity and growth throughout the 1960s, District Agencies introduced more aggressive sales techniques and objectives, reorganized field offices into three sales regions, and promoted veteran district managers Wendell P. Hartley, Edmund S. Barrett and Joseph L. Collins to division heads in June of 1960. Each was responsible for a region of nineteen or twenty offices. At the same time, management continued to enhance the company's product portfolio, improved field compensation and benefits, and began using more sophisticated agent and management training programs.

Until the 1960s, training at Monumental Life had consisted of tactical "how-tos" detailing what an agent had to do on the job. Vincent Zirpoli, appointed supervisor of field training in 1961, understood that the goal of training should be to develop people. Observing managers who did all the talking, he realized that "without the agent's active participation, behavior would not change."

Zirpoli had followed his father, Emilio ("Leo") Zirpoli, a sales manager in Philadelphia, into the business in 1952. As a young agent he'd learned that "every No puts you closer to a Yes." As a sales manager, he'd seen that activity was the key to sales. He had devised his own tools to track and analyze activity, uncover weak skills, correct problem areas, and help his agents succeed. Using these tools as a district manager in Youngstown, Ohio—a city with 15 percent unemployment in the 1960s—he took his office from last place to ninth among the company's sixty offices.

Throughout the 1960s, high agent turnover and retention challenges plagued Monumental Life and its biggest home service competitors, Louisville's Commonwealth Life and Peoples Life in Washington, D.C. Bucking the trend, Zirpoli reduced the turnover rate in his region from 60 to 15 percent during his twelve years as a division manager.

RIGHT: *Vince Zirpoli introduced training tools and materials that helped agents develop goals and objectives and take responsibility for their own success.*

Zirpoli's training tools—including a Personal Development Interview, a Goal Card, and a detailed Agents' Development Program—helped agents develop goals and objectives. "The agent, not the manager, provides the solutions," he explained. "Agents who work hard and make more calls can control sales and their own success." Zirpoli gave them sales tracks and scripts to follow with customers to assure their success.

Empowering agents to control their personal results was a new concept in the 1960s, and Zirpoli admits that his ideas were initially met with resistance. Even so, he says:

> The insurance industry was way ahead of other industries in those years in terms of training, resources, market research and sharing of information and ideas among competitors. I believe it's because insurance is an intangible product that is difficult to sell. Agents sell a "vision for the future," using both logic and emotion. That's why training is so critical. We must show agents how to help themselves and the families they insure bring their vision and goals to life.

"Both Fred Wehr and Frank Baker, Jr. were committed to increasing average size policy and to moving agents into higher income homes," adds Zirpoli, who retired in 1982 after serving as Monumental Life's director of training, vice president of Marketing Services, and vice president of District Agencies. Thanks to his efforts and the hard work of committed field trainers like John T. Allen, Richard Love, Joseph Roche, and Wilbert H. ("Spud") Ring, who succeeded Zirpoli as director of field training in 1964, Monumental Life's agents began to acquire the knowledge and skills needed to set their sights higher and make larger sales.

UNIONS STIFLE INITIATIVE, GROWTH

In some industrial cities and states, individual agent effort, initiative and production were stifled by union-negotiated contracts. That's why the insurance industry continued to regard agent membership in the Insurance Workers International Union (IWIU) so negatively. The life insurance business was not an industrial or manufacturing operation, and the role of its agents nothing like that "the typical trade union worker," Commonwealth Life president Morton Boyd had argued in 1947.

> The place of trade unionism is properly with the factory worker, the coal miner, the mill hand—in short, the man whose earnings are not individual, the man whose earnings are identical with every other man along the same assembly line or in the same pit, and who has no opportunity to improve his own earnings or advance his own destiny save as a member of the group. Its place is not, we believe, with those who determine their own destinies, those who write their own paychecks.

Even so, hundreds of Monumental Life agents continued to vote for union representation. In January 1961, Baltimore's Highlandtown Office was put on probation for lack of production, and its union filed a grievance. In 1962, when agents in Philadelphia refused to let sales managers ride in their cars, the problem led to arbitration and a slowdown in production before it was resolved.

But the worst union-related action occurred on March 18, 1963, when Monumental agents in Missouri and Ohio went on strike, protesting the company's premium growth contract and bonus provisions. Insisting that agents needed to be more productive, management stood firm. For three months, only thirty agents in the two states went to work while over two hundred remained on strike. With the help of the company's new computer, home office employees generated letters in late March alerting policyholders to the problem. The letter asked those who could to mail in payments or bring them to their local field office. The strike was settled on June 23, 1963.

IBM-1410 IMPROVES SERVICE.

As IBM, Honeywell and other vendors rolled out new and improved computer systems, Monumental Life used senior programmers—including Paul Clifford, Frank J. Heiner and Richard ("Dick") Lippert—and data processing experts like James Grigg and Tom Boesch to help upgrade its electronic data processing capabilities.

"We began to move away from manual, repetitive jobs in those years," explains Lippert, "and needed employees with a different kind of knowledge and mindset—more logical and analytical—to develop programs, test systems and identify errors."

BELOW: *With the arrival of the powerful IBM-1410 computer, Monumental's first programmers began developing programs and systems to upgrade data processing capabilities.*

ABOVE: *In 1967, Frank Baker, Jr. and employees celebrated the retirement of the "Old Black Hen" after 45 years of loyal service by giving her a gold watch!*

Hired in 1965, Ed Lochte remembers being interviewed for a programmer/trainee position. "The process was very thorough, similar to what we might do today for a department head. Information technology and programming were new fields and departments were growing." Monumental looked for and found some very talented people.

Clifford, Heiner and Lippert created the electronic systems needed to convert Monumental Life's Weekly Premium and Regular Ordinary accounting records to the IBM-650 processor. Before long, though, the team was reprogramming again to accommodate a complete system changeover to a new IBM-1410 system and high-speed printer. Frank Baker and Charlie Hayes had recommended purchasing the 1410 for $544,275 to enable the company to run its programs in one-third the time.

"We were the first company on the East Coast to install the 1410," remembers Lippert. "We had to go to New York City, working long hours and odd shifts, to complete testing so the system could be installed." On March 1, 1962, President Fred Wehr pressed a button to begin the first home office demonstration run of the IBM-1410.

BELOW: *Edward W. ("Dick") Schellhas was Monumental's first advertising and sales promotion manager.*

Reporting on the important company milestone, the *Old Black Hen* noted:

Life insurance is a most highly competitive industry. The installation of the 1410 system provides us with the latest and most efficient record keeping equipment available. Greater accuracy, prompter service, the ability to do jobs not feasible on a manual basis . . . are just a few of its advantages for our field and Home Office employees and policyholders.

LOOK!

How do you think employees and policyholders reacted on December 3, 1963—just eleven days after President Kennedy's death—when they opened the pages of the popular *LOOK* magazine and saw the company's first ad in a national publication?

Agents, no doubt, were proud to be recognized as "specialists" in family protection. Hopefully, policyholders were proud to be insured by Monumental Life. And if the eye-catching ads did their job, thousands of *LOOK*'s 14.5 million readers in states where we did business picked up the phone to call a trained Monumental "specialist" to measure their family's "individual life, group life and health insurance" protection needs.

Advertising and sales promotion became such a high priority that management appointed Edward W. ("Dick") Schellhas, CLU, a twenty-two year Monumental Life veteran, as the company's first manager of advertising and sales promotion in June 1964. He reported directly to Edmund S. Barrett, vice president of District Agencies.

Monumental's next national sales campaign—promoting the company's new "Longer Life Line" product line—kicked off in September 1964. Ads that fall in the *Saturday Evening Post* promoted the policies' liberalized benefits, lower rates, and layman's language. "Because you are living longer," noted the Triple L ads, "Monumental now offers you greater advantages in life insurance protection than ever before."

Whether it was the ads, additional training, more highly motivated agents, more consistent underwriting under John B. ("Bos") Ensor, appointed underwriting supervisor in 1963, or Ensor's personal visits to forty field offices during these years no one could say for sure. But something "clicked" in 1963 and 1964. When insurance in force grew $93.8 million in 1963 and another $146.7 million in 1964, they were the best two sales years to date in the company's history. The positive sales trend continued in 1965 when a special advertising campaign aimed at women produced $50 million in new coverage.

Though sales in the Weekly Premium marketplace were declining, as they had throughout the industry since 1956, sales of Regular Ordinary (RO), Monthly Debit Ordinary (MDO), and Group business reached new highs. Regardless of product, payment method, or distribution system, Monumental Life remained focused on the needs of individuals and groups in the middle-income market.

GENERAL AGENCIES, GROUP DIVISION GROW

By 1962, four general agency managers in Baltimore, Philadelphia, Newark and Cleveland were training career agents to produce ordinary business for Monumental Life. Another ten personal-producing general agents (GAs) in Maryland, Pennsylvania, New Jersey, Ohio and North Carolina were also selling Monumental products. Among them was Philadelphia-based Charles Freiberg, recognized as Monumental's first member of the industry's prestigious Million Dollar Round Table. In April 1963, President Wehr announced to directors that General Agencies would open a new office in Detroit.

Group business also grew during the Sixties. In 1960, the company appointed Dwight K. Bartlett as group actuary. A Fellow in the Society of Actuaries, Bartlett had graduated cum laude from Harvard University in 1953 and had several years' experience pricing group products. Elected Monumental Life senior vice president and chief

actuary in 1967, Bartlett remained with the company until 1979, when he was appointed chief actuary for the Social Security Administration. He served as insurance commissioner for the State of Maryland from 1993 to 1997.

ABOVE: *President Fred Wehr and Frank Doetzer were pleased with sales resulting from a special ad campaign aimed at women.*

LEFT: *Dwight K. Bartlett, FSA, was appointed group actuary in 1960.*

Samuel H. Shriver joined Monumental Life in 1961 as Marketing's Group representative with responsibility for assisting local field agents in soliciting and placing group business. By mid-1962, the Group Department had processed over one hundred cases representing $50 million in Group Life and Group Accident and Health coverage.

Sam Keller, who retired in 1998, wrote one of the company's first programs to process Group Health claims. "I left space for only four digits," he remembers. "Who would have thought that benefits would ever be more than $99.99 per day!"

One of the first group cases written in the early 1960s provided $4.9 million of coverage on members of the U.S.

Air Force Sergeants Association. The case helped Group increase its insurance in force by $1 million in April 1963. In 1964, Shriver helped close another large group case. The policy issued to the Baltimore & Ohio Railroad provided $21 million in death and disability coverage for over 25,000 railroad workers and retirees previously covered by B&O's Employee Relief Fund. Shriver's father, George M. Shriver, had served as vice president of the railroad until his death in 1942.

By year-end 1965, the Group Department reported $319 million of insurance in force—including $78.8 million in Servicemen's Group Life coverage on the lives of soldiers serving in Vietnam. By July 31, 1967, the company had paid a total of $272,748 in Vietnam-related death claims.

Connie Taylor, promoted to supervisor of Group Services in 1968, saw the group business grow throughout the 1960s from just a few employees in Baltimore to six group offices in Chicago, Philadelphia, Cleveland and Baltimore, Atlanta and Cincinnati. She remembers Shriver bringing his daughter, Wimbledon tennis star Pam Shriver, into the office as a little girl. "She had such beautiful curls!" But Taylor's most vivid memory of those early years was the day in November 1963 when President Kennedy was killed. "Sam called all of us together, told us Kennedy had been shot, and then closed the office."

INDUSTRY FIGHTS MEDICARE, JOINS JOHNSON'S WAR ON POVERTY

President Kennedy was assassinated before Congress could enact many of his proposed tax and social welfare reforms. Though popular with many voters, his administration's program to provide federally subsidized medical care for the aged was opposed by insurance industry executives. Extending Social Security, they argued, would create an even larger, more intrusive federal bureaucracy.

On the other hand, life insurance agents and the industry were pleased when in 1962 Kennedy signed the Keogh bill allowing the self-employed to establish tax-deferred personal retirement accounts. In fact, the American Life Convention, the Life Insurance Association of America, and the National Association of Life Underwriters (NALU) had actively participated in the development of the bill. Their efforts assured that Congress fairly treated the use of life insurance, endowment and annuity contracts in retirement planning.

By the time Lyndon B. Johnson was sworn in as president in late 1963, the country's mood had changed. During his first year in office, LBJ worked closely with Congress to pass a tax cut and the Civil Rights Act of 1964. On the campaign trail later that year, he urged the nation "to build a great society, a place where the meaning of man's life matches the marvels of man's labor." He won the November 1964 presidential election with 61 percent of the vote—the widest popular margin in U.S. history.

Johnson's Great Society program of 1965 proposed aid to education, disease prevention, enactment of Medicare legislation, and a broad-based "War on Poverty" that included urban renewal, development of depressed areas, control of crime and delinquency, and removal of obstacles that impeded a citizen's right to vote. Congress rapidly passed all legislation with few amendments or changes. But despite these efforts to relieve poverty, eliminate segregation and end discrimination, the administration could not prevent the social unrest and anti-war sentiments that were brewing in 1965, or the riots and protests that erupted across the country in 1967.

Following the 1967 riots in Detroit and Newark, the life insurance industry committed one billion dollars to help President Johnson halt urban decay and fight poverty. With sales climbing, 140 life insurance companies, including Monumental Life, controlled 87 percent of the country's life insurance assets. The company's $2,275,000 share of the industry's $1 billion investment in urban renewal helped create jobs, finance low-income housing, and improve nursing home facilities for senior citizens in Baltimore and other U.S. cities. Monumental's Don Wilson served on the industry subcommittee that developed the program's guidelines, eligibility standards and reporting procedures.

'ISLAND' IN A CHANGING INNER CITY

During the 1960s, Monumental Life was a much-respected presence in Baltimore, and Monumental agents were recognized and welcomed in just about every working-class neighborhood in the city. The company's imposing and impressive headquarters at Charles and Chase Streets symbolized permanence and strength in "the Monumental City." Its office provided employment, income, opportunity and excellent benefits for almost three hundred Baltimore-area residents.

But the company's once elegant Mount Vernon neighborhood and much of Baltimore had changed. The city that had contributed so much to the postwar economic boom was showing serious signs of neglect. Local government and businesses had pumped so much money into war-related industries, highways, and suburban growth that inner-city neighborhoods, schools and services suffered.

As housing and neighborhoods deteriorated during the 1950s, families who could afford to move abandoned the city. Established downtown businesses and restaurants closed their doors as customers found it easier to park, shop and eat at suburban malls. Boarded up buildings became symbols of urban decay, causing property values to fall even further. Before long, only Baltimore's poorest black families who had nowhere else to go remained in the city's most economically depressed and dangerous neighborhoods.

LEFT: *Lyndon B. Johnson became president in November 1963 after John F. Kennedy's death in a Dallas motorcade.*

BELOW: *Monumental contributed over $2.2 million in 1967 to help Johnson fight his War on Poverty in neighborhoods like this one in Baltimore.*
Greg Otto, 2008, "Corner House," oil and acrylic on painting board, collection of Petey & John O'Donnell.

ABOVE: *Despite increasing decay and "white flight" to the suburbs during the 1960s, Frank Baker, Jr., Monumental's newly elected president, and Fred Wehr, chairman of the board and CEO, made the difficult decision to keep the company's home office in downtown Baltimore.*

COMMITMENT TO CITY, BALTIMORE CITIZENS

As many Baltimore-based companies moved to the suburbs, Monumental Life's officers and directors made the courageous decision to stay in the city. The company bought the remaining buildings on the northern end of its 1100 North Charles Street block, began plans to add a third building, and increased investment in the growth, development and future of its Mount Vernon/Mount Royal neighborhood.

In January 1965 directors elected Fred Wehr Monumental Life chairman of the board and CEO, and Frank Baker, Jr., president and chief administrative officer. Wehr had just completed a two-year term as president of the Chamber of Commerce of Metropolitan Baltimore, and Baker would be elected to the board of Baltimore's Better Business Bureau later that spring.

Baker began attending neighborhood meetings with representatives from several civic improvement organizations—including the Greater Baltimore Committee, the Charles Street Association, the Mount Vernon Area Neighborhood Council, and the Baltimore Department of Planning—to discuss ways to revitalize the city's commercial and cultural centers. The four organizations co-sponsored a comprehensive Inner City Central Core Study funded by area businesses. Monumental Life's share of the study's $125,000 cost was $3,200.

In 1965 directors also agreed to provide $1 million in mortgage funding to help build a downtown theater planned as part of the One Charles Center/Inner Harbor urban renewal project. Ground-breaking in many ways, the Charles Center project began an era of public/private partnership and investment in downtown office buildings, apartments, hotels, theaters, parks, commercial offices, overhead walkways and underground parking garages. The new Morris Mechanic Theater opened January 16, 1967, with the road show version of *Hello Dolly* starring Betty

Between 1950 and 1970, Baltimore's population declined from 948,754 to 905,759 residents. At the same time the number of black residents almost doubled from 225,099 (24 percent) to 425,922 (47 percent).

Monumental sold its West Baltimore district office building at 1905 Bloomingdale Road for $53,200 in 1963 and its large Baltimore East office at the intersection of North Avenue and Gay Street for $23,500 in 1965. The neighborhoods had changed so dramatically that agents no longer felt safe entering and leaving the buildings with large sums of collected cash. The East Baltimore office moved out of downtown to leased space on Harford Road.

By the middle of the decade, it had also become increasingly difficult to recruit qualified employees, because workers were afraid to come downtown. A bail bondsman, a palm reader, pornographic bookstores, the "Les Girls" strip club, and the "Cat's Meow" massage parlor—advertising "We make house calls!" in blinking lights—had all opened within two blocks of the home office. When asked about those years, one retiree noted that our building sat like an isolated and "well-fortified island" surrounded by blocks of decaying rundown storefronts.

Grable.

That same month, two highly respected Baltimore businessmen—Alonzo G. Decker, Jr., president of the Black & Decker Manufacturing Company, and Austin E. Penn, chairman and president of the Baltimore Gas & Electric Company—joined Monumental Life's board of directors. Fred Wehr had announced his intention to retire, effective August 1, 1967, and the board welcomed the two men's city-wide experience and connections.

On July 28, 1967, directors elected Frank Baker, Jr., chairman and CEO and Donald H. Wilson, Jr. president and chief administrative officer. One of their first decisions as executive officers was to approve a $1,500 contribution to the city's new Operations Industrialization Center (OIC). Developed by the Chamber of Commerce and the Voluntary Council of Equal Opportunity, the new program provided vocational counseling and job training for unskilled workers.

Nineteen-year-old Diane Meredith joined the OIC program in April 1968. "The program taught me secretarial skills, filing and typing, and light accounting skills such as completing ledgers," she notes today. "I needed those skills to succeed as a [single, young] black woman in corporate America." Remembering her first weeks in Monumental's Actuarial Department in October 1968, Meredith says: "It was scary and uncomfortable at first, working in an environment with mostly whites. But

this being my first job, I was determined to make it."

Back issues of the *The Old Black Hen* document that the company had begun to provide jobs and career opportunities for the city's minority students in 1966. For the first time in the company's long history, the smiling faces of young black women appeared in photos of the Actuarial, Key Punch and Policyowner Service Departments celebrating their "Oriole Spirit" during the 1966 American League pennant race.

Purchasing's Donald Davis, a young black man, was also pictured in a 1967 issue of the publication. He was one of the company's first employees to be drafted to serve in the escalating Vietnam War.

As soldiers fought in Vietnam and protests erupted on city streets and college campuses, management tried to keep its field and home office employees focused on positive company milestones and achievements—$2 billion of insurance in force in August 1967, installation of a new "third generation" Honeywell H-1200 computer system in January 1968, entry into the Group Pensions market, the Group Department's first "mass marketing" mailing to a bank's mortgage customers, a new investment policy announced by financial vice president Frank A. Cappiello, Jr., a "retirement" ceremony honoring *The Old Black Hen* for forty-five years of faithful service, and the debut of *LIFE LINE,* a new quarterly publication.

ABOVE: *The Civil Rights Act of 1964 changed the appearance of many businesses. For the first time in its history, Monumental began to provide career opportunities for minority students.*

BELOW: *Management celebrated another "monumental" milestone—$2 billion of insurance in force—in April 1967 by serving lunch to employees.*

LEFT: *Diane Meredith, pictured here in 1979, was hired by Monumental in 1968 through the city's new Operations Industrialization Center program.*

Architect's rendering of the 1968 home office addition. It extended Monumental's presence on Charles Street to a full city block and included an employee garage.

ABOVE: *Architect's rendering of the 1968 home office addition. It extended Monumental's presence on Charles Street to a full city block and included an employee garage.*

RIGHT: *Frank Baker, Jr., and Fred Wehr broke ground for the new building on December 8, 1966.*

NEW BUILDING ON CHARLES AND BIDDLE

But what seemed to interest employees as much as anything in early 1968 was the new five-story building, garage and park-like plaza nearing completion on the corner of Charles and Biddle Streets. Modern, massive and surrounded at street level by polished red granite it belonged to Monumental Life!

Employees had watched the corner's transformation since the summer of 1966, when a wrecker's ball demolished existing rowhouses. On December 8, 1966, they attended a ground-breaking ceremony where Mayor Theodore R. McKeldin praised the company as "one of Baltimore's proud assets" and its directors as forward-thinking leaders dedicated to revitalizing the community.

THE RIOTS

By the time the building's windows and white stone walls were put in place in early 1968, employees were dreaming about lunch on their bright, sunny terrace. But those dreams and others were dashed at least temporarily by Martin Luther King's murder in Memphis on April 4.

Two days later, the tension that had been building in Baltimore's black neighborhoods erupted. A weekend of fires and looting destroyed businesses and homes on both the east and west sides of the city, including the neighborhood near North Avenue and Gay Street where, until 1965, the company had had a branch office.

"Old timer" Gail Matzen, who joined Monumental Life in 1963, remembers Sunday, April 7, 1968. "You couldn't be on the streets anywhere in the city." Though the company never closed, she says she was "scared to death" riding to work with Wylie Hopkins that Monday morning. "It was eerie. Not many cars. Not much activity. Some streets were still closed and many police were still on patrol."

Several Monumental Life officers went up on the roof that Monday, remembers Jim Gentry. Seeing smoking buildings on both the east and west sides of the city, they advised employees to go straight home after work.

ABOVE: *Baltimore mayor Theodore McKeldin praised company executives and proudly announced that Monumental's addition would be "the center of the neighborhood's rebirth."*

LEFT TOP TO BOTTOM: *Construction took almost eighteen months. Excavation began in early 1967. Exterior walls and terrace appeared a year later.*

The building about to go up, he declared, would be a center of the neighborhood's rebirth. "I am proud that Monumental Life has demonstrated faith in the future of Baltimore," he concluded. "This building is the company's latest and possibly most significant vote of confidence in the future of our city."

As construction crews put up fences, dug the foundation and erected the steel framework, no one expected the building site itself to be beautified . . . but it was! In the spring of 1967 the company invited art students from Baltimore's Catonsville Community College to submit paintings of city landmarks. The winning designs decorated the construction fences for several months, drawing favorable comments from neighbors and local businessmen.

Competitors Create Holding Companies

BY the mid-1960s it was becoming obvious to everyone in the industry that staying competitive would require experienced investment, actuarial and computer professionals. Many smaller life insurance companies were finding it difficult to attract and retain talented people. For companies like Monumental Life and its home service competitors with captive career agents operating out of local field offices, distribution costs were already high. By sharing resources, two or more smaller companies could join forces and benefit from what management teams called the "economies of scale."

As members of the "counter culture" began to form communes at the end of the decade, life insurance company executives also began to look for partners willing to come together under the umbrella of a larger holding company.

Monumental Life's directors approved the creation of Monumental Corporation as a vehicle to permit expansion, growth, and acquisitions in 1968. It was incorporated as a general business holding company in Maryland on July 15, 1968.

Less than a year later, in March 1969, the Capital Holding Corporation was incorporated in Delaware as a holding company for Louisville's Commonwealth Life. Selecting the new holding company's name presented more problems than one might imagine, explains Commonwealth Life historian Victor Gerard:

> The problem was to adopt a name that was sufficiently comprehensive to permit acquisitions of various kinds. It was also felt that the name should not in any way point to Commonwealth Life. . . .

Companies might be willing to have their stock exchanged for that of a company with a nondescript name like Capital Holding but would resist becoming an affiliate of a former competitor.

William H. Abell, president of Commonwealth Life since 1958, was elected Capital Holding's first president. Homer Parker was its first vice president and treasurer. As the holding company made acquisitions over the next few years, Parker became full-time president of Capital Holding and Abell became its chairman.

Like Monumental Life, the Capital Holding companies all started as small home service companies with agents and customers concentrated in one or two states. Commonwealth Life expanded into Indiana in 1963 when it acquired Indiana's Empire Life and Accident Insurance Company. Since 35 percent of Empire's business was in African American homes, Commonwealth became the first Capital Holding company to integrate.

Capital Holding acquired Peoples Life of Washington, D.C., and the National Trust Life Insurance Company of Memphis in 1969. Orlando-based National Standard Life Insurance Company, with a large block of minority business in Florida; Home Security Life Insurance Company in Durham, North Carolina; and the First National Life Insurance Company of New Orleans became Capital Holding affiliates early in the 1970s.

Capital Holding would continue to acquire and grow, diversify, consolidate, reorganize, share resources and change its name to the Providian Corporation over the next two decades.

BELOW: *The Monumental name and logo were well-known to home service competitors that became part of Louisville's Capital Holding Corporation.*

RIGHT: *Retired former Capital Holding Corporation executives (left to right) Tom Schnick, John Grubb and David Sams met in Orlando in 2007 for a reunion.*

On April 10, 1969, Baker was finally able to announce that Volunteer State Life's stockholders had approved affiliation with Monumental Life under the Monumental Corporation holding company. And, he noted, officers of both Monumental Life and Volunteer had already met to establish plans for the two companies to work closely together to complement one other's operations.

WHITE KNIGHTS

Baker found it hard to dismiss the 1968 takeover attempt. It could happen again, he knew, unless Monumental Corporation found a major stockholder in Baltimore to invest in the company and prevent it from being taken over by an unfriendly, out-of-town buyer.

Working through investment officers at Alex. Brown & Company early in 1969, Baker contacted Joseph Meyerhoff, the highly respected Baltimore-based commercial real estate developer, to see if his firm might be interested in becoming Monumental's "white knight." "Our family firm," notes Harvey M. ("Bud") Meyerhoff in his memoirs, "filled that role."

Joseph Meyerhoff knew Frank Baker from their joint efforts on behalf of the Baltimore Symphony. The younger Meyerhoff explains why being the "white knight" appealed to his father:

> First, it guaranteed the diversification of our estates, especially Dad's, because we would own Monumental stock instead of privately held real estate companies. . . . Owning part of a public company was a very attractive feature of merging. . . . Second, from a business point of view, Monumental was stable, with good cash flow, and its top executives understood real estate completely. . . . In the investment real estate business, cash flow equals value. . . . Third, the chemistry looked right to us because of our knowledge of the company and of Frank Baker, and his confidence in us.

And finally, we figured that if we made a mistake in judgment, we would be only half-wrong since we would own nearly one-half of the combined enterprise. The cash flow from our company and the value it represented were about the same as for Monumental. So if Monumental's business dropped, we at least knew our business and were comfortable that we would still be making money on our side of the arrangement. On the other hand, if we stumbled, we had the comfort of knowing that Monumental, which had always made money, would be there on our behalf.

Negotiations were conducted in "neutral territory," says Meyerhoff, to prevent leaks to employees, the Baltimore business community, and the press. Two weeks before Astronaut Neil Armstrong stepped onto the surface of the moon, the Meyerhoffs and Monumental took a "giant leap" of their own. Their July 1969 announcement took the community completely by surprise.

The unique and unexpected merger—between a family-owned real estate company, headed by a business-savvy Russian-Jewish immigrant and recognized as one of the best run in the country, and the state's oldest, "old moneyed," southern-leaning life insurer—was completed on December 31, 1969, with the Meyerhoff family owning 44 percent of the corporate stock.

Monumental Properties, Inc. (the real estate company's new name) joined Monumental Life and Volunteer State Life as subsidiaries of Monumental Corporation. "Anyone who tried to buy the insurance company would also have to buy the real estate operation, and vice versa," said Meyerhoff.

On January 28, 1970, Frank Baker welcomed Joseph Meyerhoff, Harvey M. Meyerhoff, and J. H. Pearlstone, Joseph Meyerhoff's son-in-law, as Monumental Corporation's newest directors, acknowledging that the just completed merger "was the finest possible affiliation and one which offered great potential for the future."

ABOVE: *Frank Baker, Jr. (seated, left) and Donald Wilson (standing, center) welcomed J. H. Pearlstone (standing, left), Harvey M. ("Bud") Meyerhoff (standing, right) and Joseph Meyerhoff (seated, right) as directors of Monumental Corporation on January 28, 1970.*

CHAPTER 10

Stayin' Alive
(1970–1979)

"EVEN NUMBERS ONLY! WAITING TIME . . . 60 MINUTES," reads the hand-lettered sign. The Monumental district manager pulls into line behind the last car. Up before dawn, he had hoped to beat the crowd, but it appears many of his neighbors with even-numbered license plates had the same idea. The gauge on his dashboard confirms what he already knows—his gas tank is almost empty. He cannot waste the little fuel he has driving around trying to find shorter lines or lower prices.

"This is getting out of hand," Don Allison thinks to himself. "How can oil companies charge 55 cents for one gallon of gas? I'm paying 20 cents more today than I did last fall." Frustrated but resigned to the wait, he turns on the radio.

"Today is Friday, February 8, 1974," says the news announcer. "Prices at the gas pump continue to climb as we enter the fifth month of the Arab oil embargo. American families in the Midwest are lowering home thermostats to 60 degrees and wearing sweaters to conserve heating oil. Schools are closed in many parts of the country. Factories have cut production and continue to lay off workers. If this embargo goes on much longer it could have far-reaching effects on our U.S. economy."

The gas crisis is starting to cost Allison's agents time as well as money. They can't afford to wait in these lines twice a week. His office is responsible for serving Monumental Life customers in and around Louisville. Facing competition from

Commonwealth Life Insurance Company, several of Don's agents with semi-rural, books of business drive almost a hundred miles daily to make sales and provide in-home service.

Today is going to be a longer day than usual. He's promised a new female agent he will join her on an appointment in the suburbs scheduled for 8:00 p.m. Like 40 percent of American families in the early Seventies, the agent's prospects—both 1968 college graduates—are a two-income couple. They cannot meet with him until the wife gets home, makes dinner, and they put the kids to bed.

Since returning to Louisville as a manager in 1970, Allison has recruited agents to fill the office's open positions, reduced agent turnover, and worked closely with agents and staff managers to help them succeed. He's accompanied veteran agents on sales calls and proudly introduced rookies

ABOVE: *Like many Americans, Louisville manager Don Allison and Elizabeth "Corky" Corcoran, his office administrator, waited in gas lines in 1974.*

to their existing customers. "If you take care of your debit," he tells them, "your debit will take care of you."

Opened in 1922, the Louisville office is one of Monumental Life's oldest outside Maryland. It has served area policyholders for over fifty years. Though some policyholders pay monthly or by automatic bank draft, many older couples still expect an agent to stop by every week to collect.

Last week, the president of their local NALU (National Association of Life Underwriters) association reported that, industry-wide, the amount of paid-weekly life insurance in force continues to decline. Allison is not surprised. Even Monumental Life now calls itself a "combination company"— with agents selling both small Weekly Premium policies and larger Ordinary policies paid monthly, quarterly or annually. Some agents in the office have even placed a few group cases recently.

"The industry is changing," the old timers say. "Fewer and fewer of us are walking neighborhood streets, collecting and talking to policyholders around the kitchen table." It's true. Some agents in their association now have private offices and expect clients to come to see _them_. But many—like the "home service" agents at Monumental Life and Commonwealth— continue to spend hours in their cars every day, driving from home to home in the communities they serve.

"That's why this crisis is hitting us so hard," thinks Allison as he moves up in line. "We depend on gas to see clients who need us." The current rise in fuel and heating oil prices also makes it difficult for clients on fixed incomes to keep their insurance in force. "Just three or four years ago" says the announcer, "economists were predicting that the Seventies would be another record-breaking decade for economic growth. The first Baby Boomers were graduating college, getting married, buying homes, and starting families of their own. Between 1960 and 1970, the number of households headed by young adults doubled. Then, last year, Watergate, the pullout from Vietnam, the Yom Kippur War in the Mideast, October's oil embargo and the resulting energy shortages all wreaked havoc with those predictions. Many families today are worried about rising prices and job layoffs."

"Looks like 1974 might be a challenging year for our industry," thinks Allison. "Pump a little faster, up ahead! I have to get to our training class. Every agent has places to go and people to see. Inflation means that families need more coverage than ever."

POLYESTER AND PLAID

Visitors walking into Monumental Life field offices in the 1970s found agents dressed in jackets and ties, as one would expect. But what a colorful picture they made in their plaids and patterned polyesters! The bright sport coats and leisure suits were a welcome break from the gloomy economic forecasts, and a big change from the dark navy, charcoal gray, black and finely pinstriped suits of years past. Visitors also noticed that many of the younger men had longer hair or wide sideburns.

Ten years after Bob Dylan first sang "The Times They Are A-Changin'" in 1964, his words still rang true for the insurance industry and much of society. The Afros, long hair, long collars, chest-wide lapels, mini-skirts, hot pants, platform heels, white patent leather shoes and boots so popular in the Seventies defined more than a "generation gap." In many ways, they became symbolic of a cultural revolution that crossed generations, challenged long-held beliefs, and changed how many Americans behaved.

BELOW: *Polyester and plaid definitely added "color" to management training seminars in the Seventies.*

Contentious Times . . .
A SOLDIER REMEMBERS VIETNAM

*D*ECADES AFTER the Vietnam War, it is still difficult to write about and even more difficult to talk about—especially for soldiers who served there. The reasons are many and often extremely personal, but the simple explanation is that the conflict was divisive politically, socially, culturally and, most of all, emotionally. It left scars, for some, that never fully healed.

Straddling the 1960s and 1970s, the long-running conflict touched Monumental Life more indirectly than directly. There was no patriotic upwelling that found older employees rushing to don uniforms, as they had in World War II. And the concerns expressed by home office employees were more for their young sons, nephews and grandchildren who could be drafted into military service. So unpopular was the war that the Selective Service would later employ a lottery based on day and month of birth to fill depleted military ranks.

All the while, pictures from Vietnam were being beamed nightly in living color into millions of homes by every major TV network. There were protests on local college campuses, picketing, and more. In Baltimore nine activists—including priests Daniel and Philip Berrigan (known later as the "Catonsville Nine")—walked into the Catonsville draft board in 1968 and removed hundreds of draft records, which they burned outside.

When the young men and women who had served in Vietnam came home, they often had to make their way through jeering crowds at airports and train terminals. Though many were unsung heroes who had served their country well, and whose bravery and patriotism could not be questioned, none were greeted with parades or a hero's welcome. Instead, most went home, quietly packed away their uniforms, and tried to meld back into society.

A number would eventually join Monumental Life.

One of those was retired Army Lieutenant Colonel Tom Wiles, who joined Monumental Life in 1983 as an agent in the Annapolis, Maryland field office. Wiles, a career infantry officer, was in the service from 1963 to 1983 and served two tours in Vietnam five years apart. During his first tour, from 1966 to 1967, then-Captain Wiles was a military advisor to a South Vietnamese battalion. Later, during his second tour, from 1972 to 1973, Major Wiles was part of a joint military commission that tried to bring together all regional parties for exploratory peace talks.

Contentious times were the order of the day here in America.

"I was on the last airplane when they pulled the last troops out of Vietnam in '73," says Wiles. It would be more than a year before Saigon fell and U.S. embassy personnel would follow.

The leadership and negotiation skills he learned as a career officer served Wiles well in the life insurance business. Promoted quickly to management in the 1980s, he served as a district manager in several Monumental field offices and worked on the company's "transition teams" following major acquisitions in the 1990s. Barbara Wiles joined her husband in the Annapolis field office in 1984 and was later promoted to sales manager. The couple moved to the home office in 1999 to become regional representatives for United Financial Services (UFS), Monumental's in-house brokerage operation. In retirement they continue to "team up" to travel around the country, educating current agents and managers about products and services available through UFS.

Wiles, like other Vietnam veterans at Monumental Life and elsewhere, still prefers not to talk about his wartime experiences. He does say that the war and the stories being depicted nightly on TV during the late Sixties—coverage that his family relied upon for news—wasn't the Vietnam he knew and experienced.

"My father was Navy in World War II," notes Wiles. "His father was Army in World War I. Everyone came together, did what they were supposed to, and then they came home. Vietnam just didn't touch us that way."

And maybe that's the best way to leave the subject of Vietnam—still capable of causing rancor, still divisive in many ways, but finally, for so many Americans, behind them.

Having served two tours of duty in Vietnam, Army Lieutenant Colonel Tom Wiles was glad to be home with his wife, Barbara, and their two children in 1979. He began his second career, with Monumental, in 1983.

The 1973 Arab oil embargo prompted Americans to begin thinking more about the earth, the environment, and taking care of our natural resources.

BELOW: *A two-income couple, Monumental analyst Wendy Lemm and her husband, Tom, lived on their thirty-two-foot boat in Baltimore harbor to save money in the 1970s.*

Soldiers, families, households, corporations, institutions, politicians—even President Richard M. Nixon, who resigned from office on August 8, 1974—fought to stay alive during the decade. The Pill, pre-marital sex, gay rights, hippies, yippies and communal living threatened traditional values. The *Roe vs. Wade* decision on abortion, the growing divorce rate, single-parent homes, and two-income households changed lives more than most couples cared to admit. And how were Americans supposed to treat fathers, brothers and sons coming home from a war that so divided our nation? Even without victory parades, families welcomed home their Vietnam veterans with pride, relief and affection.

From Watergate we learned that "Big Brother" could be watching, elections might mask hidden agendas, elected officials could not be relied upon to tell us the truth, and liars did not always get what they deserved. When banks failed and respected institutions closed their doors, we felt betrayed again, and rightly so. What was happening to our country? Who, if anyone, could we trust?

OIL CRISIS INCREASES COST OF LIVING

In October 1973 the Arab oil embargo disrupted lives, strained family budgets, and quickly began to cripple the economy. Angered by U.S. support of Israel during its eighteen-day Yom Kippur War against Egypt and Syria, the Organization of Petroleum Exporting Countries (OPEC) stopped the flow of oil to U.S. shores. Though the embargo lasted only six months, oil companies raised prices immediately. Over the next seven years the cost of gasoline more than tripled—from 38.5 cents a gallon in 1973 to $1.19 in 1980—causing decade-long inflation, trade deficits, recession, and a paralyzing slowdown in productivity.

Americans adjusted to long gas lines, fifty-five mile-per-hour speed limits, cooler homes, and "Last Out, Lights Out—Don't be Fuelish" ad campaigns. President Nixon created the Department of Energy. Congress passed the National Energy Act. Families bought smaller, fuel-efficient cars, supported energy conservation programs, and participated in annual "going green" Earth Day events.

Unfortunately, nothing succeeded in keeping inflation under control. In just twelve years rising prices cut the purchasing power of the dollar in half. By 1979, American families were paying twice as much for food, housing, heating oil, utilities and health care as they had in 1967. In some parts of the country a three-bedroom house cost $80,000, a car $7,000, and paying $30,000 for a college education was not unknown. Hardest hit by the inflationary spiral were senior citizens living on fixed incomes.

The good news? The average middle-income American family had almost twice as much to spend. Between 1967 and 1977 average household income in the U.S. jumped from $8,600 to $16,400. Many companies—including Monumental Life—gave employees cost-of-living raises to combat inflation. But working women also contributed to rising household incomes.

WOMEN, TWO-INCOME HOMES— NEW TARGET MARKETS

As inflation and the women's liberation movement gained momentum, increasing numbers of wives and mothers went to work. By mid-decade, 42 percent of U.S. families needed the wife's second income to buy and maintain their homes, but millions of other women simply wanted to get out of the house.

A 1973 insurance industry survey revealed that just 35 percent of young American women looked forward to being "average housewives," while 31 percent hoped to have a career. A similar survey three years later revealed that about one third of single women—up from 20 percent in 1970—wanted a two-income lifestyle. That dream became reality more quickly than anyone could have imagined.

In 1976 the American Council of Life Insurance (ACLI) reported that both spouses worked in half of all middle-income households earning $15,000 to $25,000 per year. By 1978, about half of all American women were employed. Using their wages to pay bills, fight inflation and meet higher lifestyle and financial goals, women, on average, soon provided up to 40 percent of their family's income.

Single, married or divorced, working women in the 1970s began buying life insurance for the same reasons as working fathers and husbands—to protect dependents, to build retirement income, to help pay college tuition for their kids, and to guarantee payment of mortgages. Between 1965 and 1976, the amount of life insurance owned by women grew 150 percent to $350 billion.

During the same period, women and two-income families became the fastest-growing target markets for life insurance. If some American families required two salaries to make ends meet, other households—especially those maintained by young, dual-income, college-educated couples—simply

had more money to spend. Both groups needed additional life insurance to protect growing needs, incomes and lifestyles.

Inflation was eroding the protection power of existing policies, but it had also created unique opportunities for life insurance agents to make new and larger sales. Writing to nervous agents and managers in 1974 the editor of *Life Lines*, Monumental's company publication, advised that business conditions had little effect on the success or failure of most agents. "The prospect of a recession or even a depression should be dismissed from our minds," he wrote. "The kind of prospects we are interested in today are exactly the same as they were in 1973 and will be in 1975 . . . *people*. The prospects are always there. Our job is still to find them and serve them."

Everyone knew he was right. For life insurers and their agents in the Seventies, "Stayin' Alive" was more than a catchy disco song. It meant seeing more people, writing more business and being better prepared to meet their customers' changing needs. Many insurance companies took advantage of the times to reorganize, "reinvent" themselves, diversify and modernize their product offerings. Monumental Life reacted to inflation and rising incomes by making a few culture-changing decisions.

POSITION: *By 1978 about half of all American women—including this group of Monumental field clerical employees gathered at the home office for a training session—held jobs.*

END OF AN ERA

Early in the 1970s the Life Insurance Marketing & Research Association (LIMRA) invited Joe Collins, then Monumental vice president of District Agencies, to speak at its annual Combination Companies Conference. The topic—"Selling Weekly Premium Insurance"— was one Collins knew well. He had joined Monumental in 1948 as an agent in Detroit, sold the company's paid-weekly "industrial" life insurance policies during their "heyday" in the 1950s, and had been responsible for regional and district office sales since 1960.

On the same conference platform with Collins was an officer from Metropolitan Life Insurance Company. After presenting Monumental's pro-Weekly Premium position, Collins received a standing ovation from his home service peers. Met Life's announcement about leaving the paid-weekly business also generated a positive response. None of the combination companies—selling both Weekly Premium and Regular Ordinary policies (paid monthly, quarterly or annually)—were sorry to see Met Life's very competitive agents leave the small policy, paid-weekly marketplace.

Weekly Premium policies had formed the foundation for Monumental Life's growth, success and profitability for one hundred years. After reaching a high point in 1954, sales of the small, paid-weekly policies had steadily declined for twenty years. By 1973, industrial insurance accounted for only 2 percent of all life insurance in force in the United States—a drop of 10 percent since 1953. For Monumental Life, paid-weekly industrial policies represented only 2.7 percent of new business sales and 11 percent of the company's $3 billion of insurance in force at year-end 1974.

Although Monumental Life agents continued to collect weekly in their clients' homes into the 1980s, an important era in the company's history ended in 1975 when management agreed to stop selling policies priced and paid on a weekly basis.

In just two years, inflation had created bigger insurance needs and accelerated the already significant costs of weekly collections. Face amounts of $2,000 or less no longer provided adequate protection for policyholders living in Monumental's mostly northern, city-centered marketplace. By 1975 the company had also developed more competitive ordinary products, and agents were introducing customers to the benefits of paying premiums by monthly automatic bank draft.

As inflation continued to erode the protection power of in-force policies, the company brought in a chief marketing officer to generate additional business. The Agency Department became District Agencies, the home service operation was reorganized into five geographic regions headed by regional sales vice presidents, and a new marketing services team began creating materials to support field sales. Monumental's new Inflation Protection Program helped agents "catch up" their clients' existing coverage to meet rising costs. Thousands of eligible policyholders accepted the company's offer of additional protection with minimal underwriting and health questions.

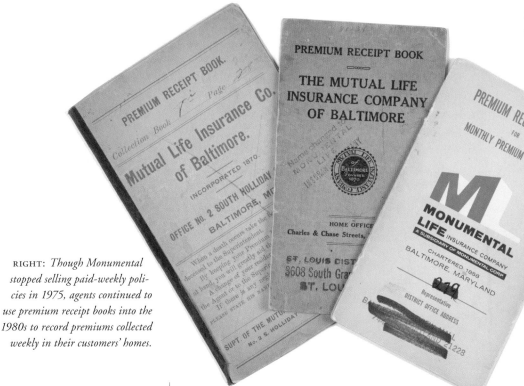

RIGHT: *Though Monumental stopped selling paid-weekly policies in 1975, agents continued to use premium receipt books into the 1980s to record premiums collected weekly in their customers' homes.*

Before long the minimum available face amount on all but a few Monumental Life policies was $5,000. Intent upon moving the company forward, management no longer accepted "but that's the way it was always done" as an excuse from agents and managers resistant to selling larger face amounts in a changing marketplace. The culture and sales climate had changed dramatically since the 1950s, with more competitive products and new distribution systems. Not surprisingly, so had potential prospects.

BOOMER CONSUMERS

The decade's college-educated "Boomer" couples were smarter, more sophisticated, more "savvy" about finances, and less trusting of "big business" than their parents and grandparents had been. Confronted with civil rights, affirmative action, discrimination and gender bias issues in the work place, recent college graduates asked why life insurance rates were higher for men and why health insurance costs were higher overall, but especially for women.

Seeing double-digit inflation and rising interest rates, they also had to decide whether to save or spend; keep their whole life policy or "buy term and invest the difference" in mutual funds, as some financial advisors recommended. Above all, as prices continued to climb, they wanted to make sure their life insurance would provide more than death and burial benefits for surviving loved ones.

Boomers asked tough questions, and they expected their life insurance agents to have the answers. To reach this growing group of better-educated prospects, agents had to be better educated themselves.

The company introduced a new self-study IDEA—Insurance Data Electronic Analysis—to improve agent professionalism and effectiveness. Using closed-circuit television technology, trainers improved sales skills by filming agents in role-play situations so they could see themselves in action. Many Monumental agents also bought portable "A/V" tape systems to educate prospects during in-home sales presentations.

More importantly, District Agencies encouraged all agents and managers to complete industry-sponsored education programs, earn the LUTCF (Life Underwriter Training Council Fellow) and CLU (Chartered Life Underwriter) professional designations, win industry awards, and join their local NALU (National Association of Life Underwriters) chapters.

NALU members benefited not only from networking at local association meetings but also from reading articles published in *Life Association News*. Article titles—including "Career Women, An Overlooked Insurance Market," "Reaching the Blue Collar Market through Group Sales," and "Solving Prospecting Problems in a Small Town"—echoed the decade's concerns and offered solutions to industry-wide challenges facing many agents.

College-educated "Boomer" couples married and started families in the 1970s. The decade's life insurance agents had to be better educated themselves to be able to answer their questions and meet needs.

BELOW: *Monumental used closed-circuit television technology to train agents and improve their sales and presentation skills.*

ABOVE: *Home office employees reflected the decade's diversity, clothing styles, and more relaxed dress code.*

BELOW: *Barbara Lucas Bryant joined Monumental in 1969.*

RIGHT: *Employee Advisory Councils composed of clerical personnel, mid-level managers and field employees helped bring employee issues and concerns to management's attention. This group included Linda Krause and Marge Imwold (seated, left), Pat Stokes (standing, third from left), and Paul Clifford (standing, fourth from right). Monumental CEO Frank Baker and President Don Wilson are standing, left and right.*

CULTURE SHOCK

During the Seventies, employees in the home office were also dealing with culture-changing human relations challenges. Since 1966 the company had employed more and more African Americans to fill administrative, clerical and support positions. If the faces of new employees pictured in company publications told an accurate story, the number of black men and women increased gradually over ten years—from a few dozen in the 1960s to almost 30 percent of new hires by the mid-1970s.

Pictures taken at company picnics and holiday dances reflected a similar startling change. Gone were separate social functions, divided by race. By mid-decade, black and white families attended the same events in nearly equal numbers.

Barbara Lucas Bryant, who will celebrate her fortieth year with Monumental in 2009, joined the company's Investment Accounting Department in 1969. "I was very young and inexperienced," she remembers. "The older employees took the young ones under their wing and taught us what we needed to know. I learned the business on-the-job thanks to their hands-on training."

An African American, Bryant says she experienced firsthand the "family atmosphere" that long-term employees continue to talk about. "We did things together inside and outside the office," she says. "We worked and played together. Black and white, we supported one another, became good friends and remain so today."

"I grew up at Monumental," she adds. "The company encouraged me to go to school at night and I developed, both personally and professionally. The people and the opportunities are why I am still here today." Looking back, Bryant notes:

> Race was never an issue for me. It was never something I felt or had to deal with on a daily basis. Race is more of an issue today because people make it one. I always treated people with respect and received it in return. Regardless of race, we need to listen to other people's ideas, agree, disagree, resolve issues and move on.

In 1970, Monumental sent Underwriting Supervisor Joan Warfield to a human resources seminar at Baltimore's Morgan State College. Other supervisory personnel from Baltimore firms with increasing numbers of black employees also attended. The program's purpose was to help increase understanding between the two races and create more harmonious work environments. Participating in seminars was just one of many ways the company coped with change and complied with new employment and anti-discrimination regulations established by the Equal Employment Opportunity Commission (EEOC).

In 1972, Chairman and CEO Frank Baker and President Don Wilson hired Edward N. Hay & Associates to evaluate jobs and develop a salary administration program for all home office positions. For the first time in one hundred years, the company put in place formal performance appraisal, salary and promotion guidelines based on position descriptions and objectives rather than on more subjective criteria like loyalty, contribution and years of service.

In the wake of industry concern about gender and age-bias lawsuits, Baker also reminded directors that language in the company's pension plan had to be changed from "wife benefit" to "spouse benefit." At about the same time, management created Employee Advisory Councils composed of clerical, mid-level management, and field employees to help bring employee issues and concerns to management's attention. As a result of recommendations made in 1973, officers agreed to implement supervisory training and approved 6 percent cost of living pay raises for all paid-weekly employees, 3.5 percent increases for managers paid monthly, and "flex" hours, as needed, for all employees.

President Don Wilson and other forward-thinking officers supported the Advisory Councils' suggestions to improve communication throughout the organization. Dwight Bartlett, senior vice president and chief actuary—responsible for several service departments in the 1970s—and Ed Brunner, vice president of

Accounting, encouraged their managers to hold more frequent department meetings and look for ways—including brainstorming sessions—to share ideas and information and update their teams regularly about corporate plans, policies and benefits. Employees used to top-down decision-making were pleased by the change to more open, interactive dialogue.

Ed Brunner,
Accounting Vice President

Opportunity Knocked...
Cheryl Brown Opened the Door!

Cheryl Brown, newly appointed Maryland assistant attorney general, in 2007.

JOINING Monumental Life as a "temp" in the Mail Pay Department in 1977, Cheryl Brown never dreamed that she would one day earn a law degree or become a partner in a well-known Baltimore law firm. Her Monumental story is proof that hard work, commitment to self-improvement, and taking advantage of opportunities can change lives in dramatic ways.

Working in the company's service departments in the late 1970s, Brown began taking LOMA (Life Office Management Association) classes to improve her knowledge and understanding of the life insurance business. By 1982 she had passed ten courses, earned the industry's "FLMI" (Fellow, Life Management Institute) designation, and begun representing her department at the company's Product Development Committee meetings.

General Counsel Jim Gentry attended the same meetings. He noticed that "Cheryl was always well-prepared," engaged in discussions, and able to answer tough questions. In 1984 he offered her a position in the Law Department.

"The department was small then, just three people," remembers Brown. Gentry encouraged her to go to college to become a paralegal. She enrolled at Villa Julie College in Baltimore County and, before long, was drafting responses to Insurance Department complaints.

Over the next fifteen years, the company changed dramatically, and so did Brown. When Gentry retired in 1993, Stacey Boyer, a graduate of Duke University and the University of Baltimore Law School, replaced him as vice president and general counsel. Because of acquisitions and increased industry regulation in the 1990s, the Law Department staff expanded to more than ten people. Brown completed college at Villa Julie, earned her law degree, with honors, from the University of Baltimore and passed the Maryland bar exam.

"It was hard going to school at night and working during the day," she admits, but the law school was only two blocks from the office and she could walk there after work. Having the company pay for her degrees through the Tuition Assistance Program also helped. "Monumental's Tuition Assistance Program makes it possible for people who struggle financially to go to college and earn their degrees," says Brown. "The program still benefits the company and its employees."

Brown remained at Monumental Life after becoming a member of the Maryland bar on December 12, 2000. Promoted to assistant secretary and compliance counsel, she was responsible for filing required forms, notifying employees of changes in state insurance regulations, approving sales and marketing materials, and preparing for insurance department examinations.

In 2001, Gentry introduced Brown to attorneys at Funk & Bolton, a downtown Baltimore law firm that represents insurance companies. She left Monumental after almost twenty-five years when Funk & Bolton offered her a position. She was promoted to law firm partner in 2006 and in late 2007 left private practice to become an assistant attorney general for the State of Maryland.

Brown appreciates Monumental Life's and Gentry's contributions to her career success. "He recognized my potential and gave me the opportunity to grow," she says today. She also values the support and encouragement she received from supervisors and co-workers who encouraged her to stay in school.

RIGHT: *Monumental's Law Department— H. Stacey Boyer, Darlene Ragan, Jim Gentry, Judy Karl, and Cheryl Brown—in 1992.*

Decisions by Monumental's board also improved employee working conditions. In 1971 contractors completed a $2.5 million "face lift" on the 1926, 1938 and 1958 home office buildings that included lower ceilings, modular lighting, carpeting, central air-conditioning, and ten thousand additional square feet of usable space for meetings and training sessions. In 1972 the company purchased a parking garage at 1209–1225 North Charles Street for employee use. A few years later, paid security guards and new sign-in procedures replaced receptionists in safer entrance lobbies.

'GO AHEAD' LEAP WITH GAAP

Until the late 1960s, employees in the company's relatively small, unsophisticated accounting department functioned primarily as bookkeepers. Their role became more strategic in the early 1970s when certified public accountants began to manage earnings. Night school students Robert McGraw and Ralph Arnold, hired by Ed Brunner in 1971 and 1972, would complete their degrees through Monumental's Tuition Reimbursement Program and become the first of this "new breed" of Monumental Life accountants.

Chris Ament Wroten joined Payroll Accounting in 1971 right out of high school. She remembers being paid weekly, and in cash—"I can still see Lenore Tranis going around the building delivering envelopes from a shoe box"—doing W-2 forms by hand, and manually typing the company's annual statements on a three-foot-wide typewriter. Wroten, who retired in 2007, smiles thinking back:

> We were also "CPAs"—cutters, pasters and assemblers! We challenged one another to see who could type the fastest, with fewest errors. We worked Saturdays and couldn't take any vacation from January 1 through mid-March. Some days, we worked from 6:00 a.m. to 11:00 p.m. to complete year-end statements.

ABOVE: *Robert McGraw joined Monumental in 1971.*

BELOW: *Ralph Arnold, hired in 1972, completed two degrees with the help of Monumental's Tuition Reimbursement Program.*

Accounting manager Bill Simmons, promoted to treasurer in 1973, remembers meeting officers Frank Baker, Dwight Bartlett, Don Wilson and Ed Brunner for lunch when they all worked Saturdays to complete year-end figures, taxes and the annual report. Among other duties, Simmons and his small staff typed bills and invoices, maintained "buy/sell" records of the company's investment securities, prepared quarterly dividend checks for stockholders, and manually updated personnel cards for eight hundred field and home office employees as their earnings, company-funded pension benefits and life insurance increased.

That's the kind of commitment it took to get things done manually in the 1970s. It's also why things had to change.

The introduction of GAAP—Generally Accepted Accounting Principles—in 1972 triggered a culture-changing shift in how Monumental Life tracked expenses and made business decisions. Prior to GAAP, the company followed statutory accounting guidelines—regulated by each state's insurance department—that required insurance companies to charge business development expenses immediately and against current earnings, in the year they were incurred. As a result, insurers sometimes put off major development projects for years to avoid "hits" to their bottom line.

GAAP made investing in expensive new technology affordable because many start-up costs could be capitalized and amortized rather than recognized immediately. Realizing that they had to modernize Monumental's systems to remain competitive in the 1970s, management committed to taking a giant leap forward. It was time to automate!

LIFE COMM—A NEW LEGACY

Like many old insurance companies in those years, Monumental was still using decades-old, home-grown manual systems to process Weekly Premium (WP) and Regular Ordinary (RO) business, accounting statements, agent performance reporting and commissions. The "legacy" systems were labor-intensive and slow, difficult to change, and expensive to maintain.

During the mid-1970s the Equimatics Division of Informatics, Inc. began marketing a comprehensive, totally integrated data processing system called "LIFE COMM III"—developed with the sponsorship of nine life insurance companies—to help life insurers administer their business. After careful research and study, a committee headed by Monumental's second vice president, John Gray, recommended that the company purchase the new system. Representatives of both organizations met, signed a contract, and began planning for the multi-year, multi-million-dollar installation and conversion.

A complex system of sub-systems, LIFE COMM could handle premium calculations, produce policy documents, and update weekly and pending status reports. All sub-systems interacted with the same policy master file. Regardless of the task—policy change, conversion, or agent pay, for example—home office personnel could access the same consolidated data.

Writing to field office cashiers in August 1978, Assistant Secretary Bert Morales noted proudly:

LIFE COMM III is the most comprehensive, advanced insurance system available today in the marketplace. It will never become obsolete because it can be upgraded and modified in infinite ways to cope with future changes in insurance accounting and the way the company operates.

This immense effort is geared for the future, to allow the home office to give faster, more accurate service at lower cost to applicants, policyholders, field personnel, management and the public. The conversion to LIFE COMM will result in drastic changes in almost everything we do, particularly in the home office, where entire departments will be changed to correspond with the insurance industry's six basic functional areas—New Business Administration, Policy Administration, Corporate Accounting & Financial Reporting, Agency Administration, Actuarial Services, and Investment Administration.

LIFE COMM ended the company's century-long practice of hand-writing or typing policies one page at a time. With LIFE COMM, policy data was stored in the mainframe, and policy pages were printed out during overnight cycles and assembled the next day. LIFE COMM also made it possible to provide comprehensive, updated policy information to field offices using an innovative microfiche storage system. Each 4" x 6" piece of fiche film held 224 pages of policyholder data.

ABOVE LEFT: *Greg Yates, LIFE COMM systems coordinator, with conversion clerks Lucy Haynie, Gail Matzen and Betty Love in 1979.*

ABOVE RIGHT: *Colleen Gizinski, administrative assistant, and Peggy Moore, supervisor, Special Ordinary Accounting, used LIFE COMM to create an agent record.*

BELOW LEFT: *Programmers Quentin Davis, Mary LeFurgy and Dave Somerville.*

BELOW RIGHT: *Consultant Kathy Horner reviewed LIFE COMM output with Ed Lochte and John Gray.*

Conversion of Monumental's manual records to the central, computerized database was a company-wide undertaking that took almost three full years to complete. Converting the Regular Ordinary business (250,000 policies) took about one year. Converting the Monthly Account Ordinary business was a much bigger challenge that took a special task force—including a consultant from Equimatics—twenty-two months to plan, complete and test. Frank Lastner, second vice president and Insurance Services Projects Officer, headed the task force. Working closely with Lastner were Gregory A. Yates, assistant vice president, Policyowner Services, and Ed Lochte, Data Processing Special Projects Officer.

LIFE COMM changed the way Monumental Life administered its business. The new system also created its own legacy. Though the company changed mainframe computers in 1978, and again in 1979, the comprehensive and flexible, patched and frequently updated LIFE COMM is still in place today.

INVESTING IN THE NEIGHBORHOOD

While teams of employees upgraded technology and data processing systems to improve output and efficiency, Vice President, General Counsel and Secretary Jim Gentry was working closely with the city and local businessmen to improve the company's Charles Street neighborhood.

Early in the Seventies, Monumental Life bought the Belvedere Hotel through mortgage foreclosure to halt its deterioration. By May 1975, Gentry was also holding regular meetings with representatives from Loyola Federal, Union Trust Bank, Mercantile Bank & Trust, the John Hanson Savings & Loan, Danny's Restaurant, Miller Brothers, and the Mount Vernon-Belvedere Association. With their backing, he negotiated with landlords to purchase all buildings on the west side of Charles Street's 1200 and 1300 blocks and signed contracts with the Frank Knott Construction Company to redevelop the properties. Monumental Life, Loyola Federal and the John Hanson

Savings & Loan agreed to share mortgage financing for the planned street-level retail stores with apartments above.

Two years later, Mayor William Donald Schaefer and the Baltimore Chamber of Commerce presented Monumental Life with the Mayor's Award for its efforts in restoring the 1200 and 1300 blocks of North Charles and for the company's attitude and assistance in helping the city renovate the Midtown-Belvedere area.

At the May 1978 dedication of the newly renovated Queen Anne Belvedere Apartments, Gentry addressed a large crowd of grateful neighborhood residents, tenants, business owners and city council representatives. "Monumental Life and Monumental Corporation," he noted, "are proud of the role they played in the resurgence to help make the city a better place in which to live and work." Three retail stores were ready to open and forty-five of seventy-one apartment units had already been leased for $200 to $325 per month.

The company's efforts sparked a revitalization of Baltimore's mid-town "cultural hub" that included renovations to Center Stage, the Lyric Opera House, the Peabody Institute, the Maryland Historical Society, the Walters Art Gallery, the Maryland Institute College of Art, the Greek Cathedral of the Ascension, Baltimore's Penn Station, the University of Baltimore, and the opening in 1982 of a new home for the Baltimore Symphony Orchestra, named after Joseph Meyerhoff, symphony president and Monumental Corporation director.

Gentry continued to serve the company and the city for many years as a member of the Midtown Community Association, the Charles Street Development Board, the Mount Vernon–Belvedere Improvement Association, and the Downtown Partnership. After retiring in 1993 he served as a consultant and lobbied for the company in Annapolis. Still on retainer in 2006, Gentry played a role in selecting Struever Bros. Eccles & Rouse to develop new condominiums, retail shops and underground parking at "Twelve 99"—just north of Monumental Life on the east side of Charles Street, directly across from the Queen Anne Apartment project he had spearheaded thirty years earlier.

DIVERSIFYING STARTS AND STOPS

With its own mortgage investments plus the apartments, shopping centers and housing projects developed by its corporate partner, Monumental Properties, the company was becoming well-known and respected in real estate, mortgage and investment circles. Under the experienced eye of Frank Cappiello, Jr., Vice President of Finance, the investment portfolio's return frequently beat returns posted by the Dow Jones and Standard & Poor's indices. In view of the Investment Department's depth, expertise and success, Frank Baker proposed that Monumental Corporation establish a separate investment advisory service.

The board approved the idea in July 1973 and early in 1974 Monumental Capital Management, Inc. was born. Employees in Monumental Life's Investment, Mortgage and Securities Departments—including investment advisors Ron Nagler, John Harring and Wylie Hopkins—began offering outside clients the same investment advice and services they continued to provide for Monumental Life and Volunteer State Life.

When the operation dissolved five years later—because the team, though talented, lacked the depth and size to compete with the big money managers like Legg Mason—corporate officers once again sought additional sources of income.

Monumental Life's District Agencies operation, which provided the company's "bread and butter," had not shown significant growth in years. Optimistic about new opportunities, management created the "Golden Seventies" campaign to encourage agents to expand into the business marketplace. The Special Markets Department developed "E$P"— Employee Savings Plan—for employees to pay premiums through payroll deduction, but results were disappointing. The General Agencies operation, begun in the 1960s and operating at a net loss in 1970, closed its remote offices at year-end 1971 and brought local business into the home office.

ABOVE: *The company's efforts to revitalize Charles Street sparked a cultural renaissance in the Midtown-Belvedere neighborhood that included construction of a new home for the Baltimore Symphony Orchestra. It was named after Joseph Meyerhoff (inset), symphony president and Monumental Corporation director.*
[Photo by Sam Friedman, courtesy of BSO]

Financial Vice President Frank Cappiello, Jr.

Monumental Capital Management, Inc., was formed in 1974 as an investment advisory service.

Early in the 1970s, Monumental Life's Group Division had marketing offices in seven major U.S. cities focused on selling Group Health and related products. With 950 Group cases and $716 million of insurance in force, Group accounted for 29 percent of the company's total annual premium at year-end 1970. Group policyholders in Baltimore included Samuel Kirk & Sons, Silversmiths, the Maryland Historical Society, Hutzler's Department Store, a local pharmaceutical company, and Danny's Restaurant at the corner of Charles and Biddle Streets.

As health care costs skyrocketed along with inflation in 1975, so did Group Health claims. At a board of directors meeting that year, Director Joseph Meyerhoff suggested that the company get out of the group health business. Officers took his advice and refocused the Group operation on selling group life and long-term disability insurance.

Having seen a few of Monumental Life's recent marketing initiatives start and stop quickly, Meyerhoff also recommended that each Monumental Corporation subsidiary prepare a long-range plan and five-year earnings projection to manage and control its business. Because the Meyerhoffs ran multiple lines of real estate business—one with manufacturing income (building and selling houses), and two with recurring rental income (shopping centers and apartments)—they were experienced at making five-year income projections for each of their operations.

But even "master planners" and project managers like the Meyerhoffs could not have predicted how a Securities and Exchange Commission (SEC) ruling would change their future, and their relatively new partnership with Monumental Corporation.

MEYERHOFFS MAKE MONEY FOR MONUMENTAL STOCKHOLDERS

Writing about "The Monumental Years" in his memoirs, Bud Meyerhoff notes:

> Our own business continued to do well. We were then building apartments in four states and were beginning to expand our shopping center operations to the Midwest and Southwest. . . . Our apartment program had also picked up speed. Throughout the early and mid 1970s, we consistently built 1,000 to 2,000 apartments each year.
>
> Then somebody rained on our parade!

In 1973 the SEC changed the reporting rules for real estate companies and others reporting cash flow as part of or in place of earnings per share. The new ruling stated that cash flow could be reported in footnotes or in a small explanatory section of the annual report but not in the main body of the report as an alternative to book earnings. The ruling, said Meyerhoff, was devastating to all publicly held real estate companies:

> They had little or no reportable earnings. Their earnings were sheltered by depreciation, and in our company's case, cash flow that might have been reported at $10 million would be reduced by 90 percent for book earnings. Instead of a dollar per share, it would be ten cents per share.

Coupled with the oil embargo's inflationary impact on the economy in general, the ruling caused the price of Monumental Corporation stock to tumble. Selling at just $12 per share in the mid-1970s, the reported value of the corporation's fourteen million outstanding shares—representing two insurance companies and the real estate business—was just $168 million in the public eye. "That total price," adds Meyerhoff, "was less than *one-half* of what the two businesses, when appropriately valued, were worth."

The Meyerhoffs watched in frustration as the value of Monumental Corporation stock declined while their real estate earnings continued to rise. The situation was compounded by the fact that two sets of analysts—one for real estate, one for life insurance—tracked corporate performance. Analysts tracking one business didn't necessarily understand the other, explains Meyerhoff, and no one took the time to understand the "hybrid" nature of Monumental Corporation.

Meyerhoff offered a unique solution to the challenge—sell the Monumental Properties real estate business and keep the life insurance business. "This stock price situation is killing our business," he told Frank Baker, "and it makes no sense. I've got an idea for you. If it works, it'll make a ton of money for our stockholders, and we'll still have a significant business remaining." Baker was interested.

The proposed plan—to separate Monumental Corporation into two distinct entities—required what was called a "private letter ruling" from the IRS. If approved, stockholders would receive two pieces of paper to replace each share of stock—one would represent shares in the life insurance companies remaining in Monumental Corporation; the other would represent the value of the real estate put into the new Monumental Properties Trust, managed by four outside trustees and three Meyerhoff officers. The trust would sell the real estate properties; the net proceeds of the sale would be distributed through the trust, taxed at capital gains rates.

The plan was announced in April 1977, and the stock price jumped immediately. Outside appraisers valued the life insurance companies at $286 million and the real estate business at $302 million—almost equal, and $600 million together. On paper, at least, the value of the fourteen million shares grew again to $42.80 per share—up from $12 to $13 per share before the announcement.

The trust received the private letter ruling from the IRS in 1979 and immediately announced the sale of the eighteen regional shopping centers and forty-two apartment complexes. The final liquidating distribution, made in December 1985, netted $576 million (almost double the appraised value!) to holders of almost 7.8 million Monumental Trust certificates—about $74 per share. Additionally, each share of Monumental Corporation was valued at $24. In just eight years, the value of one share of Monumental Corporation stock had increased 800%—from $12 per share in 1977, when the plan was announced, to $98 in 1985 for the combined Monumental Trust/Monumental Corporation holdings.

"If the price we got for the property seems stunning, it shouldn't," says Bud Meyerhoff proudly. "Monumental Properties was, in fact, one of the best-managed real estate companies in the entire country. We had a very profitable and predictable business that was attractive to many buyers."

Monumental Corp. Plans To Sell Assets Of Properties Inc.

By John T. Ward

Monumental Corporation announced a sweeping change in its organization through a plan adopted at a directors' meeting today. There had been no inkling that such a program was under consideration, and the financial district was somewhat startled at the announcement.

Frank Baker, Jr. chairman, said it was approved in principle by the full board to liquidate and distribute to stockholders the assets of its wholly-owned affiliate, Monumental Properties, Inc.

Chief reason, it was said , for the proposal was "to terminate in an orderly manner the company's real estate operations and to enable stockholders to realize in liquidation the cash values that have been created by Monumental Properties."

Only a few days ago, the figures of a realty appraisal company showed that Monumental Properties, Inc. had a net worth of $183,285,000 as compared with th $12,123,000 based on traditional accounting, a difference of $171,162,000. This revaluations was in addition to the stockholder equity of $174,-057,000 in Monumental Corporation's consolidated balance sheet prepared on an historical cost basis.

If all conditions are met, the plan adopted by the directors would begin in January 1978.

The program is subject to various conditions, incuding a favorable tax ruling, compliance with federal regulations, and approval of the shareholders.

Also, the plan is subject economic conditions, and should they be adverse, it could cause termination of the proposed program.

The corporation has 14,113,-000 shares outstanding. On the over-the-counter market, they have been selling around 13 and 13½.

On hearing the news, the stock market reflected the possibilities, the stock going to 15.

Monumental Corporation is made up of Monumental Properties, Inc., Monumental Life Insurance Company, Volunteer State Life Insurance Company, and two financial affiliates.

The life companies and the real estate company were joined by merger in 1969. Monumental Properties has been enormously successful in its many shopping centers and apartment groups. In 1976 that portion of the combined firms had a profit of $2,588,000, and non-cash charges of $14,933,-000.

The assets are to be placed in a liquidating trust, with the proportion to each shareholder yet to be determined. The trust would operate over a period of three years in accplishing the assets sale, according to the plan.

It is said there would be no federal income tax at the corporate level. Stockholders would get "units of interest" in the trust.

Accomplishment of the complicated plan would leave the life companies to pursue the insurance business under the wing of Monumental Corporation.

Monumental Properties, as such, would disappear It was emphasized that the action approved by the directors was not a spin-off, but a sale of assets.

ABOVE: *Monumental Corporation's April 1977 announcement that it planned to sell the assets of its Monumental Properties subsidiary stunned the financial community.*

Leslie B. Disharoon, CLU, was elected chairman and CEO of Monumental Life on February 1, 1977.

Stewart Clifford, Jr., a Monumental Corporation director and senior vice president with Citibank of New York who served on the board with the Meyerhoffs during the 1970s and 1980s, agrees that analysts and shareholders never understood the connection between Monumental's life insurance and real estate businesses. Even so, he says, "it was a very successful partnership for both organizations."

During those years, the stock began to increase in value and some real wealth building took place. When Monumental Corporation divested itself of the real estate operation, it was the largest single real estate transaction to date in the United States.

Monumental Corporation kept none of the money generated by the real estate sale. The proceeds passed directly to stockholders, based on their percent of ownership. As majority stockholders, the Meyerhoffs received 44 percent. But as Bud Meyerhoff had predicted, *every* stockholder made "a bundle of money."

Jack Pearlstone remained a Monumental Corporation director until his death in 1982. Joseph Meyerhoff passed away three years later. Monumental Corporation's Frank Baker, then president of the Baltimore Symphony Orchestra, announced Mr. Meyerhoff's death on February 3, 1985 at a Meyerhoff Symphony Hall concert. "We have lost a very, very dear friend," he said. "I have been most fortunate to have been associated with him, both in a business way and with the symphony. He has left us a legacy of service and generosity."

Bud Meyerhoff remained on Monumental Corporation's board until 1986. He was named chairman of the U.S. Holocaust Memorial Council the next year. His six-year

effort—including a generous $6 million donation from the Meyerhoff family—was largely responsible for the building and dedication of the U.S. Holocaust Memorial Museum in Washington on April 22, 1993.

DIRECTORS SELECT DISHAROON

During their years as Monumental directors, the Meyerhoffs demonstrated again and again that they were ethical and astute entrepreneurs who knew how to make money. Called "feisty street fighters" by one retired officer, they pushed for quick decisions, based on current market conditions, and were less concerned with promoting from within than with finding the best people to do the job.

As the decade drew to a close, the "Board of Directors realized that the company's lack of growth was not a financial problem," notes Don Wilson, Monumental Life's president from 1967 to 1978, "but a lack of sales leadership and expertise." The company's four most recent presidents—Loweree, Wehr, Baker and Wilson himself—had all come from auditing, accounting, finance or investment backgrounds. It was time, the board advised, to pump fresh life into the organization by bringing in someone from the outside with a successful sales and marketing track record.

In December 1976, the directors of both Monumental Life and Monumental Corporation agreed that Leslie B. Disharoon, CLU, possessed the experience and vision needed to help the organization meet current and future challenges. A graduate of Brown University with a masters degree in business administration from Columbia University, Disharoon entered the insurance business in 1956 as a general agent with Connecticut General in Richmond. He accepted a position with Connecticut Mutual in 1960 and increased his Norfolk agency's premium per year from $80,000 to $350,000 in just six years. Moving to Hartford in 1970, Disharoon headed the company's Agency Department and was elected senior vice president in 1974, with responsibility for marketing operations and 3,000 Agency personnel.

BELOW: *Monumental Corporation board members Bernard C. Trueschler, Owen Daly, II and Richard P. Sullivan in 1978.*

"When Frank Baker, Jr. approached me about coming to Monumental Corporation in 1977," he says today, "I saw it as a new challenge and a step closer to getting back to my roots in Virginia." At the time, Monumental Life was one of the forty-five largest stock life insurance companies (by assets) in the country. It received consistently high ratings from A.M. Best & Company insurance rating service. Monumental Life and Volunteer State Life were doing "all right," says Disharoon, but both organizations "needed to break through the status quo and change their cultures."

Elected chairman and CEO, effective February 1, 1977, Disharoon brought new energy and ideas to Monumental Life. In April he realigned the entire management team to create broader areas of responsibility and to familiarize each member of management with the company's entire operation.

At about the same time, he hired Paul Granger as vice president of Group Administration and Hap Fairburn as second vice president of Group Sales. Together they would develop and support employer-employee group business in the Philadelphia-Baltimore-Washington corridor. He then merged the Special Markets operation into a new General Agencies Department, headed by James Murphy, which included personal producing general agents, the Mount Vernon General Agency, and general agents from the Whitestone Corporation who approached middle-income consumers through associations and employers via payroll deduction.

At the time, general agents were also marketing to military personnel in the U.S. and Europe and selling Monumental's whole life, annuity and retirement income products through the Government Employee Insurance Program (GEIP). By June 1977, Disharoon was able to report to the board: "the proportion of new business being written in markets other than traditional home service is on the upswing."

Disharoon also took steps to reenergize District Agencies. At the Chairman's Round Table Conference in May 1977, he challenged Monumental Life's "Top Ten" highest income-producing agents to increase their earnings by 15 percent or more. In September 1977 he brought all field managers to Baltimore to share ideas and commit to better-than-ever fourth quarter results. To help agents reach that goal, Marketing Services delivered eye-catching, high quality new sales tools for meeting Single Needs, Total Needs, and Women's Needs—cleverly packaged in a Needs Fulfillment "tote-velope."

Recognizing that the growing number of female prospects might feel more comfortable talking to women, District Agencies also began recruiting more female agents. In 1977, Field Vice President Spud Ring held the company's first "Ladies Day" in Baltimore for veteran and rookie female agents in his Chesapeake Region. Two years later, eight female agents qualified for the industry's prestigious Women's Leaders Round Table.

Thanks to these efforts, District Agencies ended 1977 almost 11 percent over its annual objective—with $3.8 million of new net premium, "best-ever" 72.7 percent first-year persistency, and revenues of $77.1 million, which exceeded 1976 by 6.8 percent.

Female agents came to the home office in 1977 for the company's first Ladies Day.

Kolker and the Colonel . . .
Start of a Long-Term Partnership

*Roger R. Kolker, CLU
Retired Air Force
Colonel Carroll Payne*

ONE DAY in 1979, Monumental Life president Roger Kolker, a West Point graduate, picked up the phone and called retired Air Force Colonel Carroll Payne at USPA & IRA's headquarters in Fort Worth, Texas. USPA & IRA (United Services Planning Association, Inc. and Independent Research Agency for Life Insurance, Inc.) hired former military officers to provide insurance and investment products to military families on U.S. military bases. Traditionally, Payne's sales representatives wrote business with two or three insurance carriers. Monumental Life, Kolker explained, wanted to be one of those companies.

Frank Lastner, promoted to vice president of General Agencies a few years later, was in Kolker's office that day. Hearing only one side of the conversation, he remembers Kolker saying "Here's what I propose" and, a few minutes later, "we'll come down there with everything you need."

The next day a team of ten Monumental Life decision-makers—including Kolker, Lastner, attorney Paul Latchford, actuary David Ricci, and Jim Murphy, vice president of General Agencies—flew to Texas to meet with twenty military officers. There was no time for advance planning or preparation. "The two teams listened to one another, negotiated differences, and reached an agreement on products and rates that satisfied the military's needs and convinced Monumental's management team that we could make a profit," says Kolker.

Frank Lastner

"No one said no," remembers Lastner, "and we wrote the contract that day." Before leaving Texas, Kolker told the colonel that Lastner would be in charge.

"Colonel Payne insisted that we remove war exclusion riders from our contracts," notes Lastner, "because USPA & IRA was writing insurance on officers, not enlisted men fighting on the frontlines." Within six weeks, Monumental had filed and received approval for seven new life insurance policies for USPA & IRA. The turn-around was a filing first for the Maryland State Insurance Department.

Kolker's quick thinking and Lastner's determined follow-through created the start of a win-win partnership with USPA & IRA that prospered throughout the 1980s and 1990s.

"Monumental received a 'lion's share' of their business," notes Kolker, "because we understood their needs and built a dedicated service team to meet their expectations."

Lastner also built a relationship with Colonel Payne based on mutual respect and trust. "He expected us to tell the truth, talk straight, provide excellent service, and do what we promised."

Because Monumental Life did just that, military sales increased from $2 million, to $4 million, to $8 million in just three years in the early 1980s. More than a decade later, policies written on the military continued to be the most persistent and consistently profitable block of business on Monumental Life's books.

MORE CHANGES AT THE TOP

Early in 1978, the company's 120th year, Roger R. Kolker, CLU, was elected Monumental Life's executive vice president and chief marketing officer. A graduate of West Point, Kolker came to Monumental Life with twenty-four years of insurance sales, marketing and management experience from Mutual Life of New York (MONY) and North American Life & Casualty Company, its Minneapolis-based subsidiary. Although he knew little about the home service side of the business, Kolker says he saw the move to Monumental as an opportunity to build on his "mass marketing" experience to "get the company going."

Later that year, Kolker and Disharoon introduced a new three-year marketing strategy, titled "Geared for Growth," that outlined profit goals, target markets, measurable objectives, products and strategies to take the organization into the 1980s.

By November 1978, however—shortly after Disharoon was elected president of Monumental Corporation—management was distracted by a second hostile takeover attempt within ten years. Kaufman and Broad announced through its subsidiary, the Sun Life Holding Company, that it had acquired 4.9 percent of Monumental Corporation's common stock, with an option to purchase 11.9 percent more. Baker, Disharoon, Kolker, and Monumental Corporation's directors immediately took steps to prevent the unfriendly takeover. The situation was resolved in 1979 when both organizations signed an agreement that called for Monumental to buy back its shares of common stock from Kaufman and Broad.

Anticipating Frank Baker's retirement on April 30, 1979, after forty-seven years of service, directors elected Disharoon chairman of the Monumental Corporation on February 1, 1979. Disharoon retained his position as Monumental Life's chairman of the board, Don Wilson moved to Monumental Corporation as senior vice president for corporate development, and Roger Kolker became president and CEO of Monumental Life.

qualified to tackle the challenge. Working with Dana Elliott, he implemented changes in the 1980s that encouraged employee growth and development, increased professionalism, and helped create a culture committed to management excellence.

ORGANIZATION REORGANIZATION

In March 1979, Kolker unveiled a major realignment of the company's functions and responsibilities to better utilize human resources and to provide the best support possible for Monumental Life's three marketing divisions—District Agencies, General Agencies, and Mass Marketing. Each marketing division became a distinct profit center with its own marketing officer.

At about the same time, the company's directors approved a new senior officer position to rebuild the Personnel Department. Frank S. ("Bud") Piff was elected Monumental Life Vice President and Organization Development Officer in the spring of 1979. A "people person" who had made his mark at Penn Mutual Life Insurance Company, Piff was well-

NEW LOOK, NEW LOGO . . . LOOKING AHEAD!

"Monumental Life has entered a new era of growth and development to meet the needs of a dynamically changing environment," Kolker announced in mid-1979. The commitment to the future was communicated effectively through a new corporate look, a new logo, and an identity program built around the theme and tag line "*Tomorrow's Insurance . . . Today.*"

Bold and strong, the distinctive red and gray logo, logo type and tag line were effective symbols to reinforce Monumental Life's forward-looking focus. The new logo soon appeared on all policies, promotional materials, business cards, letterhead, internal memos, T-shirts, and on the masthead of the new employee publication, the *ML News*, which had debuted a year earlier.

At year-end 1979 the company reached a major milestone—$4 billion of insurance in force! In just five years, insurance in force had grown by $1 billion. Much of that growth had come from new or expanded initiatives and sales in the mass marketing and payroll deduction marketplace.

ABOVE: *The company's bold, new forward-leaning red and gray logo and "Tomorrow's Insurance . . . Today" tag line communicated the company's focus and direction.*

LEFT: *In 1979, Monumental Life chairman Les Disharoon with Roger Kolker, newly elected Monumental Life president, unveiled a three-year marketing strategy titled "Geared for Growth" to take the company into the 1980s.*

Fueled by inflation, the entire insurance industry also experienced unprecedented growth. By the end of the decade 1,890 legal reserve life insurance companies employed two million people, insured two of every three Americans, and reported $3.2 trillion of life insurance in force—$1.6 trillion Ordinary and $1.4 trillion Group. The average, middle-income family owned $37,900 of protection.

The 1970s gave the life insurance industry and Monumental Life their last moments of stability and predictable returns. Looking ahead to the 1980s, the company was better positioned than ever to meet the growing needs of America's middle-income consumers. But who knew what the future might hold as interest rates edged into the double-digits?

Employees who had lived through the Seventies remembered the decade's Afros, peace symbols, folk songs and tie-dyed clothing during Employee Appreciation Week events two decades later.

Monumental Gentlemen . . .
Baltimore Born and Bred

AS THE 1970s drew to a close, the curtain also closed on the insurance careers of two dedicated and hard-working members of the Monumental Life and Monumental Corporation executive teams—Frank Baker, Jr., and Donald H. Wilson, Jr., CLU. Though remembered for their industry leadership, their commitment to the community, and their genuine concern for employees, both probably would be more pleased today to hear themselves referred to as "classy, top quality, ethical gentlemen" by former colleagues.

Frank Baker, Jr.

Frank Baker, Jr. . . .
Good Scout, Quarterback or Both?

Born in Baltimore in 1913, Frank Baker, Jr. graduated from City College and studied accounting at the Baltimore College of Commerce. During his forty-seven-year career, he saw Monumental Life's assets grow from $17 million in 1932 to more than $559 million in 1979 while insurance in force climbed from $159 million to $4 billion.

Elected Monumental Life assistant secretary in 1941, Baker served as a company officer and director for more than thirty years. He was named president in 1965, and chairman and CEO in 1967. He was responsible for the company's decision to remain in downtown Baltimore, for building the home office addition at Charles and Biddle Streets, for creating Monumental Corporation, for acquiring Volunteer State Life and Monumental Properties, and for Monumental's successful partnership with the Meyerhoff family during the 1970s. Under his

RIGHT: *Frank Baker with perennial leading agent Frank Binetti and Mrs. Binetti at Baker's retirement party in May 1979.*

Monumental retirees and close friends—Vince Zirpoli, Jim Davis, Ed Barrett, Dick Schellhas, Bos Ensor and Frank Baker—gathered for a reunion in 1985.

leadership, the company achieved national prominence within the insurance industry and in the real estate, investment and development arenas.

Visible and influential in the community throughout his career, Baker was a director of the American Red Cross, the Chamber of Commerce of Metropolitan Baltimore, the C&P Telephone Company, the Savings Bank of Baltimore, the Independent College Fund of Maryland, and the Life Insurance Association of America. He also served on the Volunteer Council of Equal Opportunity, the YMCA board of trustees, the University of Baltimore Board of Trustees, and was appointed General Campaign Chairman of the United Fund of Central Maryland in 1971.

In 1980, Baltimore mayor William Donald Schaefer asked Baker to serve as co-trustee for the city's investment development funds. In 1984 the Baltimore Area Council of the Boy Scouts of America honored the retired Monumental executive with its "Good Scout Award." Appointed to the Baltimore Symphony Orchestra's board of directors in 1970, Baker was serving the BSO as chairman of the board at the time of his death in 1988.

"Everybody in town knows Mr. Baker!" said one proud employee during his May 1979 retirement celebration, attended by almost 120 Monumental Life and Monumental Corporation officers, employees and field leaders. Of all the gifts and testimonials presented that day, Chicago agent Frank Binetti's was the most unique. The company's leading agent for ten consecutive years, Binetti gave Baker $13,000 of annualized premium—a "Baker's Dozen"—all written during the retiring chairman's last full week on the job.

Looking back at his own leadership record, Baker compared himself to a quarterback: "You call some plays where you get thrown for a loss, but unless you play aggressively you will never get to the goal line."

RIGHT: *In 1978, Ed Brunner, Jim Gentry, and Dwight Bartlett presented Don Wilson (second from right) with an award for completing the twenty-six-mile Maryland Marathon in less than four hours.*

Donald H. Wilson, Jr. . . .
Going the Distance

Donald H. Wilson, Jr.

Like Baker, Donald H. Wilson, Jr., understood the importance of setting goals and working hard to achieve them. A long-distance runner, he reached his personal goal of completing the twenty-six-mile Maryland Marathon in less than four hours in 1977. Still active and going strong in 2006, Wilson is proud he was able to help the company "stay in the race" during his thirty-three years of service.

A graduate of Baltimore's Friends School and the Johns Hopkins University, Don Wilson taught accounting at his alma mater for four years before joining Monumental Life in 1947. When he arrived, the postwar economic boom was just beginning. Hired as a securities analyst, he says "I was the Investment Department!"

Elected vice president and investment officer in 1959, Wilson assumed responsibility for Monumental Life's entire investment portfolio. He improved its performance by adopting T. Rowe Price's "buy and hold" strategy of investing in growing companies and by taking on more risk in mortgages, bonds and private placements. By the time he was elected Monumental Life's president and chief administrative officer in 1967, the portfolio was achieving above-average results.

Wilson was also sensitive to EEOC employment issues. He worked closely with Personnel Director Brenda Shelly to introduce changes in the company's personnel policies—including Management by Objectives as a performance measurement tool, "flex-week" scheduling, and "floating holidays" to meet the needs of an increasingly diverse employee population. Though employee efforts to create a home office union were defeated, he says the attempt served as management's "wake up" call to improve communication throughout the organization.

When Les Disharoon was elected chairman and CEO of Monumental Life in 1978, Wilson's career took an unexpected turn. He moved to Monumental Corporation as senior vice president of corporate development and chaired the Investment Committee. Retiring from that position in February 1980, he knew that his high ethical standards had made a difference.

"I am thankful for the opportunity Monumental gave me to do civic work and contribute to the community," said Wilson in 2006. In addition to serving on many insurance industry committees, he was chairman of the Greater Baltimore Committee, chairman and trustee of the Maryland Realty Trust, a director of the Mercantile–Safe Deposit and Trust Company, a trustee of Goucher College, and president of the Johns Hopkins Alumni Association.

CHAPTER 11

The Challenge of Change
(1980–1989)

Monumental Corporation chairman and CEO Les Disharoon addressing field managers in 1982.

STANDING before a sea of anxious faces in November 1982, Monumental chairman Leslie B. Disharoon admits: "I have been associated with the life insurance business for twenty-six years and realize I have only three or four years' experience. So much has happened, so much has changed that much of my experience is not relevant to the world we live in today. If you have the energy . . . the optimism . . . and the vision . . . this is probably the most exciting, stimulating period in industry history."

In the audience, Monumental Life's field managers listen intently. Big changes have occurred at Monumental in the last five years. A new home office management team is in place. To compensate for rising costs, the company has consolidated field offices, reduced agent counts, introduced more flexible products, and increased expectations. Many managers are concerned about the future, their careers, and their sales teams' ability to succeed in an inflationary economy.

Invited to Baltimore by Disharoon and President Roger Kolker, they've traveled from as far away as Chicago and St. Louis to participate in this important three-day meeting. The program—focused on the theme "The Challenge of Change"—includes presentations explaining the company's direction and goals, and describing its new marketing plans and products. While they are in Baltimore, managers will participate in workshops, share ideas, and meet two new officers—Executive

Vice President B. Larry Jenkins and Ron Brittingham, newly appointed vice president of District Agencies. Both men have recently joined Monumental Life following successful careers with Peoples Life Insurance Company in Washington, D.C.

Disharoon has brought Jenkins on board to motivate and help Monumental Life's home service sales force take advantage of growing opportunities in the marketplace. Jenkins's attitude, energy, determination, and firsthand experience as an agent, field manager, corporate officer, industry president and CEO have prepared him well to tackle the task.

"The Eighties will be a mixed bag of challenge, change and frustration," Jenkins tells managers. "We are going to have to take a hard look at the way we've been conducting our business. This means adapting to some rather dramatic

B. Larry Jenkins served as president of Peoples Life in Washington, D.C. before joining Monumental in 1982.

FACING PAGE: *The Eighties presented many challenges for the insurance industry. For Monumental, the biggest change was becoming part of AEGON's international family in 1986.*

changes. Many of the things that worked for us in the past aren't good enough to meet the challenges of the Eighties. Other things may continue to work, but radical surgery is essential. For those who put forth the effort, learn to work smarter and harder, and take full advantage of opportunities, success will continue to be very much within their reach."

"Do you really want to succeed in this business? Are you willing to pay the price?" asks President Kolker during his turn at the podium. "We will change whatever needs to be changed. There is nothing sacred except our sense of values. They have been constant for one hundred twenty-four years and will remain steadfast regardless of pressures generated by volatile times."

Ron Brittingham was appointed vice president of District Agencies in 1982.

Later in the program, Ron Brittingham summarizes suggestions and questions he's received from the field management team. "You have challenged us to give proper direction and leadership. You have challenged us to provide improved field support. You have challenged us to deliver competitive, consumer-oriented products. We accept these challenges. They will be met as we mix tradition with innovation . . . new product development with fair compensation . . . proper support systems with modern sales techniques . . . so that together we can prosper and grow while catering to the security needs of our clients."

BELOW: *Regular training sessions educatd managers about the decade's many changes and innovations.*

Filled with optimism, enthusiasm, and a positive attitude about things to come, managers leave Baltimore excited

and energized. "It became apparent from day one of this meeting that someone is listening," notes one manager. "More importantly, the home office is exerting time, energy and knowledge to furnish us with the tools needed to succeed in a changing and innovative marketplace."

SPENDING . . . OUT OF CONTROL!

Two years earlier, many of these same officers and managers had voted for Ronald Reagan in the 1980 presidential election. Frustrated by rising prices, double-digit interest rates, business failures, rising unemployment and uncertain futures, they, like many U.S. businessmen, were looking for a strong, optimistic and decisive leader to take the country in a new direction. In the former Hollywood actor and charismatic former governor of California they had found a man, they hoped, who could bring home the hostages from Iran, restore confidence in government, cut taxes and stimulate economic growth.

By 1981 crippling inflation threatened not only family budgets but also the value of life insurance policies and the solvency of many life insurance companies. Rising prices continued to outpace incomes. Interest rates made borrowing from banks and savings and loans prohibitively expensive. As a result, more and more families were tapping their life insurance policies for needed cash.

Between 1979 and 1982, Monumental Life processed $71 to $106 million per year in policy loans. Policyholder requests for cash surrenders and policy loans—fixed, by contract, at low 4.5 to 5 percent pre-inflation rates—created such a strain on the industry that some insurers were forced to borrow money at much higher rates to pay benefits and meet contractual obligations.

In an attempt to relieve inflationary pressures and help insurers recoup some of their losses, the NAIC (National Association of Insurance Commissioners) adopted model legislation in 1981 that permitted life insurance companies to issue whole life policies with a flexible loan interest rate. The same year, Monumental Life joined many of its

competitors in supporting a consumer-focused national advertising and public relations campaign—"Inflation. Together We Can Self-Control It"—launched by the American Council of Life Insurance.

As it turned out, neither insurance industry efforts nor President Reagan's call for a return to simpler values succeeded in bringing spending under control.

CHANGING LIFESTYLES

Between 1980 and 1987 average U.S. household income rose 20 percent. Stock values tripled. Though the poor still struggled to make ends meet during those years, the top 10 percent of American families increased their wealth by 24.4 percent. When the Reagan administration cut taxes to stimulate the economy, many families had more money to spend. And spend they did!

At all economic levels, Americans began to buy "nice to have" items as well as necessities on credit, using "plastic" to put off or spread out their payments. For the first time in U.S. history, the growing use of credit cards brought the purchase of higher priced cars, jewelry, designer clothing, household items, computers, electronic gadgetry and other status symbols within the reach of lower and middle-income families.

The decade's status seekers—dubbed the "Splurge Generation" by author Tom Wolfe—made binge-buying and their shop-'til-you-drop mentality a way of life. Though 70 percent of U.S. households still earned less than $35,000 annually in 1984, the mantra "if you've got it, flaunt it" pushed personal credit card debt to unprecedented heights.

Inflation and Ralph Nader's consumer movement also contributed to a dramatic change in buying habits. Better educated, more self-confident, discriminating buyers looked for quality, value, durability and service to match their rising incomes and higher quality of life. For the decade's hard-working two-income couples, single moms and busy young professionals, convenience was often more important than price. Shopping at night and on Sundays, they frequented new, one-stop mega-stores and began to purchase selected goods and services through the mail and newspapers or over the telephone.

As personal growth, self-fulfillment and physical fitness took on new importance during the decade, spending on hobbies, travel and leisure activities also increased. Baby Boomers, pre-retirees and senior citizens wanted to look, act and feel younger. Women signed up for aerobics classes, men started jogging; and the sale of self-help books, exercise tapes, running and hiking gear, warm-up suits, treadmills and bicycles took off like one of NASA's rockets.

The rising affluence of middle-income consumers in the 1980s, coupled with changing consumption patterns, presented financial institutions and insurance companies with challenges as well as unique opportunities to meet needs.

Americans had begun to base many of their buying decisions on lifestyle, work style and interests as much as on income. Within just a few years, "one size fits all" financial products and strategies had become almost obsolete. "Canned" sales approaches that agents had used for decades no longer produced the same results. Consumers were "segmenting" themselves into lifestyle-based "niches" and affinity groups, and they expected marketers to do the same—by customizing sales tools and approaches, considering unique needs, and serving individuals and families, not only in their homes but also where they worked, shopped and banked.

ABOVE: *As consumers began to buy PCs for their personal use during the Eighties, Monumental did the same for employees in many of its home office departments.*

INSET LEFT: *Status seekers who bought gas-guzzling SUVs in the Eighties seemed to have forgotten the prior decade's oil embargo and resulting shortages.*

33 USA Sport Utility Vehicles

COMMITMENT TO MIDDLE INCOME CONSUMERS

Observing the marketplace carefully in the early 1980s, the company's forward-thinking executives aligned its marketing strategy with emerging trends. At a meeting of home office managers in February 1982, Kolker and Disharoon emphasized that success depended on planning, teamwork, respect, communication, the ability to deliver innovative products, and the flexibility to deal with both economic unpredictability and the blurring of differences between banking, investment and insurance companies.

"Management must have the information needed to act quickly in a changing environment," added Henry G. Hagan, assistant vice president of New Market Development. Brought on board in 1981 to help the organization meet changing needs, expand existing activities and develop new concepts and approaches for reaching consumers, he was promoted to second vice president, Payroll Deduction Marketing, in 1982.

As Monumental Life neared its 125th anniversary in 1983, meeting the diverse needs of America's middle-income consumers was a high priority. So was finding more efficient, less costly ways to distribute products.

Traditional field agents continued to visit customers in their homes to make sales and provide face-to-face service and collections. To accommodate changing lifestyles, they scheduled more evening appointments, looked for non-traditional sources of leads and sales, and encouraged clients to save time and money by paying premiums through "Mon-U-Matic" automatic bank drafts from their savings or checking accounts.

General agents were also working through employers to provide Monumental Life products to government employees, military personnel and employees of private industry. As the demand for employee benefits grew along with employers' rising costs, the company and its

new fulfillment subsidiary, American Benefit Counselors, Inc., helped meet the challenge with new products, sales tools, training programs and payroll deduction plans that identified employee needs and simplified the purchase process. The company placed its first large payroll deduction case, for $5.3 million of insurance coverage, at the North Arundel Hospital in Glen Burnie, Maryland, in 1982, utilizing an innovative new product concept called "Universal Life." By 1985, ABC's enrollment teams were achieving a 70 percent success rate per employee meeting.

In 1980, Monumental Corporation had acquired two large insurance marketing agencies—Alsop & Elliot of Virginia, Ltd. and the Sid Murray Agency (Administrators and Consultants International, Inc.) of Corpus Christi, Texas. Both specialized in mass marketing insurance products through endorsed mailings to members of association groups.

The same year, Arch Parker—known in industry circles as the "creator of association group marketing"—joined Monumental Life as mass marketing officer after twenty-four years with Chicago-based CNA Insurance. "The American propensity for joining has provided us with an established avenue for marketing supplemental life and health insurance products," Parker explained shortly after arriving in Baltimore. Later in the decade, the Fraternal Order of Police, the American Federation of Teachers, the Commercial Law League of America, the American Legion, and the Lockheed Aircraft Credit Union would all become association group clients.

Hired in 1981 as assistant vice president of New Market Development, Henry G. Hagan was charged with helping Monumental meet changing consumer needs.

RIGHT: *Mass marketing experts Ted Mudge, Arch Parker and John Revelle joined Monumental in the early 1980s.*

Two other industry specialists—John Revelle and Ted Mudge—also joined the organization in the early 1980s. Revelle had extensive contacts in the banking and mortgage marketplace. Mudge had experience marketing credit life insurance through auto dealerships. The addition of mass marketing expertise expanded the company's methods for penetrating the middle income marketplace and had an immediate impact on sales. In 1981 the Mass Marketing Division contributed almost 50 percent of the company's total new premium.

Larry Jenkins was elected Monumental Life president in May 1983.

JENKINS JUMPSTARTS SALES

Joining Monumental Life on September 1, 1982, Executive Vice President Larry Jenkins wasted no time in making a similar, positive impact on results.

After many years without significant growth, "the organization needed his strong will, determination and drive," notes Robert McGraw, Monumental Life's vice president and controller in the early 1980s. "Jenkins was good for the company. He knew the home service business, he understood agents, and he knew how to motivate the field through compensation. He moved the organization forward by the force of his personality!"

Field Manager's $9,000 Investment . . .
A ONE MILLION DOLLAR GAIN!

Field manager George Mueller was one of the first employees to buy thirty shares of Mutual Life stock when the company changed from a mutual to a stock company in 1928.

"YOU'LL BE millionaires one day if you hold onto this Monumental stock," predicted George Mueller, retired Monumental Life district manager, before his death in 1968. Speaking to his daughter and son-in-law, he made them promise never to sell the shares of Monumental stock he had recently given to them and their daughter, Cynthia Hoffarth Dreckshage.

Eighteen years later, Harriet and Del Hoffarth of Missouri *were* millionaires, with the value of their Monumental stock portfolio estimated at almost $1,139,000.

"We kept our word to George and never sold one share," said Mr. Hoffarth when interviewed in 1986. "My father-in-law lived and breathed Monumental. He had watched the company grow from its early days as the Mutual Life of Baltimore. He moved his family many times during the 1920s and 1930s as the company opened new district offices in St. Louis, Chicago, Louisville and Kansas City. "He only took early retirement in 1940 or so," noted his daughter, "because my mother was tired of moving and wanted to stay in St. Louis."

When Mutual Life changed from a mutual to a stock company in 1928, George Mueller was one of the first employees to buy thirty shares of the stock. In 1932, during the depths of the Great Depression, he purchased another two hundred shares. Mueller's total investment in the 230 shares was $9,000. Yet—thanks to 100 percent stock dividends issued in both 1932 and 1934; a 50 percent dividend in 1944; and subsequent stock dividends in 1949, 1952, 1958, 1961, 1964, 1971 and 1973—his original number of shares kept growing.

During the 1950s and 1960s, Mueller divided his shares evenly between his son, William, and his daughter, Harriet, to lower the value of his estate for tax purposes. Mueller's son eventually sold his half of the shares, but Harriet and her husband held onto theirs. By 1977, when Monumental Corporation sold Monumental Properties, its real estate subsidiary, the Hoffarths' half of Mueller's original stock portfolio had grown to 14,391 shares.

"Monumental stock proved to be a very good investment for all the company's original shareholders," said Del Hoffarth in 1986. At the time of the Monumental Properties' sale, each stockholder received units of beneficial interest in proportion to their investment in the corporation. The Hoffarths received 7,827 units, which ultimately paid them $74.09 per unit between 1978 and 1985. "Those proceeds combined with our family's remaining shares in Monumental Corporation, will give us a total return of $1,139,000 at the announced AEGON merger price of $56 per share."

"Because of my father-in-law's $9,000 investment almost sixty years ago," said Hoffarth, "my retirement years and my family's future are secure. We will always be grateful to George and Monumental for the check we'll receive when the AEGON merger is complete. My wife, however, is upset that she cannot keep her promise to her father. The company has been a part of her life for a long time. Having to sell the shares will create a big void in our lives."

the Professional
September, 1983

Paying competitive interest rates on policy cash values, Universal Life policies appealed to the decade's income-oriented, interest-savvy consumers.

The "How Much is Enough?" brochure helped agents educate families about needs.

BELOW: *Les Disharoon submitted the first application for a Monumental Universal Life II policy in 1985.*

Jenkins realized that Monumental Life's future depended as much on agent productivity and internal growth as it did on acquisitions and expansion into non-traditional markets. He got rid of the unions and eliminated a crutch that had paralyzed productivity for over forty years. "Union members had a collection mentality," explains retired general counsel Jim Gentry, who handled union contracts and grievances for many years. "Even though the agent's primary job was sales, union members looked for guaranteed pay and benefits and expected high service commissions to retain existing business. Jenkins said he'd rid the company of unions within one year, and he did."

Larry Jenkins also refocused the entire organization on increasing home service sales. He and Ron Brittingham pushed for new products, new sales tools, new compensation contracts and incentive campaigns. "The home office supported us one hundred percent in everything we did," says Brittingham. "We worked together to develop products and systems that answered the question: 'How can we help the agent?'"

To get sales off to a fast start in 1983, District Agencies introduced an automatic issue campaign. Clients age fifty-five and under who had purchased $2,000 or more coverage in 1978 or 1979 were given the opportunity to add inflation-fighting coverage with a simplified application and on-the-spot underwriting. A similar campaign was introduced later that summer to help higher income clients combat rising costs.

Such innovative offers gave agents places to go and people to see. They generated activity and, as expected, boosted results. January's deluge of applications increased sales by 74 percent over the same month in 1982. So did the sale of innovative products like Flex 20, an inflation-fighting term product, and Universal Life (UL)—both introduced to District Agencies in 1983.

Dynamic I for the middle-income market debuted in December 1984. With high face amounts, low premiums and an optional Deposit Fund that paid 11 percent interest, Flex 20 helped agents open doors. Paying competitive interest rates on policy cash values, the new UL policies appealed to the decade's income-oriented, interest-savvy consumers. "UL is the industry's first truly innovative product in one hundred years!" said Jenkins.

Also increasing productivity were a new Financial Needs Analysis Program, brochures asking "How Much is Enough?", handheld computers and customized policy illustrations that educated consumers about needs, plus print ads, press releases, pre-approach letters and giveaways that helped agents generate goodwill.

By the time Larry Jenkins was elected president and chairman of Monumental Life in May 1983, the company was headed toward its most successful year ever. "New sales highs were set. Broken. Then topped again," declared the *ML News* at year end. "Agent-marketed individual life insurance premiums were up 39% over the same nine months in 1982. Mass marketing and credit insurance premiums were also up 48% and 27%."

Monumental Life issued $1 billion of insurance in 1983, making it one of the most exciting and productive years in the company's history, but another 56 percent increase in sales the following year made 1984 even better. Jenkins was making a difference—with higher productivity, lower agent turnover, and plans for expansion into new states in the South. Despite a costly lawsuit later in the decade that charged Monumental Life with "pirating" the best managers away from its competition, the expansion program provided much-needed field management expertise for a growing and rejuvenated field force.

NEW FACE IN THE MARKETPLACE

Organizational changes undertaken at the corporate level also made 1983 a turning point and milestone in the company's history.

In July 1983, Monumental Corporation acquired First Federated Life Insurance Company, a Baltimore-based, family-owned credit life insurance business with $38.4 million of assets. The acquisition provided the impetus needed to create a new and totally separate mass marketing entity as a sub-holding company under the corporate umbrella.

Officially "born" on July 18, 1983, Monumental General Insurance Group, Inc. was formed from three entities—Monumental Life's Mass Marketing Division, First Federated's credit life business, and the credit life operation of Monumental Corporation subsidiary Volunteer State Life. First Federated, licensed to write credit and other types of life insurance in forty-five U.S. states and the District of Columbia, was renamed Monumental General Insurance Company. It would serve as the underwriting company for the new group, which would market life insurance and related products through employers, associations, affinity groups and financial institutions.

Speaking to employees that summer, Les Disharoon explained:

Reorganizing our mass marketing efforts will enable us to improve the efficiency of these operations by capitalizing on mass marketing's inherently low fixed overhead costs, without affecting our strong agent marketing posture.

Monumental's marketing strategy is to reach insurance consumers in ways that make the most sense for them. Thus, we have continued to develop several marketing channels through agents: home service agents . . . flex-time agents . . . general agents, and brokers. Each has a distinct way of reaching consumers.

But we also know there is a growing segment of the insurance marketplace that chooses to purchase through direct mail, through their employers, or through associations, professional societies and other groups of which they are members. Consumers also buy $90 million of credit life insurance annually on consumer loans through financial institutions.

Monumental recruited experienced managers and opened new offices in North and South Carolina in the mid-1980s.

William N. Sanders was named president of the Monumental General Insurance Group in October 1984.

BELOW *Monumental General's products were marketed through auto dealers, direct-mail services, and networks of financial institutions serving credit card, mortgage and consumer loan customers.*

Roger Kolker was named Monumental General's first CEO. First Federated's Richard A. Eliasburg was named its first vice chairman. In October 1984, Monumental General's board of directors elected Volunteer State Life's William N. Sanders to replace Kolker. With Sanders in charge as president and CEO, the company began its rise to success as one of the country's top direct marketers of life and health insurance products in the middle-income marketplace.

As Monumental Corporation shed its less profitable lines of business in the mid-1980s, Sanders concentrated his new company's efforts on efficient, high-profit products that could be marketed through auto dealers, direct-mail services, and networks of financial institutions serving credit card, mortgage and consumer loan customers. Credit life sales jumped 231 percent in 1984. By mid-1985, Monumental General was providing a full line of supplemental life, accident and health, credit and mortgage-related insurance products to the customers of over 750 financial institutions in the Mid-Atlantic, Midwest and Southeast.

The creation of Monumental General meant that employees of Monumental's two distinct companies shared the same home office building at Charles and Chase Streets. Over the next twelve months, departments moved, space was reconfigured, and offices were created for newly appointed executives, managers, and support teams. When Monumental

General assumed responsibility for Monumental Life's Group accounts, several dozen employees who had administered that business—plus others looking for new challenges—moved to the "other side of the house."

With different products, markets, distribution systems and customer service needs, each company maintained its own sales, marketing, product development, administration, and service teams as well as separate legal, actuarial and accounting specialists.

Paul Latchford, a member of Monumental Life's Law Department since 1973, was elected Monumental General second vice president, general counsel and secretary in 1984. Bart Herbert, Jr., succeeded Bill Sanders as Monumental General president in 1991. Marilyn Carp—now president and CEO of Monumental General's successor, AEGON Direct Marketing Services, Inc. (ADMS)—first joined Monumental Life's Actuarial Department as a consultant in 1978. Current ADMS officers Dave Rekoski and Martha McConnell and retired officer Ed Lochte also started their careers with Monumental Life and moved to Monumental General as its direct mail/mass marketing operations continued to grow. The entire company moved to a new location on Park Avenue in Baltimore in the late 1990s.

By 1984 a few new officers had also joined Monumental Life. Wallace ("Wally") DeMille, executive vice president and chief operating officer, arrived in 1980. Within a short time, Hubert ("Herb") Collins, second vice president,

Wallace ("Wally") DeMille

ABOVE: *Monumental General officers Paul Latchford, Martha McConnell and Ed Lochte began their insurance careers with Monumental Life.*

RIGHT: *Dave Rekoski and Marilyn Carp—current president and CEO of AEGON Direct Marketing Services, Inc.—also worked for Monumental Life early in their careers.*

Administration; Kenneth C. Klueh, senior vice president and chief actuary; and Richard Sarudy, vice president and chief information officer, were also hired and Jim Gentry was elected Monumental Life's vice president, general counsel and secretary.

Serving both organizations in the mid-1980s was a Corporate Services Support Unit that included Semmes ("Buck") Walsh, executive vice president, Corporate Finance and Administration; Larry G. Brown, vice president and corporate secretary; Edward Brunner, vice president and treasurer; Ron Nagler, senior vice president, Investments; Don Chamberlain, vice president, Securities; Bud Piff, vice president, Organization Development (Human Resources); Jack Taylor, senior vice president, Market Development; and Rosemary Kostmayer, assistant vice president, Planning and Corporate Communications.

"Disharoon brought an uplifting style and 'management energy' to the entire organization," notes Bob McGraw, elected Monumental Corporation senior vice president and treasurer when Brunner retired in 1984. "For the first time, compensation was related to stock performance. The long-term incentive plan was based on increasing the value of the company. His innovations brought the company into the twentieth century and were well-received" by officers and directors.

Disharoon made numerous trips to New York to speak to analysts and investors. He told Monumental's story—

"Home service was good, stable business. We are looking for growth in other areas"—while McGraw presented the numbers. Analysts began to take notice.

Monumental was no longer the average, laid-back, easy-going life insurer it had been for almost a century. In both 1968 and 1978, it had survived two hostile takeover attempts. It had survived the divestiture of almost $600 million in Meyerhoff family real estate assets. It had weathered stiff competition, price wars and, most recently, policyholders pulling cash out of their policies when interest rates skyrocketed.

By year-end 1985, Disharoon had completed a major corporate restructuring, sold off unprofitable business, and refocused the organization's vision. Earnings were up at both Monumental Life and Monumental General. Premium and investment income had increased, while expenses for benefits and claims had decreased. During the fifteen months ending December 1985, Monumental Corporation's stock price rose 50 percent. That was good news for investors, and for the 70 percent of employees who believed in Monumental and owned stock through the company's Employee Retirement Savings Plan.

Even more impressive was an article in the *National Underwriter* by Thomas K. Maken that described Monumental as a "well-managed old company" with a "distinctive new look which investors find attractive" and noted that its stock had reached new heights.

Hubert ("Herb") Collins

Kenneth C. Klueh

Richard Sarudy

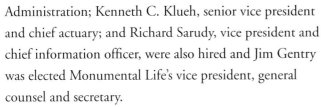

NOT FOR SALE

In February 1986, Les Disharoon received a call from Dick Strickler, managing director and head of financial institution mergers and acquisitions at Morgan Stanley & Company in New York City. Strickler wanted to speak with Disharoon about a possible merger idea. Having fielded similar calls in recent weeks, Disharoon was less than enthusiastic. The company was not for sale.

Nevertheless, Disharoon owed it to stockholders to at least hear what Strickler had to say, and he was scheduled to attend an analysts' meeting in New York anyway. He also had not forgotten that he and Strickler had worked together on Monumental's sale of Volunteer State Life in 1984.

Strickler explained that Dutch insurer AEGON, born in 1983 through a merger of the AGO and Ennia insurance companies, was looking for a "flagship" operation on the East Coast. With almost $50 billion of life and health insurance in force, it was running out of market in the Netherlands and had begun investing in the U.S. In 1985, 40 percent of the organization's more than $3.1 billion revenue had been derived from two U.S. subsidiaries—Life Investors Life Insurance Company of Cedar Rapids, Iowa, and National Old Line Life Insurance Company of Little Rock, Arkansas.

Since Morgan Stanley had helped AEGON raise $63 million in equity from the U.S. market in July 1985, AEGON chairman Jaap Peters had looked to the firm again to find an appropriate and successful merger partner.

Monumental Corporation was at the top of Strickler's list. It was the right size, with $250 million in revenue and $14 billion of life insurance in force. It was well-managed, had stable lines of business and some interesting distribution channels for selling insurance. It also operated in a different region of the country from AEGON's two existing U.S. subsidiaries.

"Gentlemen," Disharoon said to Strickler and AEGON's William Foster, "if you truly mean what you say, the only thing you have to ask yourselves is . . . how much do you think the company is worth?"

IT'S A DEAL!

In April the call came from Piper & Marbury's Andre Brewster. Jaap Peters and Disharoon were to meet at Brewster's office in Baltimore. Seeing the charts, graphs and reams of analysis, Disharoon knew immediately that AEGON was serious, and Brewster presented the case very well. AEGON's offer—$50 per share when Monumental Corporation stock was trading at $37—could not be ignored. Disharoon and his board of directors had agreed they would consider an offer if the "right situation" presented itself.

Disharoon understood Monumental's importance in Baltimore and its place in the insurance world. So did the company's directors, who did not need to be reminded that insurers Sun Life, Fidelity & Guarantee, Maryland Casualty, and the much-loved Baltimore Colts had already abandoned their city.

What should they do? Look out for shareholder interests or keep Monumental as a Baltimore-based, home-grown and still home-owned institution? In the end, says Disharoon today, "I feel we made the right decision—for our shareholders, our employees, our customers, the company, *and* the city."

Taking only two weeks to iron out the contract, AEGON agreed to pay $56 per share, all in cash, for 6.5 million outstanding shares of Monumental Corporation stock. The selling price, $364 million, was 1.7 times the corporation's book value. While lawyers worked out the details, the two CEOs got to know one another. Long after the deal was signed, says Disharoon, he took Jaap Peters on a tour of Baltimore—into Mayor William Donald Schaefer's office on the last day of his gubernatorial campaign, through the Walters Art Gallery, and behind the shark tanks at the National Aquarium.

"So many people . . . seem to forget that a company is about people," Disharoon noted during a media interview in 1987. "Price occurs only once—business relationships last forever."

The merger with AEGON was announced to a shell-shocked group of employees during a May 27, 1986, meeting at Baltimore's Belvedere Hotel. No one was expecting the announcement. They did not know what to think about being sold at all, much less to a foreign company. Most employees in Baltimore associated the Netherlands with tulips, windmills and wooden shoes. At the time, few realized that the Dutch are among the most savvy, forward-thinking and sophisticated businessmen in the world. For centuries the tiny size of their country had forced Dutch merchants and traders to become comfortable dealing with many foreign countries and cultures.

Speaking to employees (in English), Peters noted that the agreement with Monumental marked the achievement of an important step in AEGON's growth strategy. Monumental, he explained, had been AEGON's first choice of U.S. merger partners. "With your compatible book of business, strong management and operating bases, and highly complementary marketing and distribution setup, Monumental more than fulfills our original search criteria and represents an addition to our North American activities."

When asked about the future of Monumental's 1,800 employees, another AEGON executive replied confidently: "Your jobs are as safe as they would have been if the merger had not taken place." Though owned by AEGON, there were no plans to restructure or consolidate the organization. Monumental Life would remain autonomous, independent and, most important of all, based in Baltimore.

"TOGETHER ON OUR WAY TO A BRIGHT FUTURE"

ABOVE: *AEGON's brochure introduced the Dutch organization to Monumental employees.*

BELOW: *Monumental Corporation and AEGON executives in Baltimore in 1986—Bill Sanders, Monumental General; Jaap Peters, AEGON; Kees Storm, AEGON; Les Disharoon, Monumental Corporation; Larry Jenkins, Monumental Life; and Bill Foster, AEGON.*

Leslie B. Disharoon

Leading by Doing . . .
Les Disharoon's Legacy

WHEN ASKED about his years in Baltimore and what memories make him most proud, Les Disharoon answers without hesitation: "Putting Monumental in a position to be noticed by the Dutch." Though the 1980s were a challenging and often tumultuous time—both for the company and the industry—seeing the organization develop and grow gave him much satisfaction. So did working with what he calls "a super Board" of talented, dedicated, and knowledgeable business associates.

Disharoon will be remembered not only for what he did for Monumental, which by itself was significant, but also for what he did for the "Monumental City." Though not a Baltimore native, he was passionate about the Baltimore Symphony Orchestra, the Orioles, the company's Mt. Vernon–Belvedere neighborhood, and the business potential of the resource-rich Baltimore/Washington corridor.

In 1984, BSO directors had asked Disharoon to help them raise $14 million to get the orchestra back on its feet. Monumental's chairman and CEO didn't think their goal was high enough. Having committed years earlier to help revitalize the neighborhood, and worried about losing another major Baltimore "institution," he set his sights much higher—$40 million.

"A penthouse condominium at Harbor Court costs $1 million; an entrée at the Prime Rib is $23.50; a shrimp cocktail is $6.95; and a symphony orchestra costs $40 million," he insisted. The list was part of a marketing plan and presentation he prepared, with the approval of Conductor David Zinman and Executive Director John Gidwitz, to sell the BSO to business leaders, fundraisers, and donors.

Making his first call in December 1985, Disharoon raised $38.7 million in less than a year. After years of selling insurance, his pitches were convincing and polished, and with regard to the BSO, he knew the "touch points" that would get results. "It was probably the most remarkable job of fundraising that's ever been done locally," said Bud Meyerhoff in a 1987 interview for *Warfield's* magazine. "He . . . is . . . an . . . *incredible salesman*," noted business associate and friend, Piper & Marbury's Andre Brewster, in the same article.

Monumental Corporation received a National "Business in the Arts" Award in 1987 for Disharoon's "Endowment for Excellence" BSO fundraising efforts. BSO directors also invited Les and his wife, Ann, to join the orchestra in London, Moscow and Leningrad as part of their fourteen-city "world class" 1987 European tour which his efforts had made possible.

When his "Birds" needed a new home, he worked passionately with city and state leaders to develop plans and get the funding needed to build the new two-stadium complex at Camden Yards. He was also part of a team of local business leaders consulted about developing the Baltimore-Washington corridor—home of the Johns Hopkins Hospital, the federal government, the Port of Baltimore and three international airports—as an East Coast bio-tech, sci-tech and hi-tech center.

Between 1985 and 1988, Monumental Corporation donated over $400,000 annually to support health, education and the arts in the Baltimore area. One of the larger grants, for $250,000 in 1986, was given to the Johns Hopkins Medical Institutions. Made through the Life and Health Medical Research Fund, it was ear-marked for MRI (magnetic resonance imaging) research.

"Monumental was always a good corporate citizen," says Disharoon. In terms of giving back to the community from which it grew, the organization "more than did its share." The same could be said about its chairman and CEO Les Disharoon.

BELOW: Baltimore mayor William Donald Schaefer and Edgar M. Boyd, president of the Baltimore Chamber of Commerce, present the Mayor's Award to Monumental Life chairman and CEO Les Disharoon in 1977 in recognition of the company's efforts to revitalize the 1200 and 1300 blocks of North Charles Street.

BELOW RIGHT: In 1986, Monumental Corporation donated $250,000 to the Johns Hopkins Medical Institutions to support MRI (magnetic resonance imaging) research.

DUTCH TREAT!

Three months later, Disharoon stood before a group of AEGON officers at their worldwide headquarters in The Hague. *"We zijn blij met jullie te . . ."* he began, but before he could complete his first sentence the audience was on its feet, applauding.

Warm, friendly and intensely proud of their country, the Dutch were obviously surprised and appreciative of Disharoon's attempt to speak to them in their own language. "I guess I couldn't have chosen a better opening," he said later.

Joining Disharoon in the Netherlands for three days of meetings before the merger's September 3, 1986, effective date were corporate executives Larry Jenkins, Monumental Life president and CEO; Bill Sanders, Monumental General president and CEO; Buck Walsh, Monumental Corporation executive vice president and CFO; and Ron Nagler, Monumental Corporation senior vice president, Investments.

"We responded to a surprising number of questions," says Disharoon. AEGON's executives were especially curious about Monumental's corporate culture and its strategy for achieving a competitive edge in the marketplace. Good corporate citizens themselves, the Dutch expressed genuine enthusiasm about Monumental's connections to Baltimore and Maryland and its involvement in the community. They explained that AEGON was quite visible in the Netherlands—as sponsors of the Dutch Olympic speed-skating team and because the train station in The Hague, the country's capital city, was connected to their building.

The group from Baltimore toured AEGON's new headquarters and government buildings in The Hague and traveled by car for sightseeing in Amsterdam. "Our Dutch hosts were anxious to have us learn about their country, their culture, and their artistic heritage," Disharoon remembers, "and to have us feel good about the Dutch people and our new business relationship with their company."

That artistic heritage—symbolized most often by the work of seventeenth-century "Golden Age" painters

Rembrandt and Vermeer—was shared with the people of Baltimore later in 1986 when Monumental and AEGON co-sponsored a major two-month exhibit at the Walters Art Gallery featuring fifty "Dutch Masterworks." Attended by representatives from the Dutch embassy, the World Bank and Dutch cultural associations as well as by many of the area's civic, cultural and educational leaders, the exhibit helped Monumental and AEGON publicize their new partnership.

On December 3, 1986—just days before children in Holland traditionally celebrate the arrival of Kris Kringle—the Walters opened its doors to the Baltimore community for a special day-long program titled "Dutch Treat" that included art projects, tours, Dutch food, film shorts about Holland, and the sale of Dutch gifts.

"We hope that these will be the first of many such cultural exchanges resulting from our merger," said Disharoon. Not surprisingly, it was. Two years later, dozens of Monumental Life sales conference leaders flew to Holland to celebrate their success, meet AEGON officers, and tour the same streets and sites company officers had in 1986.

LEFT: *Shortly after the merger announcement, this picture of AEGON headquarters in The Hague, the Netherlands, appeared in the ML News.*

RIGHT: *Every Monumental employee received a hand-painted replica of the AEGON headquarters made of "Delft blue" Dutch china.*

BELOW: *In November 1986, Monumental and AEGON co-sponsored a two-month exhibit at the Walters Art Gallery in Baltimore that included fifty "Dutch Masterworks" by artists such as Rembrandt and Vermeer.*

Dutch Masterworks
From The Bredius Museum: A Connoisseur's Collection

THE WALTERS ART GALLERY, BALTIMORE
NOVEMBER 26, 1986 - JANUARY 18, 1987

Many AEGON employees in the Netherlands walk or bike to work.

Kees Storm's running shoes were featured on the cover of AEGON's worldwide employee publication!

RIGHT: *AEGON executives Kees Storm (third from left), Jaap Peters, Bill Foster (fifth, sixth from left) and Larry Brown (third from right) frequently competed in European marathons.*

HEALTHY LIVING

After seeing their Dutch counterparts at AEGON make room for jogging and 5k runs in their multi-day meeting agendas, Monumental executives soon realized how important leisure, healthy living and exercise were to the Dutch. Like many Europeans, AEGON employees walked, biked, or took public transportation to work. They enjoyed ice skating, running and the outdoors. Though many Dutch men and women smoked, few were truly overweight. They worked regular hours and took their vacations. Meaningful work was important, but enjoying life was even more so. Leisure time, shared with family and friends, had been an important part of Dutch lives for generations.

U.S. managers and employees might learn a lot more from their new Dutch partners than anyone had expected!

Throughout the decade, company publications encouraged employees to walk during lunch and participate in "Jazz-Y" aerobics classes, co-sponsored by the Baltimore YWCA, at a nearby church. In 1985, seventy-seven-year-old Fred Niemeyer, a Monumental retiree, recruited home office employees to help him kick off the city's "Brisk Walking Is No Sweat" campaign. After retiring in 1960, the treasurer of the Baltimore County Commission on Physical Fitness had served as a Swedish walking instructor for fifteen years.

In January 1986 the company introduced an Employee Assistance Program to help employees and their families cope with problems caused by marital, financial or work-related stress, emotional illness, alcoholism, and drug abuse. The goal—happier, healthier people living more productive lives—benefited the company and each individual who used the service.

As the dangers of smoking began to make big news, the company sponsored "Smoke Free Days" and smoking cessation programs. In January 1986 smoking was limited to personal offices and work spaces, the canteen lounge and designated areas in the cafeteria. One year later, an announcement by Disharoon prompted many employees to quit smoking:

> As a life and health insurer, we are committed to promoting good health and the prevention of disease. With so much evidence pointing to the dangers of smoking for smokers and non-smokers alike, we feel we cannot continue to allow smoking within our offices and work areas. We have an obligation to all our employees and associates to help safeguard their rights and health.

By January 1988, the Monumental workplace was smoke-free. Employees who wished to smoke had to leave the building and light up only in designated areas during their breaks.

UNPREPARED FOR AIDS

AIDS (Acquired Immune Deficiency Syndrome) was also making headlines in the 1980s. When the first U.S. case was diagnosed in 1981, insurers knew little about the disease, but as the number of cases increased along with the size of AIDS-related health care claims, the virus commanded the attention of the life and health industry.

Between 1981 and 1985, the U.S. Center for Disease Control (CDC) reported 13,611 cases. By 1985, 50 percent of those diagnosed were already dead. Within two more years, the number of reported cases quadrupled to 42,300, while the estimated count of undiagnosed but infected individuals rose to over 1.5 million. By 1991 the CDC predicted that 325,000 Americans would be dead from AIDS.

The killer virus was like a ticking time bomb not only for its victims but also for the industry's life and health insurers. Though exposure to the virus did not mean certain death even in the 1980s, insurers had not factored the risk of AIDS into their product pricing or claims liability for existing contracts. No insurer knew or could predict who or how many of their policyholders might contract the disease. Once infected with the HIV virus, victims usually developed the AIDS syndrome within two to five years. By 1985 health care claims were averaging $100,000 to $150,000 per victim.

Something had to be done or the cost of AIDS could put many insurers out of business. Because Monumental Life and Monumental General had little business in the "high risk" areas of the country where the virus first appeared, they had very few AIDS-related claims.

However, all insurers were drawn into the controversy as federal and state governments considered challenging the industry's right to administer blood tests to determine if an applicant for life or health insurance had been exposed to AIDS. The stigma, fear of the unknown and the irrational behavior then associated with AIDS created questions and concerns about the confidentiality of private health information used by insurers to determine risk and insurability.

In 1985, the American Council of Life Insurance (ACLI) and the Health Insurance Association of America (HIAA) jointly issued a report explaining the industry's position: "Insurance companies seek to preserve the privilege of administering medical tests—including ones that test for antibodies to the AIDS virus—and of using the results of such tests in the same way that they use other medical information."

Everyone agreed that the American people needed information—about how the virus was spread and not spread, who was at risk and how to change behavior. Insurers like Monumental took the lead in educating employees and the public about the disease.

Within a few years a question about HIV was included on Monumental Life's applications for insurance. Legislators and the public continued to challenge the industry's right to charge applicants for insurance based on their age, sex, medical history, or risk of dying.

PRE-NEED, PRE-PLANNING

As the industry wrestled with risk classification and life expectancy issues, more and more retirees and senior citizens looked forward to longer, healthier, still active lives. Though the cost of living had risen, so had their bank accounts—thanks to double-digit interest rates—and many couples wanted to "take care of things" while they were still clear-headed and had the financial resources to do so.

In 1985 a group of funeral home owners approached Monumental Life about providing life insurance to help older Americans pre-fund funeral expenses. Monumental, they believed, had the expertise to meet their needs and criteria. Monumental's executives liked the idea of having funeral homes market the company's products. The product they developed was sold most often as a single

During the Eighties, the red ribbon came to be the recognized symbol of the fight against AIDS.

J. Ben Jenkins helped build Monumental Life's PreNeed business beginning in the late 1980s.

BELOW: *Ron Nagler (left), senior vice president, Investments, and Don Chamberlain (right), vice president, Securities, made money for Monumental and AEGON when the stock market crashed on "Black Monday" 1987.*

premium contract. The consumer bought his or her policy from the funeral director or a funeral home agent and listed the funeral home as beneficiary. An increasing death benefit feature kept the policy on pace with inflation.

Monumental Life's PreNeed products hit the street in 1986, marketed by members of the National Selected Morticians (NSM), an association of funeral home directors. For 1987, its first full year of operation, the division reported $4 million of insurance in force.

Twenty years later, "aging Baby Boomers continue to be a growing target market for the company's PreNeed products," noted J. Ben Jenkins, vice president of PreNeed Sales, in 2006. "Though more insurers today are selling insurance policies to pre-fund funerals, Monumental Life is the highest rated company in the PreNeed marketplace. We offer a combination of fair rates, good policy growth and competitive commissions. But it's up to our sales reps to convince funeral directors—both independents and current members of the Selected Independent Funeral Home organization (formerly NSM)—that we are the best!"

'BLACK MONDAY' TURNS ROSY

On Monday, October 19, 1987, the stock market fell 508.32 points. The value of common stocks continued to slide as investors in increasing numbers sold off equities. On Wall Street and in major stock exchanges around the world, analysts were stunned. What was happening to the market?

Outside their offices on Monumental's fifth floor, Les Disharoon, Buck Walsh, Ron Nagler and Don Chamberlain checked stock quotes every ten minutes. In the frenzy of Wall Street's "Black Monday," they agreed they could invest $3 to $4 million, without impairing the company's surplus, in six of the strongest and best capitalized companies in the country—Eastman Kodak, Proctor & Gamble, IBM, MERCK, 3M and Sears Roebuck. Two days later, with the market strongly recovering, they sold the same portfolio for a 20 percent gain.

Had they received an inside tip? "No," replied Chamberlain. "We simply watched closely as the slide began and soon realized that here was an excellent opportunity for a significant short-term gain. When we felt the market couldn't go much lower, we bought— then sold two days later as prices climbed."

Though the market lost 22.9 percent of its value on October 19, making it the worst one-day stock market decline in U.S. history, "Black Monday" did not produce the devastating results many expected. No depression followed. Few businesses failed. Instead, noted Disharoon, "the downward adjustment of the market created a unique opportunity for people to buy a piece of America at prices that appeared quite sensible."

Many investors and companies like Monumental increased the percentage of their portfolios invested in common stocks. Middle-income consumers who could afford to take some risk began to put their money into mutual funds, IRAs, stocks and more market-sensitive life insurance products.

One month after the "Crash of 1987," Monumental Life unveiled a restructured, repriced portfolio and flexible new term products to meet the distinct financial protection needs of lower, middle and upper middle-income families. In a rapidly expanding and competitive global economy, American consumers were demanding value in the products they bought, and expected quality in the service they received.

Speaking to employees about quality, Larry Jenkins asked:

Don't you prefer dealing with businesses and people who listen, anticipate your needs, answer your questions, do what they promise, and solve your problems with politeness, care and respect for your time? That's good service—the key to success for banks, restaurants, travel agents . . . and insurance companies. With products varying only slightly from company to company in our business, how we serve our customers and each other determines our fate.

THE QUALITY LIFE COMPANY

Beginning in January 1988, the company's 130th year, "Quality" became Monumental's byword. Rededicated to providing quality service and to helping American families protect the quality of their lives, the company added the word to its name and committed to improve everything it did. By mid-year, the company's new "Monumental, the Quality Life Company" logo appeared on pins, letterhead, brochures, awards, training manuals, field signage and billboard advertising.

"Quality means doing things right the first time," said Jenkins. Throughout the year, management invested in improving communication, programs, systems, tools and processes to deliver more efficient, customer-focused, responsive service.

On November 11, 1988, the company celebrated 130 years of success with a "Birthday Bash" mini-conference in Baltimore attended by more than two hundred agents, managers, home office employees and spouses. For the first time in the company's long history, all conference leaders—Leading Agent Joanne Martin, Leading Sales Manager Robert Morgan, Leading Branch Manager Wayne Gagalski, and Leading District Manager Dan Gibson—came from Maryland.

Raising his champagne glass in a toast, Henry G. Hagan, vice president and chief marketing officer, announced: "130 years is a great history to build on, not sit on!" As expected, Monumental continued to change and grow.

During the winter of 1989, the company installed PCs, customized software in every field office and gave field clerical personnel access to policyholder data through PRISM (Productive Routines to Increase Sales Momentum). Meanwhile, in the field and in the home office, the company prepared for the "monumental" task of direct-billing all customers for the first time in 131 years.

PCs and policy illustrations, Quality Life Check-Ups and quality control, data bases, networks, direct bill and electronic mail—PRISM changed forever the vocabulary and scope of field office activity. "Direct bill was a big

Monumental added the word "QUALITY" to its name and logo in 1988.

Employees gathered on the home office terrace in 1988 to reinforce Monumental's company-wide focus on quality.

A MONUMENTAL MINI-CONFERENCE

Our 130th Birthday Bash in Baltimore!

FRIDAY, NOVEMBER 11 – SUNDAY, NOVEMBER 13, 1988
STOUFFER HARBORPLACE HOTEL, BALTIMORE, MD.

ABOVE LEFT: Monumental celebrated its 130th year with a "Birthday Bash" weekend in Baltimore.

ABOVE RIGHT: More than two hundred agents, managers, home office employees and spouses attended the formal event.

BELOW LEFT: Sue Drury (center) was part of the home office training team that introduced PRISM (Productive Routines to Increase Sales Momentum) automation—including data bases, direct billing and new work stations—to clerical employees in every field office.

culture change for all of us," said Phil White, then PRISM coordinator and second vice president, Marketing Services. Brought into the home office by President Roger Kolker and Vince Zirpoli, vice president of District Agencies, in 1980—after only six months as a district manager—White had been the youngest regional vice president in the company's history.

Mailing bills from the home office, he explained, eliminated most in-home collections and gave agents more time to meet people, make sales, build relationships, provide needed service, and complete regular reviews on every policyholder family. By giving field offices easier access to more accurate, timely policy information, added White, "PRISM's changes enabled each field person to work smarter and more professionally."

By early 1989 management had also introduced a new company publication, *Partners,* produced using state-of-the-art MacIntosh desktop design technology, and two new programs —"Star Quality" and "Frontline Partners"—to recognize quality service and increase teamwork, understanding, and communication between the home office and the field.

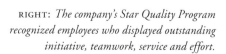

RIGHT: The company's Star Quality Program recognized employees who displayed outstanding initiative, teamwork, service and effort.

AEGON's Jaap Peters Surprised . . .

Monumental Leading Agent is a Lady!

JOANNE MARTIN, retired Monumental Life agent from southern Maryland, was a consistent leader, award winner and conference qualifier during her impressive two-decade sales career. The company's leading agent from 1985 to 1990, she earned the insurance industry's National Quality Award year after year and was a lifetime member of the prestigious Million Dollar Round Table.

She was a success, she says, because she always put her clients and prospects before her own pocketbook. "We must educate, disturb, excite and inform people sufficiently to earn the right to place the proper amount of insurance on their lives," said Martin before her retirement in 1998. "As insurance agents, we have an awesome responsibility."

In addition to the satisfaction Martin received from meeting her customers' needs, she and her husband, Bob, always enjoyed the conference trips that the company planned for qualifiers. But the one she remembers the most was the 1988 trip to The Hague in the Netherlands two years after Monumental merged with AEGON.

During one of their evenings in the Netherlands, AEGON hosted a dinner for Monumental Life's officers and sales leaders at a unique organ museum in Utrecht. Joanne had the pleasure of sitting next to AEGON chairman and CEO Jaap Peters. She says that Peters, who like most AEGON officers was Dutch by birth, was a most enjoyable host.

At one point he turned to her and asked if she could point out where Monumental's leading agent was sitting. Mrs. Peters, seated on the CEO's other side, nudged her husband and noted that he was sitting *next to* the leading agent. Peters was embarrassed, remembers Joanne, "but he made it up to me in a most extraordinary way."

On his next visit to the United States, Peters made arrangements to accompany Joanne on her southern Maryland debit for several sales and service calls. The area Joanne serviced in the late 1980s was home to Maryland's Amish population and many of the state's watermen and tobacco farmers. Most families lived very simple lives.

When Joanne introduced Peters to her policyholders— "What a handsome, elegant man he was!"—she thought it must have been quite intimidating for them. For all but one, that is. "We were in a farm home and I was explaining the benefits of a particular policy to a young couple. At one point I looked over to see how Mr. Peters was doing and saw the farmer's young toddler daughter curled up on his lap!"

AEGON employees had noted that, despite his position, Peters was very approachable. Obviously this young child thought so too!

Monumental leading agent Joanne Martin and her husband, Bob, were seated with AEGON chairman and CEO Jaap Peters at a conference banquet in Utrecht, the Netherlands in 1988.

AEGON USA!

Like Monumental Life, AEGON was also preparing to announce changes at year-end 1988. Since purchasing Monumental Corporation in 1986, the number of AEGON business units operating in the U.S. had grown, and efforts were underway to centralize the Investment Department and a limited number of other services.

On November 4, 1988, AEGON's executive board, officers from Monumental Corporation, Monumental Life and Monumental General, as well as the heads of other U.S. operating units gathered at the Four Seasons Hotel in Washington for a two-day meeting. The big news was the formation, effective January 1, 1989, of a holding company for U.S. subsidiaries to be called AEGON USA. With 3,900 employees and $5.1 billion in assets, it would be ranked among the top twenty stock life insurance companies in the United States.

In discussing plans for the future, Les Disharoon noted that "operating companies will continue as business units with a high degree of autonomy." Jaap Peters emphasized that business units would have responsibility for their own strategies and results. Leo Berndsen, just announced as chairman of the AEGON USA board, said he would be looking for opportunities to strengthen and build existing U.S. operations.

Also announced was the election of Cedar Rapids–based Don Shepard, senior executive vice president and chief operating officer of Life Investors, as AEGON USA's chief executive officer. The new organization, he said, would continue to encourage "entrepreneurship, independent and competitive thinking, knowledge of the market and customer, bias for action, accountability and development of people."

Retiring as chairman of Monumental Corporation in December 1988, Les Disharoon sent the following message to Monumental Life employees:

> In this, my last official holiday message, I extend my most heartfelt thanks to each of you for your help, your energy, your loyalty and your commitment in making Monumental the fine company it is today. We have been through a lot together, we have taken a lot of risks, we have had a few disappointments and, happily, many more successes. We have built a fine company that is a leader in our chosen areas of specialization, a company that is a responsible corporate citizen in our community. I'm proud of our accomplishments and each of you.

At mid-year 1989, Monumental Life contributed 21 percent of AEGON USA's pre-tax earnings. For the first nine months of 1989, the company reported $25.2 million actual earnings—excluding capital and surplus—almost 18 percent ahead of budget.

But the biggest news of 1989 for Monumental Life was yet to come. In late December 1989, Larry Jenkins surprised employees by announcing the acquisition of the home service business of Washington National Insurance Company of Evanston, Illinois, effective January 1, 1990. It was a fitting end to a year and a decade marked by challenge and change.

Don Shepard, newly appointed CEO of AEGON USA, and Leo Berndsen, chairman of the AEGON USA board, met in Baltimore in 1988.

Yesterday and Today . . .
WE STILL MAKE HOUSE CALLS!

Throughout Monumental's 150-year history, our agents have focused on prospecting, sales and face-to-face customer service. Industry education has improved their professionalism. Automation has reduced response time and put more tools at their fingertips, but the agent's job is still about building relationships, meeting needs and serving people in their homes. Monumental agents continue to be solidly connected to the communities they serve and are often on a first name basis with clients and their families.

Early in the twentieth century, agents wore out shoe leather collecting small weekly premiums in Baltimore's densely populated rowhouse neighborhoods. Agents on Maryland's Eastern Shore once had to take ferries and ride bicycles to collect from customers, including crab pickers, living on islands in the Chesapeake Bay. Today, agents might wear out tires driving 400 to 500 miles weekly to serve a scattered suburban and rural clientele. But the job is still the same. "You work 'til it's done," successful veterans say, underscoring a work ethic that finds them on the job from 8:00 a.m. to 9:00 or 10:00 p.m. most weekdays and making service calls on weekends.

Until the mid-1960s, policyholders traditionally paid their premiums in cash, to agents who called at their homes. When customers began mailing payments to the local office, agents still had to reconcile accounts before turning money over to managers or administrators for forwarding to the home office.

Each agent had a big, bulky ledger called a "debit book" in which to record collections for the accounts assigned to his or her "debit." Much like today's laptop, debit books were an agent's lifeblood. In the hands of a skilled salesman, they served as an at-a-glance means of identifying each household's insurance in force, payment history, sales opportunities, and referrals to family and friends who might need coverage. The task of transferring names, account numbers and collection figures from an old debit book to a new one was tedious and time-consuming.

Agents sat down weekly with their debit books to review accounts, plan their work, and decide whom to see each day for collections and sales. A star next to a name could suggest that an agent might be invited to join the family for dinner, if he timed his arrival just right!

Until the Depression, agents turned in collections at the end of each day. By the 1940s, weekly or bi-weekly staff meetings and turn-ins were more common. The demise of the weekly industrial policy in the 1960s and 1970s—coupled with the shift to ordinary insurance policies paid quarterly, semi-annually and annually, as well as the increasing use of mail pay and automatic bank drafts—have now reduced turn-ins to key strokes on a laptop and computer-generated reports. But laptop data is reviewed as carefully as debit book pages were a century ago.

The weekly sales meeting is still a staple in every field office. Managers still focus on sales ideas, results, motivation and professional development; and today's recruits still undergo weeks of extensive hands-on training, including joint fieldwork with managers, to develop expertise in making laptop presentations and sales. Though some agents continue to use printed brochures, most of the information they need—including rates, product specs, illustrations, and tools to manage accounts and generate leads—is now on their computers. The time once spent collecting premiums or waiting for proposals to arrive from the home office can be spent more productively seeing clients to review needs and reinforce the purpose of having coverage.

Yes, after 150 years, Monumental agents *still* make

▲ GIVE THE BEST THERE IS IN YOU

Celebrating his thirty-second year as a Mutual Life agent in May 1925, John L. Sebald remembered when the company had only nine Ordinary and five Industrial agents in 1893. "I am delighted to observe the spirit manifested here today," he said. "The company depends on you to carry on its work. I exhort you to give the company the best there is in you."

house calls. Day after day they continue to meet families face-to-face in their homes to educate, uncover needs and build relationships based on respect and trust. They advocate for loved ones who might be left behind, should tragedy strike. They help keep insurance in force and deliver benefit checks when they are needed most.

Agents also continue to be Monumental's face, its goodwill ambassadors. More valuable than million-dollar ad campaigns, they show local citizens that we care by *being there*, in the communities we serve—to volunteer, chair fund-raising committees, coach Little League teams, serve as Scout leaders, sing in church choirs and deliver food to the needy.

This focus on giving back and helping people is as alive today as it was when Mutual Life agents first collected weekly premiums in Baltimore's immigrant, working-class neighborhoods in the early 1870s.

▲ **WRITE 'EM WITH A SMILE**
Austin Savage, working in Washington, D.C., in 1925, gave this advice to fellow agents: "Whether it be a 5-cent Industrial or $5,000 Ordinary, write 'em with a smile. They will not forget you."

▲ **AUDITING AGENT RECORD BOOKS**
The Auditing Department was responsible for field office accounting, including regular reviews of individual agent record books. "The record of any individual man is an open confession by a turn of the page," noted the *Old Black Hen*.

▲ **AGENT ON HORSEBACK**
Louisville agent R. Miller was not about to let policies lapse for late payment, not even during a severe snow storm in 1940. When roads became impassable by car on his large rural debit, he borrowed a farmer's horse, tucked his debit book under his arm and continued collecting!

FOOT SOLDIERS ▶
Mutual Life's earliest agents in every neighborhood were foot soldiers who built the weekly premium business by knocking on doors. In Chicago, managers like Nicholas Monteforte and Dominic Zombo hired "canvassers." When they had enough business, they created a new book. That's how the company got started in Chicago in the 1930s and how offices like Chicago #3, pictured here and managed by Zombo in 1956, continued to be Monumental's weekly premium leader in the Fifties. (Agents Celeste and Gaetano, second row, center, are profiled elsewhere in this book—Gaetano on pages 131–132, Celeste on page 236)

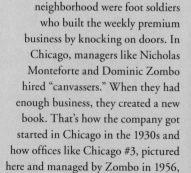

▲ BOARD CALL!

The weekly "board call" became a tradition for most U.S. home service companies. Every field office had one, including Monumental's new Baltimore East office on Harford Road, pictured here in 1966. At weekly meetings, managers called names and agents reported their results—appointments, new applications, coverage amounts and premium dollars. No agent wanted to see his or her name listed lowest on the board!

▲ CHANGING LIFESTYLES

Throughout the 1960s agents and sales managers continued to schedule daytime sales and service appointments in the homes of prospects and policyholders, often meeting with housewives and young mothers who were usually at home. This would change in the 1970s as more and more women joined the workforce.

▲ FIRST CAR!

Baltimore East agent Vince Leonard began working for Monumental Life on February 18, 1946, ten days after being discharged from the U.S. Navy following service in World War II. He borrowed money to buy his first car, a 1941 Plymouth convertible, and bought a new suit with his first paycheck. He remained on the job for more than forty years.

◀ NEW SALES TOOL!

In 1966 every man in the Evansville, Indiana, district was using Monumental's new audio-visual machine and filmstrips as part of his in-home sales presentations. "With A/V, we have a 70% closing ratio and bigger sales," said P. J. West, kneeling at right. "A picture is worth a thousand words."

Serving the Inner City, the 'Burbs' and Beyond . . .
DIFFERENT STROKES FOR DIFFERENT FOLKS

Retired Chicago agent Frank Hernandez is still proud to display his sales and conference awards earned in the 1960s

AN GIBSON likes spicy crab soup loaded with home-grown vegetables; Frank Hernandez favors a zesty salsa with hot peppers. Very hot peppers.

In many ways, Monumental Life is a microcosm of the "melting pot" we call America. The geographic, ethnic and cultural richness and diversity that has made our nation great is reflected in our agents' different tastes, in their diverse backgrounds, and in the different ways they sell and service Monumental Life's products in communities across the U.S.

Dan Gibson and Frank Hernandez exemplify those differences. Now retired, both had long and successful careers with Monumental that overlapped during the 1960s and 1970s.

Born in Mexico in 1923, Frank Hernandez moved to Chicago when he was a child. In 1960 he was working as a supervisor in the steel mills, struggling to speak better English. When his parents' Monumental agent told him the company was looking for a Spanish-speaking agent to serve a predominantly Hispanic inner-city neighborhood, he seized the opportunity.

Hernandez recalls working long weekday hours—often from 8:00 a.m. to 10:00 p.m.—and collecting on Saturdays. He also offered to accompany the office's non-Spanish speaking agents on sales calls. His sales area, or "debit," as it was called then, included several city blocks. Most of his customers had small $500 paid-weekly policies. Though they earned modest incomes, he says most could afford to pay $15 to $20 a month for life insurance—especially when he stopped by faithfully each week to collect the premium.

Hernandez was proud to show the close-knit families he served how the cash value growth and protection afforded by life insurance could help secure their hopes and dreams. He knew everyone, cultivated business by creating his own "Special Offers," and bought ice cream cones for neighborhood children so frequently that they called him the "Ice Cream Man." His hard work qualified him for sales conferences and many of the company's sales awards.

Like Baltimore and many other U.S. cities, Chicago had large Hispanic, Polish, German and Italian neighborhoods, all populated by poor but proud working-class families.

George Benavides, another Spanish-speaking Chicago agent and consistent sales leader, says customers were so concentrated in these ethnic neighborhoods that agents could make twenty to thirty collections a day. "One Saturday," he says, "my manager worked with me and we made one hundred calls between 9:00 a.m. and 9:00 p.m."

If Hernandez, Benavides and other inner-city agents gauged sales success by their worn shoe leather, stairs climbed to third-story two-flat apartments and weekly collections, it was a different story for agents like Dan Gibson.

When twenty-year-old Gibson joined the company in 1958, his sales territory was spread across parts of three rural southern Maryland counties. With Annapolis to the north, the Washington suburbs to the west and the Chesapeake Bay to the east, his customers were primarily farmers, watermen and construction workers separated by miles of quiet country roads and, sometimes, wide expanses of water.

Like the bay, Gibson's days had their Chesapeake-flavored ebb and flow. Doing business there meant being sensitive to the seasons as well as the changing needs of his customers. It was difficult catching a farmer during the planting or harvesting season. The crabbers and oystermen were also up and out on the bay before dawn. Unlike the blue-collar industrial world, most of his customers had no boss to pay them every Friday.

"There weren't many breakfast meetings for us," says Gibson. "We caught them at day's end when they came in from the fields or got off boats loaded with bushels of crabs or oysters. We planned our collections and sales calls carefully."

The daily routines, the distances and the seasonal dips in income determined when he saw clients and how he managed his business. "We didn't do weekly collections like they did in the city," says Gibson, who would later become a sales manager and then a district manager. "Many of our accounts were paid three or four months or a year in advance."

Gibson's staff met weekly at a hotel in LaPlata—many miles from their district office in Annapolis. He recalls doing "turn-ins" of collected cash, balancing his large ledger book, and then going to the local post office with other agents to purchase money orders the manager could hand-deliver to Annapolis.

When Monumental discontinued selling Weekly Premium business in 1975, recalls Gibson, it simply reinforced the way agents in his office had already been doing business for many years. Being able to spread collection calls over an entire month also meant more time to prospect for new customers—in Gibson's case, the increasingly affluent customers from nearby metropolitan areas drawn to southern Maryland by the bay, its rivers and its relaxed lifestyle. Rising incomes, coupled with attractive new Regular Ordinary products, provided new opportunities for everyone in his office.

During the 1960s, Gibson wrote many individual life insurance policies with $5,000 or higher face amounts—larger than the average policy being written in many metropolitan markets. When the company began selling group life insurance, he also embraced that initiative and used it as an opportunity to insure more people.

"I still remember coming into the office with a five or ten thousand dollar app during those early years," says Gibson. "Agents would come up to me and say, 'Let me touch it.' And a $25,000 policy, well, that was big money back then."

Near the end of the decade, when Gibson submitted nine life insurance applications on three lives totaling $375,000 of "key man" business owner coverage, the sale put an exclamation point on what many already knew—Monumental Life, true to its origins, was successfully meeting the ever-changing needs of its inner-city, suburban and rural customers.

Officially retired in 2000, former agent and field manager Dan Gibson is still writing policies and servicing Monumental customers in southern Maryland.

▶ SERVING MINORITY FAMILIES

In the late 1960s and 1970s the number of minority agents and policyholders increased industry-wide. Making "cold calls" in inner-city and rural neighborhoods, Monumental agents continued to discuss life insurance needs while sitting face-to-face with prospects in the comfort of their living rooms and kitchens.

▼ STILL CLIMBING BALTIMORE'S WHITE MARBLE STEPS

Monumental agents have served Baltimore's working-class rowhouse neighborhoods since the company first began collecting weekly premiums in 1873. Many lower- and middle-income customers depend on personal relationships with agents—including in-home sales and service—to meet their protection needs.

▲ HIGH TOUCH, HIGH TECH

As life insurance products became more complex in the 1980s and 1990s, industry professionals put away yellow pads and pencils and began pulling out laptops to make sales presentations. The transition was challenging for some veterans, but no one could deny that their new laptop tools and programs provided faster access to rates, and product and client account information. Prospects and policyholders were equally impressed!

▼ PROTECTING FARMERS, BUSINESS OWNERS

Times change, but "when you work with families over the years," said Monumental agent Jack Dyer in 1996, "you get to know them pretty well. As their children grow up and their protection and savings needs change, it's good to know that we can offer them products and services that meet those requirements." One of Dyer's clients was Mark King, whose father owned Aldus King Farm in rural Lancaster County, Pennsylvania.

▲ KEEPING FAMILIES TOGETHER

"Mr. Romano is a good agent," said Tia Harrington in 1998. "He used to visit us regularly to collect Mom's premiums. We would also see him often around our neighborhood visiting other customers." He made sure that Tia and her three siblings were insured by a Children's Term Rider on their mother's policy. When Terry Harrington died unexpectedly of a brain aneurism at age forty, Ralph Romano (right) and Jersey City District Manager Sam Bucca (left) were there with benefits for the family. Twenty-one-year-old Tia (right center) moved her family into a single-family rental home. "I don't want my sister and brothers to live with anyone else," she said. Romano also helped her allocate funds so that she and her younger sister, Shannell (left center) could enroll in a local community college.

▲ CLOWNING SHOWED HE CARED

Carlos Rodriguez, a Sunday school teacher and agent in Monumental's Jersey City office, reached out to help children and community organizations through his clown character "Shoo Shoo." He is pictured here entertaining family members stranded by Hurricane Andrew at Monumental's 1992 "Play to Win" conference on Paradise Island in the Bahamas. Before the storm hit, he also visited hospitalized kids in downtown Nassau.

▲ GIVE A LOT, GET A LOT.

"Selling and community service go hand-in-hand," said General Agent Bill Tait in 1999. "People recognize my name because I am very visible in the community." They gave him their business because he was very good at giving back. An agent with Commonwealth and Monumental for over thirty years, Tait is a life member of the Million Dollar Round Table. He helped found the Memphis branch of the Make-A-Wish Foundation in 1985. He's manned voter registration booths at malls, signed up Red Cross blood donors, and adopted needy families at the holidays. As a volunteer deputy sheriff for over ten years in Shelby County, Tennessee, he also participated in the Senior Citizens Crime Watch Program. Pictured here with Tait (center) in 2001 are his son Bill Tait III, now a Monumental manager, and Office Administrator Veta Hailey. "I don't feel that my schedule is full unless I do something good."

▲ LAPTOP NOT A LUXURY
By the year 2000, when Nikol Kelly joined the company, agents didn't go anywhere without their laptops. Kelly drives about 350 miles per week to meet with clients who live within sixty miles of her York, Pennsylvania, field office. Wherever she goes, she knows that technical support from Help Desk representatives like Derrick Odoms, pictured here in 2002, is only a phone call away. The company's continuing investment in technology has made possible such innovations as electronic applications, forms and signatures to help agents boost productivity and deliver faster, more efficient customer service.

▶ REWARDS FOR CONSISTENT EFFORT
Plan your work. Work your plan. Take care of your people. Do it every day. These are the keys to success for a home service agent, and Pikeville, Kentucky, agent Donna Ratliff opens many doors. There when families need her, she earns their respect, trust and referrals. An industry veteran and Million Dollar Round Table qualifier, Ratliff has won numerous company awards. She's pictured here in her National Honor Associate red jacket with Monumental President Henry G. Hagan.

CHAPTER 12

Merger Mania!
(1990–1999)

THE RETURN ADDRESS on the envelope . . . Monumental Life Insurance Company, 2 East Chase Street, Baltimore, Maryland . . . catches her eye. Here we go again, she thinks. Another company trying to sell me insurance. Finding these letters in her mailbox every week is becoming bothersome. She has enough coverage to take care of her final expenses. She rents her home, pays cash for most purchases, doesn't own a computer or use credit cards, and hasn't bought or financed a new car in many, many years. "How do marketers get my name and address?" wonders the widowed African American woman in her mid-sixties.

But something about this envelope is different. No "FREE OFFER!" or "OPEN ME NOW!" promotion gimmicks jump out in bold type. It's addressed to her personally and looks like it might be important. She's seen several TV news stories recently about company mergers and failures. Looking at the envelope again, she notices a number below her name and address. Maybe her insurance company has been bought, merged or changed names. Maybe this letter is notifying her of the change. Maybe she should open it.

"Dear policyholder," the letter begins . . .

> *We're proud to inform that on November 30, 1998 Capital Security Life Insurance Company will be merged into Monumental Life Insurance*

Company. As a result of an acquisition completed in June 1997, both Capital Security Life and Monumental Life are members of the AEGON Insurance Group.

> *Please note that the merger will not change your policy features, benefits, payment schedule or premium payment due. The local agent and office assigned to service your business will continue to be nearby in your community, ready to meet your needs. Please attach the enclosed Merger and Name Change Endorsement document to your current policy. It changes your insurance policy to reflect our company's new name as a result of the merger.*

Many customers received letters during the 1990s informing them that Monumental Life had assumed responsibility for their policies.

This is the third such letter the Orlando, Florida, resident has received since purchasing her policy from National Standard Life Insurance Company in 1971. The first arrived after Commonwealth Life Insurance Company of Louisville, Kentucky, acquired National Standard in the late 1980s. The second, dated 1991, notified her that the Capital Holding Corporation, Commonwealth Life's parent, had consolidated its business in Florida, South Carolina and Georgia to form the Capital Security Life Insurance Company. She's been paying her premiums to a Capital Security agent ever since.

She looks at the letter in her hand and shakes her head. "These sure are confusing times. Mergers and acquisitions. Companies changing names. How is a retiree like me supposed to keep it all straight? Monumental Life is now responsible for my policy. I guess I can call this new toll-free number if I have questions. In the meantime, at least my agent isn't changing. That's good news!

A GLOBAL MARKETPLACE

As the Berlin Wall tumbled in 1989—triggering the end of the Cold War, the break-up of the Soviet Union, and the subsequent creation of the European Union in 1993—corporations on both sides of the Atlantic also broke through barriers to form new business alliances. AEGON continued to expand its international reach, acquiring companies or pursuing start-up ventures in Spain, Scotland, Germany, Hungary, Mexico and Taiwan. Before the rise of capitalism in Europe's communist states, Hungary's new AB-AEGON had been a state-controlled insurance monopoly. During the 1990s, AEGON sent Hungarian managers to the U.S. to learn how to market in a free enterprise economy.

Meanwhile, the recession of the 1980s had caused many U.S. businesses to fail. By the early 1990s, the rapid growth of technology, the Internet, the World Wide Web,

and e-commerce had improved productivity, efficiency and turn-around times. But the introduction of PCs, employee "work stations," websites and office networks also meant that companies needed better-educated, higher-paid analysts, programmers, and technical experts to update and maintain more sophisticated systems.

In less than a decade, the cost of remaining competitive in an increasingly high-tech, global marketplace had become too expensive for many smaller companies. More and more, success depended on size. If a company had adequate financial resources, it could acquire its competitors, grow through merger, consolidate operations, and benefit from what financial analysts called "the economies of scale."

When two insurance companies merged, for example, the cost of developing expensive, state-of-the art computer systems and networks could be spread over more policies and balanced with additional premium and investment income. Newly acquired policies, premium and other assets reduced an organization's per policy cost of doing business and, ultimately, the price it charged consumers for its products.

HOME SERVICE LEADER!

Entering the 1990s, Monumental Life was positioned not only to survive but to become a leader and pacesetter in the home service marketplace. Strong, stable and well-managed for many decades, the company had celebrated 130 years of success in 1988. Since becoming part of the AEGON Insurance Group in 1986, it had the financial backing and support of one of the world's largest insurance organizations. By 1989, AEGON executives in the U.S. and the Netherlands were committed to helping Monumental Life grow.

And grow it did, beginning on April 2, 1990, with the $100 million acquisition of home service business from the Washington National Insurance Company of Evanston, Illinois.

"I have long believed that size is one of the essential keys to long-term success in our market," said President Larry Jenkins when announcing the acquisition on December 19, 1989. "The addition of Washington National's home service business more than doubles our size, increases the number of states where we do business, and makes us one of the largest home service life insurers in the mid-Atlantic and Midwest. This is the biggest acquisition ever for Monumental Life and AEGON USA." Just as important, added Jenkins, "the quality of Washington National's business is well-suited to our present and future goals."

The addition of Washington National's $70 million of annual premium, sixty-four field offices, and more than 1,000 home service agents—predominantly in Illinois, New Jersey, Pennsylvania, Texas and California—also reinforced Monumental Life's long-term commitment to the career agency distribution system and in-home sales and customer service. As a result of the acquisition, Monumental Life had $165 million of in-force premium, $11.5 billion of insurance in force, $250 million of annual revenue, nearly $1 billion in assets, and more than 1,600 field personnel in over one hundred field offices in seventeen states.

The announcement signaled the start of a challenging and productive year for the entire organization. By year-end 1989, management had appointed a transition team to begin planning the conversion and assimilation of 1.3 million Washington National customers and accounts. During January 1990's "Road Show," executives crisscrossed the country by corporate jet to introduce AEGON and Monumental Life to groups of Washington National field personnel at meetings in Chicago, Philadelphia, Houston and San Diego.

As attorneys submitted product plans to state insurance departments for approval, the company's in-house print shop began printing two million pieces of paper—including agent employment kits, product manuals, rate books, sales brochures and training materials—for

ABOVE: *Monumental's Emilie Harris and Brian Gilchrist coordinated packing and shipment of over eight hundred boxes of sales and training materials for newly-acquired Washington National offices. Retired sales manager Jack Ripple came in to help.*

LEFT: *Don Shepard, CEO of AEGON USA, and Monumental Life President Larry Jenkins discuss the Washington National acquisition in January 1990.*

shipment to newly acquired field offices. More than eight hundred boxes arrived at training sites just in time for 107 training sessions held that March. Meanwhile, letters, press releases, and phone messages announced the news to policyholders, prospects and the public.

In April, just four months after the acquisition was announced, a group of Washington National agents drove from Pennsylvania to Baltimore to hand-deliver their first Monumental Life applications to home office underwriters. Training of the company's newest "assets"—Washington National's experienced agents, managers and field clerical personnel—had been completed in record time. The goal was to keep as many of them as possible, and Monumental succeeded.

In fact, the New Jersey offices—all inherited from Washington National—helped Region 3 lead the company in 1991, 1992 and 1993. Experienced managers like Ben and Lou Dahdah, Sam Bucca, George Betar and

Joe Yankowski were hands-on leaders who set goals, commanded respect, and held agents accountable for results. Because their sales team made money and earned awards—including the company's coveted National Honor Associate red blazer—these offices consistently reported low agent turnover rates.

By the time Iraq invaded Kuwait in the August 1990 Gulf War, Monumental's Marketing Services Department had sent embarkation orders of its own to officers and Washington National's leading agents and managers for a promised week-long cruise to the Caribbean. Announced in early 1988, the "Sovereign of the Seas" sales conference was their reward for two years of successful sales results.

Throughout 1990, the acronym "PRIME" (Partnerships/ Relationships in Marketing Excellence) defined the transition and conversion process and symbolized Monumental Life's philosophy and approach to success in the 1990s. Working together—home office and field—employees in the newly combined organization focused on building and maintaining solid, long-term relationships with customers and one another.

"The merger has meant big changes for Monumental Life," said Jenkins that December. "Bigger market share, enhanced positioning and visibility within the industry, more business, more sales, more agents and offices to serve, more applications and claims to process. (Files sent from Evanston, Illinois, filled two seventy-foot "18 wheelers!") It's been a year where both the home office and the field have met challenges head-on to achieve most of the goals we set for ourselves last year."

For its outstanding effort in successfully merging two cultures, two sets of customers, two billing systems, and two field compensation and recognition programs within an extremely tight timetable—a task many insurance companies would not dream of trying—Monumental Life received AEGON's International Award. Accepting the award for the entire company in the summer of 1991, Larry Jenkins noted: "I sense a new spirit of oneness and pride as a result of last year's achievements. Pride in one another. Pride in Monumental Life. I feel very positive about our future."

HIGH TECH, HIGH TOUCH

By 1992, the decade was living up to its "the Age of Instants" nickname. Bank customers punched in numbers and out popped cash. Consumers pushed a few buttons and . . . PRESTO! . . . instant food, instant photos, and instant faxes appeared! Faceless machines talked to one another, forwarded messages, compiled, sorted and spit out everything from numerical data to matches for a Saturday night date.

Technology had begun to dictate needs and increase expectations. Consumers demanded better, faster service while "connecting" less and less. With computers, faxes, mobile phones, satellite transmissions and teleconference calls, it was even possible to conduct a full day's business without ever seeing or talking face-to-face to a live person!

"High tech eventually demands high touch," wrote author John Nesbitt in *Megatrends.* People need human contact, he pointed out, to balance the cold, impersonal emphasis on technology and machines, productivity and profits. Consumers were fed up with computer errors, poor service, talking to machines, and disrupting calls from telemarketers. After a decade of being sidetracked by spreadsheets, interest rates and illustrations, they were once again looking for value, security, and good, old-fashioned service.

ABOVE: *Reporting to Dick Huffman (standing, far left), vice president of District Agencies in 1992, the company's regional vice presidents—including (standing, left to right) George Cabaniss, Dave Bugno, Rich Picardi and (seated, left to right) George Marteslo, P. J. West, Don Allison and Bob Grosholz—helped trainers introduce Reliable and Commonwealth agents and managers to the "Monumental way."*

LEFT: *Monumental Life received AEGON's International Award in 1991 for its successful merger and conversion of the Washington National business.*

Through acquisitions during the 1990s, Monumental Life and its home service career agents became responsible for serving policyholders whose policies had originally been issued by 260 life insurance companies.

As Monumental merged high tech with high touch in the 1990s, employees were proud to say "Quality service starts with ME!"

RIGHT: *All Monumental agents received powerful new "laptop" computers in the spring of 1992.*

"Customers know service when they miss it," noted Tom Peters in his best-seller, *In Search of Excellence,* "and now they want it back."

Monumental Life had never stopped delivering that kind of good, old-fashioned service . . . right to the customer's front door! Even in the fast-paced Nineties, the company believed there was no substitute for an agent's product knowledge, regular visits, responsiveness and caring, courteous service. Staying in touch with customers, giving the service they expected, and keeping the company's promise to be there to meet needs was critical to an agent's success. The most successful agents built relationships that earned them their customers' loyalty, trust, referrals and repeat sales.

Monumental thrived in the 1990s by merging high touch with high tech—investing millions of dollars in technology to help agents and home office employees do what they had always done, better than ever before.

"*Quality service starts with ME!*" shouted the company's new sweatshirts, coffee mugs, and field office welcome signs. More than empty words, the commitment was supported by training, new employee recognition programs, a powerful new home office mainframe, and new

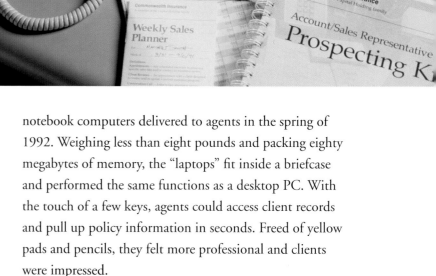

notebook computers delivered to agents in the spring of 1992. Weighing less than eight pounds and packing eighty megabytes of memory, the "laptops" fit inside a briefcase and performed the same functions as a desktop PC. With the touch of a few keys, agents could access client records and pull up policy information in seconds. Freed of yellow pads and pencils, they felt more professional and clients were impressed.

The upgrades were needed, said management, to support the company's expected future growth. At the time, only a select few knew how quickly that growth would come.

President Larry Jenkins leads employees in a "QUALITY" cheer during a mid-1990s pep rally on the Charles Street terrace.

ON THE ROAD AGAIN!

Later that spring, officers began to communicate in code. Managers whispered in corners. Members of a "special project team" attended weekly meetings behind closed doors. Before long, telephone lines were buzzing from coast to coast. "What have *you* heard about another acquisition?" employees asked. Speculation hit a high note when the company's field trainers were notified to "free up" several weeks for travel. Still, no one would confirm if negotiations were in progress, with whom, or for what blocks of business.

By mid-June executives had completed merger negotiations and agreed on a purchase price. News of the three-way deal was released in two installments, two weeks apart, on June 12 and June 26, 1992.

On June 12, Monumental Life announced it had signed an agreement with the Reliable Life Insurance Company of St. Louis to acquire its home service operations in Illinois, Iowa, Indiana, Wisconsin and Arizona. In exchange, Reliable would receive Monumental's home service business in Texas. On June 15 and 16, Larry Jenkins, Henry Hagan, and Dick Huffman, vice president of District Agencies, met with field managers in Springfield, Illinois, and Dallas.

Two weeks later a second press release announced that Monumental would acquire another block of home service business in Illinois, Indiana and Ohio from Commonwealth Life and Accident Insurance Company of Galveston. As news reached the media, Jenkins, Hagan and Huffman headed to Indianapolis to meet with Commonwealth's field managers. The Reliable and Commonwealth acquisitions further solidified Monumental Life's position as a home service leader and dominant presence in the Midwest. The acquisition also signaled the beginning of Monumental's relationship with the Galveston-based Independent Mutual Fire Company and its officers Bill Rider and Frank Moravec. The company's fire product, which protected a home's contents,

helped agents open doors at the lower end of our target market.

In making the announcement, Jenkins noted:

> At a time when the strength, stability and integrity of our industry are being questioned by the press and public alike, Monumental Life is bigger, stronger and more competitively positioned than at any time in our history. While some of our competitors are struggling to succeed, we have acquired additional blocks of business and grown. While other insurers seem to be unclear about their vision and direction for the future, we have reaffirmed our commitment to home service and taken steps to become a leader in our marketplace.

Committed to another tight conversion timetable, the experienced Monumental team was up for the challenge. "We spent weeks gathering and exchanging information, comparing systems and arranging for transfer of all necessary records and data," reported Susan Reier, Project Team leader and second vice president, Customer Service, that July. Because of the successful Washington National conversion, and the team knowing exactly what to do, they quickly updated project notebooks and got to work. At times, said one team member, the 1992 conversions seemed almost "routine!"

Converting acquired business was a challenge many companies put off for years, noted Rich Sarudy, vice president and chief information officer. "But Monumental made conversion a high priority and committed to provide the resources, money and people, to get the job done."

Training teams—including Monumental's Sue Drury, Jay Kendzierski, and Rudy Zacarias as well as field vice presidents, experienced managers and field clerical personnel—traveled throughout the Midwest to introduce

Susan Reier, second vice president, Customer Service, served as project team leader for the Reliable and Commonwealth conversion.

suddenly larger Monumental Life. "The job is not just moving paper from here to there," said Collins in 1992.

new employees in twenty-four Commonwealth and Reliable offices to Monumental's automated PRISM (Productive Routines for Increasing Sales Momentum) computer system. As in 1990, the effort demonstrated the company's commitment to professionalism, a smooth transition, and using technology to enhance customer service.

With increased workloads in his Administration departments in Baltimore, Vice President Herb Collins also scheduled training sessions to make sure his employees clear

We talked about Administration's influence on the bottom line . . . Monumental's products, computer systems and distribution systems . . . AEGON's structure, and how becoming part of AEGON allowed Monumental Life to expand and do what we do best. We've devoted a lot of time and effort to developing people. We want them to be thinkers, not just doers. That's what enables them to deliver quality service. The demand for good service exists. Customers don't care about average service times. They do care about how long it takes for *their* problem to be resolved.

Without employee commitment and teamwork in the 1990s—including the actuarial support staff (above right) and the Print Shop team (below)—conversion and assimilation of newly-acquired business would not have been possible. Officers Larry Jenkins, Herb Collins and Ralph Arnold said 'thanks for a job well done' by serving hamburgers to all employees.

MEETING NEEDS
IN A BRAND NEW WORLD

For Reliable and Commonwealth's agents and managers, becoming part of Monumental must have felt like pushing the "Fast Forward" button on the decade's new VCRs. They were used to keeping manual records and collecting their own accounts. When acquired, they had no laptops, no computerized agent systems, and no access to databases. During 1992, Monumental trainers introduced them to new products, direct-billing systems, and Personal Financial Planning (PFP) software that would allow them to analyze needs and deliver customized sales solutions in every home.

Clearly, Monumental Life was ahead of the home service curve in terms of creating sales tools to give agents a competitive edge. Considering the high rate of consumer spending in the 1990s, they needed as many tools as possible to overcome objections, point out insurance needs, and convince customers to protect their futures.

"As insurance professionals in the United States," wrote Henry Hagan in 1993, "it is important for us to recognize that in almost all cases our competition is not agents from other insurance companies, but our 'live for today' consumer lifestyle. Just think how much money we spend each week on video rentals, movies, soda, beer, cigarettes, snack food, CDs, and electronics."

Saving only 5.4 percent of their income in the early 1990s, American consumers were far behind their peers with similar earning power in Italy (a 15.6 percent savings rate!), Japan, Germany, France, Canada and the United Kingdom. "Our customers' plans must now include self-sacrifice and more self-reliant solutions for protecting incomes and accumulating retirement funds," said Hagan. "It is up to us—using tools like Monumental's Quality Life Check-Up and Personal Financial Plan software—to help our customers recognize needs and meet the challenge. No longer can we depend solely on government and employer-funded programs to protect our futures."

At the company's 1993 "Rocky Mountain Round-Up" Chairman's Round Table Conference in Snowmass, Colorado—the first Monumental Life conference for which Commonwealth and Reliable agents and managers could qualify—Larry Jenkins challenged qualifiers to do more to serve the growing numbers of families who had no personal life insurance agent or individual life insurance protection.

"Our market is huge!" said Jenkins. "Forty-two percent of American households reported income of $25,000 or less per year in 1991." Studies by the Life Insurance Marketing and Research Association (LIMRA) confirmed, "The families you serve, your blue collar and white collar prospects, haven't lost faith in life insurance. And when they make critical decisions about financial security, about protecting themselves and their loved ones, one fact comes through loudly and clearly—they want to do it face-to-face with an agent they know and respect."

LIMRA studies also confirmed that families in the lower and middle-income brackets welcomed new product information and sought informed help when planning for retirement, their children's educations and other financial security needs. "If you do not provide it," noted Jenkins, "sooner or later someone else will. It may be another agent, it might be someone selling insurance by mail or phone . . . it might even be a bank, but someone will fill the need. I'm determined that the 'someone else' . . . is going to be Monumental Life."

Members of the 1992 Reliable and Commonwealth conversion team received brass coasters to commemorate an effort that made overcoming merger challenges seem almost "routine."

Dennis Phillips . . .

He Practiced What He Preached

Monumental sales manager Dennis Phillips and family before his death in 1994.

*A*S A Monumental Life sales manager in Indianapolis, Dennis Phillips knew that being prepared for unexpected events made good sense. He used to tell his wife, Janie, that if anything were to happen to him she wouldn't have to worry about finances. When Phillips died suddenly in 1994 at the age of forty, his death was unexpected, but his family's future was secure.

Most important to Janie was that she and her children could remain in their home. "When we built our house," she explained in 1995, "we each bought $80,000 worth of life insurance. In case one of us died, the other would be able to keep the house. Neither one of us had enough income to keep the house on our own without life insurance to cover our mortgage." At the time, Phillips was a new agent and Janie was teaching school in an Indianapolis suburb.

But Janie was able to do more than keep the house with the proceeds from her husband's insurance policy. After paying bills and paying down the mortgage balance, she purchased an annuity for her retirement and opened educational trust funds for each of her three children—Melissa, then age fifteen; Jennifer, fourteen; and son Ryan, eleven.

Monumental Life's Rookie of the Year in 1990, Denny Phillips always made sure his clients had the coverage they needed. He'd once told Janie: "When I had clients who were in arrears with late payments, I tried to get right over to explain the risk they were taking. I'd make sure they got caught up. Clients see you're helping them out, and they appreciate it."

Phillips was promoted to sales manager in April 1991. A positive man who worked hard, he attributed his success to setting goals, planning, good work habits and good sales techniques.

In 1994 he qualified for Monumental's sales conference at Disney World in Orlando and had booked reservations for his entire family. He died the night before their scheduled departure. A year later, Monumental helped Janie and her children take that trip. "That the company thought enough of Denny to send us to Orlando really made us feel wonderful," she said. "It says a lot about Monumental, and the way they care about people. I received so many telephone calls, cards, letters, flowers and expressions of condolence."

"Denny was a nice guy who could take any bad situation and find some good in it," said friend and fellow Indianapolis agent Paul McMichael in 1995. "He was fun to be with, a great competitor. We had a good time competing against one another. We miss him in the office."

Dennis Phillips was a professional. He believed in the products he sold. He recognized the need for insurance and how it helped people. He took care of his customers and his family. In the end, his family's future was secure because he practiced what he preached.

LIVING UNDER A MICROSCOPE

Junk bonds, bad real estate investments, bank failures, and "bad apples" in the insurance marketplace—by the middle of the decade, regulators, insurance rating agencies, the media and the public had all put the industry under a microscope. As investigations, litigation, and heavy fines for agent misconduct and deceptive sales practices made the news, policyholders began to wonder whom they could trust, what practices *their* insurer was condoning, and where they should put their money. The industry responded with tighter controls.

H. Stacey Boyer, Monumental Life vice president, general counsel and secretary

"Stringent enforcement of insurance regulations should result in more ethical agents, better informed consumers, and better customer service," said H. Stacey Boyer, Monumental Life vice president, general counsel and secretary in 1995. As the company's compliance officer, Boyer was responsible for making sure Monumental Life complied with all industry laws and regulations. The Law Department enforces a written compliance policy, reviews and approves all policy forms and marketing materials, manages litigation, responds to customer complaints, and works directly with insurance department investigators to complete regular market conduct examinations of the company's policies, practices and procedures.

Council (LUTC). In 1996, after almost two years of design and testing, a cross-functional project team headed by Gary Willan, then second vice president, Underwriting and New Issue, rolled out the company's new state-of-the-art "E-Z App" electronic application.

E-Z App made it possible for agents

LEFT: *Between 1994 and 1996, Monumental distributed a code of ethics and required all agents and managers to complete a "Piecing Together the Ethical Puzzle" course offered by the Life Underwriter Training Council (LUTC).*

ETHICS, INDUSTRY EDUCATION, E-Z APP

Between 1994 and 1996, Monumental Life distributed its own code of ethics, published a brochure titled *Ethics and Customer Service*, and communicated the company's clearly defined mission, vision and values to all employees.

"We are committed to helping American families improve the quality of their lives," said Henry Hagan. "That's our mission. We value talent, integrity and personal responsibility. Our vision is to be the best life insurance company in America, in our chosen markets. We will reach these goals by focusing our efforts and resources on people, persistency, professionalism, productivity, progress and profitability. These 'six Ps' will become our measures of success."

"We can only be the best," added Jenkins, "if we insist on doing business with the utmost honesty and integrity, if we strive to always respect our customers' concerns, if we listen and understand their problems, and if we provide fair and equitable solutions."

By January 1, 1995, all Monumental Life agents and managers were required to have laptops, commit to customer-focused, needs-based selling, and complete industry education courses—including *Piecing Together the Ethical Puzzle*—offered by the Life Underwriter Training

to transmit applications electronically to the home office—toll-free, twenty-four hours a day. It made printed applications and rate books obsolete. It reduced agent error by calculating premiums automatically. It assured accuracy of policyholder information by eliminating illegible handwriting, missed questions and forms. If a client

Trainer Sandy Campbell (standing) conducted E-Z App training for agents and managers in Southern Maryland in 1996.

J. T. Garrett, Auditor and Compliance Investigator . . .

SIXTY YEARS, SIX COMPANIES!

Still working at age seventy-nine, J. T. Garrett has the distinction of being Monumental and AEGON's oldest full-time employee. He celebrated sixty-one years of continuous company service in 2007.

THE YEAR was 1946. Harry Truman was president of the United States. World War II was over. Winston Churchill had just stepped down as prime minister of Great Britain. In Durham, North Carolina, eighteen-year-old J. T. Garrett began his insurance career. Of the three, only Garrett is still alive today. After sixty plus years, he is still working for an insurance company in the same town and shows no signs of slowing down.

Hired as an office boy by Durham's Home Security Life, Garrett literally grew up in the insurance business. The small, family-owned company had only sixty-five home office employees when he arrived, and before long young "Jimmy" knew them all. "I offered to help everyone I met," he remembers. The visibility, contacts, and his sense of commitment resulted in regular promotions—to purchasing agent, department supervisor, field accounting auditor, senior field auditor, field audit specialist and, most recently, to compliance investigator.

At age seventy-nine in 2007, Garrett still travels to investigate fraud and interview agents, managers and policyholders. "In our business," he explains, "field management is required to inspect agent records regularly to look for shortages and misconduct. If discrepancies are found, they call in an auditor to investigate further. I review the information gathered by local managers. Depending on what I find, I might have to file a report with the state insurance department, law enforcement officers, or a local prosecutor. And if a case goes to trial, I am often called as an expert witness."

Based in North Carolina, Garrett's responsibilities can take him to fourteen or fifteen different states within a year. "I thoroughly enjoy what I do. It's personally rewarding," he says. "Though most agents are ethical and professional, there are always a few who try to take advantage of their position. My job is to find them, get them out of the business, and make sure that the company and our policyholders' interests are protected."

Working in several departments over sixty years, Garrett has been exposed to many aspects of the life insurance business. He's seen agents and policyholders become better educated as insurance products have become more complex. He's seen direct billing, mail pay and automatic bank draft replace agent-collected premiums. Though he has never changed companies or left his original Durham location, he's experienced five mergers and six decades of innovation, automation and new challenges. He's also seen Home Security's name change to Peoples Security and later to Monumental Life after the company was acquired by Capital Holding Corporation (later Providian Corporation) in 1973 and by AEGON USA in 1997.

"I enjoy the challenge. No two days are ever the same," he says. "I have a home on a lake where I relax and watch the ducks, but I have no plans to retire . . . ever. My life is my work."

We know of no Monumental Life or AEGON employee in the world with a longer record of continuous company service than J. T. Garrett.

wanted to make a change . . . no problem! With a few keystrokes, the agent could type in new information. Most important of all, E-Z App improved customer service by reducing the time needed to deliver valuable insurance coverage.

After three weeks of intense, hands-on training, District Manager Jack Buttacavoli was impressed. Reporting to fellow managers in the Chicago area, he noted: "The computer lists all requirements right on the screen. Agents don't have to worry about missing important information, miscalculating premiums, or even misspelling!"

As earnings grew in 1996, Monumental continued to innovate—introducing an automated claims system in the home office and new Pentium color laptops and illustration software to the field.

Phil White chaired LIMRA's marketing services committee.

Rosemary Riesett was elected national president of the Life Communicators Association.

LIFE . . . SPEAKING WITH ONE VOICE

Like Monumental Life, industry associations worked hard throughout the 1990s to educate consumers about the need for life insurance, improve the industry's image, and assure ethical conduct in the marketplace.

Serving on industry association committees and boards, Monumental officers provided valuable input about industry challenges and how to address them.

Henry Hagan chaired LIMRA's Home Service Executive Committee in 1991. At about the same time, Phil White, then vice president, Marketing Services, chaired LIMRA's marketing services committee. In 1995, Hagan was elected to LIMRA International's board of directors. In 1996, Rosemary Riesett, then assistant vice president, Marketing Communications, was elected national president of the Life Communicators Association for a one-year term.

"Consumers know more, see more, and have access to more information than ever before," noted Hagan in a presentation at the LIMRA Home Service Conference in 1997. He advised industry associates:

> To compete in this kind of environment, we had better know our customers well and respond to their preferences. The explosion of information technology within the last decade has given consumers better facts, more knowledge, more choices and more power. Informational power is flowing down from the traditional centers of power, out to the people. . . . Distributing the information, to the people, will cause the pace of change to quicken even more. If it's happening in the marketplace, it must *also* happen in our companies.

In late 1994, Monumental Life and AEGON USA joined a small group of insurance companies and seven life and health associations in the U.S. and Canada in becoming "charter" members of the industry's new Life and Health Foundation for Education (LIFE). AEGON,

in fact, was the first U.S. life insurer to commit its support. Banding together to speak with one voice, competitors acknowledged the need to educate the public about the benefits of life and health insurance and the invaluable role of the agent in providing financial security.

As David Woods, LIFE president and CEO since its founding, tells the story, LIFE sent its "top team"—industry veterans and award winners Robert V. Verhille and William B. Wallace —to Baltimore to meet with AEGON USA's Don Shepard and Larry Jenkins. (Shepard knew both men. Verhille was then a Cedar Rapids–based leading general agent for Kansas City Life. Wallace, former CEO of Home Life, had just retired as Phoenix Home Life's chief operating officer.)

After explaining LIFE's purpose and mission, the two men asked AEGON for $250,000. Responding with "considerable energy," says Woods, Shepard said, "$250,000!!! Hell, we have a crisis on our hands. I'll give you $500,000!"

Woods happened to be in Washington that same day. Two other "recruiters" were trying to convince him to become LIFE's president. When Verhille and Wallace burst through the door with their news from Baltimore, Woods remembers, "I was convinced it was a setup to get me to take the job! But they assured me it really had happened just that way. As I got to know Don [Shepard] later, he confirmed the story. AEGON's $500,000 was the first contribution LIFE received. It opened the door to all the success we have had since."

David Woods, CLU, president and CEO of LIFE since its founding in 1994, retired at year-end 2007.

LIFE AND HEALTH INSURANCE FOUNDATION FOR EDUCATION

Monumental Life and AEGON USA became "charter" members of LIFE, the industry's new, non-profit Life and Health Foundation for Education.

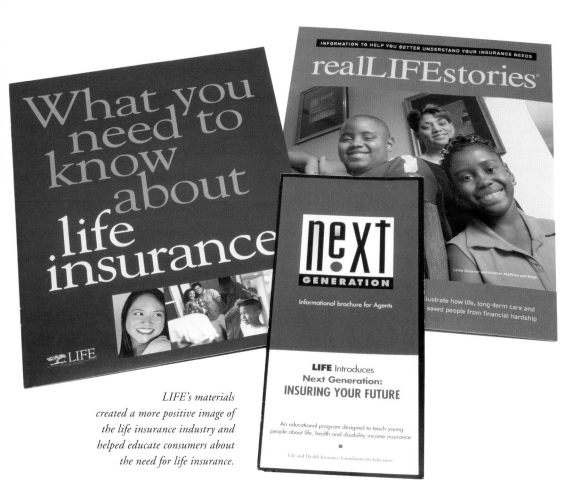

**INSURANCE
MARKETPLACE
STANDARDS
ASSOCIATION**

*Only life insurers that meet and monitor
high ethical standards for dealing with
customers are eligible to qualify for
IMSA's "seal of approval."*

*LIFE's materials
created a more positive image of
the life insurance industry and
helped educate consumers about
the need for life insurance.*

By its tenth anniversary in 2004, more than ninety life and health insurance companies were LIFE-supporting members. Leading the way in terms of both financial contributions and participation on LIFE's Advisory Council were AEGON USA and Monumental Life. When LIFE designated September 2004 as the industry's first Life Insurance Awareness Month, Monumental was one of the first organizations to commit its support. In 2005 and 2006, AEGON USA president and CEO Pat Baird served on LIFE's board of directors, representing the American Council of Life Insurance (ACLI).

Beginning in the 1990s, donations by Monumental and AEGON USA also supported an educational program, called "Learning for Life," developed by the Boy Scouts of America for boys and girls in elementary, middle and high school. Taught by classroom teachers, it focused on ethical behavior, life skills and career choices.

IMSA SEAL OF APPROVAL

Later in the 1990s, Monumental Life and AEGON's U.S. subsidiaries were among the first life insurance companies in the country to apply for membership in the new Insurance Marketplace Standards Association (IMSA). The independent, voluntary organization was created by the life insurance industry and the American Council of Life Insurance (ACLI) to establish industry-wide ethical market conduct standards. Only companies that promote and monitor ethical behavior and meet high ethical standards for dealing with customers are eligible to qualify for membership and receive IMSA's "seal of approval."

The qualification process requires rigorous self-examination and commitment from the entire organization. Outside examiners interview employees, review the company's documented policies and procedures, and request samples of employee

LIFE's eye-catching ads and materials first appeared in early 1996. The "realLIFEstories" program, also introduced to agents and industry associations in 1996, succeeded in creating a more positive perception of the industry by publicizing—in an eight-page section of *Newsweek* magazine—real stories of people whose lives had been helped by agents and the products they sold. As hoped, these efforts succeeded in boosting agent morale and restoring agent pride in their role and profession.

Later in the decade, LIFE introduced the "Next Generation" program to educate high school students about the importance of life insurance and financial security. LIFE also created an interactive website, "Insurance Matters" kits, CDs and DVDs, posters, radio ads, fact sheets, "advertorials," and annuity and long-term care brochures to assist agents, managers, their companies, and the industry in delivering public education programs.

communication pieces, sales brochures, advertising, laptop software, and marketing and training materials, among other things.

Monumental Life passed the test! The company had policies and procedures in place to assure honesty and integrity is its sales and service contacts with customers. It communicated those policies and practices regularly to employees and distributors. Its sales processes and materials complied with industry regulations, and it competed fairly in the marketplace, in compliance with state and federal laws.

Since the late 1990s, Monumental Life has passed two subsequent IMSA examinations and proudly includes the IMSA logo on its website and on materials marketing its individual life insurance products.

INDUSTRY MILESTONE!

Justifiably proud of its achievements, the company's biggest deal of the decade was yet to be announced. In every way possible, the next merger made the 1990s a "monumental" decade for Maryland's oldest life insurer!

On Monday morning, December 30, 1996, the front page of the *Wall Street Journal's* "Business and Finance" section announced that AEGON and the Providian Corporation of Louisville had signed an agreement under which AEGON USA would acquire Providian's insurance operations for $3.8 billion. The proposed acquisition represented one of the largest to date in the history of the U.S. life insurance industry. It was big news for the industry, big news for financial analysts, and big news for AEGON and Providian stockholders. It would make AEGON USA the ninth-ranked life insurer in the U.S.—a jump of six places!—based on premium income.

AEGON released the news from its headquarters at The Hague at 8:00 a.m. (Netherlands time; 2:00 a.m. in New York) in order to make early morning editions of the major U.S. daily newspapers. By 8:30 a.m. East Coast time, e-mails and memos announcing the acquisition had been

sent to employees and associates by Donald J. Shepard, AEGON USA chairman, president and CEO; Larry Jenkins, Monumental Life president, chairman and CEO; Bart Herbert, Jr., AEGON USA chief marketing officer; and Providian officers in Louisville. At 11:30 a.m., CNN and *Baltimore Sun* reporters and cameramen arrived at the Monumental Life/AEGON USA headquarters at Charles and Chase Streets in Baltimore.

In announcing the merger, Larry Jenkins commented:

> . . . the acquisition clearly demonstrates AEGON's continuing commitment to the growth of our home service business as a solid, stable base for the AEGON Insurance Group's more interest-sensitive, rapid growth pension and asset accumulation business.

On December 30, 1996, the Wall Street Journal announced that AEGON would acquire Providian's insurance operations.

Reprinted from THE WALL STREET JOURNAL.

MONDAY, DECEMBER 30, 1996   © 1996 Dow Jones & Company, Inc. All Rights Reserved.

Aegon to Acquire Insurance Operations Of Providian in $2.62 Billion Stock Deal

Purchase Signals Eagerness Of European Insurers To Expand Into the U.S.

By LESLIE SCISM
Staff Reporter of THE WALL STREET JOURNAL

Dutch financial-services giant **Aegon NV** is expected to announce today that it is acquiring the insurance operations of **Providian Corp.** in a $2.62 billion stock transaction, the latest sign of European insurers' eagerness to expand their U.S. presence.

People familiar with the matter said the pact also calls for the Dutch company, one of the world's 10 biggest insurers, to assume nearly $880 million in Providian debt and preferred stock. The transaction would be one of the largest to date in the rapidly consolidating life-insurance industry, which is beset by high costs and fierce competition for consumers' savings from banks and mutual-fund companies.

Under the complex pact, Louisville, Ky.-based Providian would spin off its banking operations to its shareholders. It would then merge the remainder of the company—the insurance operations—into Aegon's U.S. unit. For each original Providian share, Providian owners would receive Aegon stock valued at $28. The transaction would be tax free to Providian shareholders.

The deal, approved by boards of both companies over the weekend, is subject to shareholder and regulatory approval, the people said. If completed, the pact would allow a streamlined Providian to focus on a fast-growing consumer-lending and banking business, including an innovative credit-card operation.

Aegon's shares trade on the New York Stock Exchange as American depositary receipts. In composite trading Friday, the depositary receipts fell 12.5 cents to close at $57; Providian's shares also slipped 12.5 cents to $32.75.

As reported in The Wall Street Journal, Providian quietly hired Goldman, Sachs & Co. this fall to find a buyer for its insurance operations. While those operations delivered more than two-thirds of the company's 1995 pretax operating profit, the insurance results have been flat for three years.

Providian officials couldn't be reached yesterday, while an Aegon spokeswoman declined to comment.

Despite the frustrations many American insurers are experiencing with lack-luster life-insurance sales, analysts said European companies like Aegon want bigger U.S. footholds. "Large European financial-services organizations, in general, see long-term opportunities here," said Larry Mayewski, a senior vice president with A.M. Best Co., an insurance-ratings firm.

Already, Aegon owns about a half dozen U.S. insurance companies with assets totaling $32.43 billion. The Providian transaction would add more than $20 billion in assets.

The well-heeled Aegon, with $93.87 billion in world-wide assets, has made no secret of its desire to expand in many parts of the world. Earlier this month, Aegon Chairman Kees J. Storm said he hoped to strike a pact in Europe or the U.S. shortly and expected an acquisition or start-up in Asia by late 1997.

Other European companies expected by analysts and investment bankers to make significant acquisitions over the next year include International Nederlanden Group, a Dutch company that earlier this year lost a bidding contest for a large Virginia insurer, First Colony Corp. Other deep-pocketed, likely acquirers: Groupe Axa, a French insurer that owns 60% of New York's Equitable Cos., and Zurich Insurance Group, a Swiss behemoth that two years ago paid about $2 billion for Kemper Corp., of Long Grove, Ill.

Analysts view Aegon as a solid company with a successful history of acquisitions. Several Providian operations are considered a good fit with existing Aegon units in the U.S., and merging them would provide economies of scale and cross-selling opportunities.

For example, Providian has a large operation that, like the Dutch company's Monumental Life Insurance Co. unit in Baltimore, markets life-insurance policies mostly to lower-middle-class households. It is a stable, profitable but stagnant insurance segment, under which sales agents often go door-to-door to collect premiums.

Providian's innovative guaranteed-investment-contract business, meanwhile, would provide Aegon with brainpower to

significantly expand efforts to sell pension plans to employers. Aegon also would gain a unit to boost efforts selling various insurance coverages to consumers via telephone, television and the mail. The so-called direct-response business is considered one of the industry's most promising for growth.

For Providian, a sale culminates a decade-long transition from its origins as a conventional insurer to banking, under the direction of Shailesh J. Mehta, currently president and chief operating officer. Mr. Mehta is expected shortly to be named chairman and chief executive officer of the shrunken Providian, while Irving W. Bailey II, who currently holds the jobs, will be named a vice chairman of Aegon USA, the company's U.S. unit.

Providian's banking unit is now one of the nation's largest issuers of secured credit cards. Relying heavily on sophisticated direct-response marketing techniques and advanced computerization, the unit's 1995 pretax profit surged 25% to $188 million. Following industry trends, however, the unit has been plagued recently with some consumer-credit problems. Still, its third-quarter pretax profit rose 17% to $56.1 million.

Aegon at a Glance
1995 data; all figures in U.S. dollars

Major businesses	Life insurance, pensions, investment products, property-casualty coverage
Countries of operation	The Netherlands, U.S., Britain, Hungary, Spain, Mexico, among others
Year-end assets	$93.87 billion
Total revenue	$13.07 billion
Net income	$824 million
U.S. revenue	$3.95 billion
U.S. pretax income	$351 million
Headquarters	The Hague

Note: All figures in accordance with Dutch accounting principles.

JournalReprints • (609) 520-4328 • P.O. Box 300 • Princeton, N.J. 08543-0300
DO NOT MARK REPRINTS • REPRODUCTIONS NOT PERMITTED

A well-respected and highly regarded home service competitor, Providian's $403 million of home service premium in force and 2.2 million premium-paying life and health policies will strengthen our position in the competitive middle income marketplace and make Monumental Life the second-largest home service operation in the country.

Providian Agency Group marketed through three statutory life insurance companies—Peoples Security Life, Commonwealth Life and Capital Security Life. The addition of Providian's approximately one hundred field offices would significantly enhance Monumental's presence in the Mid-Atlantic and southeastern United States.

BEST OF THE BEST

The merger of the two large, well-respected and successful organizations created a new "giant" in the home service marketplace—with $4.8 billion in home service assets, $37.8 billion of home service insurance in force, and over four thousand employees in 142 field offices. Combining resources created a new top priority for 1997—getting to know one another!

Products, systems, software, strategies, organizational structure, size and space—all had to be reviewed, discussed and evaluated. Who had what? How did it work? Did it *really* work? If so, why was it important? How did organizational culture and priorities impact performance? How were agents paid? What systems were in place to recruit, train, prospect, sell, service and administer the business? The two organizations' home service operations were basically the same, but also quite different. Over the next year, management was committed to selecting the "best of the best" from each operation to create the strongest, best-educated and equipped, most competitive home service organization in the country.

The first meeting of the joint Home Service Project Team work groups was held in Louisville in early February 1997. Two weeks later, a similar set of exchange visits were held in Baltimore. Throughout the spring of 1997 teams continued to travel, meet, share information and identify issues to be resolved. Two facts became clear almost immediately. First, this would be the most complex and challenging acquisition and conversion to date for both organizations. Second, meeting the needs of policyholders and the existing field force were top priorities.

1996 Annual Report

With one bold stroke at the end of the year, **PROVIDIAN** announced the spin-off of high-growth **Bancorp** and a merger of insurance operations with **AEGON USA** – two opportunities for shareholder value creation.

Deal a boon to Providian shareholders

"Our conclusion was that the best way we could create value for the future was to let Bancorp become a free-standing company, and merge the insurance businesses with a strong partner."

Chairman and
Chief Executive Officer
Irving W. Bailey II

Providian Plans to Spin Off Credit Card Bank and Sell Insurance Units to Aegon

PROVIDIAN

MOVING TOWARD MERGER

On June 10, 1997, attorneys from Providian Corporation and AEGON USA met in Louisville to close the deal. On paper at least, the merger of the two organizations was complete!

In Baltimore, Louisville and Durham, North Carolina—the three locations where Monumental and Providian Agency Group had home office personnel— banners and cakes celebrated the signing. In the lobby of One Commonwealth Place in Louisville, Executive Vice President Henry Hagan welcomed Louisville home office employees to the AEGON/Monumental family. In Durham, Senior Vice President and Controller Ralph Arnold delivered a similar message.

The next day, Larry Jenkins formally announced that Hagan would have responsibility and authority for integrating the combined home service operations. At Providian's Leaders Club Conference in Las Vegas later that month, both Jenkins and Hagan introduced themselves and discussed Monumental's home service tradition and AEGON's history of success. Hagan also announced the formation of a Field "Best Practices" Team composed of agents, managers and regional officers from Monumental, Capital Security, Commonwealth and Peoples Security.

That summer, management made two major and much-anticipated announcements.

At Monumental's Chairman's Round Table Sales Conference in August, Jenkins introduced Hagan as the new president of Monumental Life, Capital Security, Commonwealth and Peoples Security. He (Jenkins) would continue on in a consulting and advisory capacity as chairman and CEO. On August 26, Jenkins, Hagan and Arnold held separate meetings in Baltimore, Louisville and Durham to announce AEGON USA and Monumental Life's decision regarding location of the merged organizations' home office operations.

"Going forward," they said, "our home service operations will be headquartered in Maryland and

Larry Jenkins introduced Henry G. Hagan as the new president of Monumental Life, Capital Security, Commonwealth and Peoples Security in August 1997.

insurance services for the four home service 'brands' will be split between Baltimore and Durham." In reaching their decision, management had considered the need to minimize disruption of service to customers and field offices; the ability to retain, attract and/or relocate talented people; the business climate and quality of life in each location; and the risks and costs of assuring an effective and efficient transition and conversion of $3.2 billion of Providian Agency Group assets and its $27.4 billion of insurance in force.

In early September, Hagan appointed a Project Team, headed by Providian's Carol Davies, with responsibility for converting the four company "brands" to a single set of sales and administrative systems. The master plan for the conversion and consolidation was divided into four "milestones" with late 1997, 1998 and 1999 target dates.

On September 19, 1997, Hagan unveiled the new name for the combined home service operations— "Monumental Agency Group"—as well as new logos colors and guidelines for letterhead, business cards and field office signage. "Keeping the Monumental name will allow us to continue building on Monumental Life's proud past and 140-year old reputation for strength and success," he explained. "The Agency Group name and blue logo will tie us closely to AEGON and identify the four brands as a single entity."

Carol Davies served as project team leader for the Providian merger and conversion.

ABOVE: *All employees received a brass bookmark to celebrate Monumental Life's 140th anniversary in 1998. The bookmark featured the new "AEGON blue" logo, introduced in September 1997, to build on Monumental's past, create a closer association with AEGON and to unite the four Monumental Agency Group "brands" as a single entity.*

As the leaves changed colors that fall, so did Monumental and Providian. In less than eight weeks, the Baltimore Print Shop printed and delivered more than 3,800 sets of "AEGON blue" business cards, 486,000 sheets of new letterhead, and 410,000 envelopes. By December 10, 1997, designers, printers and distribution teams in Baltimore and Louisville had deleted the Providian name—as required by the merger agreement—reprinted sales materials and shipped hundreds of boxes to the company's field offices.

With the approach of the holiday season, both organizations promoted "discount sales" to eliminate "Monumental red" and "Providian green" logo merchandize. At the same time, teams of marketing and communications employees began meeting regularly to discuss merged honors and award programs, employee publications, product portfolios and sales materials. Another high priority item was selecting the site for the first joint Monumental Agency Group sales conference in 1999.

As families completed holiday shopping and wrapped gifts, home office teams packed and shipped agent contracts and training materials. The first group of Commonwealth field agents and managers was scheduled to begin training on January 5, 1998!

ALL ABOARD . . .
TO CELEBRATE 140 YEARS!

On March 5, 1998, Agency Group employees around the country joined to celebrate Monumental Life's 140th anniversary. Each employee received a brass bookmark inscribed with the company logo and the "1858–1998" anniversary dates. In Baltimore officers served crab cakes and birthday cake. Similar celebrations were held in Louisville and Durham.

Field offices also got involved, with parties and open houses for policyholders and the public. As training continued that week, the company's field managers, regional vice presidents, and home office officers headed to Baltimore's Inner Harbor for Monumental Agency Group's first two-day managers' meeting.

President Henry Hagan opened the meeting by reporting on merger progress. "Each of our organizations has deep roots in home service," he said. "Each has experienced great success and built a heritage of its own. Going forward together, we have the talent and the opportunity to become the very best in our industry and marketplace." Then Larry Jenkins joined him on stage to recognize 1997's leading "brand" managers from Capital Security, Commonwealth, Monumental and Peoples Security.

RIGHT: *"All aboard!" shouted the conductor, as employees, retirees, spouses and dinner guests boarded the "Monumental Express" for a multi-media trip back through time celebrating the company's 140-year history and traditions in Baltimore on March 7, 1998.*

The weekend's most festive event was a 140th anniversary gala at the Renaissance Harborplace Hotel on Saturday evening, March 7. Sales leaders for the company's five-month "All Aboard" Mini-Conference joined officers, Baltimore home office employees, retirees, spouses and guests for an elegant dinner and dance. Attendees boarded the "Monumental Express" for a multi-media trip back through time—led by a costumed "conductor," musicians and dancers. Then, as hotel employees rolled in a large birthday cake and lit candles on hundreds of individual mini-cakes, company officers led the group in singing "Happy Birthday."

CHAIRMAN'S LAST CHALLENGE

A few months later, retiring chairman and CEO Larry Jenkins announced the final sales challenge of his forty-year career. His "Chairman's Challenge" pitted sales sluggers from Monumental and Providian offices against one another in a three-month contest involving hits, runs, wins and strikeouts.

On November 14, 1998, Jenkins—who had played minor league baseball as a young man—hosted the company's top one hundred hitters to a "Breakfast of Champions" at Baltimore's Camden Yards. Each qualifier received a team jacket and baseball-themed gifts representing the company's home office locations—a Baltimore "Orioles" cap, a "Louisville Slugger" bat, and a Durham "Bulls" baseball. Breakfast was followed by a behind-the-scenes tour of the ballpark, a tour of the Babe Ruth Birthplace & Museum, and a six-inning softball game for qualifiers. The regional vice presidents served as coaches, Henry Hagan called balls and strikes behind home plate, and the chairman himself was warm-up catcher.

"Chairman's Challenge" qualifiers played a softball game in which "umpire" and president Henry Hagan called balls and strikes from behind home plate.

That evening more than four hundred field and home office employees, retirees, AEGON officers, civic leaders, business and industry associates, family and friends gathered to salute, toast and roast Larry Jenkins's lifetime career and achievements.

RIGHT AND BELOW: *Larry Jenkins celebrated his upcoming retirement with a three-month "Chairman's Challenge" that pitted Monumental and Providian offices against one another. The company's top sluggers attended a "Breakfast of Champions" at Baltimore's Camden Yards in November 1998.*

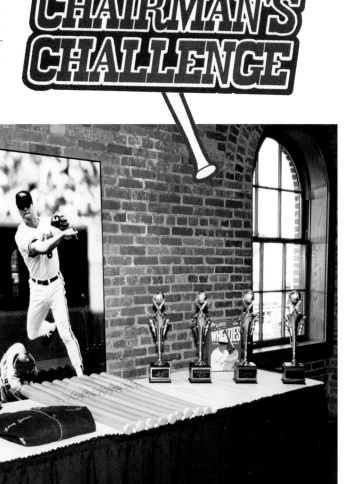

Jenkins Family . . .

A Legacy of Leadership

B. LARRY JENKINS, president, chairman and CEO of Monumental Life Insurance Company from 1983 to 1999, has always spoken proudly of his early career as a successful agent and manager with the Peoples Life Insurance Company of Washington, D.C. Hired at age nineteen to work in Peoples Life's field office in Waldorf, Maryland, Larry followed his uncle, Regional Vice President Thomas Jenkins, and his father and district manager, Benjamin J. Jenkins, into the business. Like both of them, he became a "Peoples Man."

Rising through the ranks, Jenkins was elected president of Peoples Life in 1976. He remained president until Capital Holding Corporation merged two of its subsidiaries—Peoples Life and Home Security Life—to create Peoples Security Life Insurance Company. When the companies' home office operations were consolidated in Durham, North Carolina, Jenkins chose not to move his family. In 1982 he accepted an executive position with Monumental Life in Baltimore.

Just recently, Jenkins was surprised to learn that his family's roots in the life insurance business are much deeper than he thought. They go back to Monumental Life's founding years as the Mutual Life Insurance Company of Baltimore, long before his father joined Peoples Life in 1936. Digging through old insurance applications, executive board minutes, Maryland census records and the Jenkins family archives, we discovered that Larry Jenkins is related to John Willcox Jenkins, the Mutual Life board member who was issued the company's first, documented policy after it reorganized and changed names in 1870.

Larry Jenkins and his younger brother John Benedict "Ben" Jenkins, a current Monumental Life officer, are ninth-generation descendants of a young man named Thomas Jenkins who came to Maryland from Wales in 1670. Thomas Jenkins received one hundred acres of land from Cecil Calvert, second Lord Baltimore, "for transporting himself and his wife Ann into the province." Land grant documents dated 1670 certify that Thomas Jenkins's land was in Charles County, on a hill overlooking the point where the Potomac and Port Tobacco Rivers meet.

Thomas and Ann Jenkins lived in Charles County for nearly sixty years. Their children married into prominent families in the province and had many children of their own, who also married and reared large Catholic families. As the Jenkins family expanded, so did their land holdings in Maryland. By the time the U.S. government designated the District of Columbia as the nation's capital in 1791, the family owned much of the land along the east bank of the Potomac River in Charles and Prince George's Counties, including acreage annexed from the state to build the District. In fact, before the U.S. Capitol was built on it, Capitol Hill was known locally as "Jenkins Hill."

Thomas Jenkins and his wife had six children—three daughters and three sons. Larry and Ben Jenkins are descendants of Thomas Jenkins' oldest son, George. John Willcox Jenkins, born in 1829, and his cousin, Thomas Warner Jenkins, born in 1839, were sixth generation descendants of Thomas Jenkins' youngest son, William. George Jenkins' descendants stayed in southern Maryland. William Jenkins' three sons migrated to the Long Green Valley of Baltimore County in 1757. One of those sons, Michael C. Jenkins, who lived on a plantation of nine hundred acres bequeathed to him by his older brother, was great-grandfather to both John Willcox Jenkins and Thomas Warner Jenkins. Michael C. Jenkins and Larry Jenkins' great-great-great grandfather were distant cousins.

Merchant and landowner John Willcox Jenkins was elected a director of the Mutual Life Insurance Company of Baltimore on January 27, 1870. Completing an application for life insurance on March 1 of that year, his policy was recorded as Mutual Life policy #1—the first issued following the company's reorganization after the Civil War. Before retiring from the board in 1873, Jenkins served on both the Finance and Auditing Committees. He died in 1921 at the age of ninety-two.

LEFT: *Hired as a Peoples Life agent at age nineteen, Larry Jenkins (third from left) followed his father and uncle into the life insurance business.*

Thomas Warner Jenkins, a cabinetmaker, was elected to Mutual Life's board of directors on July 1, 1886. He served on the board for thirty-six years as secretary, vice president and as a member of the Auditing and Executive Committees. He died in 1922 at the age of eighty-three.

In 1983, their distant cousin, B. Larry Jenkins, was elected president of Mutual Life's successor, Monumental Life Insurance Company. As the company's chief executive officer, he continued a legacy of hands-on leadership, community service, support of the Catholic Church, and commitment to the life insurance business in Baltimore—the city where members of the Jenkins family tree had made a similar commitment a century earlier.

Having served as president of two home service life insurance companies during his forty-year career, B. Larry Jenkins retired from Monumental Life in 1999. He lived almost twenty years in Baltimore's Greenspring Valley and purchased property in St. Mary's County in 1990. His home in Clements, Maryland, on the banks of St. Clements Bay, is not far from where the state's first Catholic colonists arrived in 1634, and where the Jenkins family of Maryland first put down roots.

ABOVE: *As chair of the United Way of Central Maryland's annual fund-raising campaign in the early 1990s, Larry Jenkins (right) continued his Maryland family's legacy of hands-on leadership, community service, support of the Catholic Church and commitment to the life insurance business.*

LEFT: *Brothers Ben (left) and Larry (center) Jenkins, with Larry's wife Kitty (right), enjoyed a joke during the retiring Monumental Life chairman and CEO's retirement dinner and "roast" in November 1998.*

ABOVE: *"Together, We're Better"*
was the theme of the March 1999
managers' meeting in Baltimore.

RIGHT: *Despite merger distractions*
and challenges, the company's "Back
to the Basics" message never changed
throughout the 1990s. Agents and
managers had to stay focused on
sales and customer service.

TOGETHER, WE'RE BETTER!

Two weeks later, on November 30, 1998, the statutory merger of the four Monumental Agency Group companies was completed, as scheduled. On New Years Eve 1998, after two solid years of meetings, programming and testing, Carol Davies' Project Team completed what many industry experts considered an impossible task—the "monumental" conversion of Providian's three huge blocks of home service business.

"This conversion could not have been accomplished," noted Davies, "without the many employees who were totally committed to the effort and who took great pride in their work. Monumental was organized, hired the right people early on, and was well prepared for this tremendous undertaking."

Throughout the transition, communicating and answering policyholder questions, conserving business and providing responsive service had created challenges for both the home office and field. That first year was especially "painful" for many former Providian Agency Group

agents and managers, admits former Regional Vice President Frank Merrill, now retired. A Peoples Life veteran and successful district manager in Pocomoke, Maryland, for many years, he had experienced several Capital Holding/Providian mergers and name changes during his thirty-year career. Even so, says Merrill, who retired from Monumental Life in 2003, there were many "bridging" issues in 1998—including compensation, new incentive programs and consolidation of accounts and offices—that affected agent performance and pay. But the end result was very positive. "After the storm," he said, "there was sunshine!"

At the March 1999 Managers Meeting in Baltimore, Hagan saluted the organization's two-year effort and the 1998 leaders and award winners from all four field divisions. Despite the challenges and distractions, they had remained focused on sales and service. "Together, we're better," he announced proudly after five days of sharing and teamwork. As they boarded buses for the ride to the airport, most managers, award winners and spouses agreed.

In mid-August 1999 more than nine hundred sales leaders, plus an additional 1,600 spouses and guests, gathered in Hawaii for the first conference celebrating the combined sales success of the fully integrated Monumental Life/Providian Agency Group field force. By year-end, Phil White, vice president, field operations, could report in an *AEGON Wise* article, distributed internationally to all AEGON employees, that more than 3,300 Monumental Agency Group agents and managers were operating under "one growth-based compensation system, a single product portfolio, a common set of administration, laptop and personal computer systems, sales tools and training programs—each derived from among the group's best practices." With this solid platform now firmly established, he added proudly, "we are poised to achieve our vision of being clearly identified and perceived as the best life insurance company, in America, in our chosen markets."

COUNTDOWN TO Y2K!

But one more big challenge remained for Monumental Life, AEGON and the world before everyone bid farewell to the 1990s. The issue, dealing with dates and data in the Year 2000 and beyond, was nicknamed "Y2K."

"Moving forward to the Year 2000 promises to be an exciting challenge for our organization," wrote Donald Shepard, chairman, AEGON USA, Inc. in March 1998. "Preparing our information systems for this pervasive and complex change is one of the most important business initiatives we've undertaken. Preserving the integrity of our data and system capabilities through the Year 2000 Project is critical to our ongoing success."

Why was "Y2K" such a big deal for a large, worldwide organization like AEGON? For one thing, just about every calculation and transaction used by insurers to process business and serve customers involves years and dates. Using two digits to identify years, which programmers had begun to do early in the development of computers and continued to do through the 1990s, would no longer be possible after January 1, 2000. (The digits "07" in a date, for example, could refer to either 1907 or 2007.) To assure that dates and data were accurate, every system—millions and millions of lines of programming code throughout

the entire worldwide organization—had to be identified, tested and possibly upgraded or replaced.

By March 1999, all AEGON USA operating companies, including Monumental Life, were able to announce that their mission-critical systems were Year 2000–compliant. As the world waited anxiously that December to see what would happen when computers encountered Y2K, AEGON wrapped up its final planning and testing. At 10:00 p.m. on December 31, 1999, processing on all systems was slowed to begin full backup of all data. At 11:45 p.m. all processing stopped to allow system clocks to roll over to the four-digit date. At 12:15 a.m. systems were restarted as technicians completed checklists. By 6:00 a.m. on January 1, 2000, all AEGON USA business units could start logging on to check their data.

Shortly after midnight, a Monumental Life policyholder in West Virginia gave birth to a new baby boy. The newborn was the first child born in Grant County in the year 2000. When proud parents Roger and Rebecca Ours took out a policy on his life, newborn David Ours became the first and youngest insured client of the new century for Cumberland, Maryland, agent Bill Blankenbeckler and Monumental Life.

When employees arrived at their Monumental offices on Monday morning, January 3, 2000, they logged onto their computers and got right to work. No systems crashed. No data was missing or corrupted. Eighteen months of Y2K planning, preparation and effort had assured a smooth transition.

Just as important for U.S. workers and their families that morning, alarm clocks worked, ATMs dispensed needed cash, traffic lights changed on cue, and coffee pots set to begin brewing at precisely "07:30 AM" on "01/03/2000" had begun to drip. No challenges in the new millennium loomed too large so long as U.S. employees and their Dutch associates had their morning coffee!

LEFT: *The light-hearted cartoons never minimized the importance or critical nature of the company's Year 2000 initiative. For AEGON's worldwide family, eighteen months of planning and preparation assured a smooth transition to Y2K-ready data and systems.*

ABOVE: *By year-end 1999, AEGON associates in Europe were bracing not only for Y2K, but also for the introduction of a common monetary unit, called the "euro," to be used by all countries in the new European Union.*

Agent Larry Celeste . . .

Monumental Music Man Plays at Caesars Palace!

*B*ORN in Italy at the stroke of midnight on January 1, 1900, Larry Celeste immigrated to the United States with his family in 1907. Shortly after arriving in New York, the family moved to Chicago—but not before his mother changed her son's name from Lorenzo to Lawrence. "She thought it sounded better since we were going to live in America."

In Chicago, Celeste started taking trombone lessons at the Jane Addams Hull House, a kind of Boys Town for underprivileged immigrant kids. Just eleven years old, Celeste made friends with a "skinny little nine-year-old who was learning to play clarinet." Later, during America's "Swing Era," that clarinet player became world-famous. His name was Benny Goodman.

Though Celeste never became world-famous, making music and making people happy defined much of his life. Just after the Great Depression, he worked with a local band playing in parks, tuberculosis sanatoriums and area hospitals. "I earned $75 every two weeks," he remembered at age ninety-five. "We got paid out of WPA funds—one of those social programs during the Roosevelt era. But I wanted to get into business. Something with potential."

In 1939 the manager of Monumental's Chicago #3 office hired him as a "canvasser." He went door-to-door in Cicero selling $1,000 insurance policies for a nickel a week. "I knew the sales lingo," he said, "but I was always straight with every customer. Even back then, you had to put in the hours if you wanted to make it. You had to like people to sell insurance."

Celeste's determination to succeed was tested early in his career. "When my first wife died, I had to raise two young sons on my own. I cooked lunch for them, then went out to sell. I came home to make dinner, and went back out to sell at night. Many days, I worked in boots. New neighborhoods were being built and there weren't any sidewalks. When it rained, there was mud everywhere."

The biggest thrill of retired Monumental agent Larry Celeste's long life was playing the organ at Caesar's Palace in Las Vegas in 1996 at age 96. Monumental officers presented Celeste with an honorary NHA red blazer to mark the occasion. Left to right: P. J. West, Henry Hagan and Larry Jenkins.

Celeste's customers genuinely liked him—for his personality and his honesty—and the feeling was mutual. He'd often drop off homemade meatballs or lasagna when making collections. Retiring after twenty-four years in 1963, he went out on a high note. His office, then managed by Dominic Zombo, was the weekly premium increase leader for the year.

Celeste continued playing music in retirement. At age seventy-two he began taking organ lessons from Wurlitzer, eventually giving lessons himself and playing regularly for a church in Maywood, Illinois. "The first organ I bought had three keyboards," he said. "When the church needed a new one, I sold it to them for $4,000." Later, he bought one with pipes and played for at least an hour every day.

Diagnosed with chronic obstructive pulmonary disease after years of smoking cigars and chewing tobacco, Celeste moved to Las Vegas in 1978. The dry climate was better for his health. At age ninety-five in 1995, he was still composing, playing his pipe organ, and recording tapes to give to friends, family, hospitals and nursing homes. "Friends offer me cash to play at special events," he said, "but I always refuse to take the money. Playing music is now my single pleasure in life because it makes people happy. The money doesn't matter."

In 1996, during that year's sales conference in Las Vegas, Monumental Life recognized Celeste as the company's oldest living retired agent. Larry Jenkins, Henry Hagan and Regional Vice President P. J. West presented the former Chicago agent with one of Monumental Life's custom-made National Honor Associate red blazers and a citation from Pope John Paul II.

But the meeting's biggest thrill occurred a few minutes later when hotel staff rolled in a large organ. Celeste—the "music man" with a heart of gold, who had been giving to others all his life—sat down at the keyboard and played for everyone in the room. When Celeste died a few years later, just shy of his one hundredth birthday, his live-in nurse called to thank the company for what it had done. Being able to tell friends he had "played at Caesars Palace" had been one of the highlights of his life.

Monumental Across America . . .
OUR TOWN, OUR FAMILY

DRIVE INTO ANY ONE OF 150 or more communities across the United States today and you will find local Monumental Life field offices—in Chicago high rises, on Main Street in a small Midwestern town, in a suburban mall in Florida or Pennsylvania, and near corn fields on Maryland's Eastern Shore. The agents working there might be American-born men and women, but it's just as likely that some will be immigrants—born in Mexico, Jamaica, Italy, Turkey, India, Russia, Vietnam or Nigeria—whose families came to our country looking for a better life. The Monumental customers they serve might live in trailer parks or government-subsidized housing, on farms and rural country roads, in upscale townhouses or condos, or in single-family homes, both large and small, in suburban neighborhoods.

As the company has grown through mergers and acquisitions, there is no longer any such thing as a "typical Monumental town," a typical "Monumental home," or a typical "Monumental family." Today, our town is "Any Town USA," and our policyholders might be any lower- or middle-income family in America.

Our employees and policyholders represent a diverse "melting pot" of races, cultures, religions and ethnic backgrounds. They might speak any one of a dozen languages and wear traditional saris, dashikis, yarmulkes or head scarves.

In many areas of the country, we insure several generations of the same family. Sons and daughters follow fathers and siblings into the business, and it's not unusual to find members of the same family competing against one another for sales and leadership awards. Parents seem proud to pass along their decades-long, career-defining tradition of helping people, and our "Monumental family" includes hundreds of field and home office employees who have celebrated thirty or more years of service to the company, its customers, their co-workers, and their communities.

The following profiles form a picture of "Monumental across America"—the communities and families we serve, and the generations of field and home office employees who have fulfilled our promise to be there to help policyholders when they needed us the most.

◀ GRANDFATHER, GRANDDAUGTHER

When this picture was taken of Andrew ("Andy") Zeiler and granddaughter Kathy in 1950, no one ever would have dreamed that one day they would both retire from the same company. Zeiler joined Mutual Life at age sixteen in 1918 when the home office was still on South Street. One of his first assignments was to write all non-printed policy information, in longhand, on each policy. He did this until someone finally said "Let's get a typewriter!" Promoted to manager of the Auditing Department in 1931 and appointed assistant secretary in 1939, Zeiler earned ninety dollars a week in 1944. "My grandfather was always well-dressed and impeccably groomed," remembers Kathy Younkin, who joined the company as a programmer in 1970. Like many of Monumental's middle managers in those years, Zeiler lived in a small rowhouse, never owned a car, and commuted to work by bus or streetcar from Baltimore's Belair-Edison neighborhood. He retired in 1965 with forty-seven years' service.

Like her grandfather, Kathy Younkin has also risen through the ranks, accepted increasing responsibility, and made significant contributions to the company. Still some years from retirement herself, she is an Information Systems assistant vice president and team leader.

◀▶ LIPPERT LEGACY

A member of the Lippert family has been working in the Charles and Chase Street home office building ever since it opened in 1926. Milton Lippert was working for the Real Estate Trust Company when it moved into Mutual Life's new building. As assistant secretary until his 1961 retirement, he had frequent contact with Monumental officers. Milton's son Richard joined Monumental in 1958 as its first programmer on the IBM-650. Dick Lippert remained in Data Processing for twenty years and retired as second vice president, Agent Compensation and Performance in 1996. Dick's wife, Susan, worked as a secretary in the Accounting Department from 1961 to 1969. Her twin sister, Gail Matzen, joined the company as a mail pay clerk in 1963 and is still working in Field Operations. Dick and Susan's son, Eric, remembers coming to the home office as a child. He joined Marketing Services in 1992 and today is assistant vice president, Field Personnel and Reporting Systems. Eric's sister, Stacey, met her husband, Jim Benzing, when they both worked summers at Monumental during their college years.

Father and son played softball, basketball and soccer on Monumental teams, and Dick remains connected to his Monumental friends through the Baltimore-area "Silver Eagles" retiree association. After forty-five years, Gail can still be counted on to help with any project. "Our family life centered around company-sponsored activities for many years," says Gail. "Employee picnics and dances, team sports and bowling nights—all built close friendships that enhanced our working relationships in the office." Eric is proud of his family's contributions, commitment and years of service to Monumental. "Dedication and a strong work ethic enabled them to achieve a great deal and build long, successful careers. I would like to continue that tradition."

◀ FATHERS, SONS IN THE FIELD

Al Jecker joined Commonwealth Life in 1946 after serving in World War II. As an agent, field manager and director of manpower development, he experienced firsthand the industry's progression from selling funeral policies, to family plans, to joint-life coverage on dual-income couples, to large term contracts in the 1980s. Intensely proud of his profession and called "Mr. Commonwealth" by industry friends, Al Jecker still serves on the Commonwealth Retiree Association board. He encouraged his son, Steve, to enter the business in 1977 and remains his son's mentor and coach, supporter and biggest cheerleader. From him, says Steve, a Monumental senior regional vice president, "I learned that attitude, passion and purpose make a difference." As he gets older, Steve also realizes the truth of something his father said many years ago. "Looking back after retirement, you'll realize it won't be about the treasures, the trinkets and trash you collected along the way. The things you will remember the most, will be the people you met, the relationships you built and the memories you shared."

▼ FOLLOWING IN HIS FATHER'S FOOTSTEPS

William H. ("Bill") Davies joined Commonwealth as an agent in Owensboro, Kentucky, in 1949. He managed the company's Findley, Ohio, field office when Al Jecker was a sales manager there. The two retirees and their sons have been friends ever since. In 1967, Davies was promoted to vice president of the company's eastern territory. Additional promotions followed, including being named president of Capital Holding's Palmetto State Life. He retired as Commonwealth's president and chief operating officer in 1983. By then his son Duane had been with the company as an agent and sales manager for nine years. "Hearing a company name all your life provides a sense of security," said Duane in 1978. "Thanks to the education my father's generation spread through the country . . . we are able to sell larger policies for mortgages, estate planning and income replacement." They are pictured here on a 2006 fishing trip to Canada. Duane is now Monumental's vice president, Sales Support—a position similar to one his father once held.

▲ ▶ BROTHERS COMPETE

When he was named Monumental's leading district manager for 1992, Lou Dahdah expected to hear "Way to go, Dad!" Instead his three sons cried "Dad, what about Uncle Benny!?" Lou's biggest competitor for the title was his brother Benny Dahdah, perennial leader and district manager in northern New Jersey's Hackensack office. "Neither of us would give up. It was a fight to the bitter end,"

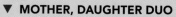

says Lou, who joined Washington National in 1960. Ben followed him into the business in 1961. The brothers' friendly but fierce rivalry that began at "WNIC" continued after Monumental acquired their offices in 1990. The brothers talked almost daily by phone throughout their careers—to share ideas, results, challenges, and training issues—until Benny passed away in 2001. Their wives were both office administrators. Their sons and nephews followed them into the business, helping to create two of Monumental's highest paid, most consistently successful and stable sales teams. At conferences, the Dahdah "extended family" of qualifiers and spouses traditionally filled several banquet tables.

▼ MONUMENTAL DAD, DAUGHTERS' ROLE MODEL

Retiree Joe Roche distinctly remembers his first sale—a 74-cent weekly premium policy for $500. He was twenty-two years old and a new agent in Pittsburgh in 1957 with two small daughters. Promoted to sales manager in 1961, he moved his family to Detroit in 1965, then to Baltimore in 1967. During his forty-four-year career, he served as district manager of several officers; as a regional vice president; and as ProSource recruiting manager following the Providian merger. "Monumental was a great place to work, with great benefits," Roche says. "It continues to provide career opportunities for women, minorities and recruits young and old who are comfortable with the laptop technology."

Roche's daughters remember their dad singing in the shower every morning. Always happy, motivated and looking forward to the new day, he provided an excellent "work ethic" example for all of them. Today, daughters and daughter-in-law all have challenging careers with Monumental and AEGON. Pictured with Joe in Ravens' jerseys at a recent family crab feast are (left to right) daughter-in-law Stephanie Roche, Monumental model office coordinator; Luanne O'Brennan, Monumental LAN (Local Area Network) team leader; Mary Pat Rourk, Payment Administration; and Colleen Gizinki, who began her career in Monumental's Service Center in the 1970s and is now part of AEGON Direct Marketing Services' successful management team. "We all work hard," they agree, "because we don't want to let down the family."

▼ MOTHER, DAUGHTER DUO

When Diretha Harper joined Monumental as a weekly premium processing clerk in 1973, there were no computers. She manually checked paper summaries to verify that agent calculations were correct. Today, her staff of twenty-four rarely touches paper. Thanks to AWD (Automatic Work Distribution), assignments are doled out electronically and Diretha checks progress from her desktop computer. When Shalonda Harper joined the company after graduating from college in February 2000, her first real challenge was establishing herself as an individual separate from her mother. "Many people felt I would be exactly like her, but our personalities are different. I had to prove that I was capable of handling my job, without her influence." In the last seven years, Shalonda has been challenged, grown, and succeeded in positions of increasing responsibility. Today they each manage critical customer-focused Administration departments— "Mrs. Harper" is responsible for New Business/Post Issue; "Ms. Harper" is responsible for the Customer Service Center. Monumental offers "opportunities to move up— regardless of race, religion or gender—to those who work hard, want a career and are willing to learn new things," says Shalonda.

▶ THREE GENERATIONS EARN RED JACKETS

Howard Bock was one the first agents to earn Washington National's coveted National Honor Associate red jacket in 1971. His son, Robert, became a WNIC agent in 1973 and received his red jacket in 1978. Twenty-two years later, Robert's twenty-year-old daughter, Nikol Kelly, followed her father and grandfather into the business as an agent in Monumental's York, Pennsylvania, office, where her father was then working. "She had the ability, the initiative, and the drive to make it," says Bock. By 2003 she was earning over $100,000 a year and had qualified for three consecutive sales conferences. In February 2006 she received a standing ovation from her peers for being the third generation of her family to earn the coveted NHA red jacket. A few months earlier she had promised her dying grandfather, who was buried in his decades-old blazer, that she too would earn the NHA award. Her proud father joined her on stage for the presentation.

PROUD PROFESSIONAL ▶

Born and raised in Jamaica, Glen Malcolm began working at age ten when his mother died and he had to help support his family. After teaching there and in the Bahamas, he married his childhood sweetheart and moved to Miami. In 1976 he became a life insurance agent with Orlando-based National Standard Life, then a Capital Holding subsidiary. Several mergers and acquisitions later, Monumental president Henry G. Hagan saluted Malcolm as a company leader and role model. Throughout his career, Malcolm was committed to his customers, his company and his industry "family." Working in predominantly immigrant and minority neighborhoods, he enjoyed educating people about life insurance. He excelled in sales and customer service, exemplified the word "professional," and qualified repeatedly for the Million Dollar Round Table. He served as president of his local chapter of the National Association of Insurance and Financial Advisors, and the Florida state association. Between 2001 and 2003, he personally visited field offices to recruit 250 new members. Whether promoting the benefits of NAIFA, serving on the industry's diversity task force, or educating congressmen on Capitol Hill about the value of life insurance, Malcolm made sure his message was heard. He retired from his full-time career agent position with Monumental after being elected a national NAIFA trustee in 2004.

◀ SUCCESSFUL SISTERS

Kathy Dickerson became a Commonwealth agent in Winchester, Kentucky, in 1983. Over the next eighteen years, she qualified for every Commonwealth and Monumental sales conference, usually at the Pinnacle Club level. Her sister, Noreen Strickland, became an agent in Ashland, Kentucky, in 1986 and was promoted to sales manager three years later. In 1994, Kathy earned a President's Trophy as the leading account rep, and Noreen's Ashland staff won a President's Citation. It is no coincidence that the two sisters were so successful. They share a work ethic that comes from growing up in rural Kentucky, two of seven children born to a farmer, pipe fitter and Baptist preacher. "We were raised to be honest and work hard. We all pitched in to help." Today, Noreen Strickland Clemens is the much-respected manager of Monumental's Northern Kentucky district office. She still gives 110 percent of herself to help her sales teams succeed. Unfortunately—despite her "can do," competitive spirit, and consistent company leadership—health issues forced Kathy to retire in 2002 after nineteen years in the field. They are pictured here in 2005 with their brother Jim. Kathy is at left, Noreen is on the right.

◄ COOKIN' IN CAJUN COUNTRY!

They eat crawfish and roux, a spicy Cajun stew, love dancing to a fiddle, serve French-speaking customers in Louisiana's bayou country, and don't need a reason to express their natural "joie de vivre." They are caring life insurance agents, perhaps, because their heritage encourages lending a hand, a "coup de main," when neighboring families need help. Sales Manager Ben Prince (center front), his wife and several other members of Monumental's awarding-winning New Iberia, sales team, pictured here in 2006, grew up in Cajun country and speak English with a distinct accent. Like their spicy Cajun cooking, sales are hot and their plate is very full!

SUCCESSFUL SISTERS...TWO! ►

Monumental's agent career attracts women who want to help people, make money and are willing to work hard. It is also a stepping stone into management for some of the most successful women in our business. Dena Smith Cochran (right) joined Monumental's Kansas City/St. Joe office in 1989. Promoted into field management within six years, she continued to qualify for conferences, win many awards, and serve on the company's Field Managers Advisory Council. Since 2002, Dena had been responsible for several field offices, first as an area manager and most recently as a regional vice president. Kimberly ("Brook") St. John (left) became a Monumental agent in January 2000 and, like her older sister, has also experienced significant success. A President's Club qualifier her first year in the business, she earned the company's coveted National Honor Associate red blazer and was promoted to manager of the Kansas City/St. Joe field office in 2006.

◄ SERVING CHICAGO'S HISPANIC NEIGHBORHOODS

Growing up in Texas, the son of a Mexican-born migrant worker, George Benavides (left) picked tomatoes, delivered newspapers, and shined shoes. In 1967, working for General Motors as a welder--afraid of layoffs but never hard work--he was thinking of joining the Chicago police or fire department when Bill Daley (center), his family's Monumental agent offered him a job. George qualified for the company's sales conference that first year and never missed another during his thirty-six year career. Many of the policies he wrote on Hispanic families in the 1960s and 1970s are still in force today.

▲ THE HECKER GIRLS

The Hecker sisters started at the bottom and worked their way up. Today all three are long-term, dedicated and successful AEGON employees with significant responsibilities.

▲ DIVERSE, YET ALL SPEAK THE SAME LANGUAGE!

Monumental's programmers and analysts represent the rich mix of cultures that make up the American and Monumental "melting pot." Though they sometimes lapse into their native languages, the international members of Monumental's programming and support teams all speak the same language when discussing projects and systems needs. Pictured here are: (front) Tatyana Gordon, Yuriy Lyakhovets, and Olga Melnik, all from the Ukraine; and (back) Kazu Ohsawa, Japan; Obi Nwankwo, Nigeria; Sam Babiso, Ethiopia; Kathy Williams, whose ancestors were Cherokee, and Nat Srinivasan, India.

Carol Hecker Davies graduated from high school without a college fund and needed to find a job. Working as a reserve clerk in Commonwealth's HR department, she completed her FLMI designation in two years and posted for positions of increasing responsibility while attending night school. After successfully rolling out the Collections System to Commonwealth's field force, she was selected as project manager for the Providian/Monumental Life acquisition and conversion, completed in 1999. Currently working in Baltimore, she is Monumental Life's vice president and chief information officer.

Cindy Hecker Murphy followed her sister to Commonwealth in 1981, while she was still in high school. Starting in the Policy Loan Department, she worked in several administrative areas before switching to Information Technology testing. Today, she is lead business analyst for AEGON Financial Partners in Louisville. Connie Hecker Whitlock also worked at Commonwealth during her last year of high school. After completing her BA in accounting, she joined the Accounting Department, was promoted to management roles in Claims and Customer Service, and eventually moved to Providian's Marketing Partners operation. Following the AEGON acquisition, she was tapped to run AEGON's Financial Partners Worksite Marketing Operation in Little Rock, Arkansas, where she is currently vice president and chief operating officer.

▲ BISCUITS, ANYONE?

Family traditions die hard in rural West Virginia. Policyholder Hazel Stover sent in this photo to make sure everyone knows she makes some of the best biscuits in Clay County!

▼ DEDICATED DURHAM EMPLOYEES

Monumental's Durham-area field and home office employees gathered in downtown Durham to listen to presentations by AEGON's Executive Board during their 2003 "Optiek" visit to several AEGON USA locations. Monumental has maintained an administrative office near Durham since its merger with Providian in 1997. Many current employees began their careers with Home Life or Peoples Security and have significant years of company service.

▲ MONUMENTAL 'MELTING POT'

Surrounding President Henry Hagan (second row, center) in Las Vegas in 2005, these top-producing Pinnacle Club men and women came from all over the country and reflect the diversity of race, color and ethnicity found in today's Monumental "family" and field offices.

▲ ALMOST HEAVEN!

Her son owns the land. Policyholder Margaret Gore owns the mobile home. "I told my son we would make it to Promised Land and today we live on Promised Land Road in Watha, North Carolina!"

▲ MY HAIRCUTS ARE THE BEST!

Monumental policyholder and barber Russell Thomas has owned and operated his barber shop in Newport News, Virginia, for decades.

▲ INVESTING IN CHARLESTON'S KIDS

"We're proud to live here because we get involved. We try to decrease crime, promote involvement and educate residents," says Charleston, South Carolina, policyholder Sarah Green.

▲ AS AMERICAN AS APPLE PIE . . .

"Reading, Pennsylvania, has a long baseball history that dates back to the 1800s," wrote one policyholder in 2004. Kids play baseball and families watch their games in just about every community where Monumental agents write business.

▲ MAIN STREET USA

Monumental policyholders showed their pride in America following September 11, 2001, by submitting entries like this one, taken in Holly Hill, Florida, in the company's annual photo contest.

▼ HARVESTING THE HAY

"Morgantown, Indiana, is a small, friendly, quiet farming community. I have lived here for 56 years," noted policyholder and photographer Carol Graphman in 2004.

▲ COUNTRY ROADS, TAKE ME HOME

A Monumental agent might enter a policyholder home like this one in Fern Creek, Kentucky, in just about any rural community we serve.

Sales Conferences . . .
MONUMENTAL'S ANNUAL FAMILY REUNION

"THIS FEELS MORE LIKE a family reunion than a company meeting!" remarked one speaker at a recent Monumental Life sales conference. "Everyone seems so happy to be here. Qualifiers have found old friends. Spouses are sharing news and family photos. Even the kids know one another!"

When agents, managers and guests gather for the company's annual incentive conference, it really is a family reunion—Monumental-style! The hugs and handshakes are genuine. The greetings always warm. "Great to see you!" someone shouts across a check-in line. "We missed you last year, hope you're feeling better," says another to someone who's been ill. "How do you do it, year after year?" asks a first-timer impressed by a leading agent's production. These are people-loving but competitive men and women. They focus on sales figures but understand the importance of building and nurturing relationships. Many couples have been friends for decades and look forward to seeing one another at these annual gatherings. They provide a chance to relax, reminisce, rekindle old friendships, receive awards, and be recognized in front of their peers.

More than any other incentive, notes President Henry G. Hagan, Monumental Life conferences motivate agents, managers and sales teams to achieve their objectives. Though some destinations generate more excitement than others, conferences never fail to stimulate production and increase. Sales conferences also help retain talented producers and solidify commitments to careers. After attending one conference, attendees don't want to miss another.

Today's qualifiers know their conference invitation will include their spouses, three or four nights at a fabulous resort, and lots of great food. Leading Pinnacle Club

◄ **AGENT OUTING**
Mutual Life's agents gathered in Avondale, Maryland, for an outing in 1905. Though outdoors in June, most attendees dressed formally in suits, ties and vests. Officers, including President Matthew Brenan, in straw hat, are seated center front.

MUTUAL LIFE INSURANCE
COMPANY OF BALTIMORE

Vol. 11　　BALTIMORE, MARYLAND, MARCH 1935　　No. 3

DON'T MISS IT!

▲ CONVENTION SPECIAL . . . DON'T MISS IT!

In the middle of the Great Depression, qualifying for Mutual Life's annual sales convention was a high priority but much harder to do. This *Old Black Hen* cover from March 1935 urged agents to get on board the "Convention Special" by producing more sales.

▼ ST. LOUIS FAMILY PICNIC.

St. Louis agents, managers and their families looked forward to the office's annual picnic, this one held in August 1925. Hairdos and more casual clothes were typical of the "Roaring Twenties." St. Louis was one of the company's leading offices.

▲ 1925 CONVENTION DELEGATES ARRIVE IN NEW ORLEANS.
Traveling from all over the country aboard the Illinois Central's "Mutual Life of Baltimore Special"—which included an engine, baggage car, two Pullman sleepers, dining and club cars—eighty delegates to Mutual Life's first sales convention arrived at the Roosevelt Hotel in New Orleans on January 26, 1925. Throughout the four-day convention, speakers promoted the "Mutual Spirit." Second Vice President Charles C. Ewell reminded delegates: "We want the benefits of the convention to be lasting ones. Take home to those you left behind the knowledge and the Mutual Spirit you have been able to get from these sessions."

producers are also treated to side trips, sightseeing tours and special events. With rates negotiated for extended stays, many couples bring children at their own expense and build annual family vacations around popular destinations.

It has not always been so. The company's first documented field "entertainment event" was a dinner at the Carrollton Hotel in Baltimore on July 20, 1899, to which President Matthew S. Brenan invited the company's agents, officers and directors. Board minutes note that "eighty persons were present" and that "the dinner [costing about $100] was paid for by the President out of his own personal funds."

Over the next two decades, local offices held annual banquets and outings, which sometimes included family members. In the early 1920s, larger annual banquets were held in Baltimore. When President

Paul Burnett welcomed qualifying "delegates" to the company's first official four-day "convention" in New Orleans in January 1925, some agents and managers had never traveled so far or stayed in a hotel. Then, as now, conferences expanded horizons and introduced producers to places they may have never visited on their own. Even more important, conference speakers, meetings and workshops provide opportunities for agent education, motivation, networking, and sharing ideas.

Conferences have become such a tradition that qualifications, awards, and destinations were among field management's top concerns when Providian Agency Group merged with Monumental in 1997. Ten years later, the location of the next conference site continues to be one of the company's most anticipated annual announcements.

▲ LEADER TROPHY

Confronted with restrictions on all but war-related manufacturing during World War II, officers somehow managed to secure five silver-finished trophies to award to the company's 1943 leading offices.

CONFERENCE FUN! ▶

In this undated photograph, probably from the 1950s, conference attendees "ham it up" with funny hats, mustaches and a few bottles of beer.

◀▼ CHAIRMAN'S ROUND TABLE

By the late 1960s, the annual conference was called the Chairman's Round Table and recognition included pins and rings for repeat qualifiers. Rubies and diamonds were added as conference years added up. Conference awards were later expanded to include "Top of the Table" blazers for top producers.

▲ GRAND TIME IN THE BAHAMAS!

During the 1970s, the company held its first conferences outside the continental U.S. President Frank Baker welcomed Chairman's Round Table qualifiers to Grand Bahama Island in 1974, where each qualifier received a commemorative plate.

PRESIDENT'S CLUB IN NEW YORK CITY ▶

Monumental Life President F. Harold Loweree (seated on the floor, front left, in bow tie) created the first President's Club in 1954. Three years later, the company recognized 112 qualifiers in New York City. Upon arrival at the Governor Clinton Hotel, all wives received corsages. The conference included "red carpet treatment" for all attendees, business sessions, sightseeing tours of Manhattan, a "floor show" featuring talented qualifiers and spouses, and dancing one night until 3:00 a.m.

▲ MIAMI BEACH IN 1961

Beautiful sunny days, a poolside water show and a new president named Fred Wehr welcomed qualifiers to Monumental's 1961 President's Club in Miami Beach. Presentations included a panel of wives whose support at home helped their husbands qualify annually for conferences.

▶ CRUSING TO BERMUDA

Cruises have always been some of the most motivating conference destinations. During the Home Security Life cruise to Bermuda in the 1960s—long before the company merged with Peoples Life or became part of our Monumental family— qualifiers in life jackets waited for a drill while others dozed on deck.

◀ TOPPERS TOUR HOLLAND

In 1986, Dutch insurer AEGON acquired Monumental. To celebrate its new "Atlantic Connection," the company rewarded conference-leading agents and managers with a trip to AEGON's headquarters in The Hague, the Netherlands in 1988. Qualifiers had dinner while riding a boat on Amsterdam's canals and toured the Dutch countryside by bus.

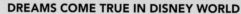

▲ CAUGHT IN A STORM!

Hundreds of sales conference attendees were at Merv Griffin's Paradise Island Resort and Casino in August 1992 when Hurricane Andrew hit the Bahamas and southern Florida. After trying to reschedule flights for more than three days, the company chartered a plane to fly stranded qualifiers to Atlanta.

DREAMS COME TRUE IN DISNEY WORLD

Realizing that Monumental agents often have to sacrifice time with family to succeed, the company scheduled its first official "family conference" at Disney World in Orlando in 1994. The family-focused events, discounted theme park tickets, and appearances by Mickey and Minnie Mouse were so well-received that the company returned to Disney World in 2000 to celebrate "Magic Moments" in the new millennium. More than 2,000 Monumental qualifiers, spouses and family members filled the Swan and Dolphin hotels!

◄ ROCKY MOUNTAIN ROUND-UP

Looking mean and determined, Monumental's regional vice presidents spent a full year on the trail rustling up qualifiers for the 1993 conference in Snowmass, Colorado. It was the first conference for which Reliable and Commonwealth's newly acquired agents and managers could qualify. Left to right (rear) are: George Cabaniss, Dick Huffman (vice president of District Agencies), Dave Bugno, George Marteslo and Bob Grosholz. Seated are Rich Picardi, Don Allison, and P. J. West.

A CAPITAL AFFAIR ▶

Monumental's 1997 Chairman's Round Table was in Washington, D.C. Elegant and impressive, the Awards Banquet included individual recognition for each conference leader. Two months earlier, Monumental officers had saluted Providian Agency Group's leaders and newly acquired associates at Caesars Palace in Las Vegas.

Lorenzo's Gondola in **VENICE**

▲ LORENZO'S ADVENTURE IN ITALY

President Larry Jenkins celebrated his announced retirement with a special conference "trip of a lifetime" to Italy for top-producing agents and managers in November 1997. The qualifiers' reward for two years of outstanding sales was seven days of sightseeing (without meetings!) that included gondola rides in Venice, shopping in Florence, and visits to the Coliseum, the Vatican and St. Peter's Square in Rome.

ALOHA!

More than 2,500 conference qualifiers, home office attendees and family members filled the Hilton Hawaiian Village in Honolulu in August 1999. The sea of people included agents and managers from all companies acquired during the 1990s—the largest group of Monumental qualifiers ever. At the Pinnacle Club "Biker Party" on Maui, leaders Jack and Rita Buttacavoli enjoyed riding on a "Harley."

▲ EVERYONE MADE IT!

Every agent and sales manager in Lou Dahdah's Wayne, New Jersey, office qualified for Hawaii in 1999. Recognized as the company's #2 manager, Lou (kneeling center front) is the only Monumental district manager to have ever achieved that distinction.

MAKING AN IMPRESSION. ▶

Thousands of conference attendees left their "ML" mark in the sand on Waikiki Beach in Honolulu in 1999.

▼ PRESIDENT'S CLUB FOR FIRST TIMERS

As the number of conference qualifiers grew with each merger, first-timers began to get lost in the shuffle. In 2000, a new President's Club focused attention on successful new agents, introduced them to Baltimore and steamed crabs, and reinforced the benefits of the agent career. Autograph collecting contests helped qualifiers meet officers and other agents.

▲ NATIONAL HONOR ASSOCIATES, A NEW TRADITION

Monumental inherited the National Honor Associate award program when it acquired Washington National in 1990. District Manager Benny Dahdah is pictured here in 1991 wearing his old WNIC red blazer with Monumental's new NHA crest featuring Maryland flag symbols and Baltimore's Washington Monument. To honor their NHA tradition, Monumental framed the old WNIC crests and presented them to veterans. Today, more than two hundred agents and managers wear their red jackets proudly at conferences. Dozens of honorees with ten or more conference-qualifying years have also been inducted onto the prestigious National Honor Associate Board. Many continue to receive annual conference invitations as retirees.

▲ MONUMENTAL CHALLENGE

With 750 qualifiers and 1,600 registered attendees, Monumental's 2001 Chairman's Round Table Conference in Cancun was one of the most anticipated in the company's history. When terrorists crashed planes into the World Trade Center on September 11 and airports remained closed days later, President Henry Hagan postponed the conference, planned for the next week. The planning team met immediately and rescheduled for January 2002. "Monumental qualifiers come from almost 200 locations throughout the US," noted AEGON Travel's Leslie Herald. With a group this size and the reduction in flight schedules after 9/11, it was difficult finding enough seats. Her team worked nights and weekends for six weeks to rebook more than 1,200 flights.

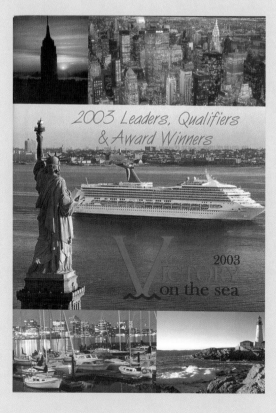

2003 Leaders, Qualifiers & Award Winners

Victory on the sea 2003

◄ BLACKOUT DELAYS 'BON VOYAGE'

Monumental had reserved half the ship and filled 750 cabins. Qualifiers were on deck waiting to leave on August 14, 2003, when a massive blackout hit much of the northeast. Thanks to quick-thinking longshoremen who cut the power cable needed to release the gangplank, the "Victory on the Seas" was able to leave port. Every other conference scheduled that week in New York City was cancelled. As the ship left New York harbor and headed to Nova Scotia, qualifiers photographed the Statue of Liberty and the unusually dark "City that Never Sleeps."

▲ PINNACLE CLUB PRODUCERS

Reaching for the top brings special rewards to Monumental's Pinnacle Club qualifiers—including extra days at conference, special dinners, extra money for sightseeing or shopping, and annual Pinnacle Club trophies, shirts, and group portraits such as this one, taken in New York in 2003.

▲ FUNERAL HOME DIRECTORS FETED.

Monumental also recognizes its top-producing funeral directors in the PreNeed marketplace. Pictured here are qualifiers, regional directors and home office attendees during the 2003 PreNeed conference cruise to Key West and Cancun.

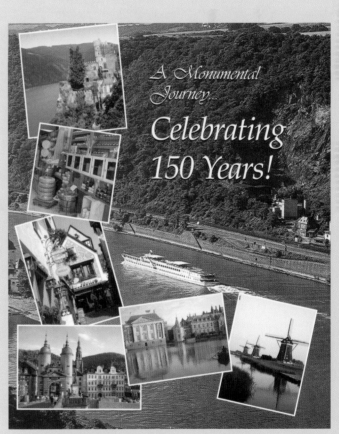

A Monumental Journey...

Celebrating 150 Years!

▲ MONUMENTAL JOURNEY

In June 2008, ninety Monumental agents and managers will be rewarded for three years of consistent effort and results with a week-long 150th Anniversary cruise on Europe's Rhine River. Visiting eight cities and four countries, the trip will include lunch at AEGON headquarters plus tours and sightseeing at each stop before ending in Switzerland.

CHAPTER 13

Fulfilling the Promise

Sales Support's Emilie Harris and Donna Sansone are already in the office at 7:35 a.m. on Tuesday morning, September 11, 2001, preparing for another busy day (and a co-worker's birthday!), when al Qaeda operative Mohammed Atta boards American Airlines Flight 11 at Boston's Logan Airport. Within the week, Monumental Life vice president Duane Davies and his conference planning team—Rosemary Riesett, Joe John, Michael Key, Carol Matthai and Linda Anderson—are scheduled to fly to Cancun to welcome 1,600 conference qualifiers and guests. Boxes containing awards, gifts and welcome kits have already been shipped from Baltimore, but there is still much to do.

As home office employees arrive for work between 8:00 and 8:20 a.m., two more jetliners take off with al Qaeda operatives on board—one from Boston and one from Dulles International Airport outside Washington. At 8:42 a.m., a fourth plane leaves from Newark International Airport in New Jersey.

At 8:44 a.m. flight attendant Amy Sweeney on Flight 11 calls American Airlines to report: "Something is wrong. We are in rapid descent . . . ." Asked to describe what she sees, she says, "I see water. I see buildings. . . . We are flying low. . . . We are . . . way too low." At 8:46, Flight 11 crashes into the North Tower of New York City's World Trade Center at 490 mph.

When Riesett arrives at 8:55 a.m. her staff is gathered around a television in the department's conference room, eyes glued to the screen. No one notices as she walks by. Though TV and radio networks interrupted regular programming at 8:49, she is still unaware of the crash. She's in her office only a minute when the phone rings.

"Mom, have you seen the news?" Calling from Manhattan, her son is concerned about an uncle who works in the World Trade Center. "Do you know which tower or floor?" he asks. When she answers "no" to both questions, he says he'll call her back.

Joining her staff in front of the TV, Riesett sees people jumping to certain death as another jumbo jet takes aim at

FACING PAGE: *This photo of the World Trade Center's twin towers was taken from the New Jersey side of the Hudson River on September 7, 2001—just four days before 9/11's tragic events—by Monumental policyholder Deborah Steele who was visiting New York with her family.*

the Trade Center's South Tower. At 9:05, Andrew Card, chief of staff for President George W. Bush, enters a classroom in Sarasota, Florida, where Bush is reading to elementary school children. Live cameras capture the interruption. He whispers in the president's ear: "A second plane hit the second tower. America is under attack."

The Sales Support staff is still watching at 9:18 when CNN confirms "planes hijacked before crash"; at 9:32, when the Secret Service orders Vice President Cheney to evacuate the White House; at 9:41, when CNN's Breaking News bulletin reads "Fire at the Pentagon"; and at 9:45, when the FAA shuts down U.S. airspace and grounds all aircraft.

Shortly before ten, Riesett's phone rings again. She heads to her office to take the call.

One year after September 11, 2001, Americans had not forgotten the sacrifice made that day by firemen, policemen and other first responders. A policyholder submitted this photo in Monumental's "Proud to be an American" 2002 calendar photo contest.

"Mom, I'm in a client's office on an upper floor, 20th Street in Chelsea," says her son. "I can see the Twin Towers from here. Uncle Kevin should be okay. Dunn & Bradstreet is on the 14th floor of the North Tower."

Mother and son are still talking at 9:59 a.m. when he looks out the window. "One of the towers just collapsed, Mom! It's down, totally gone! All I can see is smoke!" At 10:28, the second tower falls, burying thousands of Trade Center employees, firemen, policemen and first responders in the rubble. When asked later that day to estimate the number of casualties, New York mayor Rudy Giuliani replies, "More than any of us can bear."

Before noon, another 125 military and civilian personnel die following Flight 77's fiery crash into the Pentagon. All thirty-seven passengers and seven crew members aboard Flight 93 also perish when their aircraft plunges into a field southeast of Pittsburgh. Among the day's estimated 2,974 fatalities are seven Monumental Life policyholders—six men and a woman. One is a New Jersey resident. Claim records confirm that three others died at the Pentagon.

At 8:30 p.m., President Bush addresses the nation: "Today, our way of life, our very freedom came under attack in a series of deliberate and deadly terrorist attacks. . . . These acts shattered steel, but they cannot dent the steel of American resolve." Before going to bed that night, he writes in his diary: "The Pearl Harbor of the 21st century took place today. . . . We think it's Osama bin Laden."

With airports shut down, U.S. borders closed, 50,000 reservists called to active duty, and the country on high emergency alert on Friday, September 14, Monumental Life president Henry Hagan announces that he has postponed the company's 2001 Chairman's Round Table Sales Conference in Cancun:

> This week's tragic events have touched the spirit and heart of all Americans. Never before has our nation been so viciously attacked by fanatics who seem to have so little concern for human life. Earlier, following the direction of President Bush, we had resolved not to let these acts of terrorism impact our daily efforts to conduct our business or our plans to give you the recognition you deserve.
>
> Events unfolding in the last 24 hours have caused us to rethink our position. Our primary concern is the safety of our people. We prefer to err on the side of caution rather than put you in harm's way or subject you to unnecessary risk.
>
> I wish we could all be together in Cancun next week, as planned. Instead, please use this time to be thankful for the freedoms we enjoy as Americans and to build closer ties to your family. God bless you. God bless America.

The World Trade Center site was photographed in October 2001 by policyholder and Secret Service Agent Matt Jackson, who volunteered to help with clean-up.

DISASTERS DEFINE DECADE

The September 11 terrorist attacks were the first of many disasters that touched our country and the world in the opening years of the twenty-first century. By crashing jumbo jets loaded with fuel into the World Trade Center and the Pentagon—two symbols of U.S. economic and military power—al Qaeda operatives effectively demonstrated their hatred for America and our way of life. The 9/11 attacks, coupled with the anthrax poisoning of U.S. postal workers a few weeks later, confirmed that our cities and citizens were not as safe, or as immune to attack, as we had thought.

On October 26, 2001, President George W. Bush signed into law an Act of Congress "uniting and strengthening America by providing appropriate tools required to intercept and obstruct terrorism." The Patriot Act eased restrictions on intelligence gathering and dramatically expanded the authority of U.S. law enforcement agencies to monitor telephone and e-mail communication, search medical and financial records, protect U.S. borders, and detain and deport suspect individuals.

Not all acts of terror on U.S. soil came from abroad. Just four months earlier, on June 11, 2001, Timothy McVeigh, a gunnery sergeant in the Persian Gulf War, had been executed for killing 168 fellow Americans in the 1995 bombing of a federal office building in Oklahoma City. In April 1999, two students in Littleton, Colorado, had deliberately killed twelve of their Columbine High School classmates. Both attacks provoked debate about gun control, the availability of firearms, teen violence, and the safety of our schools, streets and workplaces.

Osama bin Laden was still at large. Saddam Hussein's "weapons of mass destruction" had not been found. And militants, extremists, rebels and suicide bombers continued to murder civilians around the world. By 2007 it seemed that no place on earth—not a resort in Bali, a theatre in Moscow, a London subway, a commuter train in Madrid, or a college campus in West Virginia—was safe from attack.

Least safe of all, perhaps, were U.S. troops fighting in Iraq and Afghanistan. Though President Bush declared an official end to combat operations on May 1, 2003, three weeks after Baghdad fell, U.S. soldiers in Iraq continued to die in roadside bombings and sniper attacks. Many were National Guard reservists, men and women who had left civilian jobs when called to active duty. Others, like the army's Major William F. Hecker, III—killed in An Najaf on January 5, 2006 —were "career military" who understood the risks of being deployed to a war zone. Major Hecker was one of twenty-two officers and NCOs (non-commissioned officers) insured by Monumental Life who died in Iraq between November 4, 2003, and October 1, 2007. Monumental paid claims totaling close to $2.8 million to their families and beneficiaries.

ABOVE: *Secret Service Agent Matt Jackson and his family—Chris, Nicholas and Alexis—pictured with President George W. Bush in 2007, have been Monumental Life policyholders since the mid-1990s. Jackson was assigned to a presidential protection unit early in the decade.*

RIGHT: *Monumental Life policyholder Maxie Webber recognized this dirty and battle-worn "Face from Fallujah" as that of her son, Lance Corporal Blake Miller, when it appeared in national newspapers in 2004.*

By the time President Bush announced the creation of the Cabinet-level Department of Homeland Security on November 25, 2002, "Beltway snipers" John Allen Muhammed and Lee Boyd Malvo had also killed ten people and traumatized thousands during a three-week rampage in the Baltimore-Washington Metropolitan area. Their random shootings—mostly at gas stations and parking lots just minutes from the Pentagon—cancelled school trips and athletic events and forced many area residents to hide in their homes for days.

When the U.S. space shuttle *Columbia* exploded on February 1, 2003, killing all seven astronauts aboard, who could have blamed the American people for questioning whether it had been an accident or another act of terror?

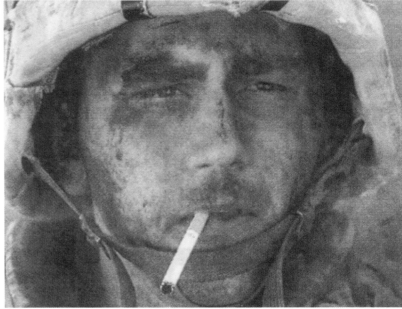

Not so prepared to face death and destruction were the thousands of victims around the world who perished in natural disasters. On December 26, 2004, a tsunami off the coast of Indonesia claimed 226,000 lives. On October 2, 2005, an earthquake in Pakistan killed another 80,000. Hurricanes, mudslides in California and forest fires in Montana also threatened lives, as did AIDS, mad cow disease and birds carrying avian flu.

But it was Hurricane Katrina—flooding New Orleans and the U.S. Gulf Coast in late August 2005, killing 1,800 and leaving millions homeless—that touched American lives most deeply. Not since the San Francisco earthquake of 1906 had a major U.S. city been so devastated by the forces of nature. Americans were shaken by the magnitude of the disaster but even more so by the poor response and lack of preparedness by city, state and federal agencies.

Despite cell phones, instant messaging, modern communications networks, satellite weather stations, and rapid response warning systems, the decade's disasters reinforced the fact that we cannot control fanatics, prevent weather-related events, or depend on the government to meet all our needs. What we can do is take responsibility for ourselves, prepare as best we can for the unexpected, and protect our families' lives, health, incomes, homes and possessions with adequate insurance.

PREPARING FOR THE UNEXPECTED

In the immediate aftermath of September 11, American families worried every time loved ones left for work, boarded planes, traveled abroad, or failed to "check in" when delayed in getting home. Staying in touch and taking care of one another became higher priorities. So did making sure family members and dependents were provided for, just in case something happened.

After a steady, twenty-two year decline in adult ownership of life insurance from 72 percent to 61 percent between 1976 and 1998, figures industry-wide had begun to inch up in 1999. By 2004, LIMRA (Life Insurance Marketing and Research Association) reported that 68 percent of U.S. adults owned either individual life insurance, group insurance, or both. The same year, LIMRA's Ownership Study reported that 44 percent of American households (48 million homes!) either did not own life insurance or realized that they needed more coverage.

Families in Monumental's chosen middle and lower-income target market—the largest but most underserved market in the United States—were among those who acknowledged that they were underinsured. Between 1999 and 2003, new life insurance issued by Monumental's Career Agency, PreNeed and Military distribution channels grew by 55 percent—from $4.0 billion to $6.2 billion.

Were ads, sponsored by LIFE (the Life and Health Foundation for Education) and appearing nationwide in consumer magazines, making the difference? Were families hearing and taking to heart the message that life insurance should be the foundation of a sound financial plan? Had the decade's tragedies prompted more families to protect their loved ones? Most probably, it was a combination of emotional and financial factors coupled with stories appearing nightly on the evening news.

LEFT: *The decade's manmade and natural disasters reminded Americans that "Life Happens" and tragedy can strike—anytime, any place—often when we least expect it.*

PROTECTING SAVINGS, PERSONAL INFORMATION

When the "dot com" bubble burst in 2001, deflating the value of many high-tech stocks, thousands of U.S. consumers lost much of their life's savings. Hoping to become "instant millionaires" in the 1990s, they had invested pensions and retirement funds in fast-growing, start-up ".com" companies. The technology stocks had soared quickly, but gains were not guaranteed. Less sophisticated investors learned the hard way that buying stocks and mutual funds involved more risk than they could handle.

Scandals at Enron, WorldCom, Arthur Anderson, Tyco, ImClone and elsewhere also prompted consumers to question how much they could trust corporate America. Who was telling the truth about income, debt, earnings and financial strength? Were pension funds safe? Whose accountants were "cooking the books" or using stockholder earnings to pay extravagant salaries, perks and executive bonuses?

As scandals mushroomed, consumers looked for safety and security. They found both in life insurance, annuities and other financial products issued by strong, regularly audited, highly regulated companies that paid *promised* benefits.

In response to well-publicized bankruptcy and fraud investigations, Congress passed the Sarbanes-Oxley (SOX) Act of 2002. The legislation addressed not only accounting rules and internal controls but also integrity and ethics, goals and values, how companies conducted business, management's commitment to employees, and assignment of authority and responsibility. It required that the CEO and chief financial officer of every publicly traded company certify and sign audit reports stating that all financial statements accurately represented the company's operations and financial condition. SOX affected corporate risk management, controls and processes at Monumental and every AEGON USA business unit.

So did the Gramm, Leach, Bliley Privacy Act, also passed in 2002, and Do Not Call legislation passed in 2003. Life insurance companies gather personal information on millions of policyholders to be able to appropriately assess risk and assign rates. Putting controls in place to protect consumers and secure the privacy of their personal medical and financial records—while at the same time creating a sense of "transparency" and trust regarding a company's financial strength—created one of the industry's (and the decade's) most time-consuming and costly challenges.

NATIONAL DO NOT CALL REGISTRY

THERE WHEN WE WERE NEEDED

"Trying times are a true test of strength," wrote AEGON executives in the 2002 AEGON Americas Annual Marketing Report. In the difficult days following September 11, 2001, Monumental and every AEGON USA business unit remained focused on its responsibilities to clients and distributors. Employees worked steadily throughout the market disruption to answer questions, meet needs, and expedite claims for families impacted by the tragedy. Financially, AEGON's losses were moderate compared to most of its peers. The pre-tax amount reported for 9/11 claims alone, net of reinsurance, was $30 million.

The 9/11 tragedy united all Americans. Monumental employees across the country testified to the generosity of the entire AEGON USA organization with a stunning outpouring of employee giving that was matched two-for-one by the AEGON Transamerica Foundation's Special Relief Fund. The campaign provided $750,000 in scholarship money for dependents of military personnel killed in the Pentagon attack or on duty in the War against Terrorism.

AEGON employees around the world also responded generously to help tsunami victims. Matching employee contributions dollar-for-dollar, the foundation donated $1.1 million to international relief efforts coordinated by the American Red Cross and Habitat for Humanity International. When hurricanes struck the Gulf Coast nine months later, employees once again dug into their pockets. Donations totaling $272,000, matched by $428,000 from the foundation, helped rebuild schools in Louisiana's storm-ravaged Cameron Parish. Wanting to do even more, teams of Monumental and AEGON employees headed for Louisiana to help teachers, school board members and residents move supplies and clear damaged buildings.

Perhaps they are thankful for what they have— challenging and meaningful careers, competitive salaries, and excellent benefits that include group life and health insurance, pensions, 401k plans and stock options, tuition reimbursement and matching funds for donations to secondary schools, colleges and universities. Regardless of the reason, Monumental and AEGON employees throughout the country regularly give back to the communities they serve.

Agents and managers from Monumental's New Iberia office were part of an AEGON USA team that helped rebuild schools in western Louisiana's Cameron Parish after they were destroyed by Hurricane Rita.

RESPECT PEOPLE. MAKE MONEY. HAVE FUN

Such benefits support AEGON's motto: *"Respect people, Make money, Have fun."* The choice of words says a lot about the company's priorities and purpose, and why today, as one of the largest insurance organizations in the world, AEGON can promote *"Local Knowledge, Global Power"* as two reasons for its continuing success.

Since acquiring Providian in 1997 and Transamerica in 1999—including the California-based insurer's soaring and symbolic San Francisco tower—AEGON had become a more visible player in the higher-income, business, asset accumulation, retirement planning and reinsurance sectors of the U.S. insurance marketplace. Its acquisition of J. C. Penney's insurance operation in 2001 made Baltimore-based AEGON Direct Marketing Services, Inc. (ADMS) the country's leading direct marketer of life and supplemental health insurance products. (Many of the products sold by ADMS and other AEGON USA business units are issued under the "Monumental Life Insurance Company" name.) By 2005, AEGON had also expanded its presence in Europe with new business units in Slovakia, the Czech Republic and Poland.

The AEGON Executive Board—including American Donald J. Shepard, the Dutch insurer's first "trans-Atlantic" CEO and chairman—visits all AEGON business units around the world every three years, through a program called "Optiek," to share AEGON's corporate vision and goals with all employees. Even with telecommunications, electronic newsletters, telecommuting and telemarketing, such face-to-face contact is an AEGON priority.

Insurance is a people-driven, people-focused business, and people continue to be the organization's greatest asset. AEGON management around the world works hard to create positive work environments where employees can succeed, enjoy what they do, make money, and grow both personally and professionally. More than ever before, success in the global marketplace depends on respecting individual differences, embracing diversity, and building positive relationships with all "stakeholders"—co-workers, distributors, business partners, customers, stockholders, and the public.

RIGHT: *The AEGON executive board visits all AEGON business units every three years. Pictured here in 1998 are American Don Shepard—the Dutch insurer's first "trans-Atlantic" CEO and chairman—Paul van de Geijn, Kees Storm, and Henk van Wijk outside the AEGON USA and Monumental Life building in Baltimore.*

LEFT: *Henry G. Hagan, Monumental Life chairman, president and CEO, addressed the company's Career Agency field managers in February 2002.*

RIGHT: *Pat Baird, president and CEO of AEGON USA in 2002.*

"Corporate responsibility is about governance, integrity, ethical behavior, compliance with laws and regulations, and taking personal responsibility for actions and results," explained Hagan. "AEGON's Rules of the Road spell out who we are and how we do business. From the top down, they guide employee behavior and decisions. We must do things right, but also do the right things." That's why AEGON requires all U.S. employees—including Monumental Life career agents and managers—to complete annual, computer-based "Integrity Ed" courses focused on ethics, workplace etiquette, privacy, information security, financial reporting, and other topics.

"We often forget the significant impact of individual actions on corporate performance," he added. "Every day, employees throughout the U.S. bring our Core Values to life by treating people with respect, by telling the truth, and by acting ethically and responsibly."

CORPORATE RESPONSIBILITY

Industry leadership and success also depend on *how* profitable and sustainable growth is achieved. "Winning means more than finishing first," noted Monumental Life president Henry G. Hagan in February 2002. Addressing the company's Career Agency field managers, he emphasized, "Winning means finishing right. Respect the rules! Guard your reputation. Avoid shortcuts. Listen to people. Empathize. Being the '*best*' in the life insurance business means putting customers first and helping families improve their lives by selling the right product . . . to the right person . . . at the right price."

In 2003, Pat Baird, president and CEO of AEGON USA, Inc., selected Hagan to chair the U.S. Corporate Responsibility Committee. Later that fall, committee members representing a cross-section of AEGON USA business units delivered "*Integrity in Action*" materials to reinforce AEGON's Code of Conduct, "Rules of the Road" and Core Values—Quality, Respect, Transparency and Trust.

RIGHT: *AEGON requires all U.S. employees to complete computer-based "Integrity Ed" courses focused on ethics, workplace etiquette, privacy, information security, financial reporting and other topics.*

Respect people. Make money. Have fun.

Treat others as we expect to be treated.

LEFT: *AEGON USA's "Integrity in Action" cube reminded employees that, when it comes to corporate responsibility, actions are more important than words.*

Practically Paperless!

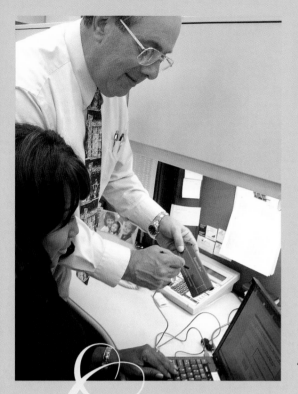

E-Z app, e-signatures and e-forms all contributed to Monumental's going "practically paperless" in the new millennium.

GONE ARE THE DAYS when applicants for Monumental Life insurance signed a dozen or more different forms. Thanks to "agent automation" and new technology, customers complete E-Z apps, E-forms and E-signatures electronically for agents to transmit electronically over phone lines. When E-Z apps arrive in Underwriting and New Business, they enter an automated queue that distributes work to department employees. The long-term goal is to streamline procedures to eliminate as much hands-on processing of applications as possible.

Likewise, policyholders no longer have to depend on the U.S. mail to pay their premiums. Many are saving time and money with automatic bank draft. In fact, since 2002, agents and policyholders rarely touch paper applications, forms, checks or envelopes. Name and address changes, beneficiary changes—all can be completed electronically, right on an agent's laptop!

"Automatic" and "electronic" are the names of today's game at Monumental. All career agents have laptops with integrated systems software. Client data is entered only once, stored and used to update laptop-based needs analysis, illustration, account management and application programs. The system can even generate leads!

In Monumental's new "practically paperless" world, potential field office recruits also complete initial interviews electronically, using an interactive voice response system. Agent personnel, training and award records are stored in an electronic database. And laptop-based training is becoming the norm. Just as important, field management no longer waits to receive printouts of monthly production reports. With Report.web, they can check the status of pending policies, arrears, lapses and placements every day and access updated reports, as needed, on their laptops.

E-mail and Intranet connectivity make it possible to deliver messages instantaneously to every home office employee and field office. Help Desk personnel also troubleshoot field laptop, PC and printer problems from their work stations in Baltimore.

However, where and when customers need face-to-face service or answers to questions, we also have live agents and Service Center representatives on call to respond. High-Tech or High Touch? Monumental provides both depending on our customers' needs.

INTEGRITY IN ACTION

Monumental Life's commitment to integrity and respect for people made news in June 2003 when the company announced it had signed an agreement with the Maryland Insurance Administration (MIA) to increase death benefits on 400,000 in-force policies and pay additional death benefits on policies that may have been issued with race-distinct rates. The practice, approved by many state regulators between the 1930s and the mid-1960s (before Congress passed the Civil Rights Act), based premiums on a race's life expectancy.

Though Monumental never charged race-distinct rates, it had—through acquisitions in the 1990s—assumed responsibility for approximately five million policies issued by more than 260 companies. Early in 2000 the company found evidence of situations, especially in the South, where acquired policies may have been priced differently based on race. Hagan and General Counsel Stacey Boyer immediately called the Maryland state insurance commissioner and commissioners in other states to inform them that policies issued in their states might still reflect race-based pricing.

Over the next two and a half years, the company worked diligently with state regulators to identify plans of insurance eligible for increased death benefits. Monumental Life's agreement with the MIA provided for payment of $35 million in additional death benefits—an average $72 per policy, at no cost to the policyholder—mostly on policies with small $200 to $500 face amounts. As part of the agreement, Monumental also set aside $2 million to be donated to charities serving the needs and interests of African Americans, as directed by state regulators.

"With the help and guidance of the MIA," said Hagan, "we have been able to reach an amicable agreement that benefits policyholders, beneficiaries, and the communities we serve." By doing the right thing,

Monumental cemented decades-long relationships with many policyholder families. The announcement caught the attention of an African American media organization meeting that week in Baltimore. "We're proud of what you're doing," said a member who contacted the company's communications officer. "Call if we can help."

LEADING FROM THE MIDDLE

Monumental Life celebrates its 150th year of serving Maryland citizens on March 5, 2008. One of the oldest, largest and most highly regarded life insurance companies in the country, it is a leader among its middle-market peers. In Baltimore and throughout the U.S., Monumental employees support the company's mission to "help American families improve the quality of their lives."

That means *all* American families—regardless of religion, race, nationality, color, age, income or social status. Monumental's millions of policyholders represent a cross-section of America. Recent immigrants and lower-income urban families who need help finding affordable coverage. Thirty-something suburban homeowners who want their children to go to college. "Empty nesters" in their forties, fifties and sixties seeking advice and solutions for retirement planning and long-term care. Elderly, home-bound policyholders living on Social Security checks who want to make sure they can die with dignity.

As other companies and agents abandon lower and middle-income families in favor of products and face amounts with higher commissions, Monumental remains committed to this market. The company's Career Agency organization—with more than 2,200 agents and managers in twenty-two states—is one of the largest in the country still making traditional "house calls" on families with $15,000 to $75,000 of annual income. Nearly 60 percent of all U.S. households fit into this group.

LEFT: *In June 2003, Monumental announced it had signed an agreement with the Maryland Insurance Administration to increase the death benefit on policies that may have been issued with race-distinct rates. The company tried to find eligible policyholders by placing ads in local newspapers.*

BELOW: *These posters, produced and distributed by Monumental in 2006, reminded agents and managers of their commitment to middle-American families.*

MIDDLE AMERICA NEEDS YOU!

BECOME THEIR ADVOCATE

Monumental's traditional life and supplemental health insurance products are designed and priced to meet basic protection, final expense, and income-replacement needs. The company also distributes products through funeral homes in the PreNeed marketplace; through First Command Financial Services Inc., an independent marketing organization (IMO) serving the military market; and through IMOs focused on meeting the final expense needs of America's senior citizens. Identifying additional marketing channels, new sources of recruits, and cross-selling opportunities to better serve lower- and middle-income consumers will remain a high Monumental priority throughout the decade.

MONUMENTAL'S "TOTAL PRODUCT"

In Monumental's market, it is advice—more than products, price or the company's financial strength—that keeps customers loyal and prompts them to refer agents to their friends and family. Year after year, industry studies confirm that "life insurance is sold, not bought."

Despite the decade's tragedies and the unexpected loss of younger friends and family members, no one likes to think about death. Many people still refuse to admit it will ever touch them personally. They procrastinate and put off making a decision, saying "I don't have the money," "I don't know what to buy," or "I'll think about it tomorrow." But death often comes without warning, as it did for thousands on 9/11.

That's why Monumental's "total product" continues to include not only death protection and cash values but also a "promise"—a promise to provide the "value-added" benefits of advice, education, service, family reviews, needs analysis, and affordable solutions. A promise to advocate for spouses, children and dependents whose lives will continue after a breadwinner passes away. A promise to meet needs, build long-term relationships, and deliver responsive service. A promise to be there when policyholders, families, and surviving loved ones need our help the most. Studies confirm that when lower and middle-income families *do* buy, they prefer to buy face-to-face, from an agent they know and trust.

As our agents and employees continued to knock on doors, deliver claim checks, automate processes, improve efficiency, and comply with increasing regulation throughout the decade, President Hagan reminded them repeatedly, "I am proud of you. I am proud of what *we* do!"

AGENTS FOR CHANGE

Life insurance is one of the most regulated industries in the world. And maybe it has to be. As life insurers, companies like Monumental Life have a responsibility to protect lives, homes, incomes, dreams and futures. In 2007, Monumental paid out approximately one million dollars *per day* in claims benefits to help the families we insure!

Industry associations—including the ACLI (American Council of Life Insurance), NAIFA (National Association of Insurance and Financial Advisors) and LIFE—continue to lobby for insurance-friendly legislation. Since 2005 a new "grassroots" association called Agents for Change has also been lobbying for an Optional Federal Charter. Meeting face-to-face with senators, congressmen and their aides on Capitol Hill and in their districts, the industry's agents point out that the current system of state-based regulation presents many challenges for insurance companies and their agents. Ultimately the system also increases the price insurers charge for their products. Insurers and agents must be licensed in every state where they do business. Getting products approved and "to market" is cumbersome, costly, and time-consuming. An optional federal charter (OFC) would eliminate the need for state-by-state review and state-specific marketing materials.

Monumental Life and AEGON are among the growing list of life insurance companies that support passage of a bill making federal legislation an option for insurers operating in many U.S. states. "Selling life insurance doesn't stop at state borders," notes Duane Davies, vice president, Sales Support. At its core, adds Peter Ludgin, executive director of Agents for Change, "this issue is about choice, competition, open markets and what is best for insurance consumers."

MEETING NEEDS

Throughout the decade, the LIFE Foundation has reminded consumers and insurers alike that "Life insurance isn't for the people who die; it's for the people who live." Moreover, "for as long as there are people who die and survivors who live," says David Woods, LIFE's president and CEO, "there will be a need for life insurance."

On Sunday evening, September 9, 2007, LIFE held its twelfth annual "realLIFEstories" banquet in Washington. Among those who spoke were Monumental Life policyholder Richelle Hecker—widow and mother of four young children, whose husband, Major Bill Hecker, was killed serving his country in Iraq in January 2006—and her agent Samantha Hilliard. Because Major Hecker provided adequately for his wife and children, their standard of living will not change, despite his death.

Another banquet speaker, college student Brinja Canter, told a very different story. Brinja's father, a business owner, died unexpectedly shortly after his life insurance policy lapsed. The family lost their home. Brinja, her mother and three younger brothers lived day-to-day for several years, in motels and inexpensive apartments, never knowing if they'd be able to pay the rent. Today her mother has a steady job and has purchased a home, thanks to friends who helped her with a down payment. Brinja is completing college with loans and a $5,000 scholarship from LIFE. However, she said, had her father kept his life insurance in

Father's Love Secures Family's Future

W

Monumental Life policyholder Susan Credle, pictured here with her grandchild, realized the importance of having life insurance when her thirty-six-year-old husband passed away unexpectedly in 2004.

HILE Susan Credle spent her days nursing patients back to health, her husband Ed worked in retail. In his free time, Ed loved to fish, play basketball and be with his two daughters—Tia, age eight, and Jasmine, age six. "He was a devoted father," said Susan. "His daughters were his pride and joy."

Like most young couples who own their own home, Ed and Susan needed both their incomes to cover everyday living expenses and provide a few extras for their girls. It was hard to save or plan too far ahead.

Through his employer, Ed was covered by a group life insurance policy. He felt more fortunate than some of his friends whose jobs provided no life or health insurance benefits. Ed also had a $10,000 permanent, whole life policy with Monumental. But he realized that, should anything happen to him, this coverage would not be enough to provide the kind of life he wanted for his family. He purchased a $90,000 term policy, which was what he could afford at the time.

Ed died suddenly, at age thirty-six, during a neighborhood basketball game in 2004. The check Susan received allowed her to pay off her home mortgage and work part-time so she could spend more time with her children. With the family's immediate and future needs in mind, her Monumental agent provided protection on Susan's life and an annuity to meet her long-term goals of retirement and college education for the children.

"Having that life insurance made a huge difference in our lives," said Susan. "My advice to others would definitely be to buy as much as you can afford. We never thought this would happen to us. Ed was only 36 years old and in apparent good health. When he died, the check I received was the single most useful thing that helped me and my daughters through the tough months that followed."

Life Insurance . . .

Protecting Hopes and Dreams

Major William Hecker, a Monumental Life policyholder, was killed in Iraq in January 2006. Because he believed in life insurance, life will go on as he planned for his wife, Richelle (above right), and their four children. The family's First Command agent, Samantha Hilliard, is pictured at top.

THEY HAD BUILT a loving life together, started a family, raised four children, ages two to ten, bought their first house, and were firmly focused on the future. Then one day in January 2006 it all came crashing down for thirty-four-year-old Richelle Hecker. Her husband, Major William F. Hecker, III, was dead—killed while serving with the army in An Najaf, Iraq, just six weeks after beginning his first tour of duty in that war-torn region.

Family, friends, neighbors, and members of the close-knit military family in the small central Texas community near Fort Hood offered support and consolation, but nothing could change the reality of what had happened. Even so, she knew her family was much better off than many others who had lost a spouse or child in Iraq.

Richelle and Bill, a West Point graduate, believed in life insurance. They recognized that financial planning was the responsible thing to do. Their shared goals were to optimize retirement options, provide for their children's education, and make sure the family would be able to maintain their standard of living should tragedy strike.

Planning was my husband's big gift," notes Richelle. "He was very good at seeing 20 to 30 years down the road. I was good at making sure we made it through the month." Whenever they had a child or another major life change occurred, the couple met with their First Command Financial Services advisor, reviewed needs, and "exercised every guaranteed insurability option possible."

As a result, today Richelle isn't worried about immediate finances, where to live, or college funding for her kids. "That area, at least, is under control." Having just relocated her family to a new home in Colorado Springs she says, "planning has enabled life to go on the same way financially." She can continue to be a stay-at-home Mom for the foreseeable future.

"The kids are all doing well," she adds proudly. "Everybody's getting "A's." Eleven-year-old Alexandra wants to go to West Point and become an astronaut. Victoria, age eight, already shows a gift for teaching. Five-year-old Cordelia has an engineer's mechanical mind and enjoys taking things apart. Three-year-old William IV is good at "putting things together and likes everything to have a place."

"We did our planning together," says Richelle, who once worked as a secretary to her father, a life insurance agent. "Bill had a combination of government insurance and commercial insurance, the latter primarily through Monumental Life. There were greater amounts of coverage on Bill, but I had enough that Bill could pay for a full-time nanny if something were to happen to me."

"Bill and Richelle did all the right things," says Samantha Hilliard, the Hecker's agent and a district advisor for First Command Financial Services serving the Fort Hood area. "They didn't expect it but they knew it could happen and they were prepared. Looking back, I think she is very proud that Bill took care of the family."

LEFT: *College student Brinja Canter's story reinforced what happens to families when they are not protected by life insurance.*

force, the benefits would have helped her family retain their comfortable lifestyle. Instead, even today, there is little money for extras.

There will always be people who won't admit they need life insurance. There will continue to be families, like Brinja's, who drop their coverage just when they need it most. There will also be couples like the Heckers—between ten and twelve million Americans every year—who understand the importance of life insurance, who increase their coverage as lives and needs change, and who make sure loved ones are protected, no matter what happens. In between these extremes are fifty million Americans annually who say they need coverage but never get around to buying it.

FULFILLING THE PROMISE

As this is being written, on September 11, 2007, six years to the day after terrorists changed our lives forever, U.S. life insurers and their agents are committed to doing all they can to safeguard the futures of America's citizens. More than ever, American families need life insurance as a "safety net" to protect against losses incurred following a family member's death, illness, or disability, or the economic instability resulting from job or income loss.

As we look ahead, finding ways to reach, serve and adequately protect America's millions of uninsured and underinsured lower and middle-income families is the life insurance industry's biggest challenge. Though we don't know what else we may face in the years ahead—economic turmoil, political change, increased regulation, cultural conflict, or life-threatening natural disasters—we do know that death is the only certain thing in life.

Our agents and employees must be prepared to meet middle-America's growing need for insurance, education and professional advice. "Education is empowerment," says Henry G. Hagan. "The information we provide enables the people we serve to make more informed decisions about their futures. As an industry, however, we can only help others if we ourselves are educated." That is why Monumental encourages its career agents to join NAIFA and requires them to earn the "LUTCF" (Fellow, Life Underwriting Training Council) designation. It's why employees in Monumental's administrative offices complete courses offered by the Life Office Management Association (LOMA) and earn the "FLMI" (Fellow, Life Management Institute) designation.

"The laws regulating privacy, security, financial reporting, taxes, and compliance continue to impact how insurance and financial service organizations conduct their business," adds Hagan. "Educated professionals are better prepared to understand and meet our industry's and our customers' changing needs."

As members of the "Task Force for Future," Hagan and life insurance industry executives from around the country have committed themselves to identifying issues, challenges, answers and solutions to meet middle-America's increasing need for financial security and protection. "Together, we must find ways for our industry to fulfill the promise we've made to help families protect their lives and futures."

Middle America needs us, and Monumental Life will be there, as we have been for 150 years, to meet those needs and help American families take care of those they love.

The LUTCF is one of many designations that life insurance professionals can earn to increase their knowledge of the industry.

A S A GROUP, they are as different as anyone could imagine from the officers who founded the company in 1858. They are also as different from one another as they could be. Companies don't use a mold any longer to turn out officers, especially when women stand shoulder-to-shoulder with men, sharing leadership and responsibility.

Entering the new millennium, Monumental's senior officers are as likely to wear high heels and leopard prints as club ties, button-down shirts and dark suits. At 7:00 a.m. you might find any of them working out at home or a gym, walking their dogs, blow-drying their hair, checking their e-mail, or answering cell phones on their way to the office. You might even find one feeding his toddler twins and another vacuuming his garage with one of his nine (got that?!) vacuums. They are an interesting and unique group of men and women.

Two have perfected the art of sunbathing and get their nails done regularly at a salon. Another is as comfortable in workout clothes and a baseball cap as she is in a suit. Two wear their Boy Scout leader uniforms proudly. One can "count cards" and is banned from several casinos. A few enjoy hunting, fishing, snow skiing and scuba. Others follow their college sports teams and regularly exchange scores. When the Baltimore Ravens won the Super Bowl, they all wore purple, and when AEGON-sponsored Zach Johnson won the Masters Golf Tournament in 2007, they ordered "Zach hats"!

Costumed Monumental officers have performed on stage to a tune from *H.M.S. Pinafore* and have been called to the "bridge" of the "Starship Monumental" for a briefing. But they rarely say "Aye, aye, Captain" without thinking carefully. An independent group, they are one of the most experienced and knowledgeable management teams in the business. And Henry Hagan, their leader, doesn't expect them to be rubber stamps. He encourages this team to challenge, disagree, express their opinions, and make decisions based on what's best for the company, its employees, policyholders, stockholders and business partners.

Six of Monumental's thirteen senior officers—including Hagan himself, Phil White, Duane Davies and the company's three senior regional vice presidents—started their careers as agents in the field. Phil White, vice president of Field Operations, joined Monumental in 1973. He is responsible for field recruiting, licensing, management succession and development as well as field budgets, leases and audits. Duane Davies, vice president, Sales Support, followed his father down a career path that began at Commonwealth Life in 1974. Today, he is responsible for products and sales systems, field training, sales incentives, communications, and creative services.

The company's three "homegrown" senior RVPs—Charles Green, Steve Jecker, and Prentice ("P.J.") West—have over 100 years of combined field experience and hands-on "know-how." Together, they share responsibility for the productivity and sales success of more than 150 field offices.

Ladies Share Leadership . . .

Management Team for the Millennium!

Ben Jenkins, vice president of PreNeed Sales, is also no stranger to the business. His father was a district manager with Peoples Life. His brother, B. Larry Jenkins, was president and CEO of Peoples Life and Monumental Life before retiring in 1999. Ben was a personal producing general agent with Peoples before joining Monumental in 1983. He helped build Monumental's PreNeed business beginning in 1986.

Another "homegrown" officer is Ralph Arnold, senior vice president and chief operations officer. Affectionately called "Tightwad," Arnold joined Monumental in 1972 and completed both his college degrees and CPA designation through the company's Tuition Reimbursement Program. Today, he is responsible for accounting, budget, treasury, human resources, compensation and benefits, administration and information technology.

Susan Reier came to Monumental from Citibank in 1985. Promoted to vice president in 1996 and chief administrative officer in 2002, her no-nonsense style and insistence on efficiency and accountability have enabled the company to quadruple in size since 1990 without significantly increasing Administration staffing. Carol Davies, another take-charge, no-nonsense leader, entered the business as a clerk at Commonwealth Life in 1979. Following the Monumental/Providian merger in 1997, she moved to Baltimore to become project leader for the Providian Agency Group conversion and consolidation. She was promoted to vice president, chief information officer in 2002.

H. Stacey Boyer, an attorney with Monumental since 1985 and vice president and general counsel since 1993, also has no time for nonsense. The company's growth—coupled with increasing industry regulation, compliance and litigation issues—keep her quite busy. On any given day, she could be drafting contracts, testifying in court, meeting with state insurance commissioners, or negotiating compliance resolutions.

Steve Cammarata, Monumental Life's chief actuary since 2000, joined the company in 1984 as an actuarial student. He is responsible for all financial reporting and product development actuarial functions and plays a central role in the company's merger and acquisition activity and IMO Final Expense marketing. Ken McKusick, vice president, Product Development and military liaison officer, also an actuary, joined Monumental in 1988. He ensures that Monumental's risks are properly priced and is responsible for the company's relationship with First Command Financial Services, an independent marketing organization that serves the military market.

Heading the organization since 1998 is Henry G. Hagan, Monumental Life's president, chairman and CEO. He learned the business "from the ground up," collecting premiums on a debit for his family's North Carolina home service life insurance company. Since joining Monumental Life in 1981 he has assumed positions of increasing responsibility. He is passionate about the business and proud of the role the company plays in helping lower and middle-income American families improve the quality of their lives.

On this team's shoulders today rests the current and future success of Maryland's first life insurer. It's a heavy weight, but one they are well-equipped to handle as the company moves ahead to make its mark in the new millennium, including celebrating 200 years in 2058!

When Phil White (standing, second from right) was honored by the Baltimore Area Council of the Boy Scouts of America in 2004, fellow officers (clockwise) Ben Jenkins (also in Scout uniform), Henry Hagan, Bob Grannan, Ralph Arnold, Duane Davies and Stacey Boyer were on hand to salute him.

Senior officers donned costumes to salute their captain on stage during the 2003 "Victory on the Seas" sales conference and joined him on the bridge of the "Starship Monumental" during a Leadership Weekend conference for managers and award winners.

Community Service . . .
LIVING OUR MISSION

*S*OME COMPANIES TALK about corporate responsibility. Monumental employees live it every day. From the agents who sell our products and deliver death claims, to the employees who respond to customer questions and requests, to the technicians who design customer-focused tools and delivery systems, to the many individuals and teams who volunteer in their communities—Monumental and its people take care of people. The company's mission "to help American families improve the quality of their lives" is more than mere words. It's the reason we've remained in business for 150 years.

Throughout its history, Monumental Life has improved lives by providing life insurance and disability benefits. But it has also helped the community by investing in railroads, roads and Baltimore's first sewer system. As soldiers fought in two world wars, the company bought war bonds and invested in companies that built the airplanes, electronics and communications systems to protect our American way of life. During the "Baby Boom" in the late 1940s and 1950s, Monumental provided jobs and home mortgages for hundreds of returning GIs.

When families and businesses fled downtown Baltimore in the 1960s and 1970s, Monumental committed to stay. Its officers played a critical leadership role in creating a coalition of local banks and businesses to help rebuild our North Charles Street neighborhood. Since then— realizing that real "quality of life" includes more than having basic necessities—Monumental and AEGON have donated millions of dollars to local schools and universities, hospitals and nursing homes, art museums, the Baltimore Symphony Orchestra and other cultural and civic institutions that enhance lives.

Monumental employees have been rolling up their sleeves to help those in need since the Red Cross "blood mobile" first parked on Chase Street during the Korean War. They've donated blood, dressed dolls, collected Toys for Tots, filled mitten trees for needy families, and delivered baskets of food and holiday turkeys to struggling policyholders. They contribute generously to the United Way every year and walk annually for the March of Dimes. They raise money for cancer research by volunteering and collecting pledges for the Susan G. Komen Foundation's "Race for the Cure." Since September 11, 2001, Monumental and AEGON employees have also donated hundreds of thousands of dollars—as well as food, blankets and other necessities—to help hurricane and tsunami victims, and the families of soldiers killed in Iraq and on duty fighting the War on Terror.

In communities throughout the United States, field and home office employees continue to donate their time and talent, as they have for decades—serving as Scout leaders and volunteer firemen, mentoring high school students, manning hot lines, visiting shut-ins, driving senior citizens to doctor appointments, coaching Little League teams, serving food in local soup kitchens, picking up highway trash, building playgrounds, and renovating Habitat for Humanity homes for new homeowners.

Our business is all about people. Since our founding in 1858, the company and its employees have reached out to help those in need. Our own jobs, livelihood and income depend on being there when families need us most. More than ever before, today's employees realize that living Monumental Life's mission also means giving back to the communities they serve.

BLOOD FOR LIFE
Monumental employees— including officers Dwight Bartlett and Ed Barrett, pictured here—have participated in annual blood drives since 1953, when Vice President Fred Wehr, chairman of Baltimore's Red Cross Fund appeal, first invited Red Cross volunteers to set up equipment in the home office. Every year since, employees have donated life-giving blood to meet the city's growing need.

◀ DECORATIONS, BASKETS FOR THE NEEDY

With candles in the windows, twinkling lights, and a holiday message over the door, the Charles Street façade looked more like a lovely old home in 1961 than the corporate headquarters that it was. Inside, generous Monumental "elves" were decorating trees, wrapping gifts, and filling food baskets, as they did every year for decades, to help the Baltimore City Police Department and other charities play "Santa" to the community.

▼ DRESSED DOLLS, TOYS FOR TOTS

In 1963 employees dressed one hundred dolls and donated over two hundred toys for needy and handicapped children. With so many gifts under the tree, Monumental's lobby soon began to look like a large family's living room on Christmas Eve. The doll program was still going strong in 1976.

▲ KEEP IT CLEAN!

Monumental's Dan Gibson and his staff formed semi-monthly Saturday "SWAT" teams in 1993 to pick up trash along a two-mile stretch of highway near LaPlata, Maryland. The State Highway Department provided signs, orange vests, hats and trash bags. Agent Cliff Boyden and Dan Gibson, pictured, and others provided the manpower.

▲ TEACHING TEAMWORK

Monumental veteran John Gulo, coach of the 1992 Little League "Yankees" in his Illinois hometown, is just one of many employees who have reached out to coach youth baseball, basketball, soccer and swimming teams during their careers. "Through sports," said Gulo, "kids master the fundamentals of coordination, teamwork and sportsmanship."

▲ DISTRICTS DONATE TURKEYS

Like many field offices, the Benny Dahdah District in northern New Jersey donated holiday turkeys and food baskets to help needy families. The sixty-three turkeys bought in 1997 were so appreciated, Dahdah (center front) reported, that the office made it an annual project.

▼ WE LEARN. WE GROW. WE GIVE. WE GET BACK. WE HAVE FUN!

Monumental formed a partnership with Baltimore's Mergenthaler Vocational Technical High School in 2000 to help the city's high school students stay in school, graduate, go to college and prepare for financially rewarding, satisfying careers. Approximately twenty "MERVO" juniors and seniors are selected annually and matched with employees representing every area of the company. One day a month during the school year, students meet one-on-one with mentors at Monumental, experience the corporate world, work on group projects, and help raise money for scholarships and service projects. In 2004 the company's program was honored as the best corporate mentoring program in Maryland. In 2007 the group pictured visited Baltimore's Reginald F. Lewis Museum of Maryland African American History and Culture.

▲ LEARNING FOR LIFE

During the 1996/1997 school year, Michigan district manager Mike Abdella (center) was one of four field managers who worked with underprivileged children through Monumental's participation in the Boy Scouts of America's "Learning for Life" program. Though taught by teachers, Abdella provided needed funding and visited the classroom regularly to reinforce the importance of a healthy lifestyle, good values and responsible citizenship.

▲ I MADE IT!

Graduating from kindergarten may not seem like such a big achievement, but graduating from college certainly is for many students. This photo of Candace Boyd won first prize in Monumental's 1997 "Faces of Our Future" calendar photo contest. Her proud parents and policyholders from Martinsville, Virginia, directed the company to make a $1,000 donation, in their name, to the United Negro College Fund. The Boyd family presented the check on TV during the Lou Rawls national telethon.

◀ ▲ MARCH OF DIMES

Every year since the 1950s, dozens of Monumental field and home office employees have solicited pledges and walked through downtown Baltimore. Though the route and distance have changed over the years, the goal is still the same—to help the March of Dimes fight polio and prevent birth defects.

▶ BUILDING HABITATS

Monumental's annual Habitat for Humanity "build teams" arrive wearing jeans, sweatshirts and hats with work gloves tucked into their back pockets. After clearing out trash, putting up wall studs and laying down floors, among other tasks, they leave dirty, sore and tired. Monumental is one of thirteen financial institutions—including AEGON USA and Baltimore's AEGON Direct Marketing Services, Inc. (ADMS)—in the Financial Services Round Table that each year jointly sponsors and renovates a house in Baltimore City. Houses are "bought" by local applicants who must put in three hundred hours of "sweat equity" labor to qualify for subsidized loans. Partnering with Habitat enables us to be a good neighbor and help families become homeowners.

▼ RACING FOR A CURE

Breast cancer continues to strike American women, but fewer are dying of the disease. Thanks to organizations like the Susan G. Komen Foundation, additional money is now available for education, early diagnosis, research and new treatments. Dozens of AEGON and Monumental employees, such as this lively group in 2004, now walk, run, raise money and serve as food court volunteers for the annual Baltimore-area Komen "Race for the Cure." Field agents and managers also man our annual booth to distribute fingerprint kids and information about Monumental's CancerCheck product.

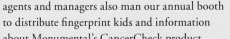

▲ HURRICANE RITA RELIEF

When hurricanes repeatedly battered eastern Florida in 2005, the company responded by helping employees and their families in Miami, Ft. Lauderdale and Belgrade who suffered losses from the storm. Pictured here are Ft. Lauderdale's Doris Riles and Regional Vice President Ray White, who drove the U-Haul truck from location to location.

▼ AEGON FOUNDATION FUNDS CANCER RESEARCH

Since 1996 scientists at the Sydney Kimmel Comprehensive Cancer Center at Johns Hopkins in Baltimore have been able to continue their research into last-stage treatments for breast, ovarian, colon and other cancers, thanks to $2.4 million provided by the AEGON/Transamerica Foundation. The foundation's current financial commitment helps provide cancer patients with some of the newest drugs and the most innovative and advanced treatments and therapies in the world. Many of the Cancer Center's patients have exhausted all treatment options. They look to the center for help in extending or improving the quality of their lives.

◄ COMMITTED TO KENNEDY KRIEGER'S KIDS

Monumental Life president and CEO Henry G. Hagan joined the Kennedy Krieger Institute's board of directors in 1999 and has been one of the Baltimore organization's biggest champions and cheerleaders ever since. Elected vice-chair in 2002 and chairman of the board in 2007, Hagan and AEGON are committed to helping Kennedy Krieger achieve its mission to help children and adolescents with brain disorders achieve their potential and participate as fully as possible in family, community and school life. AEGON is a sponsor of the organization's annual holiday "Festival of Trees" and has been a major donor to the institute since 1996.

EMPLOYEES COMPETE IN DRAGON BOAT RACES. Since 1998, forty or more corporate-sponsored teams—including Monumental/AEGON's co-ed team pictured here—have competed annually in Dragon Boat Races in Baltimore's Inner Harbor. Funds raised support Catholic Charities' programs in the Baltimore area.

◄ LIVING CLASSROOMS

Baltimore's Living Classrooms Foundation is a non-profit organization, founded in 1985 and operated for the benefit of the community at large. It provides hands-on education and job skills training for at-risk Baltimore students and young adults from diverse backgrounds. Using maritime settings, community revitalization projects, challenging environments, and an interdisciplinary, "learning by doing" approach to education, the foundation's programs teach the fundamentals of literacy, math, science, history, economics and ecology. All programs focus on career development, community service, building self-esteem, and fostering multicultural exchange. Monumental Life's Henry G. Hagan—pictured standing, back right, with Living Classrooms Fresh Start and Crossroads School students—has been a Foundation trustee since 2001 and served as chairman of the board from 2004 to 2007. AEGON provides annual financial support for the organization's mission and community outreach. Sam Friedman, photographer

Pride in Our Past — Promise for the Future

MONUMENTAL LIFE has come a long way since its founding in Baltimore in 1858. We've survived fifteen decades of growth and change. We've served policyholders born in three centuries . . . and perhaps even a few, like Monumental itself, who have survived all three.

What a "melting pot" we are! What stories we have to tell! And just think of all the families we've served.

Throughout our history, we've insured millions of American citizens. We've protected immigrants and welcomed them as employees. Our agents and policyholders today speak dozens of languages. Many come from distant countries around the globe. Since 1990, we have assumed responsibility for policies, acquired through acquisition, that were issued by more than 260 companies. Still, with more than 2,000 career agents and thousands of independent producers, we remain close to our customers.

We have every right to be proud of our history, our legacy, and our traditions. We are one of the oldest, largest, strongest and most respected life insurers in the United States. We deliver hundreds of millions of dollars annually in death benefits to help surviving loved ones. In a world plagued by violence, terrorism, disease and natural disasters, generations of policyholders continue to look to us to provide protection, peace of mind and financial security. We keep families together, help pay the bills, and make dreams come true. Looking ahead to the future, we will keep our promise to be there when policyholders and their families need us most.

Monumental, the Quality Life Company. We are proud of who we are. And *very* proud of what we do.

Monumental Milestones

1850s

1858
Maryland General Assembly grants a charter to the Maryland Mutual Life and Fire Insurance Company, making it the state's first life insurance company.

1860s

1860
Directors elect George P. Kane first president of the board. He resigns after two months to become Baltimore's marshal of police.

1861
Union troops arrest Marshal Kane as a southern sympathizer and secessionist following a riot in which four soldiers and twelve Baltimore citizens are killed. It is the Civil War's first bloodshed.

1862
Directors vote to cease writing life and fire insurance for the duration of the Civil War.

1870s

1870
Company resumes operations as the Mutual Life Insurance Company of Baltimore. Benjamin G. Harris is elected president.

1873
Mutual Life of Baltimore issues the country's first "weekly premium" life insurance policy.

Working through the Providentia Society of the City of Baltimore, a beneficial society, the company establishes a German Department and begins issuing policies to immigrants of German descent.

1880s

1883
$1 Million of insurance in force.

1890s

1900s

1910s

1920s

1892

Mutual Life establishes a Weekly Premium or "Industrial" Division in response to public demand for paid-weekly policies.

1897

John F. Harris, Benjamin G. Harris's son, is elected president but resigns after one year.

1898

Matthew S. Brenan is elected president.
Insurance in force reaches $2 million.

1903

New home office opens at 208 N. Calvert Street.

1904

Mutual Life survives the Great Baltimore Fire.

1914

First district office outside Baltimore opens in Cumberland, MD.

1917

Home office moves to 15 South Street. U.S. enters World War I. Agents sell Liberty Bonds.

1918

Mutual Life hires its first two female employees—Emily Crowley in Home Office; Margaret Connor as an agent in Cumberland.

Influenza epidemic claims 650,000 American lives, 5,000 in Baltimore. Mutual Life death claims climb.

1919

Mutual Life opens first offices outside Maryland—in St. Louis, Cleveland and Columbus, Ohio.

1923

Paul M. Burnett elected Mutual Life president.

1924

Mutual Life "Wheel of Progress" moves west as the company opens field offices in 11 states.

1925

First Mutual Life sales convention in New Orleans.

1926

New home office opens at Charles and Chase Streets.

1928

With $11 million in assets and $147 million of insurance in force, Mutual Life converts from a mutual to a stock life insurance company.

1929

Mutual Life survives the stock market crash and subsequent Great Depression.

1930s

1935

Mutual Life directors vote to change the company's name to Monumental Life Insurance Company to reflect its prominence and position in Baltimore, the "Monumental City."

1936

Leo P. Rock elected president.

1939

Monumental opens new home office addition facing on Charles Street.

U.S. Congress orders the Temporary National Economic Committee to investigate the life insurance industry. Monumental officers Paul Burnett, Milton Roberts and Harold Loweree are called to testify.

1940s

1940

As war escalates in Europe, Monumental invests $2.9 million in U.S. Treasury bills; $4.5 million in war-related manufacturing companies.

1941

Master Sgt. Donald Weeks is the first "Monumental man" from the home office called to serve in World War II.

1942

As rationing of gas and tires increases, Leo Rock announces that field agents will be "on foot" for the rest of World War II. Within the year, 360 agents are drafted or leave the company to work in war-related industries.

1944

Agents in Baltimore and other cities vote to unionize.

1946

Average agent earns $3,640 a year.

Field office count reaches 58 in 14 states.

Monumental Life introduces policies to insure the "Baby Boom" generation.

1950s

1952

U.S. life insurance companies pay $16 million in Korean War claims.

Red Cross conducts Monumental's first on-site blood drive.

1953

F. Harold Loweree elected president.

1957

Monumental purchases first IBM mainframe computer.
General Agencies Department opens to serve GAs in Maryland, Pennsylvania and Virginia.

1958

Monumental Life celebrates 100 years of service to Maryland citizens.
$1 billion of insurance in force.

Growth of suburbs pushes company investment in home mortgages to $97.2 million on 10,000 loans.

1959

Monumental forms Group Division to sell employer/employee life, medical and disability coverage.

Company installs IBM-650 computer, converts weekly premium debit records to electronic data processing system.

1960

Frederick L. Wehr elected president and CEO.

1960s

1963

Ad for company's "Family Protection Check-Up" appears in *LOOK* magazine one week after President Kennedy is assassinated.

1964

$1.5 billion of insurance in force.

1965

Frank Baker, Jr., elected president of Monumental Life.

Fred Wehr continues as chairman of the board and CEO.

1967

$2 billion of insurance in force.

Monumental Life pledges $2,275,600 to support President Johnson's "War on Poverty" and provide mortgage financing for inner city families.

Donald H. Wilson, Jr., CLU, elected Monumental Life president and chief administrative officer. Frank Baker, Jr., elected chairman and CEO.

1968

Monumental Corporation formed as a holding company for Monumental Life and Volunteer State Life of Chattanooga, TN.
New building opens on Charles and Biddle Street corner.

1969

Monumental Properties, owned by the Joseph Meyerhoff family, joins Monumental Corporation.
Monumental Group Division executes first direct mail campaign to Maryland National Bank's and Bankamericard (now called VISA) credit card customers.

1970s

1975

$3 billion of insurance in force.

Monumental Life accepts last application for weekly-premium life insurance and begins converting to LIFE COMM administration system.

1977

Frank Baker, Jr., elected chairman and CEO of Monumental Corporation.
Leslie B. Disharoon, CLU, elected chairman, CEO and president of Monumental Life.

Monumental Life receives "Mayor's Award" for helping revitalize 1200 and 1300 blocks of its North Charles Street neighborhood.
Monumental's Group Division is restructured as the Mass Marketing Division.
Monumental Corporation announces sale of Monumental Properties assets.

1978

Sun Life Company of Richmond, VA attempts hostile takeover.

1979

Leslie Disharoon elected chairman and CEO of Monumental Corporation. Roger Kolker elected Monumental Life president.
Company introduces new logo with "*Tomorrow's Insurance . . . Today*" tag line.

Monumental signs agreement with USPA & IRA (United Services Planning Association, Inc. and Independent Research Agency for Life Insurance, Inc.) to market Monumental products to military families on U.S. military bases.

1980s

1982

Monumental issues its first large payroll deduction case.

United Financial Services formed as an in-house brokerage to help agents "open doors" through endorsed sales of non-Monumental products.

1983

B. Larry Jenkins, CLU, elected Monumental Life president, chairman and CEO.

Agents begin selling Universal Life policies with the help of handheld computers.

Monumental General Insurance Company formed as mass marketing, direct mail subsidiary under Monumental Corporation "umbrella.'

1985

New Business introduces and delivers its first on-demand, laser-printed policies.

1986

Monumental enters the PreNeed marketplace, selling life insurance through funeral directors.

AEGON Insurance Group of the Netherlands acquires Monumental Corporation.
Monumental and AEGON celebrate by co-sponsoring a "Dutch Masters" exhibit at Baltimore's Walters Art Gallery.

1988

Monumental introduces its new "Quality Life Company" logo.

1989

AEGON USA formed as holding company for AEGON's U.S. operations—including Monumental Life and Monumental General.

1990s

1990
Monumental acquires home service business from Washington National Insurance Company of Evanston, IL.

1991
Monumental Life receives AEGON's International "Outstanding Business Unit" Award. AEGON listed on New York Stock Exchange as "AEG."

1992
Monumental Life acquires large blocks of home service business from Commonwealth Life and Accident Insurance Company of Galveston, TX and Reliable Life Insurance Company of St. Louis. $16.1 billion insurance in force. Agents receive laptop computers with PFP (Personal Financial Planning) needs analysis software.

1995
AEGON USA and Monumental Life commit $1.5 million over 3 years to help create LIFE, the Life and Health Foundation for Education.

1996
Agents receive EZ-App laptop-based electronic application.

1997
AEGON USA acquires Providian Corporation's life insurance operations. Capital Security, Commonwealth and Peoples Security life insurance companies are merged into Monumental Life in 1998. Monumental becomes responsible for policies originally issued by 260 U.S. life insurance companies.

1998
Henry G. Hagan elected Monumental Life president and CEO. Monumental Life is among the first U.S. life insurers to receive industry's IMSA (Insurance Marketplace Standards Association) "seal of approval."

1999
AEGON acquires Transamerica Corporation in the second-largest life insurance deal in the U.S. Y2k teams prepare computer systems for the New Millennium.

2000s

2000
President's Club conference introduced for new agents.

2001
Monumental, AEGON employees contribute $250,000, matched by AEGON Foundation, to provide college scholarships for children of 9/11 victims and men/women in U.S. Armed Forces killed while fighting War on Terror.

2002
AEGON USA requires web-based "Integrity Ed" program for all employees. Monumental equips agents with electronic signature pads and electronic forms.

2003
Henry G. Hagan, Monumental Life president and CEO, named U.S. chair of AEGON Corporate Responsibility Committee.

2004
AEGON Foundation matches $250,000 donated by employees for tsunami relief. AEGON Foundation commits to multi-year sponsorship of Susan G. Komen Breast Cancer Foundation's "Race for the Cure." Monumental recognized by Maryland Mentoring Partnership and *Baltimore* Magazine for having the state's best corporate mentoring program. Monumental supports first industry-wide "Life Insurance Awareness Month."

2005
Monumental, AEGON announce support of "Agents for Change," a grass-roots organization committed to lobbying Congress for an optional federal charter for life insurance companies. Monumental signs agreement with independent marketing organizations (IMOs) targeting the senior market. U.S. life insurance executives, including Monumental's Henry G. Hagan, form a "Task Force for the Future" to identify issues, challenges, answers and solutions to meet middle-America's increasing need for financial security and protection

2007
On average, Monumental Life pays $1 million a day in claims benefits. "RealLIFEstory" of Monumental policyholder Major William Hecker, killed in Iraq, appears in *Newsweek* magazine.

2008
Monumental Life celebrates its 150th anniversary.

Artist Greg Otto is renowned for his bright, color-filled depictions of
Baltimore landmarks and cityscapes. His painting of Monumental Life's
home office façade on Chase Street—commissioned for our 150th anniversary
in 2008—celebrates the company's solid past, its continuing strength, and the
bright future it helps create for employees and policyholders.

© Greg Otto, 2007, *Monumental Life*, acrylic on canvas, 34" x 22"

BIBLIOGRAPHY AND SOURCES

FOUNDED IN 1858 as the Maryland Mutual Life and Fire Insurance Company, the organization known today as Monumental Life was also known as the Mutual Life Insurance Company of Baltimore from 1870 until 1935, when it was renamed Monumental Life to reflect its prominence and strength in Baltimore, the "Monumental City." Monumental Corporation was formed as a holding company in 1968. It was acquired by AEGON in 1986. When "the company" or "the organization" is used in this volume, it could mean any one of these entities, depending on the decade and the context.

Much of the information included in *Pride in Our Past, Promise for the Future—A Monumental Story* comes from these organizations' board and executive committee minutes, archive files, annual reports, company publications, and interviews with current and retired employees. Following is a list of the additional sources used for background information about Baltimore and Maryland, specific individuals, the life insurance industry, and major historic events.

BOOKS, JOURNALS, PERIODICALS

Andrews, Matthew Page. *Tercentenary History of Maryland.* 4 vols. Baltimore: S. J. Clark Publishing Company, 1925. 2:48–49.

Arnold, Joseph, and Anirban Basu. *Maryland: Old Line to New Prosperity.* Sun Valley, Cal.: American Historical Press, 2003.

Baltimore City Census Records, 1860–1890. Micro film #651-820. Maryland Historical Society, Baltimore.

Baltimore City Directory. Baltimore: John W. Woods, Publisher, 1871–1872.

Beirne, Francis F. *Baltimore . . . A Picture History*, 1858–1958. New York: Hastings House, Publishers, 1957.

Brokaw, Tom. *The Greatest Generation.* New York: Random House, 1998.

Brown, George William, with new introduction by Kevin Conley Ruffner. *Baltimore and the Nineteenth of April, 1861.* Baltimore: The Johns Hopkins University Press, 2001. (Originally published in 1887).

Chapelle, Suzanne Ellery Greene. *Baltimore: An Illustrated History.* Sun Valley, Cal.: American Historical Press, 2000.

Conn, David. "Life on the Line." *Warfield's Magazine* (March 1987): 70–79.

Cordell, Eugene Fauntleroy. *The Medical Annals of Maryland.* Baltimore: Williams & Wilkins Press, 1903.

Evans, Clement A. *Confederate Military History.* Atlanta: Confederate Publishing Company, 1899.

Fee, Elizabeth, et al., editors. *The Baltimore Book: New Perspectives on Local History.* Philadelphia: Temple University Press, 1991.

Gerard, Victor B. *Commonwealth Life Insurance Company: A History of the Development Years.* Louisville: Commonwealth Life Insurance Company, 1985.

Gesell, Gerhard A. and Ernest J. Howe. *Investigation of Concentration of Economic Power.* Printed for use by the Temporary National Economic Committee, Senate of the United States. Washington, D.C.: Government Printing Office, 1940.

Hersch, Warren S. "Serving the Middle Market Can be Challenging." *National Underwriter,* (November 8, 2004): 35–36.

Hurff, Matthew. *The Millennium Time Tapestry.* New York: Pindar Press, 1999.

Jenkins, Father Edward Felix, O.S.A. *Thomas Jenkins of Maryland, 1670: His Descendants and Allied Families.* Baltimore: Maryland Historical Society, 1985.

Le Grice, Carrie, "The Silent (and Forgotten) Majority." *Senior Market Advisor* (July 2005).

La Mason, Charles A., editor. *125th Anniversary: Maryland Insurance Administration.* Baltimore: The Maryland Insurance Administration, 1997.

"Marriages, Births, Deaths." *Maryland Historical Magazine* 21 (1927): 277. Micro film #3034. Maryland Historical Society.

"Monumental Life Insurance Company Moves into New Building," *Port of Baltimore Magazine* (January 1940): 31.

Meyerhoff, Harvey M. *Memoirs.* Annapolis, Md.: privately printed, 1998.

Norris, George A. "Portrait of an Industry" *Life Association News* (December 1999): 49–120.

O'Hanlon, Tom. *The Company You Keep: 150 Years with New York Life.* Lyme, Conn.: Greenwich Publishing Group, Inc., 1995.

Petersen, Peter B. *The Great Baltimore Fire.* Baltimore: Maryland Historical Society, 2004.

Shepherd, Henry E. *History of Baltimore, Maryland.* Uniontown, Pa.: S. B. Nelson, Publisher, 1898.

Stolley, Richard B., editor. *LIFE: Our Century in Pictures.* Boston: Little Brown and Company, 1999.

United States. Temporary National Economic Committee. *Investigation of Concentration of Economic Power: Hearings before the Temporary National Economic Committee, Congress of the U.S.* Washington, D.C.: Government Printing Office, 1941.

Warren, Marion E. and Michael P. McCarthy. *The Living City: Baltimore's Charles Center and Inner Harbor Development.* Baltimore: Maryland Historical Society, 2002.

Woods, David F. "The Future of Life Insurance." *Journal of Financial Service Professionals* (January 2006): 44–48.

NEWSPAPERS

"150 People Who Shaped the Way We Live." *Baltimore Sun,* 150th Anniversary Issue, May 17, 1987.

"A Monumental Past." *Baltimore Business Journal,* September 15, 2000.

"AEGON USA: A Protective Parent." *Baltimore Business Journal,* September 23, 1994.

"America's First Suburb Celebrates 60th Birthday." *Baltimore Sun,* September 30, 2007.

"Baltimore Boosters Rallying 'Round Monumental." *Baltimore Sun,* January 14, 1979.

"Baltimore's Riots Remembered." *Baltimore Sun,* April 4, 2007.

"Burnett Tell of Loans from Insurance Company." *Baltimore Sun,* August 25, 1939.

"Commissioner Denies Sun Life Bid to Buy Monumental Stock." *The Evening Sun,* March 22, 1979.

"Early Civil War Battleground." *Baltimore Sun,* April 1, 2006.

"Gain Predicted for Monumental." *Baltimore Sun,* April 29, 1983.

"History's Tracks . . . The Route through Baltimore that Brought Union Soldiers Face to Face with Southern Sympathizers 140 Years Ago." *Baltimore Sun,* April 17, 2001.

"Immigration Debate as Old as US." *Baltimore Sun,* May 5, 2006.

"Lives in Contrast: Born at Opposite Ends of the Baby Boom Generation, Two Maryland Women Followed Different Paths." *Baltimore Sun,* January 14, 2007.

"The Military's Influence Lived on Long after World War I in Area's Houses, Camaraderie." *Louisville Courier-Journal,* November 14, 2006.

"Monumental Insurance Counters Takeover Bid." *Baltimore Sun,* November 2, 1968.

"Monumental Celebrates New Building Completion." *Baltimore Sun,* October 11, 1968.

"Monumental Life Fights Take-Over." *The Evening Sun,* May 29, 1977.

"Monumental Life Insurance Company Announces Extensive Building Program." *Baltimore Sun,* March 3, 1950.

"Monumental Plans to Liquidate Unit." *Baltimore Sun,* April 13, 1977.

"Monumental, Tennessee Firm to Merge." *Baltimore Sun,* July 1, 1968.

"Renovation Set at Monumental." *Baltimore Sun,* March 11, 1971.

"The New Lords of the Land: Baltimore Ground Rent Owners." *Baltimore Sun,* December 11, 2006.

"The Overlooked Pandemic of 1918." *Baltimore Sun,* October 20, 2006.

WEB SITES

In addition to printed sources, I consulted several web sites.

For Civil War events in Baltimore, particularly the riot of April 19, 1861:

www.civilwarhome.com/Baltimore1, *Conflict in Baltimore, Maryland,* Report of Baltimore Police Commissioners, May 3, 1861.

www.civilwarhome.com/Baltimore2, *Conflict in Baltimore, Maryland,* Report of Honorable George William Brown, Mayor of Baltimore, May 9, 1861.

www.civilwarhome.com/baltimoreriot, *The Riot of April 19, 1861.*

For information about Mutual Life's early medical directors: www.mdhistoryonline.net/mdmedicine, *Medicine in Maryland,* 1752-1920.

For World War I, World War II, the Red Cross, the Korean Conflict and Vietnam War background and timelines:

www.worldwar1.com/dbc/timeline

www.historyplace.com/worldwar2/timeline

www.trumanlibrary.org/Marshall Plan

www.redcross.org/museum/history

www.en.wikipedia.org/wiki/1970s

www.pbs.org/wgbh/amex/vietnam/timeline

INDEX

Mon-U-Matic bank draft program, 132, 186
Monteforte, Nicholas, *204*
Montgomery, Mr., 79
Monthly (Debit) Ordinary insurance. *See also*
    Ordinary insurance; Regular Ordinary life
    insurance
  conversion from manual to computer processing
    of, 172
  sales during World War II, 100
  sales in 1960s of, 149
  sales in 1970s of, 162, 166
  sales in the 1950s of, 128
Monumental Agency Group, 227, 228
Monumental Capital Management, Inc., 173, *174*
Monumental Corporation
  AEGON USA formation and, 202
  Disharoon elected chairman of, 178–179
  divestment of real estate operation from, 175–176
  donation to Johns Hopkins Medical Institutions,
    194, *194*
  factors in creation of, 158
  incorporation of, 156
  merger with AEGON, 192–193
  reorganization in mid-1980s, 189–190
  SEC's ruling on cash flow and earnings per share
    and, 174–175
  tender offer for, 157
  Volunteer State Life of Chattanooga affiliates with,
    159
Monumental General Insurance Company, 189–190,
  202
Monumental General Insurance Group, Inc., 189
Monumental Glee Club, 124, *124*
Monumental Honor Men pin, *88*
Monumental Life Insurance Company
  AEGON USA formation and, 202
  announcement of Providian Corporation merger
    with, 225–226, *225–226*
  benefits for employees, 127–128
  Burnett and name change to, 74, 82, *82*
  Centennial Celebration, *131,* 131–132
  commitment to downtown Baltimore by, *152,*
    152–153
  completion of Providian merger with, 232
  compliance with industry laws and regulations by,
    220
  construction fence project, 155, *156*
  dues-paying memberships of, 122
  family-like workplace atmosphere of, *125,* 125–
    126, *126*
  financial strength in 1946, 110, 128
  funeral expenses, PreNeed policies for, 197–198,
    257
  general agents, group insurance, and growth, *130,*
    130–131
  Half-Billion Celebration festivities, 111, *111*
  HIV/AIDS policies of, 197
  holding company (*See* Monumental Corporation)

hostile takeover attempts of, 157, 159, 178
IMSA seal of approval and, 224–225
inflation control campaign by, 184–185
investments of, 82–83, 153
labor unrest and strikes during 1960s, 147
leadership transition of early 1950s, *126,* 126–127
logistics of Providian Corporation merger with,
    226–228, *227–228*
Meyerhoffs and, 117, 159
mortgage investments of, *117,* 117–118
notice of social issues of 1960s by, 142
post–World War II hiring by, 106
as Quality Company, *199,* 199–200
reorganization of 1979, 179–180
Rocklowe Social Club and, *123,* 123–124, *124*
sales of 1963 and 1964, 149
sales of early 1980s, 188–189
SEC investigation of insurance industry and, *87,*
    87–88
segregation in, *136,* 136–137, 156
senior officers in 2007, 268, *268*
stock market crash of 1987 and, 198–199
technological innovations of mid-20th century for,
    132, 132–133
Tuition Reimbursement Program, 140
women's roles during World War II for, 95–98,
    95–98
World War II support by, 98–99
Monumental Properties, Inc., 159, 173, 175
Monumental Properties Trust, 175
Moore, Peggy, *171*
Morales, Bert, *171*
Moravec, Frank, 217
Moreland, Ann, 48, 126
Moreland, Robert M., 48, *48*
Morgan, Robert, 199
Morgan Stanley & Company, 192
Mortgage Loan Department, Monumental Life's, 118
mortgages, local, investments in, 24, 38, *117,* 117–
    118
Mount Vernon Area Neighborhood Council, 152
Mount Vernon–Belvedere Improvement Association,
    172
Mt. Clare Station, Baltimore, 19
Mt. Vernon Woodberry Cotton Duck Company, 24.
    See also cotton mills
muckraking journalists, 39
Mudge, Ted, *186,* 187
Mueller, George, 187, *187*
Mueller, Paul A., 98
Mueller, William, 187
Multiple Coverage insurance product, 145
Murphy, Cindy Hecker, 240, *240*
Murphy, James, 177, 178
Murray, Esther, *95*
Mutual Benefit Life Insurance Company, Newark,
    N.J., 3
mutual life insurance. *See also* life insurance

beginnings in Maryland of, 1–3
reasons for demutualization of, 67
Mutual Life Insurance Company of Baltimore.
  branch offices out-of-state for, 54, 62–63
  building business for, 17–18
  Burnett elected first chairman of the board, 55
  charter for, 14–15, 24, 68
  competitors for, *41,* 41–43, *42, 43*
  demutualization of, 66–68
  epidemic of 1918 and, 46
  financial safeguards in 1929 by, 69
  financial strength during Great Depression, 76–77
  financial strength in 1908 of, 38, *38*

  first policyholders of, 16–17, *17*
  first stock certificate of, *68*
  Great Depression response by, 73, 76–77
  Guarantee Capital Fund of, 15–16
  Industrial Branch, 23–24
  influenza epidemic of 1918 and, 53
  insurance for Providentia members, *21,* 21–23
  investments in support for World War I by, 47
  investments of, 24, 33
  NALU reforms of 1906 and, 40
  name changed to Monumental Life, 82, *82*
  rate book, *16*
  sales-building plans of 1920s, 63–64, 66
  sewer system financing and, 34
  weekly "board call" results 5/19/1923, *63*
  World War I and financial strength of, 50
Nagler, Ron, 173, 191, 195, 198, *198*
Napoleon I, 36
Nardini, Clare, 124, 144, *144*
National American Women's Suffrage Association, 34
National Association of Insurance and Financial
    Advisors (NAIFA), 264
National Association of Insurance Commissioners
    (NAIC), 100
National Association of Life Underwriters (NALU)
  agent education through membership in, 167
  on declines of weekly premium policies, 162
  education of GIs on retaining NSLI policies by,
    109
  insurance regulation in early 20th century and,
    39–40
  on Social Security as basis for life insurance sales,
    79
National Bank of Baltimore, 61
national economy during World War II, life insurance
    and, 100
National Energy Act, 164
National Guard. *See also* Maryland National Guard
  Baltimore Fire of 1904, protection by, *32*
  called to active duty in World War I, *44*
  riots after King assassination and, *138,* 141
  wars in Iraq and Afghanistan and, 256
National Honor Associate red jacket
  for Ben Dahdah, *250*

Rosemary Riesett Limmen, Monumental Life second vice president and communications officer, joined the organization as publications editor in 1985. A former language teacher and lover of history, she has been writing about the company, its history and traditions, its mission, vision and values for over twenty years. Promoted to assistant vice president of Marketing Communications in 1990, Limmen assumed responsibility for internal communications, advertising, public relations, sales promotion, sales conference planning and award programs. This broad experience, plus a close working relationship with senior management for almost two decades, has given her a hands-on, in-depth knowledge of the industry, the company, its people and its distribution systems.

Limmen has served on the Public Relations Council of the American Council of Life Insurance (ACLI), on the Marketing Committee of Insurance Marketplace Standards Association (IMSA), and on the Company Advisory Board of the Life and Health Foundation for Education (LIFE). An active member of the Insurance and Financial Communicators Association (IFCA) for seventeen years, she was a board member, Site Selection Chair, Annual Meeting Chair, a member of the Professional Development and Executive Committees, and the organization's national president for 1996/1997.

A native of New Jersey, Limmen earned a Bachelors degree and teaching certificate from Douglass College, Rutgers University, and a Masters degree in Publication Design from the University of Baltimore. She lives in Towson, Maryland, with her husband, Jan. She plans to retire to their cottage on the Maine coast in 2009.